STUDIES IN EIGHTEENTH-CENTURY DIPLOMACY

STUDIES IN EIGHTEENTH-CENTURY DIPLOMACY

1740–1748

BY

SIR RICHARD LODGE, M.A., LL.D., Litt.D.

EMERITUS PROFESSOR OF HISTORY IN THE UNIVERSITY OF EDINBURGH
AND HONORARY FELLOW OF BRASENOSE COLLEGE, OXFORD

GREENWOOD PRESS, PUBLISHERS
WESTPORT, CONNECTICUT

Originally published in 1930
by John Murray, London

First Greenwood Reprinting 1970

Library of Congress Catalogue Card Number 73-109771

SBN 8371-4261-X

Printed in the United States of America

PREFACE

THIS book has grown rather than been deliberately made. For the last fifty years I have lectured off and on, and for many of them on rather than off, on the relations of the European States to each other during the eighteenth century. And I took one part of those relations as the subject of my Ford Lectures in the University of Oxford. My experience as a teacher has convinced me that the darkest spot in the history of Europe in the eighteenth century is the period of the war of the Austrian Succession. Its military side may have been adequately treated by Carlyle and other writers, but I do not profess to be a military historian. But the political side of the war has been left, at any rate in this country, in great obscurity. The most notable attempts to penetrate this obscurity have been made by Arneth, in his monumental work on Maria Theresa, and by the Duc de Broglie, in the long series of volumes which he has devoted to this period. But Arneth was almost exclusively dependent upon the Austrian archives, among which he passed his life; and Broglie, though he had a larger outlook, was imperfectly acquainted with English sources. I omit the Prussian historians because they have helped to mislead the student by concentrating attention upon those periods of the war in which their hero, Frederick the Great, was a protagonist. No Englishman, since Archdeacon Coxe, had made anything like a thorough study of foreign policy during this decade, and much has been discovered since the days of the industrious Archdeacon.

v

When the termination of the Great War set me partially free from other activities, I set to work to explore some of the dark places that had long been a puzzle to me. I worked out the activities of Carteret at Hanau and Worms in his one year of greatness, 1743, and discovered that the latter negotiation helped to clear away some of the mystery that had seemed to shroud the other. My conclusions on this subject have already appeared in the *English Historical Review*, and are here reprinted from its pages, with permission from Messrs. Longmans, Green, and Co. It is a pity that Carteret has not yet found an adequate biographer. Then I turned to the Treaty of Aix-la-Chapelle, which I had always been taught to regard as the starting-point in that alienation of Austria from Great Britain which led to the great change in the normal adjustment of the European states which historians have agreed to call the Diplomatic Revolution. But I soon discovered that the alienation had begun a good deal earlier, and that the settlement of the terms of the treaty could not be really understood without a survey of the previous negotiations. This carried me back to the activities of the fourth Earl of Sandwich at Breda and The Hague, and thence to the earlier relations of the Marquis d'Argenson with Sardinia and with the Dutch. I found that the survey threw a flood of light upon the working of the Cabinet system in the period, and upon the relations of the leading English politicians with each other. This applies especially to the relations of Newcastle with Harrington and Chesterfield, and of all three with Sandwich. My study of the diplomatic activities of Lord Sandwich has been immensely aided by a perusal of his Papers, which have been carefully collected and preserved at Hinchingbrooke. For admission to this treasure-house I have to thank the kindness of the present Earl.

I have also to express my obligations to the administrators of the Carnegie Trust for the Universities of Scotland, who have given financial assistance in the production of this volume.

The difficulty of fitting in the sequence of letters exchanged at considerable distances is increased, before Chesterfield's reform of the calendar in 1752, by the varying usages in different countries. In the fifth decade of the century Great Britain, Sweden, and Russia still employed the old calendar, so that eleven days have to be added to bring their dates into harmony with those of other countries. When an English Minister writes from London he uses the old style; when he writes from Hanover, he usually heads his letters with the double dates; when he writes from The Hague or Dresden, he gives the date current there. In the present volume dates, unless expressly qualified, may be assumed to be in the new style.

RICHARD LODGE.

HARPENDEN,
 August, 1929.

CONTENTS

CHAPTER I

THE SO-CALLED TREATY OF HANAU, 1743

CHAPTER II

THE TREATY OF WORMS, 13 SEPTEMBER, 1743

CONTENTS

tion between Austria and Sardinia—Compromise about
Finale—Cessions in Lombardy—Attempt to make them
conditional upon conquest of Naples—Wording of
relative articles—Proposed exchange of Bavaria for
Naples—Sardinian negotiations with France—Signature
of Treaty—Austria demands supplementary declaration
—Carteret signs it—English Cabinet refuses to ratify—
Subsequent influence of Treaty of Worms.   31–79

CHAPTER III

D'ARGENSON'S RELATIONS WITH GERMANY AND SARDINIA

CHAPTER IV

D'ARGENSON AND THE DUTCH

CHAPTER V

BREDA AND LISBON, AUGUST, 1746, TO JANUARY, 1747

CHAPTER VI

SANDWICH AND MACANAZ AT BREDA, JANUARY TO MAY, 1747

CONTENTS

Macanaz at The Hague—His extravagant demands—

CHAPTER VII

BETWEEN BREDA AND AIX-LA-CHAPELLE

CHAPTER VIII

THE PRELIMINARIES OF AIX-LA-CHAPELLE

PAGES

CHAPTER IX

THE TREATY OF AIX-LA-CHAPELLE

CHAPTER I

THE SO-CALLED TREATY OF HANAU, 1743.

Increased British energy in the war under Carteret—Treaty of Breslau—French and Bavarian disasters secure Maria Theresa's succession—Causes of continuance of war : (1) Maria Theresa wants an equivalent for Silesia ; (2) she desires to humiliate Charles VII ; (3) aims of Elizabeth Farnese in Italy—Anglo-Prussian attempt to mediate between Charles VII and Maria Theresa—After Dettingen Charles VII appeals to England alone—William of Hesse acts for him—Proffered Bavarian terms at Hanau—Carteret drafts a project of peace and a project of assurance—William of Hesse prepared to accept—Carteret sends both documents to England—Hostile criticism by English Ministers—Carteret drops both projects—Chagrin of William of Hesse—Anger of Frederick II both with proceedings at Hanau and with their failure—Hanau controversy in 1744—Fall of Carteret.

THE war of the Austrian Succession is less familiar to all students of eighteenth-century history, and certainly to English readers, than either the Spanish Succession or the Seven Years' War. It has a considerable literature of its own, but it is for the most part in French or German. Since Carlyle no English writer has treated the land war on any considerable scale, and the inquiring student is forced to turn to Arneth or Droysen or the Duc de Broglie for a reasonably full account of a rather puzzling war. The dominating figure of Frederick the Great and the prominence of Prussia in the eyes of German historians have given special prominence to the two Silesian wars, but the period between them and that which followed the Treaty of Dresden have been comparatively neglected, even by Continental writers. It is not surprising that the war as a whole is still somewhat obscure. It lacks unity and cohesion ; it produced few very obvious results ; it has no heroic figures except Frederick and Maria Theresa ; its generals, except Frederick and perhaps Traun and Marshal Saxe, were second rate ; and the contemporary politicians were mostly as obscure as they were untrustworthy. Austria

1

had no great statesmen between Eugene and Kaunitz, and Ulfeld, who succeeded Zinzendorf as Chief Minister in 1743, was dominated by Bartenstein, the Secretary of the Conference, whose political aptitude was confined to the drafting of acrimonious and controversial notes. France notoriously lacked great Ministers in the reign of Louis XV,[1] while in England the Pelhams have almost passed into a byword for mediocrity. Walpole entered the war with reluctance, and fell an inglorious victim to its initial failures. Hardwicke may have been a great lawyer, but he had no adequate grasp of the affairs of Europe. Chesterfield was a man of letters, a wit, and an orator, rather than a statesman, and Carteret, like the Marquis d'Argenson in France, is a great name and a great enigma, remarkable rather for what he might have done than for what he actually did. He was so obviously cleverer than his successful rivals, and was so clearly their superior in diplomatic ability and insight, that he has left a posthumous reputation which cannot be disproved because it was never adequately tested.

Among the numerous puzzles which the war presents, one of the most obvious is its long duration. It opened with the prospect of speedy and revolutionary changes in the map of Europe. At the close of 1741, after the fall of Prague and Frederick's repudiation of the preposterous Convention of Klein-Schnellendorf, it seemed that the Austrian dominions must inevitably be partitioned. The shares were all plotted out, and the recipients were ready and eager to seize their respective allotments. It was at this crisis that Walpole fell in February, 1742, and the Ministry was reconstituted to admit Carteret as Secretary of State for the Northern Department. The avowed object of the change was to weaken the opposition in Parliament and to throw more energy into the war. Maria Theresa, already encouraged by the unexpected loyalty of the Magyars and by the success of Khevenhüller in recovering Upper Austria, was immensely gratified by the assurance of more men

[1] *Mémoires de Frédéric II* (ed. Boutaric), i., 149: " Ce siècle était stérile en grands hommes pour la France, celui de Louis XIV en produisait en foule."

and more money from Britain. George II, who had infuriated his insular subjects by concluding a treaty of
neutrality for Hanover and by pledging the Hanoverian
vote to Charles Albert, was gained over by taking 16,000
Hanoverian troops into British pay, and Carteret rendered what Newcastle declared to be his greatest service
to the Austrian cause by persuading the King-Elector not
to renew the neutrality which France was only too willing to grant.[1] From the spring of 1742 troops were
gradually shipped from England to the Austrian Netherlands, where they might be employed either in the
defence of those provinces, or in the expulsion of the
French forces from Germany, or—as their ambitious
commander, Lord Stair, desired—in a direct invasion of
France. But before the " pragmatic army " had begun
or was even prepared to act, the prospect of its future
activity produced a political change of the greatest mag-
nitude. Hitherto British efforts to reconcile Austria
with Prussia had led to nothing but Hyndford's abortive agreement at Klein-Schnellendorf. Carteret's more
lavish assurances enabled him to exert greater pressure
at Vienna, and the Battle of Chotusitz completed the
conversion of Maria Theresa. The Treaty of Breslau,
adjusted by Hyndford in his temporary capacity as
plenipotentiary for Austria, was a conspicuous triumph
for British diplomacy and for the new Ministry. Hyndford received from his own Government the Order of the
Thistle, while both Maria Theresa and Frederick granted
to him and his heirs the right to bear the arms of Silesia.
Carteret, however, treated him rather ungratefully by
taking the further negotiations with Prussia out of the
hands of the Berlin Embassy and conducting them
directly with Andrié, the Prussian Resident in London.
Carteret was so assured in his own mind that Prussian

[1] In a long analysis of the history of the war which Newcastle
drew up for Hardwicke on 24 October (o.s.), 1743, he admits that
Carteret dissuaded the King from making a second and lasting
neutrality treaty for Hanover, " the best thing he ever did "
(Brit. Mus. Add. MSS. 32,701, vol. xvi., of Newcastle Papers).
The narrative, one of many which Newcastle drew up from time
to time, is summarized in Yorke, *Life and Correspondence of Lord
Hardwicke*, i., 318–21.

neutrality would lead Frederick into an anti-French alliance, that he gave an immediate British guarantee to the Treaty of Breslau, without waiting for a complete agreement with Prussia, with the result that the defensive Treaty of Westminster, from which so much was expected, was not concluded until 18 November, and proved in the end to be a worthless scrap of paper.

The Treaty of Breslau—contemporaries persisted in giving it that name, although the final treaty, differing in some respects from the preliminaries, was signed at Berlin—is a notable turning-point in the history of the war. It had the effect of detaching Saxony as well as Prussia from the coalition against Maria Theresa, and their desertion left the French and Bavarian forces in a hopeless position. The main French army, under Broglie and Belleisle, was forced to retreat to Prague, where its ultimate surrender was inevitable unless it could be relieved. Maillebois was ordered to attempt the relief with the western forces which had hitherto been threatening Hanover and the Netherlands, but he found it impossible to reach the Bohemian capital, and ultimately retreated to Bavaria. Broglie escaped from Prague, before the cordon was complete, to supersede Maillebois in the command of unsuccessful and discouraged troops. Belleisle, after some weeks of energetic resistance, broke through the besiegers with the sound members of the garrison, and conducted a heroic but costly retreat to the frontier. Chevert, left to defend the city with the sick and maimed, was allowed to surrender on honourable terms, and Maria Theresa was able to assume the crown of the kingdom, which at one moment had seemed to be completely lost. Fleury had died in January, 1743, conscious that the laurels he had gained in the annexation of Lorraine were sadly withered by the frost of failure in his recent policy. Maria Theresa had good reason to be jubilant. Her outlying territories in the Netherlands, in the Black Forest, and in Italy might still be exposed to some danger, but the great main block of the Habsburg dominions, though sadly shorn by the loss of Silesia, seemed to be now solidly secure. It was not likely that the Maritime

Powers would allow her to lose either the Netherlands or her Italian provinces, and even if she did lose them for a time, she could contemplate this with equanimity as long as she held a more valuable pledge. The hereditary territories of her audacious rival, Charles Albert of Bavaria, now calling himself the Emperor Charles VII, had already been overrun by Austrian troops. If they had been for a moment partially evacuated, it had only been because forces had to be transferred to Bohemia. Now that the recovery of Bohemia enabled the Austrian armies to concentrate in Bavaria, it was unlikely that the Bavarian troops under Seckendorf and the French under Broglie would be able to defend the electorate unless France was willing to make quixotic efforts to save her ally. And, even then, the pragmatic army should be adequate to cut the French off from Bavaria. It was clear to all observers that the attempt to break up the Austrian dominions had ended, except in the case of Prussia, in absolute failure. So far as the war was waged about the Austrian Succession it should have ended in 1743.

There were three substantial reasons for the continuance of the war in and after 1743. (1) To Maria Theresa the cession of Silesia was a bitter pill. Quite apart from her hatred of Frederick and her disgust at having to reward his villainy, she regarded the maintenance of the Pragmatic Sanction as a pious duty to her father's memory. As she could not maintain it in the letter, she determined from the first to enforce it in the spirit. If Silesia had been lost, an equivalent must be found elsewhere.[1] In this search for compensation she was undoubtedly encouraged by Carteret and by George II, though they could assert that they had given no binding pledge to find it for her. Carteret, unlike Walpole, was

[1] Arneth (*Maria Theresa*, ii., 488) quotes an interesting letter from the Queen to Khevenhüller of 17 June, 1742, which shows that from the outset she had decided to seek for an equivalent: " Da Engelland mit ungemein grosser Heftigkeit auff den Vergleich mit Preussen gedrungen under ausser deme zu keiner Hülffsleistung sich einverstehen wollen, so hat derselbe anderst nicht als sehr kostbar ausfallen können. Ist also zu sehen, dass dieser Verlust anderwärts wieder eingebracht werde."

an orthodox Whig in his foreign policy. It was his primary aim to weaken and abase the House of Bourbon, and to support Austria as a counterbalancing power. Austria had already been sacrificed to Walpole's obstinate neutrality in the war of the Polish Succession : it would be contrary to Carteret's estimate of British interests to allow her to suffer another uncompensated loss. George II was equally interested. To the traditional Hanoverian jealousy of an aggressive neighbour, he added a personal hostility to an ungrateful and contemptuous nephew. If peace was made on the basis of Maria Theresa's retention of all her father's dominions except Silesia, Frederick would emerge as the sole gainer by the war, and this was intolerable both to George and to the brothers Münchhausen, his chief electoral advisers. The King and Carteret were further agreed that the desired compensation should be found at the expense of France. This would have the double advantage of crippling England's enemy and of avoiding any dangerous irritation of Prussia. It must be remembered that Frederick had no objection to an equivalent for Maria Theresa,[1] provided it was not more than an equivalent. Although he was still bound by a defensive treaty with France, he was not likely to quit a profitable neutrality merely to save the eastern provinces of France. His primary aim was the security of Silesia, and Silesia would be more secure if Maria Theresa was satisfied elsewhere, than if she was left with an uncontrollable longing to recover the lost province. It was therefore reasonably safe for Carteret to scheme for a German league to recover the *avulsa membra imperii*.[2] If he could once more seat the old line of Dukes of Lorraine, and if he could restore Naples and Sicily to Austria, he would undo the evil consequences of the Polish Succession War. If he could further wrest Alsace from France, he would

[1] Hyndford reported to Carteret on 16 July, 1743, that Frederick professed the best intentions towards Maria Theresa, " even so far as not to be against her Hungarian Majesty getting somewhere or other an equivalent for Silesia " (Hyndford Papers, ix., fo. 153).
[2] This was Pitt's phrase when he denounced Carteret's aggressive policy after the latter's dismissal.

deprive the Bourbons of one of the great bequests of Richelieu. But there was one point on which Frederick might be expected to be adamant. He would not tolerate the aggrandizement of Austria in Germany, and, above all, he would not allow the compensation for Silesia to be gained at the expense of the Emperor Charles VII by the spoliation of his electorate. Unfortunately for Carteret, Bavaria was to Maria Theresa at once the most obvious and the most attractive equivalent for Silesia. She was not averse to deprive France of Alsace, or to drive Don Carlos from Naples, but one or the other was to serve as compensation to the Emperor for the loss of Bavaria. This was destined to prove a fatal stumbling-block at Hanau.

(2) It must never be forgotten that the death of Charles VI not only opened the question of the Austrian Succession, but also created a vacancy in the Empire. The two problems were in their essence distinct, but they became almost inextricably mixed together because the principal claimant to the Succession was also the successful candidate for the Imperial Crown. The ardent Belleisle and the more hesitating Fleury failed in their attempt to partition the Austrian dominions, but they gained a counterbalancing triumph by depriving the Austrian house of an office which it had held continuously since 1438 and had come to regard as virtually a hereditary possession. To Maria Theresa the action of the eight Electors in passing over her husband was almost as great a blow as the loss of Silesia. She resolutely refused to recognize the validity of the election on the ground that the Bohemian vote had been illegally excluded, or to submit to decrees of the Diet which had been transferred from Ratisbon to Frankfort. All demands for the surrender of the imperial archives, so long kept at Vienna, were contemptuously rejected. She had already humiliated Charles VII by making him a landless and impoverished exile, dependent for his maintenance on the bounty of France, and she would continue to do so, if possible, until he submitted to her terms. The best thing he could do was to resign a dignity which he could not support; and the very least

was to consent to the election of Francis Stephen as King of the Romans. The quarrel was complicated by the fact that the Empire was technically a neutral Power. Charles Albert of Bavaria was the belligerent enemy of Austria. At Munich he might be attacked and even captured. But, if he resided as Emperor in an imperial city, such as Augsburg or Frankfort, he was immune from hostility. The problem of the Empire was not only an obstacle to peace, it was also a source of difficulty both with England and with Prussia. George II and Carteret might desire to get rid of an Emperor who was necessarily a puppet of France, but they could not evade the awkward fact that the Elector of Hanover had helped to place him on his uneasy throne. And Frederick, resenting the implied contention that the Austrian house had a vested right to the imperial office, could not allow the complete humiliation of a prince who owed his dignity in very large measure to Prussian support.

(3) While the war was continued to procure compensation for Maria Theresa and to find some solution for the problems of Germany, there were difficulties in the way of peace in Italy. There the protagonist against Austria was Spain, the Power with which England was actually at war, whereas France in 1743 was only a professed auxiliary of Bavaria. Elizabeth Farnese had provided for her eldest son by placing him on the throne of Naples and Sicily. She now undertook to find a principality for Don Philip, who was also son-in-law to Louis XV, by depriving Maria Theresa of Lombardy. To any further aggrandizement of the Spanish Bourbons England was necessarily opposed. But our naval weakness in the Mediterranean allowed a Spanish force to be conveyed by sea to Orbetello, while another army under Don Philip traversed the South of France to occupy Savoy and thence to enter Italy by the Alpine passes. If these troops could join together they would, with French auxiliaries and reinforcements from Naples, be superior to any armies which Austria could spare from her more pressing needs in Bohemia and Germany. The immediate danger was met in 1742 by the generalship

of Traun, by the invaluable assistance of Sardinia, and
by the dictatorial conduct of Commodore Martin, who
coerced Don Carlos into the withdrawal of the Neapolitan troops by a threat to bombard Naples. But if the
successful resistance to the Bourbon Powers was to continue, and still more if their hold upon Italy was to be
destroyed, Sardinia, which held the key of the position,
must be substantially paid for her services. So far
Charles Emmanuel had received nothing but undefined
assurances, and the translation of these into a definite
agreement was another of the unsolved problems connected with the war. And this was a problem which
England, as an interested and actual belligerent, could
not possibly neglect.

Although the obstinacy of Elizabeth Farnese made a
speedy settlement in Italy improbable, it did not seem
equally obvious that hostilities should continue in
Germany. What was necessary to restore peace there
was to detach Charles VII from France, to bring about
some reconciliation between him and Maria Theresa,
and to procure the withdrawal of all foreign troops from
the Empire. During the winter of 1742-43 many of the
diplomatists of Europe, amateur and professional, busied
themselves with efforts to find a solution. Frederick II,
always eager to place Prussia in the forefront, proposed
that he and George II, both of whom had voted for
Charles VII, should act as joint mediators. In spite of
his fury at the intrusion of the pragmatic army from
the Netherlands into Germany, which seemed to him to
threaten a prolongation of the war, he succeeded in
adjusting with Hyndford the outlines of a joint plan.
All French intervention was to be excluded, Bavaria was
to be raised to a kingdom with an *arrondissement* calculated to produce an increased revenue of six million
florins, no further cessions were to be demanded from
Maria Theresa, and the desired enlargement of Bavarian
territories was to be obtained by the secularization of
bishoprics (as at Westphalia) and by the mediatization
of some of the imperial cities. All Bavarian claims to
the Austrian Succession were to be withdrawn, the
Emperor was to be recognized by Maria Theresa, and

some agreement come to as to the Bohemian vote. Nothing was said about the election of a King of the Romans, and Frederick did not conceal his hostility to such a measure.[1] Neither Carteret nor Münchhausen offered any objection in principle to the joint mediation, or to the restoration of Bavaria, or to its aggrandizement,[2] or to secularization. They criticized certain details, such as the actual selection of particular bishoprics, and they objected *in toto* to the proposed mediatization on the ground that so many of the imperial cities were strongholds of Protestantism. Charles VII nearly wrecked the scheme at the outset by authorizing Haslang, his agent in London, to bring forward proposals of his own on somewhat parallel lines, but with the momentous difference that the Bavarian claims were to be bought off by cessions on the part of Maria Theresa in Bohemia and elsewhere. But Frederick and Podewils undertook to bring the Emperor to a more reasonable frame of mind.[3]

[1] Hyndford reported to Carteret on 5 January, 1743, that Frederick had said to him: "Make war on the French in their own country as much as you please, but we can't have foreign troops oppressing the chief of the Empire in his own country." And the King went on: " Écoutez, my Lord, vous pouvez à présent faire la paix pour l'Empereur, mais point de Roi des Romains " (Hyndford Papers, viii.). Later, on 1 February, Hyndford boasted that, with discreditable duplicity, he had told Valori that Frederick had advised an attack on France. The gist of Frederick's remark had been, " if you must attack France, do it in France, not in Germany."

[2] Hyndford wrote to Carteret on 18 January, 1743, that he had ventured to say that neither Maria Theresa nor her allies had any intention of keeping Bavaria. Frederick broke in: " Will you guarantee that ?" " Yes, sir, if there is no other difficulty in the way of peace, my master will guarantee that." Later Hyndford put into French for the Prussian Government a dispatch of Carteret of 1/12 March, and inserted these words: " Que par rapport à la Bavière, le Roy mon maître n'a rien a redire contre sa restitution, ni même contre son érection en royaume " (*ibid.*, fo. 314).

[3] Haslang's project is in the Hyndford Papers, vii., fo. 64, and was sent to him by Carteret on 4/15 January, 1743. Podewils' assurances that Prussia would force reasonable terms on Charles VII were reported by Hyndford on 1 February (*ibid.*, fo. 134). See also an account of the discrepancy between the Prussian and the Imperial proposals in a frank letter from Carteret to William of Hesse in Brit. Mus. Add. MSS. 22,527, fo. 93.

In spite of the appearance of substantial agreement between England and Prussia, the scheme of reconciliation would have been wrecked by the obstinate refusal of Maria Theresa to allow Bavaria to be restored, at any rate until some other equivalent had been obtained. And secularization would have proved another serious obstacle. It was easy for Protestant Powers, like Prussia and Hanover, to propose the absorption of ecclesiastical principalities, and Hanover was believed to have designs of her own on the Sees of Osnabrück and Hildesheim. But it was difficult for Charles VII to accept such proposals, to risk the alienation of the Roman Catholic princes, and to place so obvious a weapon of attack in the hands of Austria. A premature disclosure of the scheme forced the Emperor to disavow it, and in the meantime it was rendered wholly obsolete by the campaign of 1743. France was becoming more and more weary of distant fighting in Germany, and Broglie, never a very energetic commander, thought more of securing a line of retreat for his army than of defending Bavaria. The absence of all co-operation between Broglie and Seckendorf made the task of Charles of Lorraine an easy one. No pitched battle was either possible or necessary, one garrison after another surrendered, and finally Seckendorf, deserted by the French, agreed with Khevenhüller to the Convention of Niederschönfeld, by which the Bavarian troops, converted into neutral imperial forces, were to be withdrawn from the electorate. Charles VII had already departed, first to Augsburg, where he found Austrian cavalry officers carousing in the next-door house,[1] and thence to more secure seclusion at Frankfort. Bavaria was as completely in the hands of Maria Theresa as the recovered kingdom of Bohemia, to which she had gone in May to receive the homage of the estates. There might have been a chance of the recovery of Bavaria if the second French army under Noailles had succeeded

[1] The story about the Emperor's annoyance by Austrian cavalry in Augsburg is told in a letter by William of Hesse to Carteret of 18 June, 1743 (Carteret Papers, Brit. Mus. Add. MSS. 22,527). It is a curious illustration of the neutrality of an imperial city in the immediate vicinity of the actual war.

in crushing the pragmatic army at Dettingen (27 June).
But George II's lucky escape from the trap in which his
composite forces had been involved, and his success in
reaching his base of supplies at Hanau, rendered it impossible for Noailles to risk any eastward advance, and
in the end he retreated to the Rhine. Bavaria was left
to its fate.

In these humiliating circumstances Charles VII could
no longer hope to negotiate upon equal terms. He did
not entirely trust Frederick, and he did not wish to be
too dependent upon Prussian patronage. He therefore
determined to throw himself on the mercy of George II,
and to obtain through him the best terms that might yet
be extorted from Maria Theresa. His emissary, whom
he had selected on 18 May, seemed to be singularly well
fitted for the task. William of Hesse was administrator
at Cassel for his elder brother, Frederick, who had been
King of Sweden since 1720, as the husband of Ulrica
Eleanor, the sister of Charles XII. Prince William was
a sturdy Protestant, and was always exasperated by a
suggestion that France should paralyze England by
supporting the Pretender and encouraging a Jacobite
rising. But he had been from the first a consistent supporter of Charles VII, and was suspected of a desire to
obtain from a grateful Emperor the elevation of Hesse
into a tenth electorate.[1] At the same time he was closely
connected with England and Hanover, his son and heir
having married the Princess Mary, one of the daughters
of George II. He had displayed a mercenary impartiality
in the war, as 6,000 Hessians, under his brother George,
were serving in British pay with the pragmatic army,
while another contingent was in the service of the
Emperor. From an early date in 1742 he had been in
intermittent correspondence with George II and Carteret
as to the best means of detaching Charles VII from

[1] Brit. Mus. Add. MSS. 32,804 (Newcastle Papers, vol. cxix.),
fo. 45, translation of a letter from the Nuncio at Frankfort to
the Cardinal Secretary of State at Rome: " The Princes of Hesse
are well inclined to the Emperor, perhaps in hopes at some time
to attain the electoral dignity so much desired by them. For
which reason they will never openly take any engagement contrary to the service of his Imperial Majesty " (10 March, 1744).

his dependent alliance with France.[1] Hanau, where George II was now encamped, and where the momentous negotiation was to take place, was a possession of his own, and he had some acute controversies with the British Government as to the use they had made of his town. Finally, he was on intimate terms with the King of Prussia, who seems to have had a real liking for him in spite, or perhaps because, of a slight estimate of his ability.

Of the proceedings at Hanau we have a full and accurate account, not only in the Carteret and Newcastle Papers in the British Museum, but also in a narrative drawn up by William of Hesse and published by him in somewhat sensational circumstances in the following year.[2] There is no discrepancy as to the facts or the documents, though these supply no conclusive evidence as to motives on either side. But there is no reason to question the transparent sincerity of Prince William, who was evidently eager to succeed in his mission, who at one moment confidently reckoned on success, and who was equally disappointed and chagrined when his hopes were cruelly dashed to the ground. Nor is there much doubt as to the motives of the members of the English Regency, who were ostensibly responsible for wrecking the negotiation. Newcastle was no Machiavelli, and though one might discount his letters to Carteret, there is no reason to suspect insincerity in his private letters to Hardwicke and Lord Orford. The supreme difficulty is to read the inner mind of Carteret and of George II, who seem to have acted in complete accord in the matter, and who have made no confidential disclosures. It must be remembered that George II had left England at the beginning of May, that he had gone to Hanover before joining the army, that during his

[1] Brit. Mus. Add. MSS. 22,527 (Carteret Papers) contains Carteret's correspondence with William of Hesse in 1742, 1743, and 1744. The volume is of considerable interest.

[2] Copies of William of Hesse's narrative are preserved in several collections of papers in the British Museum, notably in Brit. Mus. Add. MSS. 22,527, which contains most of Carteret's papers relating to Hanau. But it can most easily be consulted in *Preussische Staatsschriften*, i. (Berlin, 1877), 633–8.

absence the administration was in the hands of a Council of Regency, of which the principal members were Wilmington, the two Pelham brothers, and Lord Hardwicke, and that these men had granted full powers to Carteret, the sole Minister who accompanied the King. In such circumstances it was inevitable that Ministers at home should regard with some jealousy and mistrust the colleague who possessed such unlimited authority coupled with the influence which personal intercourse with their royal master might confer. Even the harmless Harrington had been suspected of disloyal use of his privileged position when he went with the King to Hanover in 1741. Such suspicion was multiplied a hundredfold in the case of the brilliant and self-confident Carteret, who had never become assimilated with the former colleagues of Walpole, who did not conceal the scantiness of his respect for their opinions, who was notoriously more favoured by the King, and who did not even take the trouble to keep them well informed of his proceedings by any regular correspondence. Newcastle's letters are full of denunciations of the taciturnity of " my Brother-Secretary."

The credentials of William of Hesse consisted of a letter from the Emperor to George II, dated 18 May, 1743, in which he placed himself in the King's hands, provided the terms adjusted with Austria were consistent with his honour and with the maintenance of the imperial dignity to which George II had helped to raise him. This letter was presented at Hanover on 4 June. On his way to Hanover Prince William had been an honoured guest at Berlin from 26 May to 2 June.[1] Although we have no information as to what passed between him and the Prussian King, it is impossible to suppose that he entirely concealed from his host the object of his mission. But it is noteworthy that

[1] Hyndford Papers, ix., fo. 53, Hyndford to Carteret, 30 May, 1743: " Prince William of Hesse arrived here on the 26th in the evening; he is lodged in the Palace and has great honours showed him; 'tis said he sets out for Hanover on Saturday or Sunday next." Hyndford adds that he cannot discover the intention of his journey, and it is characteristic of Carteret that he never enlightened his envoy at Berlin.

Charles VII's letter made no mention of Prussia or of joint mediation, and this subsequently roused Frederick to suspect that he was being deliberately excluded. Nothing of importance transpired at the Hanover interview. Carteret told the Prince that (1) there could be no cessions from Maria Theresa; (2) the Bavarian claims must be given up; (3) the Emperor must detach himself from France; (4) no injury must be inflicted on any secular state, whether Protestant or Catholic. With this cold comfort William proceeded to rejoin the Emperor at Frankfort in order to discuss how these conditions could be fulfilled. To a suggested cessation of arms pending a settlement Carteret had given a decided negative. After sending a full report of what had passed to Newcastle, and also to Robinson at Vienna, Carteret proceeded with his royal master to the army, and after the Battle of Dettingen William of Hesse came to Hanau to renew the negotiation. In the interval Newcastle had replied to Carteret that the desire in England was for a general peace, and not for a mere treaty to extricate the Emperor from his difficulties.[1]

William of Hesse brought to Hanau on 5 July the preliminary terms upon which Charles VII was willing to come to a settlement with Austria. They were embodied in five articles. (1) The French auxiliaries were to be dismissed and to quit the Empire, provided that at the same time Bavaria and the Upper Palatinate were evacuated and restored by the Austrians, and that the composite pragmatic army also departed from the Empire. (2) As the Emperor's hereditary states have been ruined by the war, he must receive, pending a complete settlement, an adequate revenue to enable him to maintain both a military force and the imperial dignity. (3) The final settlement of a firm and solid peace is to be entrusted to the Empire and to the other mediating Powers. (4) and (5) There is to be a complete amnesty and a release of all prisoners. To these proposals Carteret returned a formal reply on 7 July to the

---

[1] Newcastle to Carteret, 4/15 July, 1923, in Brit. Mus. Add. MSS. 22,536, fo. 57.

effect that the King must act in complete accord with Maria Theresa, that the latter may not be unwilling to help the Emperor provided the French troops are immediately dismissed, and that no assurance can be given that Bavaria and the Upper Palatinate will be *préalablement* restored. The King will do his best both for the restoration of territories and in other matters, provided the Empire is rid of the French troops. On 8 July Carteret forwarded copies of the two documents—the Emperor's proposals and his own reply—both to London and to Vienna.[1] But in his letter to Robinson he abstained from any instructions to press for concessions to the Emperor.

Prince William carried Carteret's unsatisfactory reply to Frankfort, and returned with the Emperor's protest against the unfairness of asking him to dismiss his auxiliaries before he had obtained any assurance as to the recovery of his dominions. He reiterated his former proposals, and the only suggested concession was that he would accept an English assurance that Bavaria would be restored as soon as the French had gone. Matters had apparently come to a deadlock, and it would have caused no surprise if the negotiations had been broken off at this point. The French had already virtually quitted Germany, so that their dismissal was no longer an asset for bargaining. And the resolute omission of all resignation of the Bavarian claims on the Austrian Succession was a fatal bar to any final agreement. But, for some unexplained reason, Carteret at this stage set to work to adjust more comprehensive terms. The order of the various clauses was altered at his dictation, and by the evening of 14 July a draft scheme, under the heading " Projet et Idées," had been drawn up of the terms to be suggested to Maria Theresa. With it was associated a " Projet d'Assurance Secrète

[1] Copies of the proposals and of Carteret's reply were also given to the Austrian generals at Hanau and distributed broadcast among the Allied Courts. This publicity contrasts strongly with the comparative secrecy as to the subsequent negotiations. Robinson reported on 24 July that the Ministers at Vienna were less pleased than the generals. " This ill humour arose from the word Restitution " (State Papers, For., Germany, 160).

entre Sa Majesté Impériale et le Roy de Grande-Bretagne." These two documents constitute the so-called Treaty of Hanau. William of Hesse was so confident that Carteret's participation in drafting the articles had committed him to the scheme that he wrote a jubilant letter to Charles VII, and the Emperor, an optimist even in the darkest days, began to reckon on a speedy return to his beloved Munich.[1]

The more important of the two documents consisted of eight articles, of which the last two dealt with the proposed amnesty and release of prisoners. The other six articles were finally placed in the following order : (1) The Emperor will dismiss the French troops, and will procure their departure from the Empire. (2) The Emperor will set himself, in concord with his Britannic Majesty, to procure joint action of the Empire with the Maritime Powers to make France consent to a stable and general peace. (3) To compensate the Emperor for the loss of French supplies and for the ruin of his dominions, he is to receive an adequate monthly subsidy for his maintenance, to begin in the month following the signature of the agreement, and to continue until means have been found, in concert with the Empire, to supply him with a revenue sufficient to maintain the imperial dignity and also that of Bavaria, which is to be made a kingdom. (4) As the Queen of Hungary cannot be asked to restore Bavaria and the Upper Palatinate until she has been satisfied as to the Bavarian claims to her own dominions, the Emperor is to renounce those claims for himself and his descendants. (5) As soon as this act of renunciation has been executed, the lost provinces are to be restored. (6) Maria Theresa is to recognize Charles VII as Emperor, he is to recognize her as Queen of Hungary and Bohemia, and the Emperor is to take steps to procure the restoration of the Bohemian vote in the Diet.

As a necessary interval must elapse before these pro-

[1] Brit. Mus. Add. MSS. 22,527, Von Donop (Hessian agent at Frankfort) to Assebourg: " L'Empereur m'a témoigné une joye indescribable en apprenant que l'affaire prenoit un si heureux train " (16 July, 1743).

posed terms could be sent to Vienna and Austrian approval obtained, and as the pecuniary needs of the Emperor were pressing, it was necessary to provide for his maintenance in the meantime. This was the primary purpose of the supplementary "Projet d'Assurance," by which the British King was pledged (1) to endeavour to procure Austrian assent to the above terms; (2) to obtain, if possible, further advantages for the Emperor, but not at the expense of Maria Theresa; and (3) to pay three sums of 100,000 crowns to the Emperor, the first on the signature of the present document, and the other two at successive intervals of twenty days.

William of Hesse, by his own account, seems to have expected both documents to be signed on 15 July. But it is clear that the first document was not in a form which was ripe for signature, and could at best be regarded as raw material out of which a treaty could be constructed. But the "Projet d'Assurance," which would have committed the British Government to the championship of the adjusted terms, could have been signed, and Carteret had sufficient powers to enable him to sign it. But at the last moment, without any previous warning, he declared that he must send the documents to London in order to ascertain whether Parliament would support the scheme, that it would be unfair to the Emperor to give promises which it might be impossible to fulfil, that the delay would not exceed a fortnight, that he had no doubt that so beneficial a scheme would receive the approval of the other Ministers, that, as a sign of goodwill, the King would immediately pay the first 100,000 crowns, and that, as soon as English assent had been obtained, the King hoped to gratify the Emperor beyond his fondest hopes. Prince William was profoundly disappointed and annoyed by the unexpected delay, but it was impossible for a suppliant to cavil at Carteret's decision, and it was necessary to wait with pretended patience for the decision from London. The proffered dole of 100,000 crowns seemed rather humiliating to the Emperor, but it was deemed hazardous to irritate George II by refusal, and all that could be done to sweeten acceptance was to couple it with a request that the British King should press Austria to abstain from levying contributions upon the unfortunate Bavarians. But Carteret could hardly fail to urge that it was for the giver rather than the recipient to attach conditions to a gift, and the haggling was still going on when the return of the messenger from England put an end to the negotiation. The money was never paid, and Charles VII had to fall back upon subsidies from France.

How far Carteret was in earnest in declaring that he and the King were in favour of the proposed terms is to this day wrapped in mystery. But there is one consideration which may well have commended the bargain to George II. It was altogether his own work, and the distasteful joint mediation of Prussia had been entirely excluded. In the earlier proposals of the Emperor, Article 3 was doubtless intended to include Prussia among the mediating Powers, but no such article was inserted in the terms as finally adjusted on 15 July. Frederick had nothing more to do with them than any other member of the Empire. The Prussian King must have known about Prince William's embassy and must have had a shrewd idea of the terms which would be suggested. But the rumours from Hanau that an agreement was being adjusted without his being consulted excited his indignation. He determined to send to Hanau Count Finckenstein,[1] destined later to be a Foreign Secretary at Berlin for half a century, with a personal letter to Carteret, who was little used to such attentions from that source. Finckenstein, who arrived on 17 July, was instructed to thrust himself at all costs into the negotiations, and to insist that the British Ministry had committed itself months ago to the prin-

---

[1] Hyndford reported to Carteret that he had vainly tried to obstruct the sending of a Prussian envoy, and in his dispatch of 20 July, 1743, drew a very unflattering picture of Finckenstein. " My Lord, you cannot be too much upon your guard against this little spy, who I am certain will in all his reports put the worst construction upon things, for he is the quintessence of Prussian *fourberie*. He is extremely polite, insinuating, and affected, and I cannot make a truer likeness of him than by saying he resembles his master in everything " (Hyndford Papers, ix., fo. 164).

ciple of joint intervention.[1] But Carteret would talk of nothing but general topics, and George II treated the Prussian envoy with a discourtesy which Frederick never forgave and for which he characteristically retaliated in his own treatment of Hyndford.[2]

Meanwhile Carteret had to carry out his promise. He did not send any communication of the draft terms to Vienna. But he did transmit the two documents of 15 July to London, though William of Hesse charged him in his later narrative with never having done so. They were sent off on the 16th with a covering letter to Newcastle, in which Carteret commented upon the proposals to be made to Austria. He pointed out that Articles 1 and 2 were what we had always demanded, but might be more strongly worded; that Article 3 had been taken *ad referendum*, but the last part, about the continuance of the subsidy, must be left out; that Article 4 had always been insisted upon as a *sine qua non*; that 6 was essential and there would be no difficulty about it with the Empire; and that 7 and 8 could easily be adjusted. He concluded by declaring that, though he had full powers, he would do nothing until he had the opinion of his colleagues at home. In a private letter of the same date he informed Newcastle that the King, thinking it of vital importance to gain the Emperor or to keep him in suspense, had decided to risk 100,000 crowns under the head of secret service money, and had signed a warrant for that sum. If the Emperor accepted, we should draw him into all our measures. If he refused, the warrant would be cancelled and never heard of.[3]

It is vital to remember that this communication reached London at a time of acute Ministerial tension.

[1] *Pol. Corr.*, ii., 390, Frederick to Podewils, 26 July, 1743: "Il m'importe trop d'avoir les mains dans cette négociation. C'est pourquoi il faut que le comte de Finckenstein s'en mêle, soit à tort ou à travers. . . . Il semble, par ce que Carteret dit à Finck, que le roi d'Angleterre voudrait bien faire les choses tout seul, sans le concours des autres: mais il faut s'obstrudre et négocier en dépit de tout le monde."

[2] For Finckenstein's report see *ibid.*, pp. 390–1.

[3] Carteret's two letters of 16 July are in Brit. Mus. Add. MSS. 22,536 (Carteret Papers)

Lord Wilmington, the figure-head whom Pulteney had insisted upon promoting as First Lord of the Treasury in Walpole's place, had died on 2/13 July, and for five weeks what had come to be regarded as the first office in the State was vacant pending the decision of the King. George II was said to have virtually promised the post, when vacant, to Henry Pelham, and Newcastle, with Hardwicke and other colleagues, was eager to secure his brother's promotion. On the other hand, Carteret made no secret that he was pledged to support the claims of Lord Bath (Pulteney), and Carteret had the King's ear. In these circumstances the home Ministers viewed with more than the usual mistrust all proposals from their absent colleague, whom they suspected of a willingness to curry favour with the King by encouraging his Hanoverian predilections. The ill feeling between the British and the Hanoverian forces in the pragmatic army, which had been immensely increased by and since the Battle of Dettingen, and of which Newcastle had ample information in letters from the Duke of Richmond, stimulated this suspicion. Also Newcastle, naturally distrustful, always entertained the strange belief that Carteret was only a half-hearted supporter of the war and of the Austrian cause. He admitted his merit in putting an end to Hanoverian neutrality and in buying off Prussia, but he accused him of obstructing the march of the pragmatic army into Germany, and held him responsible for its inactivity after Dettingen. These suspicions were not only shared but were openly expressed by Lord Stair, who threw up his command in disgust at what he regarded as a deliberate decision to desert Maria Theresa.[1] The charge of Hanoverianism was an easy and obvious weapon of attack in the

---

[1] The latest biographer of Lord Hardwicke adopts this view. " In July 1743 the King and Lord Carteret, without consulting the Ministers at home, suddenly abandoned the whole policy of supporting Austria, and entered into negotiations at Hanau with the Emperor, the rival of Austria and the ally of France " (Yorke, *Life of Hardwicke*, i., 321). Mr. Yorke might have noted that the whole aim of the negotiations was to reconcile the Emperor with Austria and to detach him from France. This can hardly be described as " a total reversal of British policy," especially as it had been pursued for many months beforehand.

eighteenth century, and it was indiscriminately employed against Carteret by all his enemies, but it rests upon little substantial evidence. It is difficult to see how Hanoverian interests were directly affected by either the acceptance or the rejection of the Hanau propositions, and it is still more difficult to see how Carteret's notorious desire for an aggressive war against the House of Bourbon could be combined with a deliberate alienation of Austria. The atmosphere of suspicion, however, must be allowed for in considering Newcastle's reply and his confidential letters on the subject to his colleagues.

Newcastle wrote on 15/26 July that Carteret's letter and enclosures had been carefully considered by the Lord Chancellor, the Lord President (Harrington), Henry Pelham, and himself. They referred to a previous letter of 3/14 June, in which the late Lord Wilmington and Lord Bath had concurred, when they had pointed out that the French were more vulnerable in Germany than in their own territories, and that a separate peace with the Emperor involved the risk of bringing the war into dangerous proximity to Britain.[1] The views then expressed were confirmed by the obvious difficulty of bringing about such a treaty, which was obvious from the documents forwarded by Carteret. For example, the third article for providing a monthly subsidy presented an insuperable difficulty. And by the terms of the article it might be permanent. Who was to pay it? Obviously Maria Theresa would be neither able nor willing to pay. It was equally certain that the British Parliament would refuse to bear such a burden, and, besides, the assurances in Article 2 were not worth it. The Ministers urged that Austria should be immediately informed, and that all the allied troops should be concentrated against France so as to force on a general peace. Such a peace must include the demoli-

[1] In a private letter to Carteret of 31 May Newcastle had expressed similar views. " I dread having France and Spain singly on our hands. . . . The Emperor is the weak point of their question; he is more than half conquered already; there we must press France, and there we shall get the better of them."

tion of Dunkirk and adequate security against any assistance to Spain on the part of France.

An illuminating commentary on this letter, and on the spirit which dictated it, is supplied by the following extracts from a letter from Newcastle to Lord Orford, who was frequently consulted by his former colleagues, and on whose influence with the King they specially relied at this time to support Henry Pelham against Lord Bath. With the letter went a copy of Newcastle's reply to Carteret, and Orford was asked to send his comments and advice on the situation.

" My lively Brother abroad is not yet ripe for breaking with us. . . . German politics, German measures, and (what perhaps is near as bad as either) German manners, will make it difficult for any Ministers to go on with safety and success. . . . By all accounts there is but *one Englishman* either heard or regarded. Our general is no more consulted in the operations of war than we have been in the negotiations that have been carrying on either for war or peace. . . . The scheme abroad is certainly to set ourselves at the head of the Empire. To appear a good German and to prefer the welfare of the Germanic body to all other considerations, this is the principle upon which my Brother Secretary set out at Hanover, and this is now the sole object. In order to this the Emperor must be gained, that is bought, the French must evacuate the Empire, and perhaps some assurance be given them that they may do it with safety, which, if so, accounts for the most unaccountable in-action of our army since the Battle of Dettingen. . . . Your friends here, suspecting a little what might be the *carte de pais* there, represented so long ago as the 3ᵈ June [o.s.] against a separate treaty between the Emperor and the Queen of Hungary, whereby Germany might be cleared, and we and perhaps the Dutch exposed to the resentment of France and Spain without being assured of the effectual assistance of the Queen of Hungary. No notice was taken of this representation, but about ten days ago a letter comes from my Brother Secretary in-closing a draught of articles of a treaty between the Emperor, the King, and the Queen of Hungary, and a draught of a private convention between the Emperor and the King, whereby we were to advance immediately

300,000 crowns to the Emperor (for 100,000 of which there is now actually an order given under the disguise of contingencies for the army); and the Emperor to have besides a large monthly subsidy till he had got, in perpetuity, an increase of dominions suitable to his dignity and the honour of his house, which subsidy might have remained consequently for ever. And by whom it was to be paid I leave you to judge, though that was not yet particularly mentioned. This was referred to us for consideration : my Lord Carteret would do nothing *conclusively* without the Queen of Hungary, who knew nothing of all this, nor without the knowledge and approbation of his colleagues in England. Much was said of the great figure the King made, that this step was to engage the Emperor and the Empire *to form a concert with the Maritime Powers for the public good and to oblige France to consent to a solid peace.* Not the appearance of a reason or proof to show how France would or could be obliged to consent to a peace by this step. In short the reasonings, or rather insinuations, to induce us to approve were : If you don't do this, you now can do nothing but attack the French in their own frontiers, which will be to great disadvantage. If you do it, you will have the Emperor and Empire on your side. And a sort of insinuation that this measure was necessary either to secure peace or to carry on the war, neither of which appeared to us."[1]

It is characteristic that Orford delayed his reply till 14/21 August, and then evaded the Continental problems altogether, merely urging that if the Treasury is offered to Pelham, " however circumscribed, conditional, or disagreeable, even under a probability of not being able to go on, it must be accepted."[2]

Newcastle's letter to Carteret, reeking as it did with disapprobation and mistrust, was not in itself a veto on negotiations with the Emperor, and was not so regarded. Not only did Carteret continue to discuss a possible reconciliation with Haslang, the agent of Charles VII,

[1] Newcastle to Orford, 22 July/2 August, 1743, in Brit. Mus. Add MSS. 32,700 (Newcastle Papers, xv.), fos. 314–17. The italics are Newcastle's.
[2] Orford to Newcastle, 14/21 August, 1743, in Brit. Mus. Add. MSS. 32,701.

and with Wasner, the able envoy of Austria, but he obstinately adhered to the contention that Austria could not possibly keep possession of Bavaria.[1] In this he was in accord with Lord Hardwicke, and with Henry Pelham, the most level-headed of the Ministers at home.[2] But the letter did put an end to the so-called " treaty " of Hanau, and to the mission of William of Hesse. Carteret could not conceal the fact that it was now impossible for him to sign the " Projet d'Assurance," though he had continued to inspire the Prince with confident hopes during the intervening fortnight. After the return of the messenger he verbally informed the Prince that the English Ministers were not inclined to free the Emperor from his embarrassments, and that they preferred to leave him as a burthen upon France. He added that the Emperor had only verbally severed himself from France, and that he ought to show more confidence in the British King, whose support was his only resource. Finally, under pressure, he drew up a written reply on 3 August to the following effect : " That, as the reply from England was not what had been expected, it was necessary to turn to the Queen of Hungary to obtain something for the Emperor ; that, if the Emperor would give a confidential statement of his final conditions, an attempt would be made to get the best possible terms for him, that the Queen of Hungary would be at once appealed to for her last word, and that, once the agreement was made with her, England would be able on her side to do something for the Emperor."

[1] Robinson writes to Carteret on 27 August that Ulfeld had complained " that even by this last courier your Lordship had spoken more plainly than ever to M. Wasner of the *immediate* restitution of Bavaria " (State Papers, For., Germany, 159). And on the same date Carteret wrote to Newcastle: " As to Bavaria, gained by a providential rapidity of success, I tell the Queen she can't keep it *iusto titulo*, because not one state in the Empire will consent to her occupation of it " (Brit. Mus. Add. MSS. 32,701; Coxe, *Henry Pelham*, i., 87).

[2] Hardwicke to Mr. Stone, 4 September, 1743, in Brit. Mus. Add. MSS. 32,701: " I cannot help thinking that *opiniâtreté* of the Court of Vienna about retaining Bavaria and the Upper Palatinate intolerable, though I do apprehend the restitution has been proposed too early."

This chilling answer, less encouraging than the previous reply of 7 July, was too much for the patience of William of Hesse. He came to the conclusion that he had been deliberately deluded with false hopes, and quitted Hanau in high dudgeon. His subsidy treaty with England was allowed to expire, and in the next year he joined the League of Frankfort, became thereby virtually an ally of France, in spite of his disapproval of French encouragement of the Jacobites, while the 6,000 Hessians were transferred to aid Charles VII in that temporary recovery of Bavaria which gladdened the last days of his unsuccessful life. The desire to justify his desertion in the eyes of his English friends was the chief motive for Prince William's intervention in the fierce controversy about Hanau which arose in the autumn of 1744.

Another Prince who did not conceal his annoyance at the failure of the Hanau negotiations was Frederick the Great. There can be no doubt that the desire to keep Frederick quiet and appeased[1] was one of the reasons which led Carteret to meddle with the ticklish question of the restitution of Bavaria, and to run the risk, which Newcastle and other critics exaggerated, of alienating Maria Theresa. If he had been a free agent, he would probably have treated Finckenstein with more courtesy than George II allowed him to show. Frederick's professions of German patriotism were doubtless exaggerated and insincere, but there is no reason to question the sincerity of his interest in the cause of Charles VII, and he had ample cause to resent the threatened Austrian annexation of Bavaria and the concentration of two electorates in a single hand. For this reason, while he had resented his own exclusion from the Hanau

---

[1] Before he returned to England Carteret wrote from Hanover to Robinson about Frederick: "Maybe the greatest service that has been done the Court of Vienna this year has been brought about by knowing how to keep that Prince this year in inaction" (State Papers, For., Germany, 159, Carteret to Robinson, 7 November, 1743). When he wrote these complacent words he can hardly have anticipated what prominence would be assigned to his own conduct in this year as stirring Frederick to action in 1744.

proposals, he was none the less indignant at their apparent rejection. His wrath was visited upon thè unfortunate Lord Hyndford, who knew nothing about the matter. Carteret had received intelligence from the new Archbishop of Mainz—a partisan of Austria who owed his election largely to the presence in Germany of the pragmatic army—of a curious overture said to have been made by Hatsel, sub-intendant of Strasburg, on behalf of Marshal Noailles. This took the form of a request that the Archbishop should suggest to Austria the conclusion of peace on the basis that France would consent to the election of the young Archduke as King of the Romans and would aid Maria Theresa in the reconquest of Silesia. As a sign of goodwill Carteret instructed Hyndford to carry the news to Frederick, and at the same time to point out that it was probably only an attempt to sow dissension among the allies of Austria.[1] Hyndford, who was having a very dull time at Berlin, set out to carry what seemed to him an interesting despatch to Frederick at Glogau. To his intense astonishment he was received with a storm of indignation. Frederick made an unprintable comment on the Hatsel revelations, and then suddenly burst out with his grievance. " Est-ce qu'on ne restituera pas les pais de l'Empereur ? My Lord Carteret a oublié ce qu'il m'a promis touchant la Bavière, et il a bien joué le pauvre Prince de Hesse. De quelle manière et en quoi, Sire, car je n'en sais rien. O ! je le sais fort bien. Est-ce aux insulaires de donner la loi à l'Empire ?" To complete the astonishment of the envoy, Frederick sent for his carriage, raced Hyndford back to Berlin, beat him, and at once summoned Valori to a private conference. Hyndford, " farouche comme tous les Écossais," as Podewils described him,[2] was not prepared to submit to what he called the " brutalities " of Glogau. His

[1] Apparently more importance was attached at Vienna to Hatsel's propositions. Robinson writes to Carteret on 4 August, 1743: " I did not like Count Ulfeld's confused way last night of talking of those propositions, and his dislike of your Lordship's intention to advertise the King of Prussia of that incident " (State Papers, For., Germany, 159).

[2] *Pol. Corr.*, ii., 159.

protest extorted a sort of apology from the King, who declared that he was tired and out of humour, " and that the King my master had hid from him some negotiations which were on foot at Frankfort, and particularly a proposition which had been sent to England, although it was not approved of."[1]

There was no publicity in eighteenth-century diplomacy, so that, outside Ministerial circles, little was known about the negotiation at Hanau at the time. But in the following year the so-called " treaty " was suddenly brought into great prominence, when William of Hesse published his narrative of what had passed between Carteret and himself, and when Frederick took the treatment of Charles VII at Hanau as his chief text in the manifestoes issued to defend his renewal of the war. As Prussian intervention altered the whole character of the war and robbed the allies of their expected triumph against France, it was necessary for the English Ministers to make some answer to the charge that they were to blame for the disastrous turn of events. There were three parties who might share responsibility for the rupture at Hanau, or it might be brought home to any one of them. The Court of Vienna was notoriously averse to any reconciliation with Charles VII, and would probably have vetoed the scheme in any case. But the Austrian Ministers had a valid defence that the agreement, as adjusted at Hanau, had never been submitted to them. As far as England was concerned, the blame must rest between the Regency in London—*i.e.*, the Pelham brothers and Hardwicke—who had disapproved of the proposals forwarded on 15 July, and Carteret, who had made no great effort to convince his

---

[1] Robinson states that great interest was excited in Vienna by the news of Hyndford's ill-treatment at Glogau. Both the Austrian Ministers and Robinson himself thought " that it was clear that the King of Prussia expected that the Emperor should be restored to his country, and that he thought your lordship had only amused the Prince of Hesse " (Robinson to Carteret, 21 August, 1743, in State Papers, For., Germany, 159). Hyndford's account of his experiences is to be found in his dispatches of 15 and 20 August in State Papers, For., Prussia, 57, and in the Hyndford Papers, vol. ix.

colleagues, and who had actually broken off the negotiations with William of Hesse. That Prince and the Prussian King made no secret of their denunciation of Carteret, whose overthrow they eagerly desired. Carteret, however, who was now at loggerheads with the Pelhams, was prepared with a story which seemed at first sight to fit the available evidence. He had set himself to devise terms on which Charles VII might be reconciled with Maria Theresa, and his fellow Ministers in London had rejected them. His biographer and most English historians have accepted this simple explanation. It is in their favour that Newcastle was obviously alarmed by the prospect of having to debate this with Carteret if, as seemed inevitable, the question was raised in Parliament.[1] In the end discussion was burked by ousting Carteret from office before the session opened and by forming a coalition Ministry (the " Broadbottom ") which closed the mouths of the Opposition leaders.[2] This curious silence about an episode which had bulked so largely in Continental publications led to the obstinate tradition in England that there was some mystery about the Hanau negotiation.

Carteret tacitly submitted to be a scapegoat, and made no subsequent attempt to throw the blame upon his triumphant colleagues. This in itself is almost sufficient to show that he had no such sufficient defence as he might in altered circumstances have been forced to put forward. But there is, however, ample evidence elsewhere not only that he willingly acquiesced in the rupture at Hanau, but that he had ulterior motives for carrying the negotiation as far as he did. During his stay in Germany he was constantly pressing the conclusion of a treaty between Austria and Sardinia, to which he attached far more importance than he did to the conciliation of an impotent and landless Emperor. As this

[1] See his agitated letters to his brother and Lord Hardwicke of 25 and 28 August (o.s.), 1744, in Brit. Mus. Add. MSS. 32,703. These letters and the replies to them are partially printed in Coxe, *Henry Pelham*, i., and in Yorke, *Life of Lord Hardwicke*, i.

[2] See on the whole subject an article entitled " The Hanau Controversy and the Fall of Carteret," in the *English Historical Review*, xxxviii., No. 152 (October, 1923).

treaty also demanded sacrifices on the part of Maria Theresa, a persistence in both negotiations could only result in driving Austria to seek more lenient terms from France. On the other hand, if the less vital demand were pressed so far as to excite alarm and then dropped, the concession might make the other demand more palatable. The connection between the two negotiations was quite clear to competent contemporary observers,[1] but has been obscured to English readers by the historians' habitual treatment of the war in Italy as isolated from what was going on in the rest of Europe. If nothing else had been at stake, Carteret might have obtained the concurrence of his colleagues and forced Maria Theresa to resign Bavaria. As it was, the abandonment of the negotiation at Hanau was the price he had to pay for his success at Worms. That story is told in the next chapter. Whether, if he could have foreseen the future, Carteret would have preferred to gratify Charles Emmanuel rather than Charles VII is an insoluble problem. After all, Maria Theresa did not keep Bavaria, whereas in Italy she lost even more than she had to resign by the Treaty of Worms.

[1] Frederick of Prussia clearly grasped it. On 12 November, 1743, he wrote to Dohna, his Minister at Vienna: " Je vous dirai qu'ayant chargé le comte de Finckenstein de s'éclaircir avec le lord Carteret sur ce que—quoiqu'il l'eût positivement assuré d'avoir envoyé à la cour de Vienne les propositions de l'Empereur pour la paix—les ministres de cette cour niaient fort et ferme de n'en avoir aucune connaissance, if m'a été aisé d'apercevoir par les reponses vagues et entortillées dudit lord qu'il a en effet négligé de communiquer ces propositions au ministère de Vienne, ou, pour mieux dire, qu'il les a cachées tout exprès, pour ne pas nuire à la négociation avec la cour de Turin. Il n'a pas même fait difficulté d'avouer au comte de Finckenstein que c'était là la principale raison qui l'avait empêché de pousser la paix de l'Empereur avec la même vivacité qu'il aurait fait en toute autre occasion, n'osant surcharger la charrette, de peur de la briser; ce qui veut dire en d'autres termes qu'il avait craint d'informer la cour de Vienne des facilités que l'Empereur lui offrait pour sortir de l'affaire avec lui, de peur qu'elle ne regimbât contre les sacrifices qu'on la forçait de faire en Italie, et qu'un bon accommodement avec l'Empereur eût leur épargnés (*Pol. Corr.*, ii., 466).

CHAPTER II

THE TREATY OF WORMS, 13 SEPTEMBER, 1743

Triangular diplomacy between London, Vienna, and Turin—
Difficulty of tracing it—Importance of the negotiation—
Austria resents English attachment to Sardinia—Italian war
between Austria and Spain—Spanish claim to Austrian
succession—Establishment for Don Philip—Spanish overtures to Sardinia—Policy of Charles Emmanuel—Austrian
overtures to Turin—Terms of the two states—Spanish force
lands in Italy—Charles Emmanuel determined to oppose
Spain—Convention of Turin—Its unconventional character
—Failure of Spanish advance on Lombardy—Carteret under-
takes to promote a treaty between Austria and Sardinia—
England pays a subsidy to Sardinia—Communications between Vienna and Turin pass through London—Sardinian
demands—Draft treaty drawn up in London—Hostile reception at Vienna—Sardinia refuses aid against Naples—
Spaniards in Savoy—Renewed attack on Lombardy repulsed—English mediation between Austria and Sardinia—
Compromise about Finale—Cessions in Lombardy—Attempt
to make them conditional upon conquest of Naples—Wording
of relative articles—Proposed exchange of Bavaria for
Naples—Sardinian negotiations with France—Signature of
treaty—Austria demands supplementary declaration—
Carteret signs it—English Cabinet refuses to ratify—
Subsequent influence of Treaty of Worms.

IT is not altogether easy to trace the course of the
triangular diplomacy between London, Vienna, and
Turin which led up to the conclusion of the Treaty of
Worms. The difficulties have a double source. Communication between England and the Continent in the
eighteenth century was very slow, and in time of war
very insecure. On the coast dispatches were often held
up by adverse winds for days or even for weeks. When
they started on their voyage across the North Sea they
were exposed not only to the risks of weather, but also
to those of capture, either by an enemy ship or by a
privateer, and capture might betray the secret of a
cipher or even of a policy.[1] From Helvoetsluys they

[1] In October, 1745, a packet-boat containing secret dispatches
from Trevor to Harrington and from the Pensionary to the
Dutch envoy in London was captured by a French privateer.

were conveyed to The Hague, which was our distributing
centre, and in many ways the whispering gallery of
Europe. Our envoy at The Hague was better informed
than any other of our foreign agents, because so many
dispatches, both going and coming, passed through his
hands under flying seal. From The Hague it was a toilsome and perilous journey to Vienna. A courier might be
robbed without knowing whether it was done by thieves
for private gain or by secret agents of the state through
which he was passing. From Vienna it was a still more
toilsome journey to Turin. If in 1741 the French and
Bavarians had, as seemed likely, captured Vienna before
proceeding to the conquest of Bohemia, our envoy at
Turin might have been cut off from all communication
with England[1] unless he could induce the admiral of the
Mediterranean fleet to send a frigate round the coasts
of Spain and France. All this rendered it very difficult
to carry on any consecutive negotiation with either
Court, and especially with Turin. An instruction might
be obsolete before it reached its destination, and
information from the other end might be equally out
of date. Another difficulty which affects the historian
more directly is that, partly on account of these difficulties and partly for other reasons, the negotiations
were largely carried on in London. Thomas Robinson,
our envoy at Vienna, was an experienced diplomatist,
and in 1742 was rewarded with the K.B. for his services
in inducing Austria to consent to the Treaty of Breslau.[2]

Thus France obtained, not only a key to the English cipher, but
also a knowledge that England and Holland were trying, in despair
of victory, to devise terms of peace. The master of the ship was
severely censured for not having sunk the mails before surrender.
    [1] Villettes was afraid of this. See his letters to Newcastle of
23 September and to Harrington of 30 September, 1741, in State
Papers, For., Sardinia, 45.
    [2] Robinson had one great merit that he kept and arranged his
documents in the most orderly manner. The Robinson Papers,
ninety-eight volumes in the British Museum (Add. MSS. 23,780–
23,877), are a model collection. Their only defect, from a student's
point of view, is that the letters written by himself, beautifully
copied out, are bound up separately from those which he received,
so that it is necessary to have two volumes open at once and to
turn constantly from one to the other. The letters received are
arranged in real chronological order, and not, like most of the State

But Robinson, ever since the war of 1733, had been distrusted at Turin, and was thus not a very efficient
agent in affairs which concerned Sardinia.   And at
Turin itself we were less satisfactorily represented.
Robinson's verbosity has called down upon his memory
the maledictions of Carlyle, but it was a model of terse-
ness as compared with the maunderings of Arthur
Villettes.¹ Villettes had gone to Turin in 1732 as secretary under the Earl of Essex, and had remained in
charge without any promotion during Essex's absence
and after his departure.   It was not till 1741 that he was
raised to the still humble rank of "Resident," which,
though it increased his salary by a pound a day and
enabled him to employ a secretary, gave him neither
an adequate income nor that entrée to the Court which
was necessary in a country where the King really ruled.
At the outset Robinson and Villettes were employed in
a normal way, but later the negotiation, so far as
England was concerned — and England played a
dominant part in it—was mainly carried on by the
Secretaries of State with the Ministers sent to London
from Austria and Sardinia.   These Ministers, Ignaz von
Wasner and Joseph Osorio, were highly competent men.
But much of their task was performed in conversation,
and is more imperfectly recorded than if the policy of
our own Ministers had been formulated in instructions
to our agents abroad.   A certain amount of what passed
may be found in the dispatches of the two envoys to

Papers of the time in the Record Office, by the numerical headings,
irrespective of whether these are in the old or the new style.

¹ Villettes's dispatches frequently consist of over fifty folio
pages closely filled with ciphers, and they are rarely less than
thirty pages.   Sometimes he would send off two of these epistles
on the same day.   It was not that he had so much to say but that
he took so many words to say it.   His letters to Robinson are
almost as lengthy as those to Newcastle and Harrington.   He
himself made a sort of apology to Couraud, Under-Secretary
at the Foreign Office.   " I fancy your gentlemen of the office will
heartily curse me for the length of these letters in cypher, and
well they may, since I have cursed them more than once in writing
them " (18 January, 1742, in State Papers, For., Sardinia, 46).
No wonder he complained of overwork, especially before he had
a secretary to help him.

their own Courts, and also, so far as written documents passed, in Record Office State Papers under the heads of " Foreign Ministers in England " and of " Treaty Papers." Also, in the present case there is a good deal of material in the Carteret Papers and in the Newcastle Papers in the British Museum. But, speaking generally, it is easier for an English historian, intent upon the English point of view, to follow a negotiation conducted abroad than one which was carried on at home.

The importance of this negotiation lies partly in its bearing on the future development of Italy, which is so closely bound up with the progress of the House of Savoy-Piedmont, but also very largely in its influence upon the later relations of the great European Powers. The great central episode of European history in the eighteenth century is the so-called " diplomatic revolution," *le renversement des alliances*, as the French call it, which put an end to the secular rivalry between France and the House of Austria, and so to the traditional grouping of the chief states, the " old system," which had been based upon that rivalry. One primary force in bringing about this change was the alienation of Austria from Great Britain, which impelled Austria to seek an alliance with France. In tracing that alienation historians have very rightly laid stress upon the pressure exerted by Great Britain to extort concessions to Prussia, and upon the British refusal after the spring of 1745 to encourage or assist any effort on the part of Austria, however justified, to recover Silesia. But, even admitting the friction caused by the Treaty of Breslau, the Convention of Hanover, the Treaties of Dresden and Aix-la-Chapelle, and the hesitating caution with which Britain acceded to the Treaty of 1746 between the two Empresses, it is possible to maintain that, at any rate during the war of the Austrian Succession, still more acute irritation was caused at Vienna by the extraordinary and less explicable efforts on the part of British Ministers to promote the interests and to defend the conduct of the King of Sardinia. There were ties of relationship, there was common Protestantism, there were fears for the security of Hanover, to make Britain desirous to avoid a collision with Prussia : there were no such bonds to attach her to the Court of Turin. And to this day it is not easy to understand why Britain was so consistently and at times so enthusiastically the champion of the cause of Sardinia. It cannot be put down to any chivalrous altruism on the part of Charles Emmanuel. No ruler, not even Frederick the Great, was more openly and avowedly guided by self-interest pure and simple. What seems to have fascinated Britain was the absence of any concealment both of motives and of conduct on the part of the Sardinian King and his Ministers. They made no secret of the fact that their object was to obtain territorial expansion eastwards in Lombardy and an opening to the sea on the Genoese coast. They would prefer to get these gains by joining Austria, if they could be secure of adequate assistance and of a reasonable chance of success. But if this policy held out no hope of either success or security, then the duty of self-preservation would force them to take advantage of the overtures from the Bourbon Powers and to become their accomplices in aggression, as they had been in the last war. All their cards were laid upon the table for British inspection. Even the worst act on the part of Sardinia, which damned that Court in the eyes of Austria, the breach of the Treaty of Worms by the virtual conclusion of a preliminary treaty with France in the winter of 1745-1746,[1] was regarded with strange tolerance by British Ministers, largely because it was openly disclosed to them while it was carefully concealed from Vienna.[2] Such unusual and almost unparalleled candour, combined with an unvarying appeal for British goodwill, made even dishonesty appear almost honourable. It certainly proved attractive to the Court of London. On more than one occasion England endeavoured to procure for Sardinia at the expense of Austria more than

[1] See below, Chapter III.
[2] The only Minister who condemned the conduct of Sardinia was Lord Hardwicke, who wrote to Newcastle on 2 February (o.s.), 1746: "I cannot help thinking the Court of Turin has used the King and this country extremely ill in that affair " (Add. MSS. 32,706, fo. 93).

4

Sardinia would have been willing to accept. It is not surprising that Maria Theresa was exasperated. She had a keen eye for the weaker side of Sardinian policy. When Charles Emmanuel rendered her a service, she put it down to his own interest. When he refused to comply with her wishes, he was a deserter from the common cause and a breaker of the pledges for which he had been so extravagantly paid. That England should insist upon his retention of the gains which his treachery had forfeited was intolerable conduct on the part of a professed ally. Among the numerous misdeeds of England chronicled in the memory of Maria Theresa and Bartenstein none was blacker than the part which she played in making and upholding the Treaty of Worms.

In the Italian part of the war of the Austrian Succession the protagonists were Spain and Austria. For them the war was a continuation of the so-called war of the Polish Succession. In this previous war the two Bourbon States had undertaken to deprive Austria of all the Italian possessions which had been gained by the Utrecht settlement as modified by the Quadruple Alliance which had given to Austria Sicily in exchange for Sardinia. Thanks to the alliance of Sardinia, insisted upon by France against the wishes of Elizabeth Farnese, and thanks to the obstinate neutrality of the Maritime Powers, which enabled the Bourbon States to control the Mediterranean, they gained decisive successes in Italy. The complete expulsion of Austria was only averted by the victory of Fleury over Chauvelin, and by the consequent conclusion of preliminaries in 1735, and of the definitive Treaty of Vienna in 1738, which gave to Don Carlos the kingdoms of Naples and Sicily with the Tuscan *Presidii* (Orbetello, Talamone, Porto Ercole, and Porto Stefano, with Porto Longone on the Island of Elba), and gave to Sardinia two strips of the Milanese—viz., the districts of Novara and Tortona. On the other hand, Austria retained the slightly curtailed Duchy of Milan with Mantua, and these possessions were buttressed by the acquisition of the former Farnese Duchies of Parma and Piacenza, and by the cession to Maria Theresa's husband of the Grand-Duchy of Tuscany on condition that it should never be added to the Habsburg dominions. The settlement was not altogether unsatisfactory to Charles Emmanuel, for, though his acquisitions were far smaller than those which Chauvelin had held out to him, the balance between Habsburg and Bourbon was now much more equal than it had been, and upon that balance depended both his security and his prospect of future territorial gains. He knew that, if Austria had been driven from Italy, Spain would never allow him to remain in peaceful possession of lands which had once formed part of the great Spanish dominions. On the other hand, Elizabeth Farnese was furious at the conclusion of a treaty that not only robbed her of acquisitions which had seemed to be within her grasp, but actually transferred to the enemy the Farnese and Medici inheritance to which her own claims had been recognized after prolonged disputes by the previous Treaty of Vienna. She had provided for her eldest son, Don Carlos, but she had two younger sons, and for the elder of these, Don Philip, she was determined to obtain an Italian kingdom, or at least a principality, at the expense of the House of Austria. As Don Philip was married in 1739 to Marie Louise, the favourite daughter of Louis XV, she confidently reckoned upon the support of France.

To Elizabeth Farnese the settlement of 1738 was not a peace but a mere truce, and she welcomed the news of Charles VI's death as giving her a pretext for renewing the war which she had so unwillingly abandoned for the last five years. To justify its renewal she put forward a claim, carefully prepared beforehand, that the right of the Spanish Habsburgs to succeed on the extinction of the Austrian male line had been transferred, with the crown of Spain and the Indies, to her husband, Philip V. This preposterous pretension to revive in Bourbon hands the vast empire of Charles V was intended at Madrid, and was generally understood, to refer only to Italy and to cover a design of carving out an establishment for Don Philip. As regards the other portions of Maria Theresa's inheritance, Spain was ready to encourage any claimant who was likely to distract Austrian attention and Austrian forces from the defence of Lombardy. At the outset the Spanish claim, even though accompanied by military and naval preparations, attracted little attention, and excited less alarm at Vienna. It was taken to be one of those formal protests which were so common in the diplomacy of the period. The situation seemed to be very different from that of 1733. Spain was now involved in a maritime war with England, and was not likely to have free access to Italy by sea. Transit by land required the approval of France, and France was pledged to the Pragmatic Sanction, her policy was guided by the pacific Fleury, and he might be trusted not to upset the Italian settlement, which had been his own work. And there was another obstacle to land transit, the territories of the King of Sardinia. Maria Theresa had a shrewd and well-founded conviction that Charles Emmanuel did not want Spanish ascendancy in Italy, and that he would fight rather than submit to it. Spain, single-handed and cut off from Italy by a British fleet, by French neutrality, and, at the worst, by Sardinian control of the outlets from the Alpine passes, was not much more formidable than a single-handed Elector of Bavaria, who had also put forward a claim to a large part of her inheritance, and especially to the kingdom of Bohemia, based upon an alleged but disputed version of the will of Ferdinand I, the founder of the Austrian branch of the Habsburgs.

These assurances were rapidly dispelled in the first six months of 1741. This was effected by the wholly unforeseen invasion of Silesia by the young King of Prussia, by the certainty that France would oppose the election of the Grand-Duke Francis to the Empire, by the gradual weakening and ultimate withdrawal of Fleury's pacific professions, and finally by the discovery that France and Spain had become parties, with Charles Albert of Bavaria, to a scheme for the partition of the Austrian dominions. Spain was now assured, if not of actual French assistance in Italy, at any rate of a safe passage to the Alps of Dauphiné. And if Austria had to fight simultaneously against Prussia in Silesia, and against French and Bavarians in Austria itself and Bohemia, how was it possible to spare sufficient troops to enable the veteran Traun, now the Viceroy in the Milanese, to defend Lombardy against a Bourbon attack? Everything depended upon the British fleet and upon the possibility of obtaining active support from Charles Emmanuel. And when the news came that the British fleet had failed to block the way to Italy, that a Spanish force had actually been landed at the Tuscan ports, and that it would inevitably be joined by the troops of Don Carlos from Naples, the need of Sardinian assistance became imperative, and the negotiations with Turin, hitherto languid and tentative, were suddenly galvanized into feverish activity.

Spain had been the first Power to decide that there should be war in Italy, and so Spain had been the first Power to make overtures to Sardinia. Charles Emmanuel and his able Minister, the Marquis d'Ormea, received them coolly. They did not fear Spain, but they did fear France, and, still more, France and Spain combined. They could come to no decision until they knew whether France would support Spain in Italy. And so they refused to negotiate unless France was also a principal contracting party. By this they gained two things: delay, till they could see how the situation would develop, and also the certainty that, if they should be compelled to accept a Bourbon alliance, France would obtain better terms for them than Elizabeth Farnese would be inclined to offer. Fleury had not always seen eye to eye with Chauvelin, but he agreed with his fallen colleague in thinking that an attack on the Habsburgs in Italy required Sardinian support even when England was neutral, and required it still more when English opposition was assured. And he knew that Sardinian support must be paid for. The Queen of Spain, on the other hand, who loathed the necessity of buying Sardinia at all, would not curtail the prospective endowment of Don Philip by a foot more than she could help. And she was confirmed in this determination by feeling assured against any outbidding on the part of Maria Theresa, who regarded it as a pious duty to her father's memory to maintain the integrity of the Austrian dominions. Charles Emmanuel knew that Elizabeth Farnese was prejudiced against him; he had had ample experience of co-operation with Spain in the last war, and nothing short of extreme danger would induce him to repeat it. He had virtually made up his mind that he would join with Austria unless the risk was too great to be faced. But for his assistance he must be adequately paid, and paid in ready money, not on credit. From Spain, which controlled no territory in Northern Italy except the little Tuscan ports, he could get nothing but conditional promises, and they had an awkward habit of proving worthless. From Austria he could get actual possession, and he resolved to insist upon it. He was fully aware of Maria Theresa's reluctance to depart from the letter of the Pragmatic Sanction, but he could look to England to put pressure upon Austria, just as he looked to France to put pressure upon Spain. And so he made up his mind on four points : (1) Territorial cessions, whether large or small, must be immediate and not prospective, and must include an outlet to the sea ; (2) they must be guaranteed by the Maritime Powers, or at any rate by England ; (3) Austria must, however distressed elsewhere, maintain an adequate force in Italy to defend Lombardy ; (4) England must give him a subsidy, and keep a fleet in the Mediterranean. Until he was satisfied on these points, he could carry on the negotiations with France and Spain, which were now being conducted in Paris, and he could use their offers to justify and enforce his own demands from Austria. And so every conversation between Fleury and Solaro, the Sardinian envoy in France, was promptly retailed to Villettes for transmission to England and thence to Vienna.

At the outset Maria Theresa saw little reason for seeking Sardinian support, and less for purchasing it at her own expense. She sent Count Schulenburg to Turin, where she was previously unrepresented, with a draft in Latin of a treaty between Austria, Sardinia, and Tuscany, which was to be the basis of an Italian league for mutual security against external invasion.   There was not a word or a hint of territorial cessions.   Ormea treated it with contempt, and told Villettes that Maria Theresa seemed to think that the other Italian States would be idiotic enough to expose themselves gratuitously to what might be fatal risks in order to protect her dominions.[1]   The King of Sardinia was, it is true, the brother-in-law of Maria Theresa's husband, but he had given no guarantee of the Pragmatic Sanction nor of the Grand-Duchy of Tuscany, and did not intend to do so without adequate inducements.   So this first attempt to bring Austria and Sardinia together came to nothing.   But, as the news of Spanish preparations became more alarming, and the news from Paris less reassuring, both Vienna and Turin began to feel the need of some sort of understanding.   Neither, however, would advertise its need, and so weaken its bargaining power, by approaching the other, and so a go-between became necessary.   Villettes had neither sufficient status nor sufficient self-confidence, and the task was cheerfully undertaken by Count Flemming, the Saxon envoy at Turin, and the most assiduous and ubiquitous busybody of the Austrian Succession War.   Saxony was at the moment the avowed antagonist of Prussia, and was regarded as an assured ally of Maria Theresa on the ground that Augustus III had purchased Austrian approval of his candidature in Poland by guaranteeing the Pragmatic Sanction.   Flemming conferred with Ormea, and as the result of the conversation drew up a rough sketch of the sort of terms upon which Sardinia would be willing to give armed assistance to Austria.   It was arranged in seven paragraphs.   (1) Sardinia must receive compensation for loss of revenue, if any territories, such as Savoy and Nice, should be occupied by the enemy.   (2) Sardinia must receive an annual

---

[1] Villettes to Newcastle (cipher), 14 June, 1741 (State Papers, For., Sardinia, 45): " This may be looked upon as the first overture for a negotiation, but the Court of Vienna had better have continued silent than have given such a sample as this of their willingness to treat with the King of Sardinia, and I observe it has increased the diffidence of these people with respect to the Austrian Ministers, and raised a kind of indignation."

subsidy for the maintenance of its army. (3) In recognition of Sardinian services, the Queen of Hungary shall cede to the King what is called "Pavese oltra Po"—*i.e.*, the district of Pavia, which formerly belonged to the province of Tortona, and also the land adjacent to Novara on this side of the Po and the Ticino (*i.e.*, the western part of the county of Anghiera). (4) In order to give the King of Sardinia a harbour, and to enable him to obtain assistance from the Maritime Powers, he is to be put in possession of the Marquisate of Finale, which is to be redeemed from Genoa, and also of as much as possible of the territory of that republic. (5) England must be pledged to keep a strong squadron in the Mediterranean. (6) Austria is to join with Sardinia in inducing Venice and the Pope with other states to form a league for the defence of Italy, the maintenance of the House of Austria, and the guarantee of territories ceded to Sardinia. (7) Austria shall send to Italy and maintain for the duration of the war a force adequate to secure the King of Sardinia from any danger to his territories on the Italian side of the Alps. These articles, as drafted by Flemming, were given to Schulenburg, and sent by him to Vienna.[1]

This is the real beginning of the negotiation which ended in the Treaty of Worms. In view of the far larger sacrifices which Austria had ultimately to make, one is tempted to wonder what would have happened if the Ministers at Vienna had shown themselves eager to make an alliance on these terms. There were only two articles, the third and fourth, to which serious exception could be taken, and on the latter they were prepared to give way, in spite of Maria Theresa's scruples as to an unprovoked despoiling of Genoa. But such prompt negotiations were not in Bartenstein's way, nor in that of any other Austrian minister. Schulenburg received from Vienna a counter-sketch, based upon that of Flemming.[2]

[1] These articles were sent by Villettes to Harrington at Hanover on 5 August, 1741 (State Papers, For., Sardinia, 45). They are printed by Arneth, *Maria Theresia*, ii., 497.

[2] The Austrian articles, which were sent to Schulenburg from Pressburg on 24 August, 1741, are printed in Arneth, ii., 498.

In this Austria accepted the principle of compensation for possible loss of territories, undertook to obtain a subsidy and a fleet from England, agreed to the formation of an Italian league, and promised to maintain troops in Italy, with the one proviso that they might be transferred elsewhere at any time when Northern Italy was practically secure. As to the fourth article, no mention was made of Finale, and Maria Theresa expressed her unwillingness to injure a third party, but "il pourroit lui rester un droit bien fondé sur certain port de la mer méditerranée et territoire qui en dépend," and she is willing to cede this right to the King of Sardinia in case there is actual war in Italy, and he comes to her assistance with all his forces. The real difficulty was obviously the third article, but Austria went so far as to promise that, in the same eventuality as above, Vigevano and its district should be given to Sardinia, but not a foot of land on the farther side of the Po. Schulenburg, who had not previously had much intercourse with Villettes, gave him a copy of the Austrian *ébauche*, and Ormea added the curt comment that Vigevano was wholly inadequate, and that, as the port referred to must be Finale, Austria might as well have said so. At the same time he welcomed the articles as giving at least a basis for negotiations.[1]

Flemming's articles and the Austrian answer to them, together with Ormea's notes on the latter, were sent in October by Harrington to Robinson, who was instructed to press for Austrian consent to the Sardinian demands. He was to offer as a bribe that England would undertake in the treaty to maintain a squadron off the coast of Italy, to pay a subsidy to Sardinia, and to hire Swiss troops from the Grison league, on condition that Austria would support the application. Robinson had some difficulty with the French cipher, and had to apply to the Austrian Ministers for copies of the documents, and also for some help in understanding what were the precise territories in the north which Sardinia wanted. In the end he formulated the demands as (1) the county

[1] Villettes to Harrington, 4 October, 1741 (State Papers, For., Sardinia, 45).

of Anghiera to the Swiss mountains; (2) Vigevano and district; (3) the Pavesan oltra Po; (4) Finale. These he submitted to a full Conference on 30 December, 1741. The main objection to the demands was that the consequent loss of revenue would make it impossible for Austria to maintain the troops needed for the defence of Lombardy. Robinson curtly replied : " Point de traité, point d'escadre; point de traité, point de subside; point de traité, point de Suisse."[1] In the end the Ministers declared in a written answer that they would give the Vigevanasco with twenty-four thousand men, but, if the larger demands were insisted upon, they could only furnish twelve or thirteen thousand. As to Finale, they would grant such right of redemption as Maria Theresa possessed, and anything further must be settled between Sardinia and Genoa. It was verbally suggested that Genoese partiality for Spain would give Sardinia ample excuse for dealing with that Republic.[1]

At this stage the negotiations were interrupted. The whole situation had been suddenly changed by the news of the Spanish landing at Orbetello. It was one of a long series of disasters to the cause of Maria Theresa. Saxony, so confidently counted upon to balance Prussia, had been tempted to go over to the hostile league. George II, the most prominent champion of the Pragmatic Sanction, had been terrified by a French army into purchasing the neutrality of Hanover by promising his vote to Charles Albert of Bavaria. The French and Bavarians gained a signal triumph in Bohemia by the capture of Prague, and Frederick seized the first excuse to repudiate the Convention of Klein-Schnellendorf. A revolution in Russia put an end to all hope of active assistance from that state. In these circumstances it seemed impossible to save Maria Theresa, and still more impossible that she could send troops to Traun for the defence of Lombardy. The Austrian need of a Sardinian alliance, hitherto comparatively slight and prospective, became suddenly immediate and overwhelm-

[1] Robinson to Villettes, 31 December, 1741, in Add. MSS. (Brit. Mus.) 23,862, fo. 466. The Austrian reply is in *ibid.*, fo. 508.

ing. If Sardinia chose to raise its terms it would be
difficult to refuse.[1]

But there was one gleam of hope in the Italian situation. If the Spanish landing was a blow to Maria
Theresa, it was equally a blow to Charles Emmanuel.
In his negotiations with the Bourbon Courts he had
always warned them that he would be compelled to
oppose the Spaniards if they attempted any aggression
in Italy before the conclusion of a treaty with Turin.
Nothing could be more disastrous than to allow Spain
to occupy the Milanese without securing some equivalent for Sardinia. Even Tuscany, which Fleury would
not allow Spain to seize because it had been given in
exchange for Lorraine, was not likely long to retain its
independence when once Spain had got the upper hand
in the peninsula. As a conflict with Spain was now
inevitable, Charles Emmanuel armed himself with
another weapon, which he had hitherto held in reserve.
In December, 1741, more than a year after the death of
Charles VI, he put forward a claim to the Duchy of
Milan, on the ground that Charles V had assured the
succession, in default of male heirs, to the descendants
of the eldest daughter of Philip II, and that the eldest
daughter who had left any descendants was his own
great-great-grandmother. It was a misfortune that this
claim, though directed against Spain, was also a stumbling-block in the way of an understanding with Vienna.
To Maria Theresa Charles Emmanuel's conduct seemed
to bear a suspicious resemblance to that of Frederick
of Prussia, who had accompanied his claims in Silesia
with offers of assistance against her enemies.[2] It was
clear that the King of Sardinia would be able hence-
forward to claim cessions, not only as a recompense for
services rendered, but also as compensation for the
withdrawal of his claim.

However, for the moment all these difficulties were

[1] Villettes wrote to Newcastle on 26 December, 1741, that
Flemming's articles were declared by Ormea to be mere con-
jectures as to Sardinian demands, and to be wholly out of date
and inadequate (State Papers, For., Sardinia, 45).

[2] On contemporary comparisons between Prussia and Sardina,
see Arneth, ii., 152, and the authorities there referred to.

swept aside by the common duty of keeping the Spaniards out of Lombardy. If Austria had an imperative need of Sardinia, Sardinia had also an imperative need of Austria. This mutual need was increased when in January, 1742, a second expeditionary force was landed at Spezia, and the Duke of Montemar, the conqueror of Naples in the last war, set out through the Papal States, with at any rate the tacit permission of Benedict XIV, to meet the troops which Don Carlos, now King Charles, was sending from his southern kingdom. Fortunately Maria Theresa, freed from her worst anxieties by Khevenhüller's successes in Upper Austria, was able after all to send reinforcements to Traun, and this made Austrian co-operation more attractive at Turin. There was no need on this occasion of English mediation, nor would it have been acceptable at the moment. The startling failure of the English fleet to obstruct two successive expeditions excited the suspicion at both Turin and Vienna that Admiral Haddick had secret instructions not to interfere with the Spanish fleet if there was also a French convoy, " lest the French should use reprisals on the King's electoral dominions," and that the neutrality of Hanover was about to be extended to Great Britain.[1] A provisional convention to deal with the immediate problem was adjusted between Schulenburg and Ormea, and was signed by them on 1 February, 1742, at Turin. Charles Emmanuel, without any definite assurance of territorial gain, undertook to join Austria in the defence of Lombardy, and for that purpose to occupy the Duchy of Modena. So long as the convention remained in force he pledged himself to abstain from pressing his claim to the Milanese, and to exercise no sovereign rights within the duchy. But he definitely reserved his claim, and also his right to denounce the convention and to desert the Austrian alliance on giving a month's notice. If he should exercise that right, he promised within the month to withdraw his troops and to surrender any fortresses

[1] Newcastle to Villettes, 2 April, 1742 (State Papers, For., Sardinia, 44). Newcastle reprimands Villettes for listening to such suggestions.

which he might have occupied within the Austrian dominions. That Maria Theresa gave the Sardinian King, whom she mistrusted, so obvious an opening for the confidence trick, is evidence of her imperative need of his support. On the other hand, Charles Emmanuel's abstention from pressing his claim to compensation at the moment that he could do so with the greatest force, went far to justify the Austrian conviction that self-interest compelled him to exclude the Spanish Bourbons from Northern Italy.

The Convention of Turin, which, as Fleury said, had no parallel in diplomatic history,[1] and which reads more like a labour agreement than a political transaction, was almost startlingly successful in its immediate results. It was followed by the one period of really cordial co-operation in the war. The Sardinian troops joined Traun on the borders of Modena. Francis III of Este had believed that, with inferior forces and inferior ability, he could play the game of the buffer state as profitably as Sardinia had so often played it. But he came to too hasty a decision. Convinced by Maria Theresa's early misfortunes that her cause was hopeless, and tempted by the offer of Guastalla, he made a secret treaty with Spain, which committed him to support the Bourbon invasion. On the approach of the Austro-Sardinian troops he denied the treaty and professed his desire to remain neutral. But his secret had been discovered, and when he was confronted with an actual copy of his treaty he fled to the Spanish headquarters and thence to Venice, leaving his duchy to its fate. The citadel of Modena made a creditable resistance, but was compelled to surrender on 28 June, and the capture of Mirandola in the next month completed the reduction of the duchy. This success was decisive. Montemar abandoned all hope of invading Lombardy, refused to risk a battle, and steadily retreated southwards to Foligno. The inferiority of his forces was made more

---

[1] Villettes says (1 March, State Papers, For., Sardinia, 46) that Fleury in a letter to Ormea referred to the convention as " a piece of the most singular nature and he believes the only one to be found of its kind."

complete when Admiral Mathews, who had superseded Haddick in command of the fleet, sent Commodore Martin to Naples, and the latter, by a threat of bombardment, compelled Don Carlos to recall the Neapolitan troops and to promise complete neutrality on the part of Naples and Sicily.

The Convention of Turin was almost contemporary with the downfall of Walpole, the entry of Carteret into the Ministry, and the increased English activity in the Continental war. For the next three years Carteret became one of the dominant personages in Europe. His plan was not so much to maintain the Pragmatic Sanction as to form a great coalition, with England at its head, which should deprive the two Bourbon States of the gains which they owed, in Carteret's opinion, to the ill-advised neutrality of Walpole in the last war. It might be that Maria Theresa would be called upon to make sacrifices and to depart from the letter of the Pragmatic Sanction. In that case she must have compensation at the expense of the enemy. With this object he pressed for the buying off of Prussia, which was successfully accomplished at Breslau, and incidentally detached Saxony also from Belleisle's coalition. He failed to induce Prussia to join his league, but he got a defensive treaty, and he had confident hopes of gaining Saxony. If he was lucky he might free the Emperor Charles VII from his humiliating dependence upon Louis XV, and thus remove the greatest impediment in the way of a German confederation against France. And the success of his policy in Italy depended upon the conversion of the provisional convention between Sardinia and Austria into a real treaty of alliance. He wanted to take this matter into his own hands, and found one initial difficulty in the way. Austria was within his own province, but Italy was not. It was one of the absurdities of the geographical division between the two Secretaries of State that the supervision of a negotiation between Vienna and Turin called for the joint action of two Ministers who might not see eye to eye, and who had no Prime Minister to hold them together. Carteret could only get over this difficulty by arranging to have as much as possible of the Sardinian business conducted in London. He could not oust Newcastle from conferences with Osorio, but he could attend them, while he could conduct his own conferences with Wasner and send his own instructions to Robinson. The result was that Villettes found himself thrust more and more into the background. He had to be informed of what was going on in order that he might explain and defend English policy to Ormea and the King, but he had no control over policy and no power to make any settlement.[1] He professed himself to be pleased at being freed from responsibility, but admitted that he thereby lost the chance of distinction which he had at one time been ambitious to gain. Even as it was, his fear of Ormea's temper and his desire to gain favour at the Court where he was stationed led him into more than one scrape. Incidentally, the supersession of Villettes involved the disappointment of Kaunitz, who, after Schulenburg had joined the army and his successor had become insane, was sent as a promising young diplomatist to Turin with powers to conclude a definitive treaty. This was impossible because Villettes had no corresponding powers, and so the ultimate Austrian signatory was Wasner and not Kaunitz.

The first act of the English Ministry after the conclusion of the Convention was to intimate to Turin that £200,000 out of the £500,000 voted by Parliament for the war would be paid to Sardinia so long as the Convention was in force, on condition that, if at any time it was repudiated, the whole sum advanced should be repaid. As soon as the Convention was superseded by a regular treaty this conditional loan would become an annual subsidy. As the £500,000 had been voted for the support of her cause, Maria Theresa thought that it had all been voted to her, and therefore that she was

---

[1] Villettes reported on 4 August, 1742, that Ormea had promised to send full powers to Osorio to negotiate under English guidance. Villettes professed to be pleased, as the matter was beyond his strength (State Papers, For., Sardinia, 46). See also Villettes to Robinson, 5 September.

really paying Sardinia. However, she could not protest at the time, but some of her subsequent obstinacy was due to her conviction that Sardinia was getting money as well as other things at her expense. The terms upon which the money was granted, and the absence of any convention for repayment, gave England a direct concern in the conclusion of a treaty, and Charles Emmanuel, now completely reassured as to English policy, was quite willing to entrust his interests to English mediation. And so the negotiations, which had been in abeyance since December, 1741, were resumed in the spring of 1742 in what became for a year their stereotyped course. Osorio, at the request of England, obtained a statement of Sardinian demands. These demands, after a certain amount of manipulation by English Ministers in consultation with Osorio, were sent to Robinson (now Sir Thomas) for submission to the Austrian Ministers. The Austrian reply to Robinson, which was also conveyed through Wasner, was given in London to Osorio and also sent to Villettes to be conveyed to Ormea and the King. Their observations, usually indignant or querulous, went back to London, and thence to Vienna, in the shape either of an amendment of the draft or of a defence of its provisions. The Viennese comments or proposals returned to London, and so to Turin, where the round recommenced. On one occasion Villettes was foolish enough to soften the Austrian answer by omitting part of Robinson's letter and editing the rest. Of course the unexpurgated report came from Osorio. Villettes had to tell lies in order to excuse his conduct, and the Sardinian Court was confirmed in its conviction, formed during the last war, that Robinson was too much of an Austrian to be entrusted with the defence of Sardinian interests. Villettes, reprimanded by Newcastle, had to write grovelling apologies to the Duke, and requested to be transferred to a haven of peace like Berne. Sardinia followed Carteret's wishes by entrusting its business more and more to Osorio, and Austria, mistrusting Villettes as Turin distrusted Robinson, came to depend more and more upon Wasner. Kaunitz was increasingly left in the cold.   He got full information and instructions from Vienna, but Ormea adhered to the policy of negotiating through England instead of directly with Vienna,[1] and Kaunitz's relations with Villettes were neither cordial nor confidential.   Canales, the Sardinian Minister at Vienna, had little to do except to report the anti-Sardinian sentiments of Bartenstein, whose tongue was almost as irrepressible as his pen. The slow process of negotiation along two sides of the triangle might have continued indefinitely if Carteret had not shortened the circuit by attending George II to Germany in the summer of 1743 and compelling Wasner and Osorio to follow him.   And it must be remembered that the strength both of demands and of objections was constantly affected by the course of the war.

The second stage of the negotiations began in May, 1742.   Their object was to convert the provisional convention of 1 February into a definitive treaty.   Osorio presented the Sardinian demands to the British Ministers in the form of three alternative plans, arranged in order of preference.   The first plan demanded (1) the county of Anghiera *dans toute son étendue*—i.e., not merely the western part as in the Flemming articles; (2) Vigevano and its district; (3) the Pavesan on both sides of the Po, together with the adjacent part of the Duchy of Piacenza as far as the Trebbia; and (4) either Finale or in default the whole Duchy of Piacenza.   The other two plans contained successive reductions of the third demand, but they are unimportant as they were never communicated to Vienna.[2]   The British Ministers took the first plan, and deliberately made a substantial increase of the demands by making the Duchy of

---

[1] Villettes to Robinson, 5 September, 1742 (Add. MSS. 23,812, fo. 179).   In this letter Villettes recounts that, when he told Ormea of the Austrian offer of Sicily, the latter, "with a temper that would have startled another man," told him that he might bring news from London in the middle of the night, but if he had only a message from another Court he might save the time of both of them.

[2] Osorio's memorial is in Robinson Papers, xxxii., fo. 374, and in State Papers, For., Sardinia, 44.

Piacenza an addition to Finale instead of a possible
substitute. They then drew up a carefully drafted
memorial in French, embodying all the arguments that
Robinson was to use in order to induce Austria to grant
the Sardinian terms as they stood. These were now
(1) the whole county of Anghiera; (2) Vigevano and
district; (3) the whole district of Pavia on both sides
of the Po; (4) the whole Duchy of Piacenza; and
(5) Finale. Austria was warned that, if these demands
were refused, Sardinia would be forced to join Spain
and Lombardy would infallibly be lost. On the other
hand, if they were accepted, Lombardy would be saved,
and Austria would probably gain at the expense of the
enemy ample compensation for what she was asked to
resign. Carteret sent the memorial to Robinson on
28 May/8 June with instructions to read it to the
Austrian Ministers. He added that a draft treaty was
being prepared in London, and would be sent to Vienna
shortly.

Robinson's memorial, which he had to read succes-
sively to three Ministers, Ulfeld, Starhemberg, and
Bartenstein, could not have arrived at a more unlucky
moment. The humiliation of the preliminaries of
Breslau was just over, and here was England, after
making Austria give up the most valuable part of a
valuable province to the King of Prussia, demanding
similar cessions to Charles Emmanuel, who was the King
of Prussia in Italy. The Ministers were at first genuinely
taken aback, and could only growl out almost inarticu-
late complaints. The English manner of action was
almost as intolerable as the action itself. Why was
Austria treated like a child, to have her treaties made
for her instead of making them herself? They were
fully aware of the necessity of converting the provisional convention into a treaty, had been ready to do
so for the last six months, and had given full powers to
their Minister at Turin. The delay was due to the King
of Sardinia, who had insisted upon sending his demands
through London instead of direct to Vienna. Again,
why were the Sardinian gains to be immediate, whereas
those of Austria were prospective and were qualified by

the word "probably"? Why did not the Allies pledge themselves to continue the war until Naples and Sicily had been conquered, and why should not Sardinia wait till Austria got her equivalent? If it was urged that the revenues of the territories demanded were required to enable Sardinia to equip troops, they were equally needed by Austria for the same purpose. It would do nothing to promote the common cause if money was to be taken from one ally and given to another. Austria had already been compelled to part with £200,000 out of the £500,000 which had been voted for her needs. The only reference to the actual demands was the groan that what was left was hardly worth fighting for, and that, as Austria was to be despoiled either way, she might as well be robbed by Spain as by Sardinia.[1] As to the risk of a Sardinian alliance with the Bourbons, they did not believe that there was any real danger of the King taking a step which would be ruinous to his own interests. It was unfortunately true that Sardinia was carrying on negotiations with the enemy Powers, but did that constitute a claim to a substantial reward? In the end Bartenstein drew up a written reply in which he reiterated these complaints, after dilating in a long preamble upon the services and sacrifices of Maria Theresa and the shabby treatment she had received from her allies. He concluded by hinting that Austria had in mind a proposal of her own for satisfying Sardinia. This was interpreted to mean that, if Don Carlos was turned out by the allies, Austria would be content with Naples and the *Stato dei Presidii*, and would allow the King of Sardinia to take Sicily.

So far Austria had mainly concentrated upon the contention that the cessions and the equivalent should be *également et en même temps*. As Robinson puts it, they had insisted on the *quand* and never touched the *quantum*. But this attitude could not permanently be maintained. Even Bartenstein knew that a prospective

<hr>

[1] Old Austrian Ministers, like Starhemberg, had always looked askance at the Italian acquisitions of Charles VI, and would have been quite willing to let them go. See Robinson to Carteret, 3 July, 1742 (Add. MSS. 23,864, fo. 476); and to Villettes, 3 May, 1743 (*ibid.*, 23,867, fo. 6).

and distant acquisition like Sicily would never be accepted by Charles Emmanuel as a substitute for an immediate extension of his own territories. After all, Austria had actually offered Vigevano before a Spanish soldier had landed in Italy. And so, when Robinson received the draft treaty, the Austrian Ministers were prepared to consider matters in a more practical temper than they had hitherto shown. On 19 August they held a conference with the English Minister, who arrived with the three Sardinian alternatives stowed away in different pockets so that he could take them out in their proper order as should appear necessary in the course of the discussion. The draft treaty was considered clause by clause, and Robinson paid little attention to the minor difficulties raised, as they would have to be settled in London. His intention was to concentrate on the ninth clause, which dealt with the cessions to Sardinia. But here he found that Austria would not come near even to the minimum of the Sardinian proposals, so that the carefully prepared papers had to remain in their respective pockets until they could be safely locked in his strong box. The utmost that Austria would offer was the immediate cession of Anghiera west of Lake Maggiore and the Ticino and of the Pavese oltra Po, with the conditional promise of Sicily in the future. The greatest obstinacy was shown in refusing to part with Anghiera to the east of the lake and the river. This was justified by two arguments. One was that nobody knew what was the eastern boundary of the county, which had ceased to be a territorial unit for the last two hundred years.[1] The maps were so varied as to give no certain guide; so the words *dans toute son étendue* might be capable of undefined extension. But the real argument was that the Naviglio Grande led out of the Ticino just below its exit from the lake, and that Milan was dependent upon this canal for its trade with

[1] The county of Anghiera used to be an appanage for the eldest son of the Duke of Milan.   When Charles V transferred the duchy from the Sforzas to the Habsburgs, this practice ceased, and the county became a vague geographical expression, without any precise boundaries, like some of the old divisions of Scotland, Angus, the Mearns, etc.

Switzerland[1] and for its water supply. To cede the control of this waterway to the King of Sardinia was to make him master of Milan.[2]

The negotiations, after this unpromising start, affected, and were affected by, the military operations of 1742-1743. As soon as Modena and Mirandola had been captured, both Austria and England urged that the Austro-Sardinian army should follow up its success by pursuing the retreating army of Montemar, completing its destruction, and then invading Naples. But Charles Emmanuel would do nothing of the kind, and Traun was too cautious to attempt the adventure with the Austrian forces alone. The Sardinian King declared that he was bound by the provisional convention to protect the Austrian dominions, and he had done so. He was not bound to do anything more, and would not do so until he had got his definitive treaty. His motives were obvious. He had no real desire to see Austria once more in possession of Naples. It would be almost as bad as a Spanish Bourbon in Milan. He had expressly reserved in the Convention the right of going over to Spain, and he was not going to destroy the army of a state which might in certain contingencies

[1] Villettes to Newcastle, 16 November, 1742 (State Papers, For., Sardinia, 46): " I have all along observed Marquis d'Ormea's heart to be sett on the whole county and the town of Anghiera, with a view of being by the cession of that district masters of the vast trade carried on with the Swiss."

[2] Robinson, who was instructed to defend the Sardinian demands, obviously agreed with the Austrian objections. He wrote to Villettes on 20 August to report the conference of the day before (Add. MSS. 23,864, fo. 822). On the 21st he added a private letter: " Sir. Lay aside, for God's sake, some prejudices I have observed in you against this court. . . . You yourself were of opinion that the Piemontese should not pass the lake or the Tessin. You know the lake, you know the Tessin, you know the Naviglio of Milan. He who is master of the lake is master of Milan " (*ibid.*, fo. 836). It is to Robinson's credit that he did not always tell his employers what they wanted to hear. He warned Carteret that Naples and Sicily were not such an attraction at Vienna as they had been under Charles VI. " The present is a German government, not a Spanish government " (*ibid.*, fo. 476). And he constantly urged that, if there was a danger of driving Sardinia into an alliance with Spain, there was also a danger that Austria, if pressed too hard, might prefer to seek a reconciliation with France.

become his ally. He exasperated Austria by urging
that it was wrong to enter the Papal States against the
will of the Pope, whereas Maria Theresa held that she
had just as much right to go there as the Spaniards.
In the end he got a more valid excuse in the necessity
of repelling an invasion of Savoy by a third Spanish
contingent, which had marched through Southern
France under the nominal command of Don Philip. On
the approach of the Sardinian forces, the Spaniards retreated into Provence, and Charles Emmanuel dared not
follow them on to French soil. He had still less desire
to quarrel with France than to carry to extremes his
quarrel with Spain. In the end the approach of winter,
which would close the Alpine passes, compelled him to
choose between defending Savoy and defending Piedmont. After consultation with Villettes and Kaunitz
he decided that the loss of Savoy would be the less
harmful to the common cause and the less advantageous
to the enemy.[1] So he reluctantly recrossed the Alps,
and left Savoy to be occupied by the Spaniards till the
close of the war, thus giving them a valuable pawn to
play in any future negotiations. Of course Austria suspected that the evacuation of Savoy was the result of a
secret bargain with Spain, while England, convinced of
the King's rectitude, regretted that he had wasted on
what proved to be a futile defence troops which might
have been employed to better purpose in the peninsula.[2]
Charles Emmanuel, however, had added two arguments
in favour of getting his demands. He had proved that,
until they were granted, it was useless to think of turning Don Carlos out of Naples, and the loss of the
revenues of Savoy entitled him to compensation, as
Austria had admitted in the first stage of the negotiation.

Charles Emmanuel returned in time to meet a second
attempt on the part of Spain to invade Lombardy.
Gages, who had taken over the command from Monte-

[1] Villettes to Newcastle from Montmeillan, 28 December, 1742,
in State Papers, For., Sardinia, 46.
[2] Newcastle to Villettes, 18 January (o.s.), 1743 (State Papers,
For., Sardinia, 44).

mar, was ordered by the impatient Elizabeth Farnese to take advantage of the exhaustion of the Sardinian troops after their winter campaign. He crossed the Panaro in February, hoping to take Traun by surprise. The Battle of Campo Santo (6 February, 1743) was so far a decisive victory for Austria that the Spaniards retreated. But again the sanguine hopes in London and Vienna of an energetic pursuit were disappointed. Charles Emmanuel declared that his first duty was to defend Piedmont, which might be invaded by Don Philip from Savoy. As Traun for the second time refused to advance alone, he was superseded by Lobkowitz, who arrived too late to do anything before the treaty was signed. The lesson of 1743 was the same as that of the previous year. Sardinia held the balance.[1] Spain could not obtain the coveted principality for Don Philip unless Sardinia came over. And Austria could not crush the Bourbons unless Charles Emmanuel got his terms.

Meanwhile the negotiations continued in the hope of putting the treaty drafted by England into acceptable shape. England, which had begun by acting as the agent for Sardinia, now undertook to play the part of mediator, and to find some middle point between the extreme demands of Sardinia and the jejune offers of Austria. But the mediation was always rather one-sided. As a rule, the alterations suggested by England were concerted with Osorio before being submitted to Wasner for reference to Vienna, and Ormea warned Villettes beforehand that what would satisfy Austria would fail to please Sardinia. These two Powers started with strong convictions that obstinacy on their part would not do any real harm. Sardinia was assured that Austria would never carry out its repeated threat to abandon its possessions in Italy and to seek compensation elsewhere. Nor would Austria, in disgust with its allies, seek a separate understanding with the Bourbon

[1] See Carteret to Robinson, 8 July (o.s.), 1742 (Add. MSS. 23,811, fo. 334), where he defends the proposed cessions to Sardinia on the ground that " they are to a prince who holds the balance in Italy. If you lose him, you lose Italy: if you keep him, you may gain an ample equivalent."

Powers, even with the prospect of recovering Silesia.
On the other hand, Austria was equally convinced,
and the conviction was strengthened by reports from
Kaunitz,[1] that the Sardinian negotiations with France
were a mere ruse, that self-interest would compel Charles
Emmanuel to defend Lombardy, just as it compelled
the Maritime Powers to defend the Netherlands, and
that he would never face the alienation of England
and the necessity of repaying the English subsidies.
England, which shared neither conviction completely,
was the most eager of the three states to hasten the conclusion of the treaty. Austria complained that obstruction was unfairly attributed to her, whereas Sardinia
was equally to blame, and that English threats were
always addressed to Vienna and not to Turin. This was
quite true. Robinson was not a mealy mouthed envoy
like Villettes, and did not hesitate, when Ulfeld de-
claimed against English partiality, to tell him that
orders would be sent to Stair to stop the advance of the
pragmatic army, and that a courier to Turin would tell
the King of Sardinia that, as nothing was to be obtained
from Austria, he had better make his own terms with
France.[2] On another occasion he declared that the fleet
could not remain off the Italian coast until a treaty had
defined the purposes for which it was to be employed.
These were what he called his " emphatical arguments,"[3] and they were bitterly resented by the
Austrian Ministers.

A few of the articles of the draft treaty were accepted
without opposition. These were the first, which contained the conventional assurances of peace and alliance

[1] One of Kaunitz's arguments was that Ormea would be ruined
if the provisional convention, regarded and claimed as his peculiar
achievement, should prove to have been a mistake. Villettes to
Newcastle, 28 January and 6 April, 1743 (State Papers, For.,
Sardinia, 47).

[2] Robinson and Villiers to Carteret, 13 February, 1743 (Add.
MSS. 23,866, fo. 251). Carteret sent Villiers in 1743 on a round
of the German Courts, in order, if possible, to organize a league
of the well-disposed States against French interference. Before
starting Villiers paid a visit of several weeks to Vienna, where he
acted during his stay as joint envoy with Robinson.

[3] Robinson to Villettes, 3 May, 1743 (Add. MSS. 23,867, fo. 6).

between the three Powers; the fourth, which renewed
the obligation of Sardinia to aid in the defence of Lombardy; the seventh, which bound England to keep a
squadron in the Mediterranean, hitherto a voluntary
service; the fourteenth, which forbade any separate
peace with the common enemy, and prescribed the continuance of the alliance after the end of the war; the
fifteenth, by which Austria and Sardinia undertook, not
only to confirm all existing privileges to English traders,
but to increase them on requisition by commercial
treaties; the sixteenth, that the Dutch should be invited
to join as a principal contracting party; and the seventeenth, that other Powers might be admitted by agreement. On all the other clauses there was more or less
controversy. The second article, which enumerated a
number of treaties, especially those of 1731 and 1738,
and confirmed them so far as they concerned the allies
and were not modified by the present treaty, seemed at
first sight harmless enough. But Austria wanted to
include the preliminaries of 1735, and Sardinia objected
on the ground that this would involve a guarantee of
Tuscany. It was contended that the definitive treaty
of 1738 did not do this, because Tuscany had been
transferred to Francis in the previous year. Austria
replied that the treaty confirmed the preliminaries, and
that, anyhow, Sardinia had acceded to the latter in
1736. As that accession was still binding, no new
obligation was imposed. However, to remove all doubt,
Austria proposed a direct guarantee of Tuscany by both
Sardinia and England. Sardinia refused unless the
Grand-Duke gave a counter-guarantee, and, as Francis
declined, the matter was allowed to drop. The preliminaries of 1735 were not included. This is a
fair example of the pedantry of eighteenth-century
diplomacy.

By the third article Sardinia renounced in favour of
Maria Theresa and her heirs the claim to the Duchy of
Milan, which had been reserved in the provisional convention, and also guaranteed the Pragmatic Sanction
for the first time. As a special concession, Sardinian
aid to maintain the Pragmatic Sanction was restricted

to Italy, and at the last moment a third separate and secret article provided that the renunciation of the claim to Milan should not be valid if an heiress under the Pragmatic Sanction should marry a member of the House of Bourbon. The fifth article fixed the Sardinian contingent to the joint army at 45,000 men, and that of Austria at 30,000. Austria protested against this quota, and insisted that her military expenditure should be expressly limited to the revenue derived from her Italian dominions, after deducting the cost of their administration. This was objected to as likely to give rise to endless chicane, and was withdrawn.[1] To the sixth article, which gave the command of the allied forces to the King of Sardinia, whenever he should be present, Austria made vehement objections. Austrian troops could not be entrusted to an alien general, or at any rate not without adequate provision for their control from Vienna. England, however, insisted upon the Sardinian command, and Charles Emmanuel refused to refer his decisions to a distant capital. Austria had to be content with the assurance that the King would consult the Austrian officers in a council of war. This clause gave rise to endless friction in subsequent military operations. The eighth article was also contentious. England was pledged to pay to Sardinia a subsidy of £200,000 per annum *tant que la guerre et le besoin durera.* Sardinia insisted upon the words *le besoin* on the ground that military expenditure did not cease with the close of actual warfare, and made vain efforts to get the subsidy increased. But the chief difficulty was the Austrian demand that a similar pledge should be given for the payment of her subsidy of £300,000, which was only granted from year to year. The English Ministers replied that they could not bind future Parliaments, though it was difficult to explain why the same objection did not apply to the payment to Sar-

---

[1] On 3 May, 1743, Robinson transmitted a *Réponse* from the Austrian Ministers in which they agreed to omit the reference to the revenues from the Italian States on the understanding that Maria Theresa was not thereby condemned to reduce to ruin her German provinces (Add. MSS. 23,867, fo. 15).

dinia. Here again Austria had to give way, though, as we shall see, the demand was renewed after the signature of the treaty.

The tenth article about Finale presented almost insuperable difficulties. Both Sardinia and England attached immense importance to its acquisition. The prospect of gaining Sicily made the Court of Turin more eager than ever to acquire a port on the mainland. With Sicily, Sardinia, Villafranca, Finale, and perhaps Savona in addition, the state might become a real maritime Power, and as such an invaluable ally of England in the Mediterranean. But how could the acquisition be brought about? The mere cession of the right of redemption, which was all that Austria would offer, was worthless, because both Vienna and Turin admitted that no such right existed.[1] Sardinia wanted Austria to effect the redemption and then to cede the marquisate, but this was absolutely refused. Sardinia then proposed that the Duchy of Piacenza should be held in pawn until Finale was acquired, but Austria refused to give any pledge for territory which was not under her control.[2] In the end an absurd compromise was adopted. Maria Theresa transferred to the King of Sardinia " tous les droits qui peuvent lui compéter en façon quelconque et à tel titre que ce soit," in the expectation that Genoa would provide the necessary facilities for an arrangement that was indispensable for the future security and liberty of Italy. But neither Austria nor Sardinia was to furnish the money that might be required for the transaction, and Finale was always to be a free port like Leghorn. When Ormea

[1] The contract between Charles VI and Genoa for the sale of Finale is in Dumont, *Corps Universel Diplomatique*, vol. vii.

[2] England proposed a secret article to run as follows: " Le cas arrivant que S.M. la Reine de Hongrie et de Bohème ne satisfît point à l'article 10 de la présente alliance par le retrait et la remise du Marquisat de Final, Elle s'oblige de céder et transférer pour équivalent à S.M. le Roi de Sardaigne tout le reste du Plaisantin de la même manière que les païs énoncés dans l'article neuvième " (Newcastle to Villettes, 18 January [o.s.], 1743, in State Papers, For., Sardinia, 44). Charles Emmanuel wanted to amend this so that he should occupy the whole of Piacenza till he got Finale.

read the article in its final form, he said that he presumed England would find the money.

It was on the ninth article, fixing the cessions in Lombardy, that the most heated and prolonged controversy was conducted. Vigevano with its district, Western Anghiera, and the Pavesan oltra Po were the only agreed transfers, and Sardinia obtained the enlargement of the last by the inclusion of Bobbio and its dependencies. As to the other demands, Austria had refused to surrender (1) that part of Anghiera which lay to the east of Lake Maggiore and the Ticino; (2) any part of the Pavesan, including the City of Pavia, lying to the left of the Po; and (3) the Duchy of Piacenza or any part of it. On 30 September (o.s.), 1742, Newcastle, during a temporary absence of Carteret at The Hague, concerted with Osorio a compromise between the extreme refusals of Austria and the extreme demands of Sardinia, or rather the demands put forward by England on behalf of Sardinia.[1] This compromise became the basis of all the later discussions. He proposed to accept for Sardinia (1) Anghiera to the west of the lake and river, the middle of both being the boundary; (2) the Vigevanasco; (3) the Pavesan oltra Po with Bobbio. Austria might keep Eastern Anghiera, which was claimed as necessary for trade with Switzerland and for the supply of Milan, and, in addition, might choose between the Pavesan on the left of the Po and Piacenza. If she chose the Pavesan she must give Sardinia an equivalent in the Duchy of Piacenza. After some haggling Austria agreed to take the Pavesan (with a special stipulation for the retention of the island in the river facing Pavia), partly because it belonged to the Duchy of Milan, and partly because its cession would bring Sardinia too near to the capital of that duchy. As an equivalent the Austrian Ministers offered to cede to Sardinia a strip of Piacenza as far as the Trebbia. This gave rise to a storm. Sardinia de-

[1] Newcastle to Villettes, 30 September (o.s.), 1743 (State Papers, For., Sardinia, 44). Newcastle writes that he had submitted to Wasner the expedient " which I may in confidence acquaint you I had previously concerted with Mr. Osorio."

nounced the offer as " pitiful " and inadequate, and
demanded the duchy as far as the Nura, which would
involve the surrender of the city of Piacenza. Austria
refused to cede the city, as being the last fortress left
to her on that side of the Milanese, and as covering the
natural transit between Milan and Tuscany.[1] Maria
Theresa, who had travelled that way to visit her husband's grand-duchy, would not give the control of the
high road to a foreign state. This produced a deadlock.
England whole-heartedly backed Sardinia. When the
Grand-Duke suggested that a *milieu* could be found by
bisecting the land between the Trebbia and the Nura,
Robinson replied that " there was no *milieu* but for his
Sardinian Majesty to throw himself into the hands of
the House of Bourbon."[2] This dispute remained un-
settled until the very last moment.

Although the dispute as to the *quantum* of the
cessions to Sardinia appeared to be so irreconcilable,
the real crux of the negotiation lay elsewhere. Maria
Theresa, having once made up her mind that she could
not keep her Italian inheritance intact, never concealed
her opinion that the actual cessions were comparatively·
unimportant provided that compensation for them was
adequate and assured. In the diplomatic correspondence of the period the dominant word is *dédommagement*. The first and most persistent of the Austrian
demands was that compensation should be given *en
même temps et également* with the cessions, which
would have made the latter conditional.[3] Sardinia

<hr>

[1] Robinson to Carteret, 6 April, 1743 (Add. MSS. 23,866,
fo. 444), says it is held at Vienna that " no practicable way could
be found from the Milanese to Tuscany but by Placentia."

[2] Robinson to Villettes from Prague, 3 May, 1743, in Add.
MSS. 23,867, fo. 6.

[3] Carteret expressed the English policy in this matter to
Robinson on 18 January (o.s.), 1743, when he sent to him a
revised draft of the treaty. " The point which seems to make
the greatest difficulty at Vienna is the indemnification of the
Queen for what she shall yield to his Sardinian Majesty, upon
which they would make the validity of the cessions themselves
dependent. The King sincerely wishes such an equivalent may
be secured, will readily himself concur in the design, and cannot
question the same willingness in the King of Sardinia to oblige
and indemnify the Queen by dislodging the Bourbons entirely

would not have this at any price, and insisted that the cessions should be *dès à présent et pour toujours*, and this was prescribed in the treaty. Then Austria turned to the amendment of the twelfth article, which is of considerable importance in itself. It provided that Sardinia should remain loyal to the cause of the allies not only during the war in Italy, but also until peace was made in Germany and between England and Spain, and then continued in words which were evidently as carefully chosen as they were anxiously scrutinized: "Et c'est ici la condition principale et sine qua non des cessions ci-dessus à luy faites par les articles 8 et 10 lesquelles cessions ne recevront leur force complète et irrévocable que de son entier accomplissement, après lequel les païs cédés au dit roi lui seront censés garantis par les alliés à perpétuité comme ses autres états." Austria wanted to insert words pledging Sardinia to remain loyal until she had obtained her equivalent for Silesia as well as for her cessions in Italy. Such a provision coupled with the concluding words of the article would have given Maria Theresa a pretext for reclaiming the cessions in case the equivalent should not be forthcoming. Naturally Sardinia objected, and the objection was upheld.

Having failed in two efforts, Austria concentrated

---

from Italy, when he sees that he goes upon sure grounds as to his own interest, and has the protection of a powerful alliance on his side by the conclusion of the definitive treaty now depending, besides the farther temptation of a new and great acquisition to himself. But it can never be expected that he, who looks upon the cessions he now demands as the price of his pretensions upon Milan on one hand, and of his contributing to the immediate support of the Queen on the other, should consent to subject those same cessions to the hazard and uncertainty of future conquests, in such measure as that all the charge he shall have undertaken, all the efforts he shall have made, and all the risks he shall have run in behalf of the Queen, should go for nothing if her Majesty were not put in possession of Naples at the end of the war. This being what we can never hope to obtain of the King of Sardinia, it was necessary to conform the present stipulation to what might be practicable upon that head, and you will find the second separate article drawn accordingly." Immediate cession was also justified on the ground that the revenues of the ceded territories were to compensate Sardinia for the loss of all revenue from Savoy.

attention upon the second separate and secret article,
which referred to the possible expulsion of the Bourbons
from Italy.   Maria Theresa wanted to make the conquest of Naples and Sicily as definite an object of the
alliance as was the defence of Lombardy under the
fourth article.   She was furious when Commodore
Martin, in return for the recall of the Neapolitan troops,
seemed to recognize the neutrality of Naples.   So far
from helping her cause the English Fleet had rendered
her the greatest disservice.   Bartenstein declared to
Robinson, after the threatened bombardment, that " his
Neapolitan Majesty was as safe in that kingdom as the
King was in England," and added that this showed how
little desire England had to drive that Prince back to
Spain.[1]   The English Ministers had much trouble to
convince Austria that they were not bound in any way
by what Commodore Martin had done or said,[2] that
they had in no way recognized Neapolitan neutrality,
and that Admiral Mathews was ready to join in an
attack upon Naples as soon as the military council
should decide for the enterprise.   There can be no
doubt that the Austrian suspicions of England in this
matter were unfounded.   Carteret, like Maria Theresa,
wished to drive Don Carlos from Naples and Sicily.
England never welcomed the establishment of a Spanish
Bourbon in the middle of the Mediterranean.   Both
trade and maritime ascendancy would be promoted by
his expulsion.   But Carteret knew quite well that
Charles Emmanuel would fight shy of any obligation to
carry on the war for the purpose of giving Naples to
Austria.   An attempt was made to placate him by
offering Sicily, and by avowing that the purpose of the
offer was to equalize in Italy the dominions of Austria

[1] Robinson and Villiers to Carteret, 13 February, 1743 (Add.
MSS. 23,866, fo. 251).
[2] Newcastle to Villettes, 23 April (o.s.), 1743 (State Papers,
For., Sardinia, 44): " As that whole affair passed without any
directions from the King, and even without his Majesty's knowledge, his Majesty has always declared he did not look upon it as
in any way binding on him, or to lay him under any obligation not
to act in such a manner as the support of his allies and the interest
of the common cause should require."

and Sardinia.[1]　But the King knew that this proposed balance was wholly illusory.　Outside Italy Austria had immense resources : Sardinia had none except Savoy, and at the moment he had not even Savoy.　Nor had Sardinia any complete assurance that, once in possession of Naples, Austria would make any strenuous effort to conquer Sicily for somebody else.　The simple fact remained that Sardinia had no real desire to see Naples in the hands of a Habsburg, and would rather prefer to keep a Bourbon there as a check upon the Habsburgs, provided the Bourbon would keep his hands off Lombardy.　England, therefore, had to find a form of words which would look sufficiently like an engagement to pacify Austria, and yet be so short of a positive engagement as not to frighten Sardinia.　And so the article provided that the enterprise against Naples and Sicily should be " concerted " between the allies, and that, if it was successful, Sicily should be given to the King of Sardinia.[2]　It cannot be said that the " formula " served any purpose except the immediate one of getting the article accepted.　Naples was never conquered, Maria Theresa did not get her *dédommage-*

[1] Robinson to Villettes, 3 May, 1743 (Add. MSS. 23,867, fo. 36): " Our design in England is to divide Italy between the houses of Savoy and Austria.　The thought is English and worthy of us." Compare Newcastle to Robinson, private and autograph, 5 July (o.s.), 1742 (Add. MSS. 23,811, fo. 332): " Italy should be divided between the Queen of Hungary and the King of Sardinia, and so it shall, if your court pleases, and not a Bourbon branch remain there."　The second secret article of the treaty provided that, if Don Carlos were driven out, Sicily would be given to Charles Emmanuel, partly to cover his expenditure in the enterprise, and partly " pour luy assurer une addition de force proportionnée à celle que sa Majesté la Reine acquerra par là."

[2] From the outset the English Ministers laid stress in communications to Turin on the fact that the possible conquest of Naples and Sicily was " entirely separated from the treaty, and independent of it," and that it could only be undertaken by common consent.　Newcastle to Villettes, 1 July (o.s.), 1742 (State Papers, For., Sardinia, 44).　As the article was originally drafted, it provided that Sardinia should receive an equivalent for any gain on the part of Austria, and that, in case of dispute, England should arbitrate.　The suggestion that Sicily should be the equivalent for Naples came from Vienna, and was gratefully accepted by England as solving what might otherwise have proved a very difficult problem.

ment, and a King of Sardinia only acquired Sicily from a Bourbon ruler more than a century later and under wholly different conditions. Apart from the Austrian demands to keep Piacenza, to have a regular instead of an annual subsidy, and to have some substantial assurance as to compensation, the treaty had been hammered into something like its ultimate terms when in May, 1743, George II crossed over to Germany to take command of the pragmatic army, and incidentally to fight the Battle of Dettingen, and to superintend his Minister's tangled negotiations at Hanau and Worms. Carteret followed him, and received powers which for a time freed him from the direct control of his colleagues. Never, since the days of Wolsey, had an English Minister held such a commanding position in Europe. He had two client Princes, one an Emperor and one a King, dependent upon his good offices to obtain terms for them from Maria Theresa. He could deprive France of her whole status in the war by procuring the restoration of Bavaria to Charles VII; and he could checkmate Spain in Italy by obtaining the required cessions of territory for Charles Emmanuel. Both necessitated the consent of Austria, and Austria was dependent upon England for subsidies, for ships in the Mediterranean, and for troops either in Germany or in the Netherlands. It seemed to be a promising position. But Maria Theresa, in spite of this dependence, was no longer in such a desperate position as she had been when the negotiations with Sardinia began. Two Spanish attacks in Italy had been repelled. Bohemia had been recovered, and she had been crowned in Prague. The French armies were abandoning Germany. There was nothing to prevent an invasion of France, and little to hinder an attack upon Naples. Bavaria was in her hands, and the Elector, who had presumed to wrest the imperial dignity from her husband, and to procure the rejection of her own Bohemian vote, was now an impotent exile, condemned apparently to wander from one imperial city to another, and dependent upon French charity for funds to enable him to maintain some squalid approach to imperial state. Now, if ever, was

6

the time to claim that equivalent for Silesia, which had been vaguely dangled before her at the time of the Treaty of Breslau, and at the same time compensation for the sacrifices to be made to Sardinia. Robinson noted in June a curious inclination at Vienna to mix up German with Italian affairs.[1] But the full extent of the intermixture was not yet known. On 15 July, at Hanau, Carteret went as far as he ever went towards drafting a treaty between Charles VII and Maria Theresa, based upon a renunciation of all the Bavarian claims in return for the recovery of the electorate.[2] Two days later Wasner, who had been summoned to Vienna, started for the English headquarters with new and startling instructions. On the ground that European liberties demanded not only the abasement of the Bourbons, but also the elevation of the House of Austria, Maria Theresa ought to be compensated for the loss of Silesia by the acquisition of contiguous territory. To render this possible, Maria Theresa was willing to sacrifice her destined *dédommagement* in Italy, and to hand over the kingdom of Naples to Charles VII in exchange for Bavaria and the Upper Palatinate. The Wittelsbachs could keep their electoral rank in their new home, just as the Duke of Lorraine, also transferred to Italy, had kept his status in the Empire. Wasner might assure English Ministers that the Elector of Bavaria would doubtless give all commercial privileges to English traders in gratitude for the King's assistance in transferring him from a devastated electorate to a rich kingdom. As Maria Theresa would require no further compensation for sacrifices in Italy, and as Sardinia would still be allowed to gain Sicily, the Sardinian treaty could be concluded at once. Thus the two problems, the

---

[1] As early as 16 March Robinson reported hints that Maria Theresa would be "more easy in the affairs of Italy, were she more certain of being supported in Germany" (Add. MSS. 23,866, fo. 360). On 22 June he wrote that this Court are convinced that Sardinia would not join in driving the Bourbons out of Italy. So, as they cannot get their compensation there, they will not sign unless promised, however secretly, some compensation in Germany (*ibid.*, 23,867, fo. 162).

[2] See above, Chapter I.

Bavarian and the Sardinian, with which Carteret had
been busied during the summer, would be solved at one
stroke.[1]

This scheme, which from a modern point of view
seems a crazy suggestion, was quite in the spirit of the
eighteenth century, and was probably designed incidentally to rap the knuckles of those states which had
consented to the exchange of Lorraine for Tuscany. Of
all people in the world, the timid Villettes was singled
out as the parent of the scheme. He was said to have
broached it to Kaunitz while they were both in Savoy
before Christmas.[2] As he was an English Minister, it
was to be presumed that he did not speak without
authority from London, and, as he was an intimate
friend of Ormea, who was also said to have talked of
the scheme, it was equally assumed that he had secured
the approval of Sardinia. The agitated Villettes hastened to declare that he was innocent of any such presumption, and that the utmost he had done was to
quote in casual conversation the opinion of the man-in-
the-street that everything would be much simpler if the
Emperor could be translated to Italy. The idea of
putting it forward as a practicable scheme, and of making Naples the future home of the Emperor in place
of Munich, probably came from the fertile brain of
Kaunitz, who as yet had more imagination than experience.[3] It must be remembered that, from the point of

[1] The gist of Wasner's instructions was embodied in a *mémoire*
given to Robinson on 19 July, after exacting his word of honour
that he would not send it on, so that Wasner might have the credit
of the first disclosure. Robinson observes that this " gives a new
turn to all the measures which have been upon the anvil " (Add.
MSS. 23,867, fo. 313).

[2] See extract from a letter of Kaunitz, 29 June, 1743, in Add.
MSS. 23,867, fo. 329.

[3] Villettes's verbose expressions of humility, regret, and inno-
cence may be read in State Papers, Sardinia or Germany, or in
the Robinson Papers. See especially Villettes to Robinson,
27 July and 3 August, 1743, and Villettes to Carteret, 17 August,
in which he drew an elaborate contrast between his own character
and that of Kaunitz, and contended that the latter wanted a
father " for this darling child of his fertile brain," and chose
Villettes because his familiarity with Ormea would suggest that it
had the latter's sanction. Arneth (ii., 285) produces evidence

view of the current negotiation, the proposal could be commended as freeing Sardinia from the bugbear of Austrian domination in Italy. It was really believed in Vienna that Ormea would concur. And he might have done so, but for the awkward suggestion in the background that Austria must be assured of the retention of Bavaria before consenting to hand over any Lombard territories to Sardinia. Turin was as resolute as ever to have nothing to do with conditional cessions. As a matter of fact, Sardinia was never consulted. The scheme was submitted to Carteret, and Carteret killed it by a prompt and unhesitating veto.[1] To remove a Bavarian Elector to Naples, or, as was alternatively suggested, to Tuscany, would be startling to Germany, but to remove the elected Emperor and the titular ruler of Germany would be an outrage which even the imperfect German nationalism of that period would not tolerate. The mere propounding of such a proposal proved how completely Austria had ceased to be a really German power. At the same time, the creation of a single overwhelming Roman Catholic state in Southern Germany would be a disaster to Protestantism, while the overturning of the German balance in favour of Austria would be a direct challenge to Frederick of Prussia, who also regarded Charles VII as an Emperor of his own creation. If there had been no other argument, the inevitable antagonism of Prussia would have been decisive with Carteret. All his anti-Bourbon schemes were guarded by the reservation that at all costs Frederick must not be provoked into resuming the war. And so instructions were sent from Hanau to Robinson to declare that the scheme propounded by Wasner was altogether impracticable, and Robinson carried them out with even more than his customary bluntness. When Bartenstein, the strongest partisan of the scheme at Vienna, asked whether England would stand out if Austria and Sardinia were agreed, Robinson replied that

that Kaunitz had formulated the plan before his alleged conversation with Villettes.

[1] Carteret to Robinson, 24 and 27 July, 1743, in Add. MSS. 23,815.

the predominant partner was the state which supplied the others with the sinews of war.[1]

The rebuff administered to Vienna by the almost contemptuous rejection of its proposal, following as it did negotiations with William of Hesse, which had been regarded with jealousy and suspicion, was bitterly resented by that Court. Lord Stair suspected Carteret of a deliberate design to cut adrift from Austria and to substitute an alliance with Prussia. Newcastle, chafing in London at the impotence to which Carteret's silence condemned him, was half inclined at one moment to share the suspicion. Nothing could be more unfounded, but there can be little doubt that Maria Theresa was at the moment so alienated from England as to be inclined to welcome overtures from France. Carteret was seriously alarmed when he learned that such overtures were actually on their way through the medium of the new Archbishop of Mainz. There is still a good deal of obscurity about the propositions which Hatsel, subintendant at Strasburg, was said to be authorized to put before the Archbishop, but there seems to have been a genuine desire to test Maria Theresa's willingness to be reconciled with France on the basis of a joint effort to recover Silesia and a promise to procure the election of the Archduke Joseph as King of the Romans.[2] Carteret checkmated the plot, if there was one, by assuming that it was a mere attempt to sow dissension among the allies, and by promptly disclosing it to Frederick. This action, taken without any consultation with Austria, the Power most immediately concerned, was another grievance at Vienna, and was taken as evidence of that predilection for Prussia, which was almost a worse offence than the obvious predilection for Sardinia. Carteret tried to conciliate Vienna by dropping his negotiation with Charles VII and by tacitly acquiescing in a continued Austrian occupation of Bavaria. Whatever chance of life the draft treaty

[1] Robinson to Carteret, 4 August, 1743 (Add. MSS. 23,867, fo. 373).

[2] On the Hatsel overtures, see Arneth, ii., 288 and 523. He prints Hatsel's letters on the latter page.

of Hanau had was destroyed when Wasner broached the exchange project. At the moment when Carteret refused to allow Maria Theresa to make her own use of the conquest of Bavaria, he could not propose to take that conquest away from her altogether and to restore it to Charles VII. If he had persisted in this, the Austrian alliance would have been subjected to a strain it could hardly have borne. Even as it was, the quarrel had gone so far as to make it extremely improbable that Austria would yield to English pressure as regards the Sardinian treaty. Carteret had already been compelled to abandon one of his negotiations. It seemed extremely probable that he would fail in the other. From this humiliation he was saved by external events.

The provisional Convention of 1 February, 1742, had broken off all direct intercourse between Turin and Madrid, but it was still possible to continue it indirectly through France. Fleury had abstained from condemning the Convention because it expressly reserved the right to come over to the Bourbons. In the following May Solaro had resumed his confidential conversations with the French Ministers. France had to undertake the difficult task of inducing Elizabeth Farnese to pardon Charles Emmanuel for putting forward a claim to the Duchy of Milan, and to tempt him by the offer of a sufficient bribe in Lombardy to withdraw both his claim and his objection to the establishment of a second Bourbon prince in Italy. Fleury always advocated this policy, and after his death Amelot continued to do so. But the successive failures of Montemar and Gages did more to convince the Spanish Queen than any arguments on the part of France. After Campo Santo, and the subsequent threat to Naples, she was gradually induced to agree that Charles Emmanuel should have the Duchy of Milan with the title of King of Lombardy, while Don Philip should have Parma, Piacenza, and Sardinia, taking over the royal title with the island. If Maria Theresa gave her consent, she might keep Cremona and Mantua with the succession to Guastalla, but, if she refused, Cremona was to complete the Duchy of Milan, and Mantua with the expectative of Guastalla was to go to Don Philip. This promised Charles Emmanuel a great deal more territory than he could possibly get from Maria Theresa, but it was contingent : he had no trust in Spanish promises, and he did not want Don Philip as a neighbour. So he would only consent if Austria finally refused to accept the terms which were now settled as between England and Sardinia. In order to gain time for the application of the necessary pressure upon Austria, he invented successive demands which prolonged the negotiations in Paris and postponed the necessity for a final decision. But he could not play this game for ever without exasperating France, which he desired to avoid as long as possible. His last demands were that the Emperor should become a party to the treaty, that Savoy should be restored and guaranteed to him, that Don Philip should be pledged to gain no further territory in Italy, and that there should be no establishment for a third Infant. To his surprise France not only agreed to these demands, but undertook to force Campo Florido to assent.[1] This brought matters to a crisis. Villettes was called in, was shown the dispatch from Solaro, and was requested to write to Carteret the only letter from his pen which was of decisive importance.

Villettes pointed out that the Sardinian King and Minister were now in a serious dilemma. Either they must put Italy and themselves in the power of the House of Bourbon, separate themselves from England, and save France and Spain from that reduction of power which they regarded as the best safeguard for their own future security ; or, by refusing the treaty, they must admit that they have been cozening France by mean artifices for the last two years, and thus incur the just resentment and fury of that Power and of Spain. They could not possibly resist such a force as France and Spain could send to co-operate with the Spanish troops already in Savoy. In this dilemma Ormea had decided

[1] The draft treaty, with the relative correspondence, is in a bundle of papers sent home by Carteret on 13 September, 1743 (State Papers, For., Treaty Papers, 115).

to give the following answer to the French envoy at
Turin :

" That the king his master having been informed by
the letter brought him on the 27th inst. [August], and
by a messenger Monsr Osorio had dispatched hither,
that the conclusion of their treaty with the Queen of
Hungary depended on one single point [*i.e.*, Piacenza]
which the Austrian minister had refused consenting to
and Monsr Osorio to give up without precise orders from
his court, the King could not allow his ambassador at
Paris to sign the treaty with France and Spain till he
was disengaged with his Majesty and the Queen of
Hungary in a becoming manner. That he had therefore now directed Monsr Osorio to insist upon the point
in dispute, and, if the Austrian envoy complied, that
he should sign the treaty with the Queen of Hungary,
as they had promised to do so on this point being
granted ; in which case, the King of Sardinia must
refuse the considerable advantages now offered him by
France and Spain, as having been made too late. But
that, if the Austrian minister persisted in his refusal
to admit this controversial point, Monsr Osorio was
directed to disengage himself and break off all farther
treaty or negotiation, and immediately to dispatch a
courier to Paris, with the orders of this court to the
commander Solar (which had been sent inclosed to
Monsr Osorio) to sign the treaty with France and Spain ;
so that as little time as possible would be lost in putting
an end to this affair one way or the other."

Villettes added that the Sardinian King and Minister
left it to his discretion whether he would communicate
this state of affairs to Kaunitz, but that he thought
Kaunitz could do little good in the matter, and so had
refused unless they gave him the information in writing. He had, however, sent a courier on 31 August to
Robinson with two horses of his own, in order to keep
it secret from both Kaunitz and the French Minister.[1]
Carteret confronted Wasner at Worms with this
letter, and the instructions to Osorio as constituting an

[1] Villettes to Carteret, 2 September, 1743, in State Papers, For.,
Sardinia, 47.

ultimatum on the part of Sardinia. Wasner was placed
in an extremely difficult position. He had power to
give way in the last extremity about Piacenza, but he
knew that he would be expected to obtain in return
for this both a definite *dédommagement* and an assured
subsidy, and Carteret would give neither. When he
asked for delay in order to get final instructions, he was
told that delay meant the sending of the Sardinian
courier to Paris. He might suspect, but he had no
evidence, that the threat was concerted between
Carteret and Osorio in order to force his hand. England
had given so many warnings of inevitable Sardinian
defection which had come to nothing. On the other
hand, he knew that a Sardinian alliance with France
and Spain would be fatal to the Austrian cause in Italy,
and the evidence which Carteret produced was sufficiently alarming. With many misgivings he made up
his mind to give way, and to write home that he had
signed the treaty with the knife at his throat. Before
signing he made desperate efforts to get better terms.
But the only concessions which he could obtain were
the insertion of words in the fifth article to the effect
that Austria should only be bound to raise her Italian
troops to 30,000 men, " aussitôt que la situation des
affaires en Allemagne pourra le permettre," and the
signature by Carteret of a separate declaration pledging
England to aid Maria Theresa " pour lui procurer avec
l'assistance divine tout le dédommagement possible et
seureté pour l'avenir." In return Sardinia got the
coveted extension of its share of Piacenza to the Nura.
The Treaty of Worms, with its three separate and secret
articles, was signed on 13 September, 1743, by Wasner,
Carteret, and Osorio. The separate declaration was
signed on the same day by Wasner and Carteret.[1]

Ratification was now necessary to complete the transaction. On the part of England and Sardinia, who may
be regarded as the successful parties in the bargain, this

[1] The separate declaration was ratified by the English Ministers,
but Maria Theresa thought it so valueless that she declined to
accept the ratification. See Přibram, *Oesterreichische Staatsverträge, England*, i., 611.

was a mere formality, though Ormea grumbled that the modification in the fifth article made the military co-operation of Austria dangerously insecure. But Maria Theresa, who regarded the treaty as a diplomatic defeat, was not so ready to confirm it. She dared not run the risks involved in repudiation, but she determined to make a last effort to enforce at least one of her demands. She sent the ratification to Wasner, but ordered him on no account to exchange it unless Carteret would sign a separate declaration pledging England to pay the subsidy of £300,000 on the same terms as those given for the Sardinian subsidy—*i.e., tant que la guerre et le besoin durera.* Carteret objected that he could give no such pledge without the consent of his colleagues and of Parliament. This time it was Wasner's turn to be obdurate, and after consultation with the King, Carteret signed the supplementary convention with Wasner on 14 October, 1743. By his signature he obtained the exchange of the ratifications. But this tardy triumph on the part of Austria, though welcomed at Vienna, met with a very different reception in London. During the summer of 1743 Carteret's colleagues had watched his independent conduct of affairs with unconcealed jealousy, and he had not deigned to conciliate them by a full and frank explanation of his actions. They were not unwilling to teach him that he was not a sole or even a first Minister. When the question of ratifying the convention came before the Cabinet, a substantial majority refused to accept Carteret's defence and voted for rejection.[1] All that Wasner

[1] In State Papers, For., Treaty Papers, 115, is a record of the Cabinet meeting on 24 November (o.s.). Thirteen Members, an unusual number in the eighteenth century, were present. The convention of 14 October was read and considered, " and my Lord Chancellor, my Lord President, my Lord Steward, my Lord Chamberlain, the Duke of Richmond, the Duke of Montagu, the Duke of Newcastle, and Mr. Pelham were of opinion humbly to advise His Majesty not to ratify the said convention, but that His Majesty would be pleased to cause proper instances to be made at the Court of Vienna to substitute in lieu thereof another treaty for paying to the Queen of Hungary a subsidy of three hundred thousand pounds. And the Duke of Argyll was of opinion that this convention should not be ratified without explanation. And the Duke of Bolton, the Marquis of Tweeddale, the Earl of

could obtain was a renewal of the subsidy for another year.[1] This disappointment did not contribute to bring England and Austria closer together, or to make the Treaty of Worms more acceptable at Vienna.

The Treaties of Breslau and Worms are Carteret's two most notable achievements. Both were of supreme importance at the time, and both mark turning-points in the history of the war of the Austrian Succession. Breslau ushered in a period of startling successes on the part of the anti-Bourbon Powers. Worms marks the beginning of the later stages of the war. It led to a renewal of the Family Compact, to the entry of France as a principal into the war, to the encouragement of the Jacobites, and to the invasion of the Netherlands. And the second treaty largely contributed to the failure of the first, and so to the ruin of Carteret's policy. His schemes for the humiliation of the Bourbons required as an essential condition of their success the continued neutrality of Prussia. The Treaty of Worms may be taken as the date from which Frederick decided to return to the war. The very wording of the treaty inspired him with misgivings. The contracting Powers guaranteed a number of treaties, such as those of 1731 and 1738, which were inconsistent with the Treaty of Breslau. In the third article Sardinia guaranteed the Pragmatic Sanction without any reference to the cession of Silesia. It was possible to contend that the Treaty of Worms dealt with Italian problems, and that it would have been quite irrelevant to drag in Silesia or any other German problem. On the other hand, it was notorious that Austria had tried to drag in German problems of the first importance. And no defence could obscure the fact that the Treaty of Worms, if strictly interpreted, could be held to impose

---

Winchelsea, and my Lord Carteret were of opinion that the convention should be ratified." It may be noted that the Premier, Henry Pelham, was the only commoner in the Cabinet, which contained five Dukes. For Philip Yorke's account of this Cabinet meeting, see Yorke, *Life of Lord Hardwicke*, i., 323, and Coxe, *Henry Pelham*, i., 478.

[1] See Pribram, *ubi supra*, pp. 625–30.

upon its signatories obligations which were inconsistent with the security of Prussia's recent acquisitions. The treaty was regarded by Frederick as a grievance, and it was against the interest of England to multiply his grievances. It also alienated Frederick even more directly in another way. It was due to the Sardinian negotiations that Carteret's draft treaty of Hanau was stillborn. The failure to obtain any concessions to the Emperor, and the prolonged Austrian occupation of Bavaria, were the main pretexts, and probably the main causes, of the sudden irruption into Bohemia in August, 1744. And this renewal of military activity on Frederick's part wrecked all Carteret's schemes, and led directly to his own downfall. So to some extent he may be said to have been ruined by his own handiwork.

In Italy also the Treaty of Worms had disastrous consequences. Until its conclusion the Austrians and Sardinians had more than held their own against the Spaniards, and had done so with comparative ease. But when France replied to the Treaty of Worms by concluding the Treaty of Fontainebleau with Spain, and by undertaking to procure an Italian principality for Don Philip, this Austro-Sardinian superiority, even with the assistance of the British fleet, came to an end. When Frederick's intervention distracted Austria from Italy, the balance in the peninsula was completely reversed, and in 1745 both the Milanese and Piedmont were on the verge of being conquered. This fate and the desertion of Charles Emmanuel which would have followed were averted by the Treaty of Dresden. But even then the evil results of the Treaty of Worms were not exhausted. Its most iniquitous provision was the tenth article, which proposed, without any provocation, to despoil Genoa of the Marquisate of Finale. This compelled Genoa to abandon its neutrality and to join France and Spain by the Treaty of Aranjuez in 1745. And it was Genoese hostility which finally deprived the allies of that coveted triumph in Italy which was to balance their ill-success in the Netherlands. This decided the settlement of Italy in the final peace. Sardinia had to give up Finale and postpone its maritime ambitions. Don Carlos kept Naples and Sicily, and Don Philip established a second Bourbon branch in Parma, Piacenza, and Guastalla. To complete that principality Charles Emmanuel had to surrender that segment of Piacenza to the Nura which Wasner had so reluctantly conceded at Worms. Maria Theresa recovered nothing that had been handed over to Sardinia, and was compelled to add Parma and Guastalla to the list of her uncompensated losses. Eight years later England had ceased to be the ally of the Austrian ruler, whom Carteret had helped to alienate, and had become the ally of the King of Prussia, who had ruined Carteret's most cherished schemes. The triumphs of diplomacy are proverbially short-lived, and its results rarely correspond with its intentions.

CHAPTER III

D'ARGENSON'S RELATIONS WITH GERMANY AND SARDINIA

Inefficiency of French Foreign Office after 1740—Fleury yields to Belleisle as to Austrian succession—Louis XV dispenses with a First Minister on Fleury's death—Treaty of Fontainebleau with Spain—French expedients to meet Carteret's successful coalition—France saved;by Prussian return to the war—D'Argenson becomes Foreign Minister and Carteret falls—Prospects of peace—Death of Charles VII—D'Argenson's prepossessions—His imperfect control of French policy —Futile attempt to oppose election of Francis I—D'Argenson secures neutrality of Empire—French successes in the Netherlands—Triumph of " Gallispans " in Italy—Frederick's defence of Silesia and Treaty of Dresden—Refusal of d'Argenson to quarrel with Prussia—English capture Cape Breton—Sardinian overtures to d'Argenson—His Italian plans—First mission of Champeaux to Turin—The agreement of 26 December—Disclosure to England—The draft treaty and the armistice—D'Argenson's letter to Maillebois—Outcry from Spain—Champeaux's second mission—Narrative of Villettes—The younger Maillebois brings signed but conditional armistice—Rupture of negotiation—Fall of Asti—Quarrels of French and Spaniards—English reticence—Austria regards Sardinian ill-faith as forfeiting Worms cessions.

It cannot be disputed—and was, indeed, admitted at the time[1]—that the French Foreign Office was inefficiently guided during the war of the Austrian Succession. There had been no warning of this beforehand. At the close of the previous decade France seemed to have recovered the ascendancy in Europe which it had lost in the later years of Louis XIV. If Fleury had been so fortunate as to die in 1740, he would have come down to history with a halo as the statesman who had dealt a mortal blow to the Utrecht Settlement by concluding a Family Compact with Spain and by establishing a Bourbon King in Naples and Sicily, who had removed the last weakness

[1] Noailles to Louis XV, 8 July, 1743. Rousset, *Correspondence de Louis XV et le Maréchal de Noailles*, i., 148. " Je ne puis me dispenser de dire à Votre Majesté que ses affaires étrangères sont tres-mal conduites."

from the eastern frontier of France, who had dictated terms of peace in the East to a humiliated Austria and a malcontent Russia, and who had further shackled the latter Power by an alliance with Sweden. And he had done all this without provoking active opposition on the part of the Maritime Powers, who had been lulled by his pacific professions into forgetfulness of the maxims and traditions bequeathed to them by William III. When, in 1739, Spain became involved in a maritime war with Great Britain, Fleury was careful to insist that the treaty of 1733 imposed no obligation upon France to take part in the war. The death of Charles VI and the accession of his young and inexperienced daughter seemed at first sight likely to confirm the ascendancy of France. It presented an obvious opportunity for consolidating French influence in Germany by detaching the imperial dignity and pretensions from the family which had held them for so many generations. Maria Theresa's husband, ex-Duke of Lorraine and Grand-Duke of Tuscany, was practically landless in Germany, and could hardly aspire to wield the sceptre of the Habsburgs. He could not be endowed by his wife without flagrant breach of the Pragmatic Sanction, and if she should die before him, his position as the titular ruler in Germany would be ludicrous. By supporting the candidature in the Empire of Charles Albert of Bavaria, France would discharge its obligations to the House of Wittelsbach, without incurring blame for any departure from that guarantee of the Pragmatic Sanction by which Fleury had purchased the reversion of Lorraine.

If Fleury had been strong enough to follow his own cautious inclinations, his reputation would have been unsullied, and the whole history of Europe would have been changed. But he was too old and frail to stand up against the wave of enthusiasm excited in France by Belleisle's scheme for the humiliation of the House of Austria, and the disasters which followed France's ill-judged plunge into the Succession war almost obliterated in the minds of contemporaries, and even of historians, the memory of the cardinal's past services to France. It is true that he seated his candidate upon the imperial throne, but he might have done that without a war, and the military failures in Bohemia and Bavaria left France saddled with the burdensome obligation of maintaining an impotent and homeless Emperor, and without any hope of an adequate recompense. This obligation was Fleury's bequest to France when he died in January, 1743, and left the Government rudderless in a stormy sea. There were four Ministers in the great departments of State—Maurepas for the navy, the Count d'Argenson for the army, Orry for finance, and Amelot for foreign affairs. In time of peace they might have managed fairly well, but in war their departments hopelessly overlapped. Foreign policy either dictated or was dictated by military and naval plans; finance was either the servant or the master of the other three. A strong hand was needed to give unity and co-ordination to jarring interests and wills. Fleury, whatever his defects, had done this for sixteen years. Whether the decision was his own or imposed upon him, there had been a decision, and French policy had not lacked direction, whether wise or unwise. Now that he had gone, somebody must fill his place. Inspired by a momentary eagerness to emulate his great-grandfather, Louis XV undertook to dispense with the services of a First Minister, and to undertake in person the guidance of the ship of State.[1] It was a task for which he had neither the requisite industry nor the necessary self-confidence. In the words of Frederick of Prussia, " his ardour was extinguished in eight days, and France was governed by four subaltern kings, each independent of the other."[2] Nor was this the worst. Louis was not even honest and straightforward with his Ministers. Like many a weak man he professed to agree with a Minister in private conference, and then proceeded to betray him

[1] Noailles asserts that he persuaded Louis XV to be his own First Minister on the death of Fleury by producing the instructions which Louis XIV had drawn up for Philip V, when the latter went to Spain. " Ne vous laissez pas gouverner, soyez le maître; n'ayez jamais de favori ni de premier ministre; écoutez, consultez votre conseil, mais décidez " (*Mémoires du duc de Noailles* [ed. Petitot], iii., 300). Noailles was rewarded for his advice by being created *ministre d'état.*

[2] *Mémoires de Frederic II*, i., 178.

behind his back.   Besides the office-holders, there were
Ministers without portfolios, notably the Duc de Noailles
and Cardinal Tencin, to whom he could turn for advice.
And beyond them were courtiers, generals, mistresses,
and even valets, who might share in influencing a royal
decision.   The habit of deceiving his Ministers, once
contracted, was cultivated with such malicious ingenuity
as to give rise in the later years of his reign to a whole
system of secret diplomacy carried on outside the
Foreign Office and side by side with the normal diplomatic service.

After Fleury's death French affairs went from bad
to worse.   Noailles, who aspired to combine military
with political control, was defeated at Dettingen,
though not through his own fault.   The Bavarian army
collapsed, and was only saved from compulsory disband-
ment by transforming itself into a neutral imperial force.
Marshal Broglie, who had contributed to the French
failure in Bohemia, brought his military career to an
end by leaving Germany and Charles VII to their fate
and leading his army back to France.   It would be
difficult, after recent experience, to induce French
troops to undertake any more distant campaigns.   And
France itself, though still technically only an auxiliary
in the war, was threatened with invasion and with the
loss of the border provinces of Alsace and Lorraine.   A
formidable anti-Bourbon coalition was inspired and
guided by the genius of Carteret.   An effort on the part
of France to divide and distract her enemies by gaining
over Sardinia was foiled at the last moment by Carteret's success in extorting Maria Theresa's assent to the
Treaty of Worms.   In their chagrin the French King
and Ministers discarded Fleury's teaching, and concluded the Treaty of Fontainebleau with Spain.   By this
they saddled France with new responsibilities without
adding in any way to her resources.   They were now
pledged to gain a principality in Lombardy for Don
Philip, to guarantee Naples to Don Carlos, to recover
Gibraltar, and if possible Minorca too, for Spain, and
to free that country from the commercial concessions to
England extorted at Utrecht.   Again, as in the treaty

7

with Bavaria, France was to promote the interests of another Power without any prospect of proportionate gain to herself. It was fortunate for France that the hostile allies, after threatening for some weeks in the autumn of 1743 to cross the Rhine, decided in the end to postpone their enterprise till the next year. Even with this reprieve, however, the prospect was sufficiently bleak, and it was necessary to devise means to meet the danger.

There was no unanimity among the French Ministers as to any of the expedients that were proposed, but in the end four schemes obtained sufficient approval to be adopted. The first need was to meet the obligations which France had undertaken. Something must be done for Charles VII besides merely enabling him to maintain at Frankfort some semblance of a Court. His own army was now pledged to neutrality, and it was no longer possible to send a French force for his support. The only way out of the difficulty was to organize a league among the loyal Princes of Germany, and to induce them, if necessary by subsidies, to supply troops for the defence of the Empire and its elected head. The nucleus of such a league would be formed by the King of Prussia, who was rendered increasingly uneasy by the obvious desire of Maria Theresa to retain Bavaria, the Elector Palatine, the most loyal of the allies of France, and the Landgrave of Hesse-Cassel (also King of Sweden), who was still hankering after a tenth electorate. If the league could be formed and extended, it would make Maria Theresa hesitate to send her army on so distant an enterprise as the invasion of Alsace. The other treaty obligation was to Spain. To carry out the Treaty of Fontainebleau troops must be found to co-operate with the Spaniards under Don Philip in an invasion of Piedmont, which offered the double advantage of compelling Maria Theresa to desist from any attack upon Naples and also to divert some of her troops to the defence of Lombardy. In order to convince Spain of the genuineness of French co-operation, the command of these troops was to be entrusted to the Prince of Conti, a member of the Royal Family.

But neither Germany nor Italy could be trusted to effect a sufficient diversion of the enemy forces to save France from invasion, and something further must be devised. Tencin and Maurepas pressed for the dispatch of an expedition to Britain to aid a prospective Jacobite rising and to carry with it Charles Edward, the Pretender's son, who was invited to return to France in defiance of treaty pledges. Noailles and others doubted the wisdom of alienating Protestant allies, like Hesse, and of adding the championship of the Stewart cause to the other obligations of France, but they could not veto a scheme which held out the prospect of paralyzing George II and Carteret, the arch-enemies of France. With this was coupled the most important of the plans which were evolved in the later months of 1743, an invasion of the Austrian Netherlands. Hitherto, as in the previous war, France had abstained from this attractive enterprise, and it was still regarded with some misgivings as likely to stir the Maritime Powers to more strenuous exertions,[1] and to revive in Europe the old suspicions of the aggressive designs of France. On the other hand, it would propitiate the army, weary of campaigns at a distance from France, and it tempted the King, who aspired to emulate Louis XIV by taking part in military operations where the risk of failure was comparatively small. These schemes, and especially the last two, were inconsistent with the part of a mere auxiliary in the war, to which France had hitherto steadily adhered, and in the spring of 1744 France declared war against both England and Austria.

Not one of these enterprises achieved the success that was hoped for. Chavigny succeeded in organizing the German League at Frankfort, but nobody would join it except the obvious Princes, and Hesse was inclined to desert it when France threatened the Protestant Suc-

[1] Mémoire presenté au Roi par le Maréchal de Noailles, 10 Fevrier, 1744 (Rousset, ii., 117): " Les entreprises que l'on ferait en Flandre paraissent plus propres à animer la guerre qu'à la terminer, et fourniraient au gouvernement d'Angleterre et à la faction anglaise en Hollande, des motifs capables de déterminer ces deux nations à faire les plus grands efforts." The whole document deserves careful study.

cession in England. The League itself was short-lived
and was impotent as a check upon Austria. Conti
occupied Nice and conducted a creditable passage of
the Alps, but was compelled to retire from the siege of
Cuneo, so that Piedmont was once more secure. The
Austrian invasion of Naples was foiled rather through
the ineptitude of Lobkowitz and the refusal of Sardinian co-operation than by the intervention of
France. The naval expedition against England had to
be abandoned on account of adverse weather, and this
was in a sense fortunate, as it left Maurice de Saxe, who
was to have headed it, free to guide Louis XV in his
first military enterprise. This opened brilliantly with
the occupation of Courtrai, and the rapid capture of
Menin, Ypres, and Furnes. But, as Noailles had foreseen, Maria Theresa did not care enough for the
Netherlands, whose defence she regarded as the task
of the Maritime Powers, to save them by abandoning
her attractive plans. Charles of Lorraine crossed the
Rhine into Alsace, and the French forces under Coigny
retreated under the walls of Strasburg. Louis had to
abandon his career of conquest in Flanders and hasten
to give the inspiration of his presence to the defence of
the southern province. When on the way he fell ill at
Metz, France was in greater danger than she had incurred since the Wars of Religion.

The worst of the danger was averted by the intervention of the King of Prussia, who thus made tardy
amends for his previous desertion which had left the
French army fatally isolated in Bohemia. Frederick's
rapid advance through Saxony to Prague in August,
1744, compelled the Austrians to return hurriedly across
the Rhine and to evacuate Bavaria, with the exception
of a few fortresses. Alsace was saved, and the French
were enabled by the reduction of Freiburg to make
themselves masters of Anterior Austria, and thus to
buttress Alsace against any subsequent attack. The
unfortunate Charles VII was able to return to a precarious residence in Munich. It did not in any way
diminish Frederick's services to France that he proved
unable to retain his hold upon Bohemia and was com-

pelled before the winter to retreat to Silesia. He had
done exactly what France needed and diverted the main
Austrian forces from a western war to a war against
Prussia. The French Ministers could now renew with
some assurance of success the enterprises which had
hitherto been comparative failures. The year 1745,
while Frederick was fighting with his back to the wall,
was for the Bourbon Powers, in spite of one apparent
disaster, the *annus mirabilis* of the war. But, although
danger had been transformed into something like
triumph, this had been due to an alien intervention,
and the imminence of the danger had called attention to
the shortcomings of the French Foreign Office. Amelot,
who had held the Secretaryship since the dismissal of
Chauvelin, had been got rid of in April, 1744, largely,
it is said, because Frederick refused to deal with him.
For a moment there was a general expectation that
Chauvelin would be recalled. But the King, who was
beginning to enjoy the sense of power, refused to
employ a man who might be too masterful, and for
seven months was his own Foreign as well as First
Minister. When he went to Flanders he took with him
Noailles as his principal adviser, du Theil, the *premier
commis* of the office, to draft the necessary documents,
and the Count d'Argenson, the Minister of War, to
supply the required signature of a Secretary of State.
But the King's illness, and the humiliation to which he
was exposed by the removal of his mistress, put an end
to this sudden outburst of industry, and when Louis
returned from Freiburg he determined to employ once
more a Foreign Secretary. The vacant office was offered
in the first instance to Villeneuve, who had negotiated
the eastern treaties at Belgrade in 1739. When he
declined, it was promptly accepted on 18 November by
the Marquis d'Argenson, the elder brother of the War
Minister. The motives for his selection are obscure,
unless it was thought that fraternal unanimity would
produce the necessary harmony between military and
political plans.

The appointment of d'Argenson was followed three
weeks later by the downfall of Carteret. The two events,

taken together, seemed to presage an early termination of the war. The French Foreign Minister was known to desire it, and was nicknamed *d'Argenson de la paix* to distinguish him from his brother, who was *d'Argenson de la guerre*. And the dismissal of Carteret removed the most active and inspiring leader of the European coalition against the Family Compact. From some points of view there seemed to be no adequate reason for a prolongation of hostilities. The attempt to partition the Austrian dominions had failed for a second time. After Frederick's recent expulsion from Bohemia, it seemed inevitable that Maria Theresa must retain the great bulk of her inheritance. And the counter-effort, organized by Carteret, to compensate Maria Theresa by wresting the border provinces from France, had also, thanks to Frederick's intervention, ended in complete failure. Equally unsuccessful had been the Bourbon effort to expel the Austrians from Italy, and, as long as Sardinia adhered to the Treaty of Worms, it did not look likely to succeed. Nor, in view of the attitude of Charles Emmanuel, did it seem probable that Maria Theresa would succeed in driving Don Carlos from Naples. Thus, as regards the major issues of the war, there was a dead-lock, and a presumption in favour of something like the retention of the *status quo*. It is significant that d'Argenson's first act was to sound Louis XV as to what he would consider reasonable terms of peace, and how far he would consider himself bound by the letter of the Treaty of Fontainebleau, which the Minister regarded as the most serious obstacle in the way of terminating the war. He was much relieved when the King assured him that he had concluded the treaty against his will,[1] and that Don Philip must be satisfied with a smaller establishment than the treaty had promised him. And on 23 December, 1744, Louis wrote him a letter in which he defined the aims of France.[2]

[1] D'Argenson, *Journal et Mémoires* (ed. Rathery), iv., 252. This was certainly untrue. Broglie (*Maurice de Saxe et le Marquis d'Argenson*, i., 89) asserts that the treaty was peculiarly the work of Louis himself.

[2] *Journal et Mémoires*, iv., 254.

Charles VII must be recognized as Emperor, must recover the whole of Bavaria, and must be compensated for the withdrawal of his claims by the cession of the Swabian lands of Austria. Don Philip was to be endowed with Savoy and Nice, Genoa was to keep Finale, and the King of Sardinia should receive compensation in the Milanese. France would restore her conquests in Flanders, but in return was to be freed from the restrictions imposed upon her possession of Dunkirk. England was to be pacified by recovering the *navio permiso* and the *asiento*. These terms were regarded by d'Argenson as not out of reach, and their formulation gratified him because it displayed an intention to free France from her hampering dependence upon Spain.

French historians, following d'Argenson's guidance, have been in the habit of pointing to the death of Charles VII (20 January, 1745) as the cause of the prolongation of the war.[1] That may have been the actual result, but it was by no means a necessary result. Looked at impartially, the Emperor's death, and still more the Treaty of Füssen in April, by which the young Elector of Bavaria made his peace with Maria Theresa, ought to have brought peace nearer. These events freed France from her first and most urgent obligation to continue the war. By consenting to the Grand-Duke's election in the Empire, which after Füssen was practically assured, it would be easy to purchase Maria Theresa's assent to the territorial adjustments in Northern Italy that were required to provide Don Philip with that moderate establishment which Louis had agreed to regard as a sufficient discharge of his obligations to Spain. No insuperable difficulties were to be anticipated from the Maritime Powers. England had made little use so far of her maritime superiority. She had been compelled to keep her major fleet in European waters, and had not as yet gained any of the desired

---

[1] D'Argenson, *Journal et Mémoires*, iv., 260: " il est certain que la paix se fût signée avant l'ouverture de la campagne de 1745, si l'empereur Charles VII ne fût pas venu à décéder subitement."

conquests in America. The broad-bottom Ministry of Henry Pelham contained a number of pacific members, who would be amply satisfied if France evacuated the Netherlands, dropped the cause of the Stewarts, and compelled Spain to restore the commercial concessions of the Utrecht settlement. The Dutch were not actual belligerents, and the dominant Republican party had good reasons to desire a speedy termination of the war. On minor contentious issues, such as Dunkirk, there would be difficulties, but France was advantageously placed by her acquisitions in Flanders, which Saxe had triumphantly maintained after the King's departure had put an end to further conquests. There remained the treaty with Prussia and the contention that France was bound to continue to fight as long as Prussia was in danger. To this it could be replied that Frederick had shown no such scruples in 1742, and that it was reasonable to pay him back in his own coin.

That the war continued after 1744 on the large scale, instead of being narrowed down to an Austro-Prussian struggle for Silesia, was due, not to the death of Charles VII, but to the faulty policy of d'Argenson himself. He is perhaps the first, though not the last, example of the Professor in politics. His knowledge of European affairs was based entirely upon an assiduous study of books and other records, and he had no practical experience of diplomacy or diplomatists. He entered office with a number of pre-conceptions, which he found it difficult to modify and impossible to abandon. He had a strong prejudice against Elizabeth Farnese and her excessive demands from France. As a pupil of Chauvelin he had no desire to break away from the Spanish alliance, which had been his master's achievement, but he was resolute that, if the alliance was maintained, France must be the predominant partner. He had in his head a ready-made plan for the settlement of Italy. All foreign rule was to be put an end to, as Julius II had long ago proposed, and there was to be a federation of Italian Princes, including the Pope. If Don Carlos and Don Philip were among these Princes, they must be prepared to give up their Italian possessions in case of succession to the Spanish throne. In order to expel Austria from Italy, Sardinia must be gained over, in spite of any objections on the part of the Spanish Queen, and the King might be tempted by a sort of hegemony in the federation. The union of the Maritime Powers must be broken off by detaching the Dutch, who had historic obligations to France and good commercial reasons for disliking England. As to England, d'Argenson would have liked to injure her mercantile prosperity and to see the Stewarts once more on the throne. But he was not prepared to fight for either object, or to make any sacrifice in order to restore to Spain the monopoly of her colonial trade. To disarm the Maritime Powers and to avert any revival of European alarm, he desired France to abstain from all expansion, especially in the Netherlands. If he could have had his way, he would have put a stop to further aggression in Flanders, as he foresaw a growing reluctance to give up such attractive conquests. He admitted that he knew nothing about war, and he mistrusted the political influence of soldiers. He had grown up in the time-honoured belief that the first duty of France was to weaken Austria. The greatest blow to Austria, and therefore the greatest gain to France, had been the Prussian annexation of Silesia, and Austria must not be allowed to regain the lost province. Above all, Austria must not regain the imperial power and thus be enabled to bring a united Germany into the field against France.

In criticizing d'Argenson's policy it is only fair to remember that he very rarely had matters his own way. Like Carteret, he had a very uncertain tenure of office. Carteret, who depended in the last resort upon the House of Commons, was no parliamentarian. D'Argenson, who depended altogether upon royal favour, was no courtier. But even while in office the French Minister was far less masterful than the Englishman had been. He lacked, not only Carteret's diplomatic experience and aptitude, but also many other of his qualities. D'Argenson could put his case clearly and forcibly with his pen, or in monologue with a single listener. But he admits that he was impotent in debate with his col-

leagues. He induced the King to give up the regular
meetings of Ministers which Fleury had instituted, and
to revert to the practice of separate consultations with
the heads of departments. He thought that he had
thereby gained a great advantage, whereas, in reality,
he ensured his own failure and deprived France of all
hope of a reasoned consecutive policy. It is true that
he had a greater chance of impressing the King, and
from time to time he believed that he had done so, but
he had no power of making that impression permanent.
If he urged independence of Spain or a dictatorial tone
to the Court of Madrid, the King's apparent consent
might be overcome by counter-advice from Noailles or
Maurepas, or by imploring letters from Louis' favourite
daughter, pleading the cause of her husband, Don Philip.
And he lost all hope of guiding military operations, upon
which the success of his policy depended. The evil
results of this want of harmony between French departments is conspicuous in the events of 1745.

D'Argenson's anti-Austrian prepossessions made it
impossible for him to accept the death of Charles VII
as a stepping-stone on the way to peace. He conceived
it to be his duty to maintain the young Bavarian Elector
in the ranks of the enemies of Maria Theresa, and
deemed it still more imperative to prevent the election
of her husband as Emperor.[1] In order to achieve these
two aims, and at the same time to effect a diversion in
favour of Prussia, he urged the sending of the main
French army into Germany and the maintenance of a
defensive attitude in the Netherlands. The League of
Frankfort was virtually dissolved by the death of the
Prince for whose support it had been formed, so that
no German troops could be counted upon. Hesse
promptly applied for a renewal of British subsidies, and
the Elector Palatine had to seek safety in a sullen
neutrality. But here d'Argenson came into collision
with the soldiers and with the King. The War Office
would not send an adequate force to Germany. The

---

[1] Noailles (*Mémoires*, iii., 395) says that d'Argenson declared
that he would employ down to the last soldier of France to prevent
the election of the Grand-Duke.

generals contended that a defensive war was the most
ruinous of wars and that it was alien to the military
traditions of France. Louis was eager to renew the
sequence of successful sieges which had been interrupted
in the previous campaign. Maria Theresa was enabled
with complete impunity to pour troops into Bavaria
and to extort the Treaty of Füssen. There remained the
imperial election, on which d'Argenson was as obstinate
as Belleisle had been in 1741. But there was a fatal
difference. Belleisle had had a candidate ready to his
hand; d'Argenson had none. The only Prince who
could be reasonably put forward was Augustus III, the
King of Poland and the Elector of Saxony. But
Augustus was the Roman Catholic ruler of a Protestant
electorate, and his candidature made no appeal to the
ecclesiastical electors. He was also bound to Austria by
the Treaty of Warsaw, and was in receipt of subsidies
from the Maritime Powers. It was doubtful whether
the crown of Poland was tenable with the imperial
crown, and Augustus was notoriously eager to make the
former crown hereditary in his family. For this reason
he must retain the favour of Russia, the Power which
had placed him upon the Polish throne, and it was
practically certain that the Tsaritsa Elizabeth, now completely reconciled with Maria Theresa, would frown upon
his candidature for the higher dignity. The imperial
crown had no great attraction for the sluggish and un-
adventurous character of Augustus, and the career of
Charles VII did not give any glamour to the prospect
of receiving that crown as the nominee of France.
Above all, Augustus was engaged in negotiations with
Maria Theresa for the spoliation of the King of Prussia,
whom he regarded with mingled fear and hatred. It
was extremely unlikely that he would for a possibly
unsuccessful candidature abandon the prospect of adding
to his own territories at the expense of an inconveniently
powerful neighbour. Regardless of all these considerations, d'Argenson insisted upon urging the Saxon
Elector to come forward, and induced the more than
reluctant King of Prussia to join, at any rate ostensibly,
in the invitation. No evidence of reluctance on the part

of Augustus would be accepted by the French Foreign
Secretary, and the only defence of his credulity in the
matter is that he was not the only politician who
believed that the ambition of the Electress, eager to
emulate a younger sister who had already been an
Empress, and the egregious vanity of Count Brühl, the
dictator of the Dresden Court, would in the end overcome all Augustus' scruples and hesitations.[1]   The
Elector so far gratified his proffered patron as to declare
coyly that he would accept the Empire if it was offered
to him by the Electors and if his acceptance was necessary for the welfare of Germany.   But meantime he used
the French overtures as a means of driving the best
bargain he could with regard to the proposed partition
of Brandenburg.   In the end he got his treaty with
Austria, which proved wholly futile, and he gave his
vote for the Grand-Duke.   There could be only one end
to the comedy.   The force which had been reluctantly
entrusted to Conti to overawe Frankfort was depleted
to swell the army in the Netherlands, and, finding it
impossible to break the cordon which Traun had drawn
round the electoral city, withdrew across the Rhine.
The Bohemian vote, rejected in 1742, was now admitted.
The Prussian and Palatine plenipotentiaries protested
and departed.   The seven Electors who remained gave
their votes for the Grand-Duke, who was elected Emperor
on 13 September as Francis I.   Maria Theresa, in spite
of her advanced pregnancy, came to see her husband
crowned.   France had lost the one conspicuous gain
which Belleisle had won, and, thanks to d'Argenson's
obstinacy, had been humiliated as well as defeated.

It was no small consolation to France, though little
to d'Argenson, that this disaster was counterbalanced
by an unprecedented series of military triumphs.   Marshal Saxe, with the King in attendance, opened the campaign of 1745 in the Netherlands by laying siege to
Tournay.   Cumberland and Königsegg led the allied

---

[1] Chesterfield, who was on an embassy to The Hague from
January to May, 1745, and who was devoid neither of experience
nor of insight, constantly reiterated his conviction that Augustus
would come forward as a candidate.   See his interesting letters
to Newcastle in Add. MSS. 32,804.

army to its relief, and, after an obstinate and not inglorious combat, were defeated at Fontenoy (11 May). The news of the victory was received with exultation in Paris, where the citizens had been profoundly depressed by the previous reverses in Bohemia and in Germany.   The consequent surrender of Tournay ushered in the long sequence of successful sieges which culminated in the capture of Brussels in February, 1746. Not even Turenne and Luxemburg had won such laurels as decorated the brow of the Saxon Prince, who had previously been looked at askance as an alien and a Lutheran.   These French triumphs were rendered more easy and more rapid by the contemporary troubles in Great Britain, which found itself compelled to recall from the Netherlands its own troops and a contingent of its Dutch allies to meet the danger suddenly threatened by a Jacobite rising in the North, and by its rapid progress after the sensational victory at Prestonpans.

The news from Italy was almost as gratifying as that from the Netherlands, and, in view of previous experiences in the peninsula, was far more startling.   The Treaty of Aranjuez with Genoa opened the Riviera route to the " Gallispans," as the combined French and Spanish forces were called.   The natural difficulties of the route, which had no made road in those days, were overcome, and the British fleet, inefficiently handled throughout the war, failed to make adequate use of its power of obstruction.   By this passage the Alpine defences of Piedmont were turned, and the combined troops, under Maillebois and Gages, were able to lay siege to Tortona, which surrendered on 8 September. The fall of Tortona opened Lombardy to the invaders, and Schulenburg, who had taken over the Italian command from Lobkowitz, insisted that the primary duty of the Austrian troops must be the defence of the Milanese.   Charles Emmanuel, weakened by Schulenburg's departure, was defeated by Maillebois at Bassignana (27 September).   Valenza, Asti, and Casale fell into the hands of the French, and Alessandria, the last great fortress in Piedmont, was invested before the troops went into winter quarters.   Fortunately for

Charles Emmanuel, co-operation between the French and the Spaniards was as imperfect as between Sardinians and Austrians. The impatient Elizabeth Farnese sent imperious instructions to Gages to press on to the occupation of Parma, Piacenza, and Milan. In spite of the warnings of Maillebois that it was imperative to secure the line of communications with France and to complete the reduction of Piedmont before advancing eastwards, Gages had to obey orders, and in December, 1745, Don Philip entered Milan, which he regarded as the capital of his kingdom of Lombardy. Although serious military risks were incurred by this premature advance, there seemed little doubt that a final triumph in Italy was assured. Once Alessandria was taken, Turin would be open to the enemy, and Charles Emmanuel would have to choose between exile and submission. Alessandria could hardly be saved unless reinforcements came from Austria, and as long as Maria Theresa continued to concentrate all her forces on the Silesian war, she had no troops to spare for Italy. The expulsion of Austria from Italy, the aim of the Treaty of Fontainebleau, seemed in December, 1745, to be inevitable.

While these notable events were occurring in the Netherlands and in Italy, Frederick was fighting with his back to the wall to defend Silesia against the Austrians and Saxons. He had reason to regret with some bitterness that he had embarked in the war to serve the interests of an ungrateful ally. But for him, France, instead of reducing the Netherlands and trampling upon Piedmont, might have been engaged in desperate struggles to repel invaders from her own soil. And now, when he urged that a French army should be sent into Germany to intimidate Hanover and to divert Austria from attacking him,[1] he could get no response, because the French forces were engaged elsewhere.

[1] Frederick to Louis XV, 2 May, 1745: " L'unique remède que j'entrevois et que l'on puisse humainement employer . . . est de faire pénétrer un fort détachement de l'armée du prince de Conti jusqu'au cœur du pays d'Hanovre; c'est l'émétique qu'il faut employer dans cette agonie." Pol. Corr., iv.

Fontenoy, he declared, might, as far as he was concerned, have been fought upon the Scamander. He admitted that the war had been a blunder, and that the best he could look for was to emerge from it without territorial losses. From the beginning of the year he appealed to England to act once more as mediator between himself and Maria Theresa, and he gave the impression that he would be satisfied with a renewal of the Treaty of Breslau. The English Ministers hesitated as to what line they should take. They wanted Austria to turn once more whole-heartedly to the war with France. But they had good reason to distrust Frederick, and they doubted whether it would not be safer to allow Maria Theresa to complete the overthrow of Frederick, which would remove all danger of future Prussian intervention, as a preliminary to renewed concentration against France. The Battle of Hohenfriedberg, however, convinced them that the crushing of Frederick was not so easy a matter as they had supposed, and this put an end to their hesitation. In spite of the reluctance of George II, always hostile to his ambitious nephew, they insisted upon concluding the Convention of Hanover, by which they undertook to extort from Austria a renewal of the Breslau settlement. Maria Theresa was furious when she learned that her dictatorial ally was again demanding the resignation of Silesia, though the promised compensation for its loss had never been forthcoming. The English Ministers were equally furious when they learned that the Queen, after all they had done for her, refused to submit to their dictation. In the confident hope of assistance from Russia, both Austria and Saxony persisted in the war, even after another defeat at Soor, and it was only by the invasion of Saxony, in resolute defiance of warnings from St. Petersburg, that Frederick was at last enabled to extort from his two enemies the signature of the Treaties of Dresden. Thus for the second time Frederick broke away from the French alliance, and France, which owed so many advantages to the action of Prussia, was even more indignant that these advantages should be withdrawn than she had been with the far less defensible desertion of 1742.

This indignation, however, was not shared by d'Argenson,[1] who had been eager to give more direct assistance to Prussia, and who was genuinely pleased that Silesia had been retained.   By abandoning Prussia he might have concluded that alliance between France and Austria which was brought about under altered circumstances ten years later.   He could have purchased an extension of French frontiers in the Netherlands and the Duchies of Parma and Piacenza for Don Philip if he had been willing to consent to the recovery of Silesia by Maria Theresa.   He is blamed by some French historians, and notably by the Duc de Broglie, for not having seized an opportunity which, it is said, would not have been allowed to escape from the eagle eye of Richelieu, or the address of Mazarin, or the royal vigilance of Louis XIV.[2]   But there are two considerations which may be pleaded in d'Argenson's defence.   The same historian denounces Charles Emmanuel for his willingness to turn from an alliance with Austria to hostility to that Power, and it would be difficult to approve a Minister who should recommend to a French King a similar conduct with regard to Prussia. And the proposed treaty with Austria could not have been signed without a complete breach with Spain.   No warning had yet been given to Elizabeth Farnese that France was preparing to drop the Treaty of Fontainebleau and curtail her son's establishment, and, at a time when Spanish troops were about to occupy the city of Milan, she would never have consented to leave

---

[1] D'Argenson (ed. Rathery), iv., 367: " Les gazetiers du parti autrichien dirent alors que nous avions pris la défection du roi de Prusse ' en philosophes chrétiens,' et certes il n'avait pas tenu aux ministres du conseil que nous lui en eussions marqué le mécontement le plus vif, même en nous tournant contre lui."

[2] Broglie, *Marie Thérèse Impératrice*, ii., chap. vi., especially pp. 353–6 and 395–406.   His numerous volumes, valuable as they are in many respects, constitute a colossal pamphlet, written under the inspiration of the war of 1870–1 to denounce the criminal folly of past French Ministers in promoting the aggrandisement of Prussia.   On the Austro-French negotiations before the Treaty of Dresden see also Arneth, iii., 160.   The eminent Austrian historian must have found it difficult to reconcile Maria Theresa's willingness to sacrifice the interests of the Maritime Powers with his constant insistence upon her loyalty and honesty.

Austria in occupation of that duchy. D'Argenson might have been willing to disregard the clamours of the Spanish Queen, but Louis XV and the other Ministers would have refused at this stage to alienate France's one substantial ally. At any rate, d'Argenson did not consider that his conduct needed any defence. On the contrary, he plumed himself with some justice on having preserved amicable relations between France and Prussia after the Treaty of Dresden, and he owed to this the one conspicuous triumph of his ministry, the maintenance of imperial neutrality in spite of the efforts of the new Emperor. He complacently observes in his Memoirs that this achievement cost France far less than Chavigny's rather futile League of Frankfort.[1]

There was one salient event in 1745 which took place outside Europe and attracted less attention at the time than the Battles of Fontenoy, Hohenfriedberg, and Bassignana. It was destined, however, to have no inconsiderable influence upon the prospects of an early peace. In June a body of New England troops under a native commander, Colonel Pepperell, with the assistance of ships from the Mother Country under Admiral Warren, compelled the surrender of Louisbourg, the capital of Cape Breton, which commanded the entry to the St. Lawrence. This seemed to open the way to extensive conquests at the expense of France in Canada, which several politicians, notably the Duke of Bedford, First Lord of the Admiralty, regarded as the true objective of Great Britain in the war. Nothing came at the time of these ambitious designs, but England now had a substantial acquisition either to retain or to use as a means of extorting concessions from France. And the question of its retention interested and concerned a great colony as well as the Mother Country. From this time we can trace in England a notable slackening of the desire for an early peace.

The success of France in 1745 brought to d'Argenson overtures for peace from the two Powers most immedi-

[1] D'Argenson, *Mémoires et Journal Inédit* (ed. Jannet), iii., 112. Both these editions are defective. A really first-rate edition of d'Argenson's great work is a desideratum in French literature.

ately threatened, Holland and Sardinia. The Dutch overtures were futile at the moment because the unofficial envoy sent by the Grand Pensionary professed to speak for both the Maritime Powers, and peace with England was impossible as long as a Stewart Prince was actually disputing George II's title to the throne. Charles Edward had started on his adventurous expedition without actual French assistance, but he had with him a French envoy, and it was notorious that France watched his progress with enthusiastic admiration and would eagerly applaud and welcome his success. The Sardinian overture, on the other hand, was much more promising; it seemed for a time to be assured of a successful issue, and in the end it involved d'Argenson in the deepest humiliation of his career. Nobody in France questioned the desirability of gaining Sardinia. It had been pursued by Fleury and by Amelot with as much assiduity as at an earlier date by Chauvelin. But in 1745 it might be doubted whether the desired end could not be attained more easily by coercion than by conciliation. Coercion would have the merit of pleasing Spain, and its results might be more permanent. But to d'Argenson, who wished neither to please Spain nor to weaken Sardinia, who regarded in fact a strengthened Sardinia as a factor in his desired federation of Italy, the alternative had no attraction. He pinned his whole faith to negotiation, and he succeeded in inducing the King to allow him to try the experiment without communicating it to the other Ministers. This was the sort of underhand intrigue which appealed to Louis XV.

Circumstances were not unfavourable. Ormea, the Sardinian Minister who had concluded the Convention of Turin and the Treaty of Worms, had died in June, 1745, and his successor, the Marquis of Gorzegno, might not be so attached to a policy which he did not originate, though Villettes assured Newcastle that he would be loyal to the English alliance. Although normal diplomatic relations between Paris and Turin had been broken off after Worms, Charles Emmanuel had been careful to keep a back door by which, in time of need, he could open communications with France. The Princes of Carignano, a junior branch of the House of Savoy, held extensive estates in France, and through their intendant, Count Mongardino, it was possible to convey intelligence to Turin. D'Argenson had already employed this channel to suggest a reconciliation between the two States, but so far he had met with no response. But after the defeat at Bassignana, for which all the blame was laid upon Schulenburg, it was the turn of the Sardinian King to take the initiative.[1] If, as seemed at the time inevitable, the Bourbons gained the upper hand in Italy, it was better to have France as a friend than to trust to the tender mercies of the Spaniards, who had the larger forces in the peninsula. D'Argenson welcomed the opportunity of developing his pet scheme for the reorganization of Italy. In order to keep the matter a complete secret, he employed Champeaux, a minor diplomatist who was the French Resident at Geneva, and who could pretend to have private business with the Princess of Carignano. He divulged to Mongardino the proposal to rid Italy of all foreign rule and of the whole tradition of imperial suzerainty. Even the Grand-Duke of Tuscany, being now Emperor, was to hand over his Italian dominion to his brother Charles. The Austrian provinces were to be divided between Sardinia, Don Philip, and Venice, while the Duke of Modena was to recover his duchy, and Genoa was to have exclusive control of its Riviera coast. When a rough-and-ready balance had thus been created, federation was to follow, and a federal army, presumably under the command of the King of Sardinia, was to defend Italian independence. The scheme has been generally hailed as a remarkable anticipation of nineteenth-century ideals. As such it was a century too soon, and at Turin it was regarded as suspiciously savouring of a French protectorate. Villettes, when he

---

[1] " Ce fut donc au commencement du voyage à Fontainebleau, 1745, que le roi de Sardaigne m'envoya exprès et très-secrètement le sieur de Mongardin pour me témoigner l'envie qu'il avait de traiter avec moi, ne se fiant qu'au roi seul et à son ministre des affaires étrangères " (*Journal et Mémoires*, iv., 282).

heard of it later, thought the French King would be an Emperor in Italy, and that he would probably assume the title as a rival of the other Emperor in Germany.[1]

As Sardinia showed no inclination to accept d'Argenson's prescriptions, and as the process of sending messages to and from Turin was both slow and not conducive to secrecy, the French Minister, with the sanction of the King, determined to send his agent to Turin in spite of the continuance of war between France and Sardinia. Accordingly, Champeaux, disguised as the Abbé Rousset, made his way by devious routes across the Alps, and was secretly housed in Turin, where he arrived on 20 December, the very day on which Charles Emmanuel returned from his unsuccessful campaign. Champeaux had been instructed that he was only to stay for four days, and that if the French proposals were not accepted within that time he was to break off the negotiation. If dictatorial methods were to succeed, the moment could not have been better chosen. The King was tired and dispirited, and considered that he had been deserted and left to his fate by Austria. Without external aid he could not break through the cordon round the citadel of Alessandria, and within a limited time starvation must compel the garrison to surrender. When it fell, Turin would be defenceless. All reports from Vienna described Maria Theresa as obstinately bent upon prosecuting her war with Prussia, even if she had to give up Lombardy altogether, while from The Hague (there was ominously no news from London) came the news of the advance of the Jacobites, the spread of panic in England, and the desire of the Dutch for a separate peace with France. There seemed to be no hope of assistance from either of the Worms allies. If submission was extorted by force, Spain would insist upon seizing the Milanese, Parma, and Piacenza, and would probably demand the restoration to the Duchy of Milan of those strips which Sardinia had filched from it by two recent treaties. All hope of getting Finale was at an end either way. But

[1] Villettes to Newcastle, 31 December, 1745 (S.P., For., Sardinia, 50).

compliance with France meant comparative salvation. It would spare Alessandria and Turin, and it would give Charles Emmanuel a larger share of Lombardy than was offered by the Treaty of Worms. No doubt there were risks in the acceptance of Bourbon ascendancy, but risks were better than certain destruction. Even in this dilemma, however, Charles Emmanuel and Gorzegno were not prepared to be unbecomingly docile. Champeaux, an enthusiastic exponent of d'Argenson's doctrine, wasted two days in trying to convert them to the merits of federation and independence. To the Sardinian King and Minister these were empty words, and they objected to giving Germany a galling grievance by demanding the abolition of an imperial suzerainty, which was useful in legal disputes and was no practical hardship to Italy. Nor would they irritate Austria by insisting on the useless transfer of Tuscany from one brother to another. Champeaux denounced these objections as a virtual renunciation of the French proposals, and threatened to depart at the end of his prescribed four days. But in the end he pulled out of his pocket an autograph document in which Louis XV had written down his proposed distribution of the Austrian dominions.[1] Sardinia was to have the whole of the Milanese on the left bank of the Po, and on the right bank as far as the Scrivia. Don Philip's share was the rest of the Milanese, including Parma, the district of Cremona (the fortress of Gera d'Adda being razed), and the part of Mantua between the Po and the Oglio. The remainder of the Mantuan Duchy was to be divided by the Po between Venice and the Duke of Modena, the latter having also the succession to Guastalla. Genoa was to keep Finale and to receive the *enclave* of Oneglia, which was an old possession of the Dukes of Savoy. These practical details were far more to the taste of Gorzegno than d'Argenson's dreams of an ideal Italy, and he insisted upon time for discussing them with the King. Champeaux agreed to stay over Christmas Day, and in the evening Gorzegno drafted a memorandum

---

[1] The text of Louis XV's letter is given by d'Argenson, *Journal et Mémoires*, iv., 287.

expressing assent to the proposed distribution of territories, though he protested against the cession of Oneglia,
and demanded an immediate armistice, together with
assurance of Spain's acceptance of the terms and the
payment by the Bourbon Powers of the same subsidy as
had been paid by England. This document was signed
in duplicate by both Ministers, and Champeaux hurried
off with his copy to Versailles.

No sooner had the French emissary gone than Gorzegno hastened to carry the news to Arthur Villettes.
Charles Emmanuel had frequently promised that, even
if he had to desert the common cause, he would do
nothing without the knowledge of the King of England.
And, anyhow, the English Resident was the only channel
by which instructions could be sent to Osorio. The
dispatch of a Sardinian courier at this moment to
England would have excited the suspicions of France
and probably have hastened the disaster which it was
desired to avert. Villettes, who for the last three months
had sent constant warnings that Sardinia, if no assistance came, would be forced to make the best possible
terms with France, cannot have been surprised, and he
was prepared to accept all the excuses which the Minister
and the King, in two personal interviews, offered for the
action which ill-fortune had forced them to take.

" As to the King of Sardinia, I have the honour to
know him so well that I will venture to say he has never
taken any step in his life so much against his will or
more contrary to his inclination. The anguish of mind
I observed him to be in at both my audiences is not to
be expressed. . . . He said he had been neither concerned nor uneasy as to the manner this step of his
would be taken at Vienna, as that Court had used him
very ill, and their Ministers and Generals abandoned
him most undeservedly and shamefully to the resentment of France and Spain, so that their conduct to him
was more than sufficient to justify what he had now
done. But that what principally affected him was the
doubts and apprehensions he was in as to the impression
the news of it would make on His Majesty, that the
King was his only friend, on whom alone he had all
along relied, and for whom he should always have the

strongest and most inviolable attachment. . . . The King of Sardinia charged me more than once in my two audiences to beg of His Majesty in his name that the contents of this dispatch, or any part of it, may not be known to have been communicated to our Court, as the least suspicion of this must expose him to all the resentment and vengeance of the French.''[1]

There was one sentence in Villettes' voluminous dispatch which probably made more impression upon the English Ministers than all his assurances of Charles Emmanuel's lachrymose loyalty to England. He declared that nothing could save the situation except peace with Prussia and thirty or forty thousand Austrian troops. By the time that his letter reached London, news had come that the Treaty of Dresden had been signed, and it could be confidently expected that the thirty thousand troops would be promptly sent to Italy. This may explain why the intelligence from Turin caused so little dismay in Whitehall, and it also explains what has rather shocked French and Austrian historians—the abstention from giving any intimation to Vienna.[2] It may well have been thought that, if Maria Theresa had now returned to a sane policy, and if there was a good chance of reclaiming Sardinia, it was undesirable to make any needless mischief between the two allies.

[1] Villettes to Newcastle, 31 December, 1745 (S.P., For., Sardinia, 50).
[2] Broglie (*Maurice de Saxe et le Marquis d'Argenson*, i., 195) says that he found it so difficult to credit the absence of any communication on the subject between London and Vienna that he consulted Arneth, who replied that the Vienna archives proved that Maria Theresa had no suspicion of Sardinian defection until the end of February, and then only from rumour. Broglie did not know that Hardwicke, who judged Charles Emmanuel's conduct with the severity of a lawyer, wrote to Newcastle on 2 February (o.s.) " to suggest whether it may not be necessary or advisable to give some hint of this affair, in a proper manner, to the Court of Vienna. It seems to be of vast importance to them to be apprised of it, the rather that this is not a mere treaty of pacification, but the King of Sardinia is afterwards to take an active part in the war against France and Spain. For my own part, as at present advised, I cannot think that the behaviour of the Court of Turin on this occasion has entitled it to have its secret so religiously kept " (Add. MSS. 32,706, fo. 93). Hardwicke's more politically minded colleagues did not act on his advice.

Also, attention in London was concentrated upon Cumberland's success in driving back the Jacobite invaders.

The document signed at Turin in the early hours of 26 December was wholly anomalous : it was neither a treaty nor the preliminaries of a treaty, but merely a note of terms upon which a treaty might be based. But Louis XV and d'Argenson welcomed it as a virtual acceptance of their proposals, and the latter constantly speaks of it in his Memoirs as the " Treaty of Turin." The two conspirators now set themselves to complete their work. For this purpose it was necessary to draft an armistice and a formal treaty, and to obtain the assent of Spain. Not a moment must be lost in doing these things for fear that the situation in Italy might be completely altered by the arrival of Austrian reinforcements. It was easy at the French Foreign Office to draft a preliminary treaty, but d'Argenson, who was utterly unable to see with any eye but his own, and was incurably convinced that everybody must welcome what he considered to be for their good, insisted upon inserting all the provisions as to Italian independence, freedom from imperial suzerainty, transfer of Tuscany to Charles of Lorraine, which Sardinia had rejected, while he omitted all the Sardinian demands.[1] He tried to induce Mongardino to sign this off-hand in Paris, but the Sardinian agent replied that he had no power to deal with anything but an armistice. So it was necessary to send Champeaux, disguised this time as a Dutch merchant under the name of Kraff, to demand acceptance at Turin within forty-eight hours. The imperiousness of this demand was so far softened that the draft of the preliminaries was sent to Turin beforehand, with explanatory letters from Champeaux and Mongardino.[2] This was not unreasonable, but it obviously gave

[1] The draft of the preliminaries is printed in the appendix to d'Argenson, iv., 464.

[2] Broglie, who has written the fullest and clearest account of the whole negotiation, and who is the only historian who consulted the English dispatches, omits the important fact that Charles Emmanuel and Gorzegno had the text of the treaty in their hands before the arrival of Champeaux. But the whole thing had been communicated to Villettes, who wrote a full

time for the formulation and hardening of criticism, and thereby diminished the prospect of assent. While Champeaux was toiling across the Alps, instructions were sent to Vauréal, the able French envoy at Madrid, to demand immediate acceptance of the treaty by the Spanish King. D'Argenson proposed to give Spain four days for consideration, but Louis XV, now fully committed to the scheme, declared that two days would be ample.

There remained the drafting of the armistice, a far more difficult matter. An armistice was a military convention, and d'Argenson ostentatiously paraded his complete ignorance of all military affairs. It was necessary to call in an expert. Louis XV, who was enamoured of secrecy, wished to employ Coigny, who was outside official circles; but d'Argenson insisted upon calling in his brother, the Minister of War. The Count d'Argenson, who was senior as a Minister to his elder brother, was not unnaturally indignant that a business of such importance had been carried so far without the slightest consultation of himself and his colleagues. However, he drafted the terms of an armistice, but insisted upon the insertion of a separate article providing that it should not come into force until after the treaty had been signed on behalf of Spain as well as Sardinia, and until it had been ratified by the three Kings.[1] As there was as yet no assurance that Spain would sign at all, and as the treaty provided for an interval of a month between signature and ratification, this threatened to deprive Sardinia of all power to relieve Alessandria before the garrison was forced by starvation to surrender, which had been the most imperative motive for coming to terms with France. The Marquis d'Argenson was so alive to this, and to the danger that any aggressive action on the part of the French troops would wreck the whole negotiation, that he took the reckless, and, as

---

account to Newcastle, and forwarded the documents to Osorio on 29 January, whereas the French envoy did not arrive till the evening of that day.

[1] For the text of the armistice see Appendix to d'Argenson, *Mémoires*, iv., 470.

it proved, disastrous, step of writing a secret letter of
warning to Marshal Maillebois, whose son had married
his own daughter. By doing so he trespassed upon the
War Department, without even informing his brother,
and he sent word of his action to Turin, thereby weakening the motive for a prompt acceptance of the French
terms. The letter has frequently been printed, but it is
so vital to the story, and throws so much light upon
d'Argenson's character that it is necessary to repro-
duce it.

" A negotiation is far advanced with Turin, but the
greatest difficulty is with Spain. We are adopting a
tone which may be efficacious; it is the greatest secret
in the world, everything here being between the King
and myself. This is his will; but in meanwhile the King
of Sardinia hopes that the French army will show consideration for him. I have no order to give you with
regard to this. As to the Germans, there is to be no
consideration for them, quite the opposite. It would
be my brother's business to send you orders, but as yet
he knows nothing, nor does your son. I hope soon to
be able to speak openly to them. Meanwhile they are
working hard at plans for the forthcoming campaign,
and I hope that the only operation will be a prompt
advance to the Tyrol and the Trentino, as in 1735, in
order to cut off communication between Italy and
Germany.—*P.S.* If in the circumstances anything should
be undertaken against Lichtenstein [who had succeeded
Schulenburg in command of the Austrian troops in
Italy], the King of Sardinia might abstain from intervention, but he might suspect us of ill-faith and of a
desire to make an evil use of the delicate and secret
relations in which we stand. So that today it is
a simple defensive and tranquillity till the treaty is
signed."[1]

[1] Broglie, *u.s.*, i., 147; Zevort, *Le Marquis d'Argenson*, p. 290;
Spenser Wilkinson, *The Defence of Piedmont*, 1742–48, p. 231.
In his Memoirs (iv., 302) d'Argenson gives part of the letter,
but omits the reference to his brother, as he had already boasted
of having forced the King to admit him to the secret. It is
characteristic of d'Argenson that he begins by declaring that
there is no need to spare the Austrians, and then recommends in
the postscript that this should be done.

Disillusion was not long delayed. Even d'Argenson's
optimism cannot have expected anything but protest
from Spain. The draft treaty, for which Spain was
utterly unprepared, came like a bombshell upon the
Court of Madrid. Elizabeth Farnese, who considered
that the fulfilment of the Treaty of Fontainebleau was
the first duty of France, and who believed that the campaign of 1745 had practically secured that fulfilment,
made no attempt to conceal her fury when she learned
that the treaty was to be wholly disregarded, that her
son's principality was to be cut down to a pittance, and
that the hated King of Sardinia was to obtain the greater
part of the Milanese. Even the silent and sluggish
Philip V, who usually left all the talking to his wife,
was moved to protest, in terms which Vauréal declined
to report, against his nephew's assumption that a King
of Spain could be treated as a submissive satellite of
France. Not only did Vauréal receive an absolute rejection of the proposed treaty, but a Spanish grandee, the
Duke of Huescar, was sent on a special mission to Versailles to express the indignation of Spain at the conduct
of the French Foreign Office. This extraordinary mission
made it impossible to maintain the secrecy which had
hitherto veiled the transaction. It was necessary to
inform the resident Spanish envoy, Campo Florido, who
went in turn to all the French Ministers to denounce
the treachery of the Marquis d'Argenson. As the Treaty
of Fontainebleau had forbidden all negotiations with
the enemy without the knowledge and participation of
Spain, it was not easy to answer the charge of ill-faith.
And d'Argenson did not find any of his colleagues at all
eager to defend him. They put a much higher value
than he did upon the maintenance of a close alliance
with Spain and were not unwilling to thwart a scheme
which had been deliberately engineered behind their
backs. As long as the King supported him, d'Argenson
might go on his way without ministerial approval, but
if Louis once began to weaken, his darling scheme
would have to be abandoned. It did not materially improve matters when he discovered that Huescar, after
exhausting his fulminations, was not unwilling to con-

sider modifications of the treaty. Any change in the
partition of Lombardy which might pacify Spain would
be certain to alienate Sardinia. And to reopen the only
part of the treaty which had been accepted at Turin
would lead to a protracted negotiation, and would
render impossible that promptitude of settlement which
was of the essence of the whole transaction.

If the opposition on the part of Spain was disconcerting, the news from Turin was not much better. When
Charles Emmanuel learned that Maria Theresa had
made peace with Prussia and was sending thirty
thousand men with all possible speed to Lombardy, he
ruefully admitted to Villettes that if Maria Theresa had
been wise enough to do this two months earlier, there
would have been no need for his distasteful negotiation
with France.[1] And when the letters from France
brought the news that a treaty had been drafted in
complete disregard of the inchoate agreement of
26 December, and that the coveted armistice might be
indefinitely delayed, the British Resident began to hope
that this might furnish a pretext for repudiating that
agreement, and that Sardinia might be reclaimed to the
allied fold. In that case he himself would be freed from
the fear that he might suddenly have to quit Turin and
find a temporary abode in Switzerland, whence he might
secretly carry on that intercourse between the Sardinian
and English Courts which, he was assured, would never
be allowed in any circumstances to be broken off. The
event proved that his hope was justified. There can be
little doubt that in December the Sardinian King and
Minister were convinced that they could only escape ruin
by coming to terms with France, and that, if the enemy
had carried on active operations during the winter, or if

---

[1] Villettes to Newcastle, 15 January, 1746, in cipher (S.P.,
For., Sardinia, 51): " The King of Sardinia, in talking to me of
the body of imperial troops now coming into Italy, could not help
lamenting the obstinacy of the Court of Vienna in refusing to
listen in time to His Majesty's friendly advice with regard to the
treaty with Prussia, which he said might (had it been concluded
two months sooner) have very possibly saved Italy, and would
most certainly have prevented his entering into measures so
contrary to his inclinations and no less to his interest."

the Silesian war had not come to an end, some sort of treaty would have been made, even if Spanish pressure had diminished the Sardinian share of the spoil. But when the Gallispans remained quiescent and Maria Theresa came to her tardy repentance, this assurance ceased to exist. At some date in January or in February the Sardinian leaders must have made up their mind to break off the negotiations to which they were committed, or rather to carry them on only so far as would serve their own interests. It is not easy, and is probably impossible, to fix the exact moment when the negotiation ceased to be sincere and became intentionally fraudulent.[1] D'Argenson and his apologists would put it as late as possible; his hostile critics would incline rather to antedate it. Very possibly there was an intermediate period of genuine vacillation. On this question Villettes' evidence is of first-rate value. All other records go to show that he received very full and accurate information, and this was inevitable, as the correspondence with Osorio, whom the Court of Turin could not afford to mislead, passed through his hands and was conveyed by his messengers. From the later part of January his dispatches, in spite of their verbosity, become interesting and even exciting. There is one fairly obvious allowance to be made. The Court of Turin was naturally anxious to magnify its merits in adhering to the Treaty of Worms, and therefore to make the most of the difficulties and temptations that had to be overcome. If this be taken into account, Villettes' letters may serve as the basis of a reasonably accurate narrative, and his estimate of motives and conduct is not without shrewdness.

On 29 January, 1746, Villettes wrote to Newcastle that Champeaux (whose name he never mentions until all

[1] It is difficult to read the instructions from Turin to Osorio (dated 12 February, 1746) without coming to the conclusion that from the time of Champeaux's second mission the Sardinian King and Minister desired to free themselves from the inchoate agreement with France, and only continued the negotiation in order to save Alessandria until the arrival of the Austrian reinforcements. A copy of these instructions is in the British Museum (Add. MSS. 32,805, fo. 9).

disguise had been abandoned) was expected to arrive that evening, and continued :[1]

"It seems this Court flattered itself that, by means of the writing signed on the 26th past, and by which they accepted the partition of Italy proposed by France, a suspension of arms would be immediately settled and published. But the Court of France has objected that the suspension of arms could not take place otherwise than as the consequence of the preliminary articles signed in form on the basis of the plan proposed by this emissary and accepted here, and till Spain has likewise signified her approbation of and concurrence in them, and till this act was farther consolidated by a ratification of the three crowns. The rough draft of these preliminary articles has been sent here beforehand, and is to be finally adjusted, concluded, and signed off-hand. It has been communicated to me. These people have observed it to be very defective and altogether artfully conceived; several points they had insisted upon and which were agreed on by the emissary being omitted, and others they had eluded being added and brought in, particularly that of the association and confederacy between the several princes and powers of Italy, which this Court is so averse to that, if still insisted on by France, it may come near to produce an entire rupture of this negotiation. This, however, I do not believe, and it appears from the emissary's letters and Count Mongardin's, that the peace with Prussia has not a little alarmed the Court of Versailles, and will render it more tractable to secure the Court of Turin to her interest, and the King of Sardinia's concurrence in her measures with regard to Italy. . . . As our friends here are resolved to give His Majesty an entire communication of the sequel of this negotiation with the French emissary, I foresee I shall in a few days be obliged to dispatch another express to your Grace."

A fortnight later (13 February) a "very private" letter continued the story. Champeaux was visited by Gorzegno on 30 January, and countered the latter's

[1] This and subsequent dispatches are in S.P., For., Sardinia, 51. The folios are not numbered, so it is impossible to give any reference except the date. All were carefully ciphered.

objections to the draft treaty by roundly declaring that it must be either accepted or rejected within forty-eight hours. But he soon found that circumstances had changed, and that if the high hand had been difficult in December it was now impossible. In the end he had to accept a counter-project, drafted by Gorzegno, together with a renewed demand for an armistice, and for the insertion of a separate and secret article that the French forces would be withdrawn from Italy in case Spain should refuse to be a party to the treaty. Champeaux gave this assurance verbally, but the cautious Sardinian desired its official confirmation.[1] Finally, Gorzegno insisted that everything, treaty and armistice, must be settled before the end of February, as after that date active military operations might begin at any moment. The crestfallen emissary had to send all this to Paris by a courier whom he had left beyond the frontier at Briançon. The courier set out on 5 February, and till his return Champeaux, who had declared that the limit of his stay was forty-eight hours, had to remain in hiding in Turin, without any social intercourse, and unable to leave the house except in the dark.

Gorzegno carried the news to Villettes, and begged him " to transmit an account of it to England as a discovery of my own, without this Court appearing to have the least part in the dispatch." This promise Villettes promptly gave, and as promptly proceeded to break it, " as it highly imports this Court that, at this juncture, His Majesty should not be prepossessed with notions that the King of Sardinia is absolutely, and without any possibility of being retained, in the hands of France." And he came to the conclusion that " this Court is not without hopes of getting clear of her en-

---

[1] Broglie, *u.s.*, i., 150, quotes the vital words from Champeaux's instructions: " M. de Champeaux ne doit lui laisser ignorer que, dans le cas où la cour de Madrid ne voudrait pas adhérer au traité qui aurait été conclue entre le roi et le roi de Sardaigne, Sa Majesté se déterminerait à rappeler sur-le-champ l'armée que commande M. de Maillebois. (Cette assurance ne devra être donnée que de bouche et non par écrit.) " The parenthesis shows that d'Argenson, with all his boasts as to the merit of blunt honesty, had begun to master the technique of normal diplomacy.

gagements with that crown by the convention of the
26 December, and of seeing affairs return thereby into
their old channel, which . . . they would be very glad
of, especially the King of Sardinia, on whom the impression made by the convention of the 26 December
and by the dread of losing the friendship of England, is
visible to anyone who has the least knowledge of his
character and temper."

By 26 February his forecast was more assured than
ever. Sardinia had no direct communication with Spain,
but reports from other sources left little doubt that the
treaty was not accepted at Madrid. The sending of
Huescar was in itself conclusive proof, as Campo Florido
would have sufficed for a simple signature. Villettes
declared that the Court of Turin would gladly lay the
odium of a rupture upon Spain and upon French unwillingness to coerce their ally. " Upon the whole, this
Court looks upon the breaking of this negotiation, and
its being shortly determined by the return of the French
emissary's courier, as infallible." This optimism seemed
to be justified by the fact that Lichtenstein, who knew
nothing of what had been going on in the background,
was at the time making arrangements with Charles Emmanuel as to the opening of the campaign. It was
agreed that the primary aim must be the relief of Alessandria, and as a preliminary step an attempt must be
made to recover Asti.

On the very day after Villettes' last dispatch was
written came a letter from Mongardino which caused the
utmost perturbation among all who were parties to the
secret negotiation with France. On the arrival of
Champeaux's courier, d'Argenson, stirred by the bitter
criticisms of his brother, determined to force Sardinia
into the open. He would grant the armistice which had
been so persistently asked for, and he obtained its signature by Mongardino on 17 February. He determined to
entrust this document and the carrying out of its provisions to his own son-in-law, the Count of Maillebois,
whose father was commanding the French forces in Piedmont. This was a military, not a civil, mission, and
there was to be no secrecy about it. When the French

Marshal's son entered Piedmont with his retinue, all Europe would know that France and Sardinia had come to an understanding, the coalition of Worms would be broken up, and Charles Emmanuel, convicted of having deserted his allies, would be compelled to sign the treaty without waiting for the adhesion of Spain. If the armistice had been unconditional, it is possible that, at the last minute, Charles Emmanuel might have accepted this as a surer method of saving the hardly pressed citadel of Alessandria than a military enterprise in conjunction with alienated and justly suspicious allies. But the younger d'Argenson was, in the first place, a soldier, and his first problem was to deal with soldiers. When he had settled the armistice he might take the place of Champeaux and adjust the treaty of alliance. Meanwhile, he was the agent, not of the Foreign Secretary, but of the Minister of War. The Count d'Argenson had no trust in Sardinian honesty, and believed it possible that, once Alessandria was saved, the Court of Turin would betray their new rather than their old ally. He was not prepared to abandon his military grip on Piedmont. To the publication of the armistice he attached three conditions, of which the most vital was that Alessandria, instead of being completely relieved, was to remain invested until the treaty was signed, and, in the interval, was only to receive supplies for a week at a time. This was fatal to the whole scheme of the elder brother. If Alessandria was to remain in danger, the main motive which impelled Sardinia to accept the French alliance was destroyed. The King and Gorzegno acted with great promptitude. When the Count of Maillebois reached Briançon, he received a letter from Gorzegno saying that he was not to cross the frontier unless he was authorized to grant an unconditional suspension of arms. The reckless young soldier paid no attention and pressed on to Rivoli, only sixteen miles from Turin. There he was met by the unfortunate Champeaux and also by Count Bogino, the Sardinian Minister of War. Both explained that the conditions must be dropped. As Maillebois could not withdraw the one condition which was regarded as intolerable, he received

9

his passports to return to France.[1] This was the real
breaking off the negotiations. Events soon made their
renewal quite impossible. Yet the Marquis d'Argenson
continued to believe that the treaty might still be made,
and he maintained the possibility in his Memoirs. He
refused to pick a quarrel with Sardinia, as he had
refused to pick a quarrel with Prussia, and he actually
induced Louis XV to write a conciliatory letter to
Charles Emmanuel. The latter was quite willing to
play this harmless game, and replied that he hoped the
alliance was only postponed. Champeaux, as credulous
and obstinate as his employer, returned from Rivoli to
Turin, and remained there for another fortnight, until
at last his patience was worn out and, on 20 March, he
applied for his passport, which was forthcoming, says
Villettes, in record time.[2]

France had gained something from this futile negotiation. Even if England was pacified by the unprecedented frankness of Sardinia, of which, of course, France
had no knowledge, an apple of discord had been thrown
between Sardinia and Austria. The journey of the young
Maillebois had torn away the veil of secrecy, and it was
impossible any longer to conceal from Austria the fact
that Sardinia had been carrying on negotiations with
France for more than two months without a word to its
closest ally in Italy. All that could be concealed, and
that must be concealed, was that England had known
all about it and had been equally secretive. On 5 March,
the very day on which the younger Maillebois set out
from Rivoli, Gorzegno invited Villettes and Richecourt,
the Austrian envoy, to meet him, and gave them a
bowdlerized version of what had passed in December,

---

[1] Copies of the letters between Gorzegno and the Count of
Maillebois are in the British Museum (Add. MSS. 32,805, fos. 27–37).
The latter's excuse for crossing the frontier in disregard of
Gorzegno's order was that he did not regard the conditions as
affecting the substance of the armistice.

[2] Villettes to Newcastle, 22 March, 1746. Villettes says that
Champeaux made several attempts to renew negotiations " not-
withstanding what has lately happened and the backwardness of
Spain." But the King, on the pretext that it would excite
mistrust in England and Austria, refused to allow Gorzegno or
Bogino to see him.

explaining the reasons which had made Sardinia press
for an armistice and how the attempt had failed.
Villettes, who had been coached for his part, expressed
surprise and regret, and asked a few discreet questions.
The Austrian envoy, and still more the Austrian general,
when the news reached him, expressed indignation, and
probed the tender point as to what had been actually
signed in December.[1] Villettes astutely pointed out to
his colleague that it was a question which had better
be left unasked. If the correct answer was discreditable
Sardinia would deny it, and if the denial was true
Austria would never believe it. The sore place was
plastered over for the time, not by Villettes' casuistry,
but by the startling success which attended the joint
military operations of the two Powers. On the eventful
5 March the expedition against Asti started under a
skilful Sardinian commander, Leutrum. The enterprise
would have been doomed to failure but for d'Argenson's
fatal letter to Marshal Maillebois and for the mission of
the Marshal's son. The French commander was lulled
into quiescence by the daily expectation of the publication of the armistice. When he heard of Sardinian
preparations, he assumed that the object was to convey
licensed supplies to the beleaguered garrison of Alessandria. When at last his suspicions were aroused and
he hurried from his camp near Tortona to save Asti, he
was too late, as on 7 March the commander, who had
also heard of the imminent armistice, had surrendered,
and his nine battalions were prisoners of war. So in-
auspiciously opened a campaign which was destined to
lose all and more than all that Maillebois had gained in
the previous year. And this campaign, by counterbalancing the losses in the Netherlands, encouraged the
allies to continue the war for another two years.

If the Franco-Sardinian negotiations sowed discord
between Austria and Sardinia, they gave rise to an even

[1] When Villettes described the interview in his letter of
15 March, he was rather pessimistic about its results. " I must
observe, upon the whole, that this discourse has left such seeds
of jealousy and diffidence in the Austrian General and Minister,
that I can but look upon our alliance to be already entirely dis-
joined and unhinged by it."

more bitter enmity between Spain and France. The fall
of Asti was only the first of a series of rapid successes
which enabled Charles Emmanuel almost at once to
relieve Alessandria and to recover most of his losses in
Piedmont. Villettes, who must have been pleased that
events had justified his forecast of Sardinia's ultimate
loyalty to the alliance, gleefully chronicled these
triumphs, and at the same time laid his finger upon
their principal cause.

" It is one of the most surprising events that the
present war has afforded that, in less than eight days'
time, and with the loss of about thirty men and a
subaltern officer of artillery, we should, in the ruined and
desperate condition we were reduced to, and after so
many losses and misfortunes, have made between seven
and eight thousand prisoners, rescued a citadel block-
aded by fifteen battalions under it, and an army quar-
tered in all the villages and essential posts about it,
recovered three large towns with a very considerable
tract of country, and drove an army out of it which had
hitherto had such successes as that of France under
Marshal Maillebois. The project had long been hatching
in the King of Sardinia's brain, who was unwilling to
trust so far to his negotiation with France as not to
secure this other string to his bow; and I can't help
observing that this very negotiation has greatly contributed to the success of the undertaking, as it has
served to lull Marshal Maillebois into a kind of security
as to make him look upon peace with this Court as
infallible and concluded, as he might well by his letters
infer, that his son was actually at Turin in the public
figure of a French Minister."[1]

The Spanish troops, compelled by the French collapse
to abandon the Milanese and to give up all hope of
preventing the junction of the Austrian reinforcements
with Lichtenstein, did not hesitate to accuse the French
Marshal of deliberate treachery. Villettes again reported
that, " as for our enemies, the jealousy, rancour, and
animosity between them cannot be greater. The
Spaniards at Milan, from the general down to the last

[1] Villettes to Newcastle, 15 March, 1746.

private man, openly call the French traitors, and both
their letters and their discourses make no scruple of
saying they have bargained to sacrifice them to the
Piedmontese and Germans."[1]

At Madrid the indignation was as great as in the
Spanish camp. It did not improve matters that on
7 March, the very day of the attack on Asti, Elizabeth
Farnese sent for Vauréal and informed him that, after
a sleepless night, she and her husband had made up
their minds to yield to the solicitations of the French
King and to accept the treaty with Sardinia. This
humiliating surrender was the more galling when it was
found to have been made too late, and when the startling
events in Italy made it apparent that Don Philip, instead
of dividing Northern Italy with the King of Sardinia,
might have to go without a principality altogether, and
that the kingdom of Naples was once more in jeopardy.
It was not unnatural that Spain in her turn should
embark upon secret negotiations, and should attempt
to come to an arrangement with Austria by which Don
Philip should be endowed at the expense of Charles
Emmanuel, who had behaved so atrociously to both
Powers.[2] France found it necessary to send a special
embassy to pacify the Spanish King and Queen, and
d'Argenson was not unwilling to get rid for a time of
a persistent opponent by entrusting the task to the Duc
de Noailles.[3] His primary duty was to impress upon
the Court of Madrid the necessity of giving up the extravagant designs of the Treaty of Fontainebleau, and
of being satisfied with a more moderate establishment
for Don Philip. In this task he was aided by the
disasters of the Gallispans in Italy. As for excusing
the recent negotiations with Sardinia, and those still
being conducted with the Dutch, which caused consider-

---

[1] Villettes to Ramsden, 19 March, 1746.

[2] For these negotiations see Arneth, iii., 182.

[3] *Journal et Mémoires*, iv., 308: " Je trouvais un grand
moment de délice en faisant absenter du conseil, pendant plusieurs
mois, un ministre si importun et si brouillon." It was a Russian
custom to punish opponents by sending them on foreign
missions, but it was not a common practice in Western
Courts.

able alarm in Spain, Noailles adopted the simple method of throwing the whole blame upon the Minister whose instructions he was supposed to be carrying out. In doing this he was encouraged by Louis XV, who had repented of the lengths he had gone while he was acting in concord with d'Argenson, and was now character-istically engaged in writing secret letters to Noailles and in sending him information which the Foreign Minister had withheld.[1] D'Argenson suspected the Ambassador of being privy to and encouraging the Spanish overtures to Austria.[2] The embassy certainly helped to convince Elizabeth Farnese and her daughter-in-law that d'Argen-son was the enemy of Spain, and that no pains should be spared on their part to procure his dismissal.[3] Their power to injure him was, however, seriously diminished when the death of Philip V on 9 July transferred the crown to Elizabeth's stepson, Ferdinand VI, whose mother had been a sister of Charles Emmanuel. D'Ar-genson, convinced that his policy would have been triumphant if it had not been thwarted by ignorant opponents, attributed Philip's death to chagrin at the disastrous results of his refusal to accede at once to the " Treaty " of Turin.[4]

It remains to say a word about the influence exerted by the ill-starred negotiation upon the two allies of Sardinia. In England, where full information was regularly furnished by Villettes and Osorio, there seems to have been no great perturbation. Not only was no word sent to Vienna, but no very strenuous effort was made to reclaim the erring Charles Emmanuel. It was not till the middle of March that Harrington mentioned

---

[1] Noailles gives an account of his mission in his *Mémoires*, vol. iii., and his correspondence with the King from Spain is in Rousset, ii., 196–215.

[2] *Journal et Mémoires*, iv., 315. D'Argenson admits that the King may have secretly authorized this in spite of his own remonstrances.

[3] D'Argenson did not conceal his dislike for Spain. On 17 May, 1746, he wrote to Vauréal, at that time a friend but later a bitter enemy: " L'Espagne est un mauvais camarade en guerre, encore plus méchant en négociation " (Zevort, *Le Marquis d'Argenson*, Appendix, p. 322).

[4] *Mémoires et Journal Inédit* (ed. Jannet), iii., 122.

to Robinson the possible defection of Sardinia, and then only as reported by rumours from Paris.[1] If it should prove true, it is suggested, though Robinson is not to make official reference to it, that Austria should leave a strong garrison in Mantua, and withdraw the rest of her troops to serve in the Netherlands.[2] This suggests that English quiescence was at any rate partly due to the feeling that a collapse in Italy would not be an unmixed disaster if it led to a concentration of forces in the one scene of military operations in which England was profoundly interested. When, however, the news came that the attack on Asti had broken off the negotiation, and that Sardinia was more than ever committed to war against France, there was much rejoicing in London over the repentant sinner. Newcastle, who had not written to Villettes for several weeks, authorized him, on 26 March (o.s.), to declare that England, in spite of its immense financial burdens, would pay to Turin in the current year £100,000, in addition to the £200,000 paid under the Treaty of Worms. Thus the prodigal son received the fatted calf.

At Vienna nothing was known except by rumour during the critical months of January and February, though the reserved attitude of the Sardinian envoy justified a certain measure of suspicion. When at last the secret was partially disclosed in March, the intelligence was accompanied by the news of victories which rendered it both unnecessary and impolitic to utter any public reprobation. It was fortunate that Robinson made no use of the suggestion that Austria might abandon the Milanese, as one of the principal arguments employed by England to advocate peace with Prussia had been the necessity of defending that province. In

[1] So determined were English Ministers to conceal their knowledge of the negotiation that Harrington on 8 March (o.s.) assured Trevor at The Hague that the King had no accurate information as to the Franco-Sardinian agreement (S.P., For., Holland, 416, fo. 285).

[2] Harrington to Robinson 4/15 March, 1746, in cipher (S.P., For., Germany, 174). The caution that Robinson was not to take the suggestion about Austrian retirement from Italy as an instruction seems to have been interpolated as a result of criticism by the Cabinet.

1746 Italy became the bright spot in the allied operations, and after Genoa had fallen it was hoped that an invasion of Provence might force France to withdraw large forces from the Netherlands. In these circumstances it would not be wise to pick a quarrel with Sardinia about past backsliding. But, when the extent of the misconduct was discovered, Maria Theresa never forgave Charles Emmanuel for having actually authorized the signature of an agreement, however informal, which contemplated the expulsion of Austria from Italy. She agreed with Bartenstein that by this flagrant ill-faith Charles Emmanuel forfeited all moral right to profit by the Treaty of Worms, and this conviction not only poisoned the relations between Austria and Sardinia during the later stages of the war, but also had a marked influence on the attitude of Austria during the final negotiations at Aix-la-Chapelle.

CHAPTER IV

D'ARGENSON AND THE DUTCH

Anomalies of the war—Holland not a belligerent—Anglo-Dutch
relations—Dutch parties—First French overtures and Dutch
response—Dutch alarm in 1745—Robert Trevor and Van der
Heim sketch a plan of peace—D'Argenson's overtures to The
Hague—French threats—English dread of Dutch defection
—Larrey sent to d'Argenson—Failure of his mission—
Wassenaer sent by the States-General to France—Fall of
Brussels—D'Argenson's *Idées sur la Paix*—Rejection by
England—Gilles sent to join Wassenaer—Dutch proposals
—D'Argenson's counter-project—Its terms—Divisions in
English Ministry—Newcastle's opposition to acceptance of
French terms—His success—Communication of d'Argenson's
project to allies—Mission of Puyzieulx to The Hague—
Death of Van der Heim—Decision to send an English pleni-
potentiary to join the Dutch—Consequent transference of
negotiation to Breda—Simultaneous negotiation at Lisbon
with Spain—Choice of Sandwich for Breda—Retirement of
Trevor.

To the superficial student of the eighteenth century the
war of the Austrian Succession appears to be a struggle
between two rival coalitions. On the one side were the
Bourbon Powers, France and Spain, with their allies,
Prussia and Bavaria. Opposed to them were Austria,
the Maritime Powers, and Sardinia. The student is
taught to contrast this with the adjustment of the Great
Powers in the subsequent Seven Years' War, when Sardinia and Spain dropped out, Austria and Prussia
seemed to change sides, and Russia came in as the ally
of Austria and France. What, as a rule, escapes his
notice is the imperfection of the coalitions in both wars,
and the anomalies in the relations between the various
members of one group of Powers with the various
members of the other group. Confining our attention
to the earlier of the two wars, we may note some of
these anomalies. Spain was at war with England
before the death of Charles VI opened the question of
the Austrian Succession, and Spain remained at war
with England until 1748. Spain entered into a second

war in 1741 against Maria Theresa, nominally to enforce a claim to the whole Austrian Succession, but in reality to obtain Parma and Piacenza, with as much as possible of the Milanese, for Don Philip. This war also lasted till 1748. France refused to be a party to the first war, but became a party to the second in 1743 by the Treaty of Fontainebleau. Charles Albert of Bavaria went to war with Maria Theresa in 1741 as a rival claimant to Austria and Bohemia, but in his later character, as the Emperor Charles VII, he was not at war at all, and could reside in safety in an imperial city, although Maria Theresa's troops might also be there. Frederick of Prussia went to war against Austria in 1740, before any other Power had done so, but he was at war with nobody else, and he made peace in June, 1742. In August, 1744, he again went to war with Austria, and this time he was forced in 1745 to declare war also against Saxony. But he made peace with both Powers on Christmas Day, 1745, and he remained at peace for the remainder of the war. As he was not a belligerent in 1748, he was not admitted to the Congress at Aix-la-Chapelle, yet, by a strange anomaly, his conquest of Silesia was confirmed to him by the treaty. England was never at war with Prussia, though during the second Silesian war relations with Berlin were extremely strained, and our diplomatic representation there was cut down to an indecent minimum. England and France were not at war with each other until 1744, and the Battle of Dettingen was fought between the forces of two states which technically were not belligerents. France fought against Austria until 1744 only as an auxiliary of the Elector of Bavaria. But the most anomalous position of all was that of the United Provinces. Dutch troops from 1743 formed part of the allied armies, and Dutch money was furnished for the hiring of mercenary troops against France. Yet the Republic was never engaged in open war with either of the Bourbon States, and maintained a lucrative trade with both. While Europe saw the two Maritime Powers settling between them the proportion of joint contributions of men and money to the war,

English men-of-war were constantly seizing Dutch merchant ships, not only for carrying contraband of war, but also for conveying French and Spanish goods between those countries and their colonies. Even when French armies invaded Dutch territory on the pretext that the Austrian and English armies were encamped there, no declaration of war followed upon either side. When in 1747 a revolution organized by the anti-French party raised a son-in-law of George II to be Stadtholder, it was thought that this preposterous anomaly must at last come to an end. But still the States-General refused either to declare war or to prohibit trade with France. Technically the Dutch remained non-belligerents to the end, and yet they were such obvious belligerents in reality that they took an active part in the promotion of the final peace, and were among the three primary signatories, both of the preliminaries and of the definitive Treaty of Aix-la-Chapelle.

The Dutch alliance was regarded in England as the keystone of the "old system." The Austrian alliance was desirable but less indispensable. We had dispensed with Austria from the Treaty of Utrecht to the Quadruple Alliance, and we had actually quarrelled with Austria from 1725 to 1730. Walpole had refused to fight for Austria in the war of the Polish Succession. Even in the current war, which England had entered as the champion of Maria Theresa, it was not very easy to remain on good terms with a Power which employed so strident a controversialist as Baron Bartenstein. But no English politician could contemplate with equanimity a rupture between the two Maritime Powers, which would leave England isolated in Europe, and isolation, in view of the Family Compact between France and Spain, was regarded as equivalent to ruin.[1] The buckle which held the alliance together was the Barrier Treaty of 1715. The supreme common interest which had created and maintained the union of two Powers, which had fought three wars against each other

[1] See the elder Horace Walpole, who knew France well, on this subject in *Trevor Papers* (Hist. MSS. Commission Report, xiv., App. 9), pp. 54–9.

in the previous century, was the necessity to prevent France from establishing either rule or control in the Southern Netherlands. Apart from this, there were, as d'Argenson maintained, plenty of causes why the Dutch should dislike and distrust England. The two states were still rivals for commercial and colonial expansion, and in this rivalry England had gone distinctly ahead. It was not difficult to persuade the traders of Amsterdam that what England gained was at their expense. The Navigation Acts, which England had rendered more stringent in the previous century in order to restrict Dutch carrying trade with her ports and plantations, were still in force. And the Dutch had ample experience of the ruthless way in which England treated carriers in time of war if their activity impeded in any way the full use of English naval power. If only France could be induced to tie her own hands by giving some assurance that she would refrain from attacking the Netherlands, it should not be difficult to detach the Dutch from their patronizing ally, and to make the phrase, " the Maritime Powers," an anachronism.[1] This was a problem which d'Argenson had constantly before him in his dealings with the Dutch, and this involved him in frequent collisions with the military ambitions of France. It was, in a more acute form, the same dilemma which had arisen with regard to Sardinia. D'Argenson desired to gain the Dutch by conciliation : the soldiers would coerce them into submission by force.

The relations between allied states were not based upon altruism in the eighteenth century, and the partners were always apt to be irritated with each other in time of war. The original motive for intervention

---

[1] D'Argenson went so far as to say a good word for the Barrier treaty, which had been concluded against France: " C'est une grande question à savoir si la barrière ne nous étoit pas plutôt utile par la facilité d'une neutralité avec la république de Hollande. Cette république n'est pas foncièrement notre ennemie, elle ne l'est que par malentendu, car elle a tout à craindre de l'Angleterre pour son commerce et de l'Autriche pour sa liberté" (*Mémoires et Journal Inédit* [ed. Jannet], iii., 24). He develops the same proposition in *ibid.*, p. 75.

was the same in the case of both English and Dutch, the fulfilment of their joint guarantee of the Pragmatic Sanction. This was nothing like so powerful a motive as the instinct of self-preservation, which had driven the two states into the war of the Spanish Succession. When Maria Theresa was attacked by her first enemy, Prussia, the Dutch were as eager as England to defend her, because Prussia was, in her western provinces, an inconvenient and rather dreaded neighbour of the Republic. But when France, Spain, and Bavaria joined in the attack, the States-General, conscious that their finances were insufficient for war on a large scale, and not unwilling to bargain with France once more for the security of the Netherlands, began to draw back. The Dutch, like the Danes, were chilled by the action of Hanover in making a separate treaty with France. At The Hague, as at Copenhagen, it was urged that other Powers were entitled to provide in like manner for their own safety. When Carteret superseded Sir Robert Walpole, and England undertook a more strenuous prosecution of the war, great difficulty was experienced in inducing the Dutch to make any proportionate efforts. Endless friction arose as to the respective quotas of men and money to be furnished by the two states. In the Spanish Succession war this difficulty had been evaded because both engaged in it *totis viribus*, but the Dutch had neither the will nor the ability to make any similar effort in the later war. And when after endless delays the States-General were induced to come to a decision, it was a constant complaint that the Dutch troops came too late, as at Dettingen, or fought badly, as at Fontenoy. The delays at The Hague were often maddening. The Republic had a " crazy constitution."[1] The state was a federation of provinces, and each province was a federation of towns. In both federations the local was stronger

---

[1] This was Trevor's phrase. See Trevor to Henry Pelham, 30 November, 1744, in *Trevor Papers*, p. 103. For Chesterfield on the Dutch Constitution see his *Letters* (ed. Bradshaw), ii., p. 618. The whole question of Dutch relations with England in this period has been ably treated by Dr. P. Geyl, *Willem IV en Engeland tot 1748*.

than the central authority. Every proposal had to be referred back to the constituent bodies before it could receive formal approval. And every decision was likely to be based upon party rather than upon national interests. At the one extreme were the supporters of the House of Orange and of the closest possible alliance with England. At their head were the Bentinck brothers, William and Charles, the sons by a second marriage of William III's friend, the first Earl of Portland. They advocated an open war with France as offering the best opportunity for a revival of the Stadtholdership in favour of William IV, the head of a junior branch of the House of Nassau, who, like William II and William III, had as wife the daughter of an English King. At the other extreme were the Republican zealots, the " Amsterdammers," or the " Matadors of Holland," who detested the English alliance on account of its Orange colour, and advocated an understanding with France. Between the two extremes was the Moderate Republican Party, whose leader, Van der Heim, was the chief official of the Republic as the Pensionary of Holland. His associates were desirous of maintaining the alliance with England in order to prevent any overt measures for an Orange restoration. But they also desired a speedy termination of the war; they resisted all pressure to induce them to declare war against France; and they were always propounding schemes for a general pacification in order to extort from the English Ministers some definition of war aims to which they could be pinned down. It was equally the aim of England to evade this trap, and yet to avoid the display of any obvious desire to continue the war for fear of driving the Dutch into a separate treaty with France. The Dutch leaders were swayed by two conflicting fears. On the one hand they might lose the support of the Republican Party, which had raised them to office; on the other they might share the fate of John de Witt at the hands of an Orange mob. The events of 1672 bulked largely in the mind of both Van der Heim and d'Argenson when they came into contact with each other. D'Argenson wished

to save the Grand Pensionary from the doom to which
Marshal Saxe seemed likely to sentence him. He had
the cordial co-operation of van Hoey, the Dutch envoy
in Paris, who had an evangelical horror of war, and
constantly urged his employers to abandon all hostility
to France and to revert to an absolute neutrality. It
was another advantage that Robert Trevor, who had
gone to The Hague as Secretary with the elder Horace
Walpole in 1734, and had remained after Walpole's
departure in the character of Envoy Extraordinary and
later of Minister Plenipotentiary, was also an advocate
of peace, maintained a close understanding with Van der
Heim and the Moderate Republicans, and refused to be
mixed up with any projects for an Orange restoration.
His affinity was with Henry Pelham and the more
pacific section of the English Ministry, and he had no
sympathy with the policy of Carteret.

The Dutch were obviously the weakest link in the
coalition, to which they were far less closely attached
than the King of Sardinia, who had his own ambitions,
and was keenly interested in opposing Bourbon aggrandizement in Italy. The Dutch had nothing to gain by
the war; they had no direct concern in the disposal of
Silesia, or in imperial elections, or in the Italian
struggle. They regarded with more than coldness the
commercial and colonial aims of England, and they had
definitely refused to give their assistance in the war
with Spain, to which these aims had given rise. All
that they wanted was the security of their barrier, and
the continuance of the Protestant succession in Great
Britain, though they could wish that the Protestant
dynasty was not so exclusively devoted to the interests
of Hanover.[1] At all times in the war it was the interest
of France to persuade the Dutch to withdraw the assistance which treaties bound them to supply to Austria
and to England. And, if at any time France desired
peace, the most obvious method of approaching England
was through The Hague. As early as 1748, when the

[1] On the Dutch antagonism to Hanoverian influence in England
see Trevor to Henry Pelham, 15 May, 1744, in *Trevor Papers*,
p. 95.

main scaffolding of Belleisle's policy had collapsed,
Fénélon, the French Ambassador, and his assistant, the
Abbé de la Ville, had sounded the Republican leaders
as to their willingness to take a hand in the restoration
of general peace.   But at that time the allies were
carrying all before them.   Carteret was at the zenith
of his career, and even the phlegmatic Dutch were rather
carried away by the prospect of crippling the Bourbons,
who had been such resolute enemies in the reign of
Louis XIV.   The situation changed in 1744, when
France declared war against England and Austria, and
proceeded to do the two things which were most dreaded
by the Dutch, to break through the barrier and to take
up once more the cause of the Stewarts.   It is true
that the threat was not carried very far in this year;
the expedition against Britain did not sail, and the
invasion of Flanders was cut short by the need of
defending Alsace.   But the threat had been quite formidable enough to make the Dutch seriously alarmed,
and regretful that they had not responded more cor-
dially to the French overtures last year.   They now
sent the Count of Wassenaer-Twickel (whose cumbrous
title English diplomatists conveniently but disrespect-
fully cut down to " Twickle ") to Arras with a carefully
thought out scheme of a general pacification.[1]   The
proposals with regard to Charles VII, which necessarily bulked largely in all early plans of peace, became
obsolete in 1745, but some of the articles came into
prominence in later negotiations.   The first article provided that all conquests in the Netherlands should be
restored, and that France should be pledged never to
attack those provinces unless directly engaged in war
with Holland.   This is the parent of all those proposals
for Belgian neutrality, which gave rise to vehement discussions in England at the time, and did not obtain
recognition until nearly a century had elapsed.   France
was also to abandon the cause of the Stewarts down to
the last generation, and to restore Dunkirk to the condition prescribed by the Treaty of Utrecht and the

[1] These proposals, dated 22 July, 1744, are in S.P., For.,
Holland, 411, fo. 268.

Triple Alliance of 1717. Spain was to renounce all claims to Austrian possessions, to restore Savoy to Sardinia, and to grant freedom of navigation in American waters. If she refused, France was to withhold all assistance either in Europe or in America. These terms, it must be remembered, were put forward before it was known that Prussia was about to renew the war, before France had taken Freiburg, and before French troops had made their way into Piedmont. On the other hand, France had made her treaty with Frederick on 5 June, 1744, and had a shrewd idea as to the results of his intervention. On the advice of Noailles, who was at the time virtual Foreign Minister, the Dutch proposals were unhesitatingly rejected. They would, among other things, have involved a repudiation of the Treaty of Fontainebleau.

Matters became far worse in 1745. The Dutch were seriously alarmed by the French victory at Fontenoy, and alarm became a panic when the frontier fortresses fell like ninepins, when Maria Theresa refused to send more assistance, and even, after the imperial election, recalled Traun's troops to Bohemia, when all hope of diverting the enemy to Italy was destroyed by the successes of the "Gallispans," and when England, terrified by a Highland rising, first recalled her native troops, then insisted upon Dutch auxiliaries being sent to her aid, and finally summoned the six thousand Hessians to cross the North Sea. Only the Hanoverian troops were left, and they were regarded with distrust in Holland as being more zealously spared than employed by their electoral ruler. The Dutch Republicans began to clamour for peace, if not with the concurrence of England, then without it. And they realized that far larger concessions must be made by their allies than had been contemplated when they put forward the Arras propositions in the previous summer. In England pessimists like Henry Pelham, who had never been enthusiastic in the war, and who were exasperated by what they regarded as Maria Theresa's selfish absorption in her own interests at the expense of " the common cause," came to very much the same conclusion. It

10

was in their eyes almost a misfortune that the capture of Cape Breton gave a new stimulus and increased popularity to the advocates of a continuance of the war, and at the same time interposed an obstacle in the way of cordial co-operation with the Dutch in the pursuit of peace.[1]

Trevor, who carried on a private correspondence with Henry Pelham and shared his views, was emboldened by the " Premier's " sympathy to draw up with the Dutch Pensionary suggestions for a preliminary treaty between France and the Maritime Powers. This he forwarded to Pelham, while to Harrington, his official chief, who was at Hanover, he only sent an outline sketch with humble apologies for " the presumption and pragmaticalness of this undertaking."[2] In the covering letter to Pelham he admits that : " My chief views have been : 1. To saddle the Dutch, who are less stiff than we are upon points of honour, with this humiliating commission; as well as to leave them to stand the brunt of the first reproaches of our allies, and to bear the chief load of any national unpopularity that this saving step may possibly be hereafter attended with from the uninformed, ill-judging multitude. 2. To prevent the Dutch, by amusing them with some nego-

[1] Henry Pelham's letters to Trevor on the subject all convey this suggestion of regret. The strongest is that of 11 December, 1745, quoted by Coxe (*Henry Pelham*, i., 282): " A good peace is every man's wish; an indifferent one would be gladly accepted; a sad one, I am afraid, will be our lot. . . . Cape Breton will be a stumbling-block to all negotiation. . . . Gibraltar and Minorca have kept us for thirty years at variance with Spain; I am of opinion Cape Breton will do the same with France." This was a depressing letter to be written by the head of an English Ministry in the middle of a war, and with reference to the most notable English success in the war.

[2] The autograph letter to Harrington, " most secret and particular," and dated 18 August, 1745, is in S.P., For., Holland, 411, fo. 118. The letter to Pelham and the suggested terms of peace are in *Trevor Papers*, pp. 123–26, and were sent off more than a fortnight before the date of the letter to Harrington. By normal usage, when one Secretary of State was at Hanover, the dispatches on foreign affairs should be sent to the other. Newcastle, who always resented any incursion by his brother into what he considered his own department, was annoyed with Trevor. See Stone to Trevor, 2 August, 1745, *ibid.*, p. 128.

tiation, from being driven by the hopeless prospect of
our arms to seek their own safety, or rather reprieve,
without our participation, or even at the expense of the
common cause."

Some of the proposals, such as those about the
restoration of the Netherlands, the abandonment of the
Stewarts, the dismantling of Dunkirk, and the terms
between England and Spain, were borrowed with only
slight alterations from the scheme entrusted to Wassenaer twelve months before. Certain minor concessions were offered to France. Compensation was to be
given for French ships burned when the British fleet
pursued a squadron of Spanish ships into the harbour
of St. Tropez in 1742,[1] and France was to be excused
from repairing the damage done to the barrier fortresses.
But the chief novelties in the scheme refer to Italy. It
is now recognized that Don Philip must have some
establishment. In order to avoid mulcting for that
purpose either Austria or Sardinia, the Grand-Duke,
on his election as Emperor, is to hand over Tuscany to
the Spanish Infant. If Don Carlos should succeed to
the crown of Spain and Don Philip take over the Two
Sicilies, Tuscany is to return to the House of Lorraine
in the person of Prince Charles, and if that Prince's
male issue should become extinct, it is to fall to Sardinia, but in all cases it is to remain a fief of the Empire,
and Leghorn is to be a free port. The Duke of Modena
is to recover his duchy, and Genoa is to be invited to
exchange the Marquisate of Finale for Oneglia.[2] There
is a careful avoidance of all reference to Cape Breton,
but it is clearly implied that if France is to give up
the Netherlands there must be a general restoration of
conquests.

Harrington naturally wrote a non-committal reply
from Hanover, pointing out that it would be difficult
to ask the Grand-Duke to give up Tuscany if the King
of Prussia, as was now proposed by England, was to

[1] Weston (Under-Secretary at Foreign Office) to Trevor, 25
October (o.s.), 1745: "The article of St. Tropez I wonder you
passed, it raised indignation " (*Trevor Papers*, 132).
[2] Oneglia was already in the possession of the King of Sardinia.

keep Silesia. Fuller letters came from England. Henry Pelham wrote on 9 August (o.s.) that he, with Hardwicke, Newcastle, and Chesterfield, had gone carefully through the articles on the previous evening and considered them a good basis for negotiation with France. Chesterfield wrote more warmly that the terms suggested were not only tolerable but, considering present circumstances, excellent. Both, however, dilated on the difficulty about Cape Breton, to which Harrington had also alluded. As Chesterfield put it : " One almost insurmountable difficulty I foresee in any negotiation with France is our new acquisition of Cape Breton, which is become the darling object of the whole nation; it is ten times more popular than ever Gibraltar was, and people are laying in their claims, and protesting already against the restitution of it upon any account. But, on the other hand, I foresee the impossibility of keeping it." Henry Pelham added in a later letter, with more than usual disregard of grammar, that " our people are so mad upon it that it requires more spirit and conduct to get the better of, than I doubt our present Government are masters of."[1] The real reason, however, why nothing was done to promote the negotiation on the lines sketched out by Trevor and Van der Heim was that Harrington had just signed the Convention of Hanover, and until it was seen what effect this would have at Vienna, it would be dangerous to suggest, at the moment when Maria Theresa was called upon to renounce all hope of Silesia, that her husband should also surrender his grand-duchy.

The decision in England to hang up the proposed negotiation was by no means satisfactory to the Republican leaders in Holland. Not only was Saxe continuing to capture and dismantle the fortresses which the Dutch regarded as essential for their security, but d'Argenson on his side was holding out an artful combination of temptations and threats. In September de la Ville was authorized to make a formal proposal to

[1] The letters of Pelham and Chesterfield are in *Trevor Papers*, pp. 126–32. Harrington's letter is in S.P., For., Holland, 411, fo. 120.

the States-General that a European Congress should
be convened at The Hague to adjust the terms of peace.[1]
In the same month van Hoey reported an interview
with d'Argenson, in which the French Minister virtually
offered to evacuate the Netherlands, but insisted upon
the restitution of Cape Breton, while he dilated, as
usual, upon the folly and ingratitude of the Dutch,
who owed their independence to Henry IV, and were
now fighting to secure the colonial gains of England.[2]
All this was, as Trevor and Harrington admitted, admirably adapted to detach the Dutch from their alliance,
as malcontents at The Hague or Amsterdam could
always denounce English selfishness as the one obstacle
in the way of a satisfactory peace. They could also
declaim against both Austria and England as throwing
the burden of defending the Netherlands upon the
Dutch, while neither of them would make a sacrifice
for what ought to be a common cause. Equally
insidious were French threats. The garrison of Tournay
after its surrender had been released on a pledge that
they would take no more part in the war. When
England demanded 6,000 Dutch troops, the States sent,
among others, the Tournay garrison. France denounced
this as a breach of parole, and Trevor admits that many
of the officers were likely upon that ground to refuse
to fight.[3] This was not the only French grievance.
Three ships of the French East India Company, which
had been seized by the English, were sold at Batavia
to the Dutch East India Company. France protested
that this was an illegal as well as an unfriendly act,
and threatened to annul the commercial privileges
granted to the Dutch by the treaty of 1739, and to lay

[1] De la Ville's memorial to the States is in S.P., For., Holland,
411, fo. 213.
[2] Trevor to Harrington, 17 September, 1745, *ibid.*, fos. 262,
266.
[3] Trevor to Newcastle, 31 August, 1745 (S.P., For., Holland,
411, fo. 193). On 10 October Trevor reported to Harrington that
de la Ville, in presenting his memorial about Tournay, declared
that his master regarded this as an affair of honour on which no
compromise was possible, and " insinuated in pretty intelligible
terms that his stay in this country is not likely to be long " (*ibid.*,
412, fo. 37).

an embargo upon all Dutch ships in French ports.[1] Trevor reported that the States were not confident that they had the best of the case either in this matter or in the dispute as to the interpretation of the Tournay capitulation.[2] In view of the growing fear of France and of the French offers of seductive terms, Van der Heim significantly remarked to Trevor that he could not much longer restrain his masters.[3]

The English Ministers were so impressed by the danger of Dutch defection, and so annoyed by Maria Theresa's obstinate refusal to agree to the Convention of Hanover, that they abandoned the attitude of passive procrastination which they had adopted in August. They agreed to a general Congress, which they had at first condemned, on condition that it was accompanied by an armistice, and they approved the adjustment with the Pensionary of a plan of a general peace, based upon the Wassenaer proposals of 1744, as modified by the suggestions forwarded in August by Trevor. Thus they reluctantly accepted the necessity of finding a principality in Italy for Don Philip, and of doing so at the expense of Austria, as they insisted that " all possible care should be at the same time taken of the King of Sardinia's interests." But their insuperable difficulty arose when they came to the other essential point, the mutual restitution of conquests. The Netherlands must be restored, and Dunkirk must be dismantled, but in view of public opinion they cannot in the meantime, until Parliament has been tested on the matter, agree to give up Cape Breton upon any consideration.[4]

Van der Heim was only partially appeased by the comparative frankness of this communication. He

[1] This threat was carried out in January, 1746. Trevor to Harrington, 11 January (*ibid.*, 416).

[2] Trevor to Harrington, 5 October, 1745.

[3] Trevor to Harrington, 8 October, autograph and " most secret." Van der Heim had urged, as usual, the settling of a joint plan for an agreement with France, " adding, in a most significant tone of voice: *Il m'est impossible de retenir mes maîtres plus longtemps.*"

[4] This important dispatch of Harrington, which was evidently drawn up after prolonged discussion in the Cabinet, is dated 4 October (o.s.), 1745, and is in S.P., For., Holland, 412, fo. 52.

pointed out to Trevor that a Congress, of which Austria
disapproved, would only serve to betray the want of
harmony among the allies; that it did not necessarily
involve an armistice, witness the Congresses of Utrecht,
Ryswick, and Nymegen; and that an armistice on land
would have to be extended to the sea, which would not
suit England at all, as it would enable France and
Spain to replenish their supplies from America.   He
had no great love for Sardinia or for the Treaty of
Worms, and he had no hesitation in condemning the
article about Finale, which had discredited the alliance
and brought Genoa into the war.   But his great
grievance was the obstinacy of England in refusing to
part with Cape Breton.   One quotation from Trevor's
dispatches may serve to illustrate the prevalent Dutch
opinion on this point: " Here the Pensionary fell a
lamenting the tyranny of popular prejudices; and said
he never thought to have seen the national concern in
England for the recovery of the barrier and coast of
Flanders, for the immediate preservation of the Republick's independency, and even of our own constitution, run so low as to make those objects not be thought
worth the purchasing with the sacrifice of a loose and
precarious acquisition in America."[1]   In spite of these
lamentations, which Trevor reported with a fidelity sug-
gestive of agreement, Van der Heim was so far encouraged by Harrington's professions, as to decide on
a definite move in the direction of a joint understanding with France.   He had had this in his mind for
some time, but had hesitated between employing de la
Ville and sending an emissary of his own, van Hoey
being ruled out as too full of prejudices.   Just at this
time de la Ville was recalled to Paris to take du Theil's
place as *premier commis*—what we should call Under-
Secretary—at the Foreign Office.   This left the Pensionary no alternative to the course which he personally
preferred, and he determined to send his own man,
Colonel Larrey, on the pretext of private business to
France, and to accredit him to d'Argenson by a personal
letter from himself.   The plan was disclosed to a few inti-

[1] Trevor to Harrington, 2 November, 1745.

mates, but it was to be kept secret from the States-General, and van Hoey was to know nothing about it. Van der Heim must have had great confidence in d'Argenson's desire for peace, as he drew up a complete scheme for a preliminary treaty to be signed by France and the maritime states, and to be afterwards pressed upon their respective allies in a general Congress. The scheme was based upon that mapped out with Trevor in August, and contained the same proposal for the temporary transfer of Tuscany to Don Philip, the surrender of Cape Breton in return for the evacuation of the Netherlands, and an assurance to Genoa that there was no intention of doing more than suggest a purchase or an exchange of Finale. Larrey was to begin by sounding d'Argenson as to the intentions and wishes of France. If he found a sufficient measure of conformity with his own instructions, he might unfold his detailed proposals, which were carefully marked to show the points on which concession was allowable. As it was essential that Larrey should be able to some extent to speak for England as well as for Holland, the draft instructions had to be sent to Harrington for submission to his colleagues. They were followed a few days later by a further letter from Trevor giving a full explanation and defence of the draft instructions, and especially of the proposal for the transfer of Tuscany.[1] But Harrington, without waiting for this, had

----

[1] The defence of the article about Tuscany, which was destined to make a sensational reappearance, is interesting. (1) It is designed to prevent Austria, " but too much disposed of herself," and urged on by Courts of Dresden and Turin, from offering to establish Don Philip in the Netherlands. (2) It is the only Italian endowment which does not make a breach in the Pragmatic Sanction or conflict with the Treaty of Worms. (3) France having disavowed the treaty of 1738, it is open to make a new disposal of Tuscany. (4) Maria Theresa can compensate her husband without losing either power or revenue, and such compensation accords with her own proposal in 1741, and will save the Emperor from being portionless after her death. (5) The neutrality of Tuscany in the present war shows that it is of little value to Austria. (6) The grant is purely temporary for the life of Don Ferdinand, who can neither live long nor leave issue. (7) The King of Sardinia will be freed from the risk of having to contribute to Don Philip's endowment, and the temporary aggrandisement of the Bourbons

already written a crushing reply: "His Majesty has
no objection to the sending of an emissary to Mr.
d'Argenson in order to sound and discover, if possible,
the real intentions of the French Court, in order to our
taking our resolutions thereon. But, as to the project
now transmitted, it contains so many points of most
difficult and dangerous nature and tendency, and is in
effect so far *carte blanche* to be offered to France, that
the King cannot by any means think it expedient to
authorize you to declare at this time his agreement
therein."[1]

Van der Heim was naturally chagrined by this return
to a policy of procrastination, but, as he had no desire
to place the Republic singlehanded at the mercy of
France, he had to abandon the ambitious plan of dicta-
ting the outlines of a general peace, and to recast
Larrey's instructions. No formal scheme was entrusted to him; he was to sign nothing, and after ascer-
taining what he could of the French demands, was
simply to take them *ad referendum*.[2] To this no
serious objection could be offered by English Ministers,
nor indeed did they get the chance to do so. As Trevor
had no reply, four English mails being held up by
contrary winds, and the "Matadors of Holland" were
alarmed by de la Ville's departure, in spite of the
"unctuous terms" in which he took his leave, the
Pensionary sent off Larrey with no other English
authorization than could be taken as implied by Harrington's previous dispatch. But the mission, never
very promising, was deprived of all chance of success
by this cutting down of his instructions. Larrey had

will be counterbalanced by the prospective reversion of Tuscany
to his House. (8) This reversionary interest will serve to keep
him loyal to Austria. (9) France finds her account in this arrangement, "as it perfects her title to Lorraine by the acquisition of
Prince Charles's consent to that cession, which is to this day
wanting" (S.P., For., Holland, 412, fo. 260).

[1] Harrington to Trevor, 22 October (o.s.), 1745 (*ibid.*, fo. 225).

[2] Trevor to Harrington, 15 November, 1745 (S.P., For., Holland,
413, fo. 1). The *Mémoire pour servir d'information et d'instruction
a M. Larrey* is in *ibid.*, fos. 13–30. The document is interesting,
as it gives a sketch of previous Dutch relations with France
during the war.

three interviews with d'Argenson, sent interim reports
by a circuitous route in order to avoid publicity, and
returned with a full report in January, 1746.[1] It is clear
that d'Argenson outwitted the rather simple Dutch
soldier. The militant party in France was in the
ascendant. Marshal Saxe was preparing to attack
Brussels before the allies had emerged from winter
quarters or had even formed a plan of campaign. The
French Foreign Minister was confident that he would
gain Sardinia, and thus carry out his plans for the
settlement of Italy. No Jacobite reverse had yet been
reported from England, and it was impossible to adjust
terms with the two Maritime Powers as long as there
was even a dim possibility of a Stewart restoration.
All that was open to d'Argenson was to adopt a
threatening attitude towards the Dutch and to
endeavour to detach them from their alliance with
England. He declared that Louis XV would exact a
satisfaction éclatante for Dutch misconduct with regard
to the East India ships and the Tournay garrison, and
not obscurely threatened that France might be compelled to keep Flanders. Spain and Prussia would
doubtless have their own claims, and France could not
make peace without consulting both Madrid and Berlin.
Cape Breton would have to be restored as a matter of
course, and the Dutch, who owed their independence
to France, were both ungrateful and insane in fighting
to aggrandize a selfish ally. His last words were that
it was impossible to treat with England in present circumstances, and that the Republic should make its own
terms. Trevor summed up the results of the mission :
" The Marquis d'Argenson let him depart without re-
tracting any of his insolent insinuations with respect to
our constitution, without disavowing the itch he had
betrayed for Flanders, without abating of his ill-humour
against the Republic, without articulating the preten-

[1] Larrey's interim reports are in S.P., For., Holland, 413, fos.
242, 291, and 416, fo. 14.   The full report is in *ibid.*, 416, fos. 155–
62.   Larrey returned to Paris on 27 January, 1746, and Trevor
forwarded the copy of the report on 1 February.   The three interviews with d'Argenson were on 3, 17, and 26 December.

sions of France or her allies, without defining the vague
professions of his desire for peace, and lastly without
returning the Pensionary an answer to his letter.   If
anything precise is to be collected from the French
Minister's several conversations, it is that the Dutch
have no means left of skreening themselves from the
impending resentment of his Court, and from being
involved in the ruin of their allies, but by their speedily
separating themselves from them and adopting a perfect neutrality."[1]

There was some compensation for Larrey's failure
in the news that the Jacobite forces, after advancing
as far as Derby, had retreated to Scotland, and that
the Silesian War had been closed by the Treaties of
Dresden.   There was now a possibility that British
forces might return, that Maria Theresa might send
reinforcements, and that the continuance of the subsidy might induce Saxony to furnish 10,000 men under
the Treaty of Warsaw.   It was thought dimly possible
that Frederick of Prussia, under obligations to England
in the recent negotiations, might be persuaded, if tact-
fully approached, to come to the aid of his fellow-
Protestants, or at any rate to use his influence in favour
of a reasonable peace.   England sent Thomas Villiers,
who had gained Frederick's favour by his conduct at
Dresden, to the Court of Berlin,[2] and the Dutch sent
Ginkel to act with him.   But in all these directions
Dutch hopes were disappointed.   A Jacobite rally in
Scotland led to a further summons of troops from the
continent.   Maria Theresa was more prompt to send
reinforcements to Italy than to the Netherlands.
Augustus III refused to admit any obligations under
the Treaty of Warsaw,[3] and in the end preferred to

---

[1] Trevor to Harrington (most secret), 28 January, 1746.

[2] Harrington to Trevor, 3 January (o.s.), 1746, says it has
been decided to send Villiers to Berlin " to try whether it may be
possible to bring that Prince to employ any part of his power
and influence for the benefit of the common cause of Europe and
for the interest of the maritime Powers " (S.P., For., Holland,
416).

[3] The sixth article of the Treaty of Warsaw provided that
Saxony should, in return for the subsidy of £90,000, send 2,000

accept a subsidy from France to remain neutral. The King of Prussia would send no troops, and, though he might be willing to mediate, the Dutch had no trust in his mediation. Meanwhile, the French were not only threatening Dutch trade,[1] but were pressing Brussels, and the allies could interpose no adequate army between Marshal Saxe and the Dutch frontier. The States-General, who had no official knowledge of Larrey's mission, were convinced that invasion could only be averted by opening negotiations with France, and insisted that " some person of great weight and figure " should be sent to test d'Argenson's professed desire for peace. The Pensionary, who attributed Larrey's ill-success to the envoy's ineptitude, was eager to continue the negotiation, but insisted that the more official mission must have the approval of England, and must not create the impression that the Dutch were seeking a separate treaty for themselves.[2] The choice of the States fell upon Count Wassenaer-Twickel, who had been engaged, since his abortive mission to Arras, in negotiating with the Elector of Cologne for the supply of mercenary troops. His official instructions were contained in a resolution of the States-General of 1 February, which directed him (1) to defend the conduct of the Dutch in regard to the Tournay garrison and the East Indian ships, and to demand the revocation of the French edict against Dutch trade; (2) to ascertain whether there was any prospect of ending the

---

horse and 8,000 foot to the Netherlands or elsewhere at the discretion of the maritime Powers, " aussitôt que tout danger du côté de la Bohème et de l'Electeur de Saxe aura cessé à la satisfaction des parties contractantes." It was contended at Dresden that the war had not been closed to the satisfaction of Saxony.

[1] See dictatorial letter of d'Argenson to van Hoey, 9 January, 1746, in S.P., For., Holland, 416.

[2] Trevor reported to Harrington (28 January, 1746, most secret) that Van der Heim had assured him that " this shall be the uttermost length he will go in temporizing: that he will not take even this step but with His Majesty's privity and acquiescence, as in the case of Mr. Twickle the summer before last, and that he has already declared to the leading men amongst his masters that, if they are for going any farther, they must make use of some other Minister than him."

war on terms satisfactory to the allies of the Republic, and whether there was any hope of the summons of a Congress for the settlement of a general peace. But Van der Heim, who desired to keep the negotiation under his own control, gave to Wassenaer privately the instructions which had been given to Larrey, and which had received the approval of the English Ministers.[1] Thus the mission was in reality an attempt to adjust preliminary terms between France and the Maritime Powers, in the expectation that they would be able to obtain their subsequent acceptance by the allies of the three Powers. No communication of the projected terms was to be made in the meantime to these allies, and the mission, which was not secret like that of Larrey, was regarded with the gravest mistrust and misgivings at both Vienna and Madrid. Wassenaer set out on 10 February, no attention being paid to the remonstrances of van Hoey, who urged that France was not likely to be convinced of the good intentions of the Republic by the supersession of a resident Minister who was so agreeable to the French and so well known an advocate of restoring the ancient good relations between the two states.[2]

Little more than a week after Wassenaer's departure Brussels surrendered, and the whole garrison became prisoners of war (20 February, 1746). The stories of a heroic defence proved to be unfounded, and the delay in the city's downfall was only due to Saxe's want of heavy artillery. Trevor drew a gloomy picture of the impression produced by the news in Holland:[3]

" This event has set fire to the murmurings and heart-burnings which have for some time past been smothering in this nation and government at England's pretended relaxation of her attention to the common cause and to the very existence of the Republic. Many

[1] Harrington to Trevor, 3 December (o.s.), 1745 (S.P., For., Holland, 413, fo. 206), says that the instructions " were in general very well approved by His Majesty."
[2] Trevor to Harrington, 11 February, 1746, S.P., For., Holland, 416, fo. 223.
[3] Trevor to Harrington, 25 February, *ibid.*, fo. 257.

of our formerly most zealous friends now distinguish themselves by their declamations against us. . . . The Pensionary, indeed, keeps this humour of despondency as well as of resentment at bay as long as he can, in hopes of some speedy succour from His Majesty, and his personal objections to servile or separate counsels continues as great as ever. But he tells me he is near run down. Nor do I, my Lord, pretend, unless my hands are incessantly and most powerfully strengthened, to be able to stem the present torrent of distress and discontent in this nation, which complains that the Court of Vienna only offers troops which it cannot pay, and England pay for troops it cannot get. There are, indeed, two sorts of men here, and those of quite opposite principles, who seem to take a sullen pleasure in the agonizing state to which public affairs are now brought. The one hopes this distress might hurry the Republic into a Revolution at home and desperate vigour abroad, the other (I fear upon better grounds) into an immediate submission; whilst each of these parties has the malice to impute, alternately, to our Court the views and sentiments of the other, and to represent us as co-operating therewith."[1]

In England the fall of Brussels made no less sensation. Harrington anticipated Trevor's request for a strengthening of his hands by announcing that England would at once send back the Hessian horse and nine squadrons of British cavalry, that an additional

---

[1] This allusion to a possible revolution in Holland, followed by the news that Friesland and Groningen had protested against the employment of foreign generals and demanded that the Prince of Orange should command Dutch troops, caused English Ministers to prick up their ears. The restoration of a Stadtholder had always been a possible method of cementing the Anglo-Dutch alliance, and it specially commended itself to George II as the father of the Princess of Orange. For the last ten years British Ministers had rather ostentatiously abstained from encouraging the Orange party, but it might be necessary to promote a revolution to avert a Dutch surrender to France. Trevor, alarmed at the encouragement that might be given to the more bellicose Ministers at home, found it advisable to explain away his words, and to say that he expected "rather a movement of the governors in favour of a peace abroad than of the governed in favour of a commotion at home." Trevor to Harrington (autograph), 22 March, 1746 (S.P., For., Holland, 417, fo. 111).

£100,000 would be offered to Maria Theresa on condition that 50,000 men were sent to the Netherlands before the end of March for the whole campaign, and that England would pay two-thirds of £150,000 to be offered to Saxony for 15,000 men, and the same proportion of an additional £50,000 if these troops were sent at the earliest possible moment. But these offers were conditional upon the Dutch putting at least 50,000 men into the field, counting among them any Bavarian or other German troops that they could hire upon their own account.[1] This condition was bitterly resented by the Dutch as reflecting discredit on their past services, and the extreme Republicans continued to put more faith in diplomacy than in military effort.

Wassenaer's mission proved in the end the most important step hitherto taken towards a general peace, but its first results held out no great hope of success. The envoy, according to d'Argenson, made himself popular in Paris, and sent home optimistic reports of the French desire to put an end to the war, which he declared to be the wish even of the soldiers, notably Belleisle and Saxe. He evaded all d'Argenson's efforts to induce him to negotiate for the Dutch alone without any reference to the interests of England, and the French Minister came to the correct conclusion that the envoy had some authority to speak for London but none for Vienna. On the other hand, d'Argenson declared that he had no authority to consider the terms of a general peace, and that any such proposals would have to be submitted to the King and the Council of Ministers. Wassenaer obtained leave to discuss the problem in detail with de la Ville, with whom he had been intimate at The Hague, and the latter drew up a minute which professed to embody the Dutch proposals of peace between the various belligerents. These were drawn upon familiar lines, and rather evaded the most difficult problems. Hope and belief were expressed that England would restore all conquests in North America, no definite concession to Don Philip was sug-

[1] Harrington to Trevor, 18 February (o.s.), 1746 (S.P., For., Holland, 416, fo. 249).

gested, but Sardinia was to recover all lost territory, and Genoa was to be reassured as to its particular interests. England was to be satisfied as regards the Stewarts, Dunkirk, and the recovery of her commercial privileges from Spain. Maria Theresa was to keep all her father's possessions, except such as had been already ceded, and the Dutch undertook to obtain the approval of England for such arrangements in Italy as might be settled between her and Spain.[1] The document was described by Louis XV as "full of demands without any offers," and it was obviously too vague to serve any useful purpose. It is only important in that it served to extract from d'Argenson the first definite statement of French aims. This document, entitled *Idées sur la Paix entre Messieurs le Marquis d'Argenson et le Comte de Wassenaer*, was drafted by d'Argenson himself with much feigned reluctance, and "only as the loose thoughts of a private man."[2] It began with the proposition that Italian affairs should in the meantime be excluded from consideration, partly because they did not concern the Dutch very directly, and partly, no doubt, because d'Argenson had not yet abandoned his own plan for dealing with them. It went on to propose that France should restore her conquests in Flanders and Brabant, and that the barrier should be reconstituted as it was with a mutual guarantee of permanent neutrality not only for the barrier towns but for the whole "Pays Bas Catholiques." In return, France was to recover Cape Breton, Luxemburg was to be dismantled, and Maria Theresa must be induced to cede Limburg and Austrian Gelderland to the Elector Palatine, and *les enclaves du Hainaut* (Chimay, Beaumont, and St. Hubert) to France. Dunkirk was to remain in its present condition towards the sea, but to be fortified

[1] This minute is in S.P., For., Holland, 417, fo. 95, and was sent by Trevor to Harrington on 18 March (most secret).

[2] This is Trevor's version of Wassenaer's report, which was submitted to him by Van der Heim. There is a copy of the *Idées* in S.P., For., Holland, 417, fo. 101, and another in Brit. Mus. Add. MSS. 32,706, fo. 270. The document was forwarded by Trevor with the other on 18 March.

on the land side in order to protect its inhabitants. Peace was to be made between Spain and England on the basis of the Convention of the Pardo.

D'Argenson's *Idées* made a sensation in England and for the moment reunited the jarring sections in the Cabinet. Great indignation was expressed that the Dutch envoy had allowed his name to be associated with a project which made no provision for the security of the Protestant Succession, and offered nothing in return for the restitution of Cape Breton. It was urged that the proposed cessions to the Elector Palatine and to France, coupled with the dismantling of Luxemburg, would enable France at any time to cut off communication between Austria and the Netherlands, so that those provinces and the territories of the Republic would be at her mercy. The whole scheme was regarded as a barefaced attempt to induce the Dutch to purchase the restoration of their barrier at the cost of their allies, while the exclusion of Italy seemed to prove that France was assured of an agreement with Sardinia. Trevor was instructed to make a categorical declaration that his Majesty " cannot and will not submit to enter upon any negotiation upon such preliminaries." At the same time, in order to soften this apparent censure of Dutch procedure, he was to intimate that England had not abandoned the pacific policy which had led to the sanction of Wassenaer's mission, and that there would be no opposition to the Pensionary's " still endeavouring to procure a more satisfactory explanation of the intentions of France." But he was to accompany this assurance with a warning that England could not continue the present lavish expenditure of men and money in defence of the Dutch without a reasonable assurance of their " unalterable resolution to continue firm in the present alliance with England, and to contract no engagement whatever of peace or neutrality with France."[1]

Harrington's uncompromising dispatch was not altogether welcomed by its two recipients. Trevor, who had pinned his faith to Henry Pelham, thought

[1] Harrington to Trevor, 14 March (o.s.), 1746 (S.P., For., Holland, 417).

that insufficient attention was paid to the imminent threat of a French invasion of Dutch territory, and pointed out that no assurance of fidelity would be proof against 100,000 French soldiers upon the soil of the Republic. Van der Heim, who believed that his own security as well as that of the state was involved in the success of the negotiation, complained that the English attitude was purely negative, that no distinction was drawn between the terms that must be rejected and those that might be taken as a basis of discussion, and thus no indication was given of what England would regard as reasonable conditions of peace. And he went on to voice the suspicion—which Trevor knew to be not wholly unfounded—that there was a desire on the part of England that the Republic should make her own treaty, " to be able to saddle her hereafter with the *odium* of a peace, which at best never could, without a miraculous change in our circumstances, turn out an advantageous or popular one."[1] He gladly welcomed, however, the approval of continued negotiations, and suggested that, as Twickel had satisfied neither party, a colleague should be sent " of a more circumspect if not a more manly turn of humour," who might urge with some force how incompatible the late ideas were with the French Minister's previous professions. In spite of Trevor's caution that the presence of three Dutch envoys at Versailles would increase the jealousies and misgivings of the allies, the Pensionary persisted in his design, and selected for the purpose Gilles, the second Greffier, to whom he said that, " if the air of the French Court had the effect upon him that it seems to have had upon Colonel Larrey and Count Wassenaer, he would not even trust himself in it."[2] Gilles was

[1] Trevor to Harrington (most secret), 1 April, 1746. For the idea of using Dutch action to cover an unpopular peace see Trevor to H. Pelham, 18 August, 1745, quoted above, p. 132.
[2] Newcastle to Chesterfield, 6 April (o.s.), 1746 (Add. MSS. 32,707, fo. 21): " Our friends in Holland have procured Mr. Gilles, the second Greffier, to be sent as coadjutor to Mr. Twickle at Paris. He is represented to be a very able, very honest, and a very firm man, and one that is neither to be amused nor frightened with the insinuations or threats of the Court of France."

Van der Heim's most intimate confidant, and was destined to be his successor. His instructions were to insist upon the abandonment of the Stewarts, and to obtain by remonstrance and argument a more moderate statement of the French terms for a general peace.

Gilles left The Hague on 13 April, and found d'Argenson much more moderate than he had been in his intercourse with Wassenaer. The Jacobite cause had collapsed at Culloden, and England was free to make much greater exertions on the Continent. The Hessians and a number of native troops were sent back to the Netherlands, and Cumberland would have been willing to resume command of the allied army if Maria Theresa had not insisted upon sending her unlucky brother-in-law, Charles of Lorraine.[1] The Austrian subsidy was increased by a third, and the Sardinian subsidy by a half. While the opposition in Brabant was likely to be more vigorous, the news from Italy was in the highest degree depressing to the French Minister. His Sardinian negotiation, upon which he had based such sanguine hopes, had not only broken down ignominiously but had so strained the relations between French and Spaniards as to ruin their campaign. It was almost inevitable that the Gallispans, even if they escaped humiliating disaster, would be forced to evacuate Italy, and in that case it would be possible for the allies either to attack Don Carlos or to invade France itself through Provence or Dauphiné. The Austrian and Sardinian Ministers began to say that " it will soon be a question of what Don Carlos is to keep rather than of what Don Philip is to get." D'Argenson had no longer any interest in reserving Italian problems for a separate settlement. On the contrary, if Louis XV was to be saved from the humiliation of having made

---

[1] There was a general expectation in England that Cumberland, who had raised rather than lowered his reputation at Fontenoy, would resume his command as soon as he was free. Weston wrote to Trevor on 25 April (o.s.), after the battle of Culloden: " The cry of the battalions, immediately after the engagement, was ' Now, Billy for Flanders !' " (*Trevor Papers*, p. 145). On George II's indignation at the appointment of Charles of Lorraine see Wasner to Ulfeld, 16 August, 1746, quoted in Arneth, iii., 456.

promises which he could not keep, the only chance of obtaining any endowment for his son-in-law was to induce the Maritime Powers to put pressure upon Maria Theresa and Charles Emmanuel. So the *Idées* were thrust into the background, and in a series of interviews d'Argenson and the two Dutch envoys grappled with the detailed problems of a general resettlement of Europe. Certain fundamental points were roughly agreed upon. The Dutch insisted upon the evacuation of the Southern Netherlands, and the restoration of their barrier towns with or without their previous fortifications and artillery. D'Argenson was willing to restore artillery so far as possible, but not to rebuild fortifications which had been dismantled. Both parties wished for some measure of neutrality for the Netherlands; the Dutch for a simple neutrality, as in 1733, when the two states were not at war with each other, whereas d'Argenson wanted an absolute neutrality in all wars, so that neither the Dutch nor any other Power could invade France through those provinces, and he wanted this neutrality guaranteed by the Dutch. D'Argenson consented unwillingly to a pledged abandonment of the Stewarts down to the remotest generation. He agreed without discussion to recognize the Emperor and to renew the French guarantee of the Pragmatic Sanction, with the exception of cessions made in this and other treaties. On the other hand, he insisted upon the restitution of Cape Breton, and the Dutch made no objection on their own part, though they reserved the right of England to object or to attach conditions. There was no great difficulty about demanding from Spain a pledge *à ne point troubler ou gener* (the words had been suggested from England) the ships of other nations in American waters when travelling to their own colonies or those of their allies. Nothing was said about the *asiento* or the *navio permiso*, which neither the Dutch nor the French had any desire to restore to England. The problems on this side of the Alps, upon which no agreement was possible at this stage, were the dismantling of Luxemburg, demanded by France, and that of Dunkirk, demanded by the Dutch, and the proposed cessions in the south-east of the Netherlands to the Elector Palatine and to France. When they came to Italy, d'Argenson insisted that the allies of France, Don Carlos, the Duke of Modena, and the Republic of Genoa, should not be sufferers by the war. To this the Dutch offered no objection. There remained the difficult problem of Don Philip. D'Argenson demanded the retention of Savoy and Nice, with the possible addition of the island of Sardinia, and also the grant to Elizabeth Farnese of the Duchies of Parma and Piacenza for her life. Wassenaer and Gilles had no great interest in these Italian problems, but they knew that such a departure from the Pragmatic Sanction and the Treaty of Worms would never be accepted at Vienna or Turin, and that England would never agree to press these terms upon the two allied Courts. In order to put an end to the deadlock, and in the hope of purchasing concessions upon other disputed points, they threw out, as a private suggestion of their own, that the Republic might employ its good offices to procure for Don Philip the temporary cession of Tuscany. This, it may be remembered, was an ingenious proposal which had been put forward in the sketch drawn up by Trevor and Van der Heim in the previous August, and had been included in the original draft instructions to Larrey, which had been cancelled in consequence of English disapproval.[1] However, this draft had passed with other Larrey papers into the hands of the two later emissaries, but, as Trevor points out, merely for their information,[2] and with no expectation that use would be made of it. It is, of course, possible that they had private instructions of which he knew nothing.

This suggestion of Tuscany, as novel as it was unexpected, fascinated d'Argenson, and was attractive to the French King and Ministry. Hitherto there had been a general doubt as to whether the Dutch were not merely "amusing the carpet," in order to post-

[1] See above, pp. 139 and 143.
[2] Trevor to Harrington (most secret), 7 May, 1746.   Trevor sent off summaries of the Dutch reports from Paris as they came in.

pone a French invasion and to gain time for preparing their defence. That doubt was for the first time partially dispelled. If France could commit the Maritime Powers to the principle of an establishment for Don Philip, it would be a great diplomatic score against Austria and Sardinia, who were determined that the Infant should get nothing, at any rate at their expense. So d'Argenson announced that the project was so far relished that he would wave the demand for the dismantling of Luxemburg and would agree to restore Dunkirk to its condition in 1740 (Trevor pointed out that the beginning of the year must be fixed, as the shore batteries were erected in 1740). But he adhered to his contention that Prussia must have her guarantee of Silesia, that the Elector Palatine must have Limburg, and that the King insisted upon the *enclaves* in Hainault as the only French gain from the war. By way of protest against these demands, and in the hope of hastening a conclusion, the envoys presented their draft scheme of settlement, based partly upon their instructions and partly on their discussions with d'Argenson. Their draft, which took the form of separate treaties between the various belligerent states, made no mention of Prussia or the Elector Palatine, and while it upheld the English demands as to the Stewarts and Dunkirk, included the cession of Cape Breton.[1]   D'Argenson refused to adopt the Dutch scheme, but he agreed to have it fully considered, and undertook to present a counter-project at either Lille or Brussels, as it was impossible to arrive at a settlement before the King joined the army. In reporting the progress made up to this point, Trevor pointed out that it had been possible to prevent the Dutch from making peace on the basis of d'Argenson's original *Idées*, but that it would be extremely difficult to restrain them now that France was coming down to something like reasonable terms. He therefore begged that Ministers would "take the whole affair into the maturest

[1] This Dutch draft of a bundle of treaties is in the Record Office (S.P., For., Holland, 418, fos. 51–4) and in the British Museum (Add. MSS. 32,805, fos. 90–5).

consideration, and prescribe eventually to me or some other instrument better fitted for this arduous task, the precise limits and bounds of His Majesty's demands and concessions, in order to avert a most unreasonable and dangerous discrepance of sentiments and measures between England and the Republic."[1]

D'Argenson's Counter-Project was submitted to the two envoys on their arrival at Brussels on 9 May, was finally adjusted between them and de la Ville on the 14th, and was forwarded by Trevor to London with a long covering letter on the 20th. He was compelled to warn the English Ministers that they must always speak of it as the "Project," because the States-General had no official knowledge of the previous history of the negotiations, and must not be allowed to suspect that their envoys, who had only been instructed to ascertain the French demands, had gone so far as to formulate a scheme of their own for a general European peace.[2] The document is itself so important in the sequence of peace negotiations, and gave rise to such a ministerial crisis in England, that it deserves a rather minute examination. It was planned, unlike the Dutch scheme, as the basis of a single general treaty, which was the form ultimately adopted at Aix-la-Chapelle, and it consists of twenty-three articles. Some of the less important are omitted, but, for convenience of reference, the original numbering is retained :

1. This is the contentious article about neutrality. France is never to attack the Dutch through the Netherlands, and the Dutch are similarly pledged not to attack France, " et à concourir, *par toutes sortes de moyens,* avec S.M.T.C., pour empêcher que la France ne puisse être attaquée de ce côté là par quelque puissance, ou sous quelque prétexte, que ce puisse être."

3. The Dutch are to guarantee Silesia to the King of Prussia.

4. The French conquests in the Netherlands are to be restored with all artillery, so far as this is possible.

[1] Trevor to Harrington (most secret), 7 May, 1746 (S.P., For., Holland, 418, fo. 42).
[2] *Ibid.*, 27 May (S.P., For., Holland, 418, fo. 162).

5. In consideration of this generous restitution, Maria Theresa shall cede to the Elector Palatine all that she possesses in the duchies of Limburg and Gelderland.

6. She shall also cede to France the *enclaves* in Hainault.

7. France shall make peace with Maria Theresa on the basis of the treaty of 1738, and shall guarantee the Pragmatic Sanction except as modified by this and other treaties.

8. France shall recognize the Emperor, and he, both as Emperor and as head of the House of Lorraine, shall renew the cession of that duchy to Stanislas and to France.

9. France shall make peace with England, including Hanover, and shall extend its engagements, made in 1713 and 1717, as to *celui qui a pris le titre de Prince de Galles,* to all his posterity.

10. Dunkirk is to be dismantled so as to put that port in the same condition as at the beginning of 1740.

11. England shall restore Cape Breton with all artillery.

13. Peace is to be restored between England and Spain on the basis of the Treaty of Utrecht and the Convention of the Pardo of 14 January, 1739. The Dutch provision as to freedom of navigation in American waters is adopted verbatim.

15. Spain and England shall appoint commissioners to fix the boundary between Georgia and Florida.

17. Maria Theresa is to make peace with Spain and Naples on the basis of the treaty of 1738.

18. All conquests in Italy by Spain and its allies are to be restored.

19. Spain, Naples, and Don Philip are to recognize the Emperor and to guarantee the modified Pragmatic Sanction.

20. The Emperor is to cede Tuscany to Don Philip and his male heirs and male descendants of the present Queen of Spain, so long as they do not hold the crown either of Spain or of the Two Sicilies. On extinction of the Queen's male descendants, Tuscany is to revert to the House of Lorraine in the person of Prince Charles and his male heirs, so long as they hold no crown. On extinction of male heirs of both lines, Tuscany is to fall to the King of Sardinia. Tuscany is to remain a fief of the Empire, and Leghorn is to be a free port.

21. To compensate the Emperor for this sacrifice, Maria Theresa is to cede to him for life the *souveraineté et jouissance* of Bohemia, and this temporary grant is not to be regarded as a breach of the Pragmatic Sanction.

22. Sardinia is to recover all territories conquered in the present war.

23. The Duke of Modena is to recover his duchy, and Genoa " sera entierement rassurée sur tout ce qui peut l'intéresser, et particulièrement sur la possession tranquille du Marquisat de Final."[1]

Unfortunately for the chances of the acceptance of this project by England, d'Argenson, a clumsy humanitarian, insisted upon adding to the repudiation of the Stewarts in the ninth article the words : " Ajoutez ici une stipulation pour la sûreté de la personne du Prince Edouard et sa retraite, et pour une amnestie en faveur de ceux qui ont suivi son parti." Even the pacific Trevor was startled by this irrelevant interpolation into a plan of European peace, and would only receive the document after presenting an energetic protest. And the French Minister followed up his first *gaucherie* by another still more astounding. He wrote a strong letter advocating clemency and hinting at French reprisals if his counsels were not adopted.[2] As he had no means of communication with the British Ministry, he induced his friend van Hoey, another sentimentalist, to forward it to England with a covering letter, in which he supported the French contentions.[3] This provoked a storm in England. That a foreign and hostile state should presume to dictate in domestic affairs and to plead the cause of defeated rebels was bad enough, but it was intolerable that this intervention should be aided and

---

[1] The text of d'Argenson's project is in S.P., For., Holland, 418, fos. 132–40, and in Add. MSS. 32,805 (Newcastle Papers, vol. 120), fos. 96–105. Trevor's covering letter (most secret) of 20 May is in above volume of State Papers, fo. 121.

[2] There is a copy of the letter, which is dated 26 May from the Camp de Bouchoute, in Add. MSS. 32,805, fo. 106.

[3] Hoey's extraordinary covering letter is in *ibid.*, fo. 111 For a pungent commentary on the whole episode see Broglie, *Saxe et d'Argenson*, vol. i.

abetted by the Minister of an allied Power. No answer was sent to d'Argenson, but van Hoey received a denunciatory letter from Newcastle,[1] who also made a formal complaint to the States-General. A demand would have been made for the envoy's recall, but, in view of the Dutch fear of irritating France, it was feared that the States might be compelled to refuse, and that such a refusal would endanger the alliance between the two maritime Powers.[2]

This episode, of little importance in itself, had the unforeseen effect of almost paralyzing for the moment the pacific section in the English Cabinet. These men, notably Henry Pelham and Harrington, who had an exaggerated fear of the power of France, and had been completely estranged from Austria in the previous year by Maria Theresa's obstinate continuance of the Silesian War, were convinced that the longer the war lasted the more disastrous it would be, and believed it to be their duty to make peace as soon as possible on the best terms they could get. Their favourite parable was that of the Sibylline books. George II, who regarded their policy as discreditably pusillanimous, tried to get rid of them and to bring back Lord Granville in February, 1746. But the attempt had been an ignominious failure, and the restored Ministers had continued, with the help of Robert Trevor at The Hague, to encourage the Dutch Pensionary to adjust terms with France which would satisfy the most pressing needs of the Maritime Powers, and to which they could then, as at Utrecht, extort the unwilling consent of unconsulted allies. Their constant defence was that any other policy would drive the Dutch into a separate treaty with France. At the back of their minds there was, as we have seen, the belief that such a separate treaty, while it would be in one sense a disaster, would supply them with an adequate justification for their own acceptance of unpopular conditions. Henry Pelham in all his

[1] Newcastle's letter to Hoey is in S.P., For., Holland, 418, fo. 271, and in Add. MSS. 32,805, fo. 109.
[2] Harrington to Trevor, separate and private, 3 June (o.s.), in S.P., For., Holland, 418, fo. 277.

actions had one eye fixed upon the House of Commons, where he knew that, unless he could carry Pitt with him (and Pitt was at this time in favour of peace), he had to fight the opposition with no adequate oratorical support.

In d'Argenson's project the pacifists had got something like what they had been aiming at.   It was true that many of the articles were distasteful, but they might have been much worse, and there seemed no good prospect of getting better terms.   They were prepared to take them as a basis of negotiations, and, after obtaining such improvements as they could, to meet the obvious desire of the Dutch Ministers by signing a triangular preliminary treaty, which could then be submitted by the three Powers to their respective allies. On 16 May Harrington sent to Robinson at Vienna a dispatch which was evidently intended to prepare the way for an ultimate revelation of English defection. The envoy was to depict the melancholy situation on the Continent; the impossibility, already admitted by the Dutch and now asserted by England, of carrying on the war for another year; the certainty that, if any military advantages were gained by the allies, they would be nullified, as in 1744, by the renewed intervention of Prussia; and the consequent necessity of a speedy pacification.   A treaty which would secure a restoration of all conquests by France and Spain, their recognition of the Emperor and their guarantee of the Pragmatic Sanction, would be cheaply purchased by giving to Don Philip a sufficient establishment in Italy, even if it involved some sacrifice on the part of the Emperor or the Empress.   These last words were evidently employed to cover the projected cession of Tuscany.[1]

Harrington now proceeded to draft a dispatch to Trevor, in which he proposed to lay down the objections to be offered to the French proposals, to entrust the

[1] This dispatch of 16/27 May, which has escaped the notice of English historians and is conclusive proof of Harrington's readiness to accept d'Argenson's project, is in S.P., For., Germany (Empire), 173.

defence of those objections to the Dutch envoys, and
in the end to authorize Trevor to conclude upon the
best modifications of the terms that could be thus
arranged. But at this stage he met with a doughty
opponent in the Duke of Newcastle. Newcastle had
held the Southern Secretaryship since 1723, but had not
hitherto been a dominant figure in politics. He had
been overshadowed by Walpole as long as the latter
held office, and by Carteret for two years after Walpole's
fall. Newcastle had intrigued against both his chiefs,
and had helped to overthrow them, but he had not
gained much profit for himself. When his younger
brother had been raised to the premiership in 1744, the
Duke had not been thought of for the office. Harrington, who took over Carteret's secretaryship, was at the
outset more prominent than Newcastle. It was Harrington who accompanied the King to Hanover in 1745,
who concluded the famous convention with Prussia, and
who gave the directions to Thomas Villiers, which
helped to bring about the treaties of Dresden. Harrington, with fatal results to himself, took the lead in
the comedy of resignations which humiliated the King
in February, 1746, and he guided Trevor in his relations with the successive Dutch negotiators in France.
Newcastle acquiesced in his colleague's leadership because he had no alternative policy to suggest, and had
no assured supporter if he had attempted opposition.
He had no temptation to hold aloof in February, because the return of Granville would have been the
return of a master. But that episode seems to have
suggested a policy which he afterwards adopted. Granville's strength had lain in the favour of the Crown,
and the King still retained very considerable power,
especially in foreign affairs. Royal favour had not been
enough to sustain Granville, because he had not sufficient Parliamentary backing. But if a Minister could
combine a substantial hold upon the control of Parliament with influence in the closet, it would be possible
to gain substantial predominance. What Newcastle
aimed at was the control of English foreign policy, and
the reduction of his fellow-Secretary to subordination.

To gain this end he must wait for the emergence of a dispute in which he could be sure of gaining the support, not only of the King, but also of the King's favourite son, the Duke of Cumberland, who, since Fontenoy and Culloden, had become a popular idol in England, a position from which Scottish curses were powerless to depose him. The d'Argenson project offered to Newcastle just the opportunity which he desired. A conflict with his brother was inevitable, but Henry Pelham was no modern Prime Minister with an oversight over all departments, and he had adopted the pose that foreign affairs, except so far as they required the raising of money, were outside his competence. At the worst he could be trusted not to go too far in opposition to a brother for whom he had a genuine affection, in spite of the exasperating touchiness which so often led to fraternal quarrels. In the background were two men, Lord Chancellor Hardwicke and the mysterious Andrew Stone, Newcastle's secretary, who were equally trusted and consulted by both brothers, and could act as mediators in case of divergence with a curious but assured partiality for the Duke.

Harrington's draft letter to Trevor, which proposed to give that envoy power to conclude after further negotiations to be conducted by Gilles and Wassenaer, was submitted, not to a full Cabinet, but to " those persons whom His Majesty usually consults upon matters of importance," in this case the Premier, the Lord Chancellor, the two Secretaries of State, and Lord Chesterfield, the Irish Viceroy, who happened to be in London at the time.[1] Newcastle at once stated his objections. He took his stand on two great principles. In the first place, it was indecent to entrust the settlement of great national interests, such as the fate of Cape Breton and Dunkirk, to the Ministers of a foreign Power. And, in the second place, it was extremely dangerous to allow bargains to be made about territories which belonged to our allies without giving those

[1] There is a good account of the meeting in Newcastle to Cumberland, 23 May (o.s.), Add. MSS. 32,707, fo. 234. There are numerous references to this inner Cabinet in the Newcastle Papers.

allies a voice in the matter. He took special exception to the proposed neutrality of the Low Countries, as certain to sever the connection between Austria and the Maritime Powers, and also to weaken the alliance between the Maritime Powers themselves. And he denounced the idea of ceding Tuscany, partly because it would be barefaced robbery of a non-belligerent who had obtained the grand-duchy as the price of his patrimony, and partly because it would be handing over the greater part of the Italian coast to the House of Bourbon. He therefore demanded either that a person " of great weight and credit " (*i.e.*, other than Trevor) should be sent to negotiate on our behalf, or that we should insist upon a French answer to our objections to their project before any authority should be given to sign. And he insisted that the whole transaction as it stood should be communicated to our allies, in order that we should know their opinions. Hardwicke, on the whole, supported Newcastle, especially about the neutrality, but had some doubts as to completely changing the character of the negotiation by calling in Austria and Sardinia, whereas France had not, so far as we knew, made any communication to Spain. And it would be unfair to do this without obtaining the consent of the Dutch. On the main points Henry Pelham and Chesterfield argued in support of Harrington that any delay would drive the Dutch into a separate treaty with France, and that to call in the allies before we had settled what were reasonable terms would give rise to endless obstruction. In the end there was a compromise. No special envoy was to be sent in the meantime, and indeed no suitable person could be suggested except Chesterfield, and he refused. But it was agreed to postpone any final resolution until the French answer to objections had been received. As to the objections, Newcastle undertook to draft them,[1] and Harrington to re-write the letter with this to guide him. On the vital question of communication to the allies, Trevor was to be told to urge the Pensionary to impart the whole transac-

[1] There is a copy of his draft in Add. MSS. 35,408, fo. 232.

tion to the Austrian and Sardinian Ministers at The
Hague.

On the following day Harrington, after an intermediate failure to induce Newcastle to alter his opinions,
submitted the revised draft to the King, and Newcastle
got his desired opportunity of posing as the champion
of the royal wishes.   On all the points at issue,
George II edited the letter in the Newcastle sense.[1]
Even when Harrington resorted to the questionable
argument that a separate Dutch treaty would be followed by a French invasion of Hanover, the King paid
little attention, and the letter was finally adjusted in
the evening of 20 May.   It embodied the compromise
previously settled by Ministers.   The French project
might be taken as a basis of negotiation subject to a
number of reservations.   Dunkirk must be restored
under the supervision of English commissioners to the
condition prescribed by previous treaties.   The monstrous addition to the ninth article must be withdrawn.
The States should hesitate to accept the absolute
neutrality proposed for the Netherlands, and should
weigh the objections offered by " persons of consideration " on this side.   Spain must restore the *asiento* and
the permitted ship.   As to Cape Breton, " that being
the only acquisition made by England to balance in
any degree the vast expense of blood and treasure
brought upon this nation by the present war," His
Majesty does not absolutely refuse to give it up, but
must first know what proportionate advantage France
will offer in return.   England will agree to an establishment for Don Philip, but can only approve the
cession of Tuscany if the consent of Vienna and Turin
is obtained.   If Don Philip is endowed, all idea of
cessions by Maria Theresa in the Netherlands must be
abandoned.   Finally, the Dutch are urged to communicate the project to the allies, and the ultimate
decision of England is reserved until France has replied
to the English reservations.   Newcastle and Hardwicke agreed that the letter read as if the author did

[1] For this interview of the two Secretaries with the King see
Newcastle to Hardwicke, 21 May (o.s.), Add. MSS. 32,707, fo. 222.

not agree with its contents, but accepted it as a substantial victory over their opponents.[1]

The English reply was eagerly awaited at The Hague. Van der Heim was a sick man, and his ill-health was aggravated by agitation as to the results of the negotiation on which he considered that his own credit and the fate of the Republic depended. Trevor had endeavoured to console him during the delay by reading to him Harrington's preparatory dispatch to Robinson, which seemed to commit England to at any rate a general acceptance of the projected treaty. He was therefore bitterly disappointed when the much-debated letter with its extensive reservations was at last received. Why, he wailed, did not England state her terms beforehand, so that the Dutch envoys might have known what line they were to take? Was the restoration of the Netherlands, hitherto regarded as a supreme English interest, no equivalent for Cape Breton? How can the French, after the negotiation has been carried so far, be asked to consent to such fundamental changes? They will conclude that the whole transaction has been a blind, and they will vent their indignation upon the unfortunate Republic. It is easy for England, protected by the sea, to defy France, but the Dutch have lost their barrier. As to the communication to the allies before any preliminary agreement had been reached, it would be a condemnation of all previous procedure, would involve the scrapping of past labours, would be an additional insult to France, who had not consulted Spain, and would probably ruin the constitution of the Republic. As England obviously refused to allow the Dutch negotiators to pledge her to any conditions, and as constant references to London caused endless delays, it was imperative to have on the

---

[1] This important letter, dated 20 May (o.s.), 1746, is in S.P., For., Holland, 418. The correspondence about it between Newcastle and Hardwicke is printed in Coxe, *Pelham Administration*, i., pp. 487-90, and partially in Yorke, *Life of Hardwicke*, i., 636. A more summary account of the ministerial dispute is given by Newcastle in a letter to Cumberland of 23 May (Add. MSS., 32,707. fo. 234). For Chesterfield's views see *Trevor Papers*, p. 146.

spot an English plenipotentiary who would have some discretionary power to deal with contentious problems. With this demand Trevor, convinced by the last dispatch that the English Ministers were turning away from the policy hitherto pursued by Harrington and Henry Pelham, expressed his complete agreement.[1]

Van der Heim's agitation was increased by the equal impatience for a prompt decision shown by d'Argenson, who had sent the Marquis de Puyzieulx, previously French envoy to the Court of Naples, to test on the spot the sincerity of the Dutch desire for peace. Although Puyzieulx professed to come for the purpose of consulting the Faculty at Leyden about his health, it was generally and correctly assumed that he carried an ambassador's commission in his pocket, and his arrival at The Hague tore away the last shred of secrecy that shrouded the Dutch relations with France. The Pensionary was rather disconcerted by this sudden transfer of the negotiations to his own door, and as Louis XV was leaving the army to be present at the lying-in of the Dauphine, he called Gilles home to assist him, while Wassenaer followed the King to Paris. Gilles was as annoyed as Van der Heim had been by Harrington's dispatch, and pointed out that it would be impossible for the Dutch plenipotentiaries to urge the English objections with any force unless they could give an assurance, which they were forbidden to do, that England would sign a preliminary treaty if these objections were reasonably met. To any premature communication to the allies he was resolutely opposed. Before Puyzieulx left The Hague he had a final interview with Van der Heim, at which he reported the gist of the answers he had received on points raised in their previous consultations.[2] France refused to discuss the *asiento* and the *navio permiso* without consulting Spain; the wording of the article about neutrality might be

[1] Trevor to Harrington (most secret), 7 June, 1746 (S.P., For., Holland, 418, fo. 221).
[2] For Puyzieulx's discussions with Van der Heim see Trevor to Harrington (most secret), 21 and 24 June, in S.P., For., Holland, 418, fos. 306 and 335.

altered, provided reciprocity was maintained; but there were four articles which were *sine quibus non*: (1) the restoration of Louisbourg; (2) the cession of Limburg and Gelderland; (3) the transfer of Tuscany; and (4) the guarantee of Silesia. He added that, while he was personally convinced that the Dutch genuinely desired peace, he must report that " the state's connection with, or rather dependence upon, England would disappoint the whole, and not allow it to follow its own inclination or interests." As he did not wish to exclude England, he hoped that a sufficiently authorized person could be sent from London to act with the Dutch plenipotentiaries at Paris or with the army. Van der Heim hoped that England would accept this as the required answer from France, and intimate its promised resolution. But as Puyzieulx's statement would almost inevitably be regarded in London as too vague and not sufficiently comprehensive, Gilles was sent back to rejoin Wassenaer in France with a carefully concealed commission from the Secret Committee to conclude a separate treaty with France in case England should prove unreasonable.[1]

Meanwhile, the ministerial quarrels in England continued, but the stars in their courses fought for Newcastle. Harrington's pessimistic dispatch of 16 May (o.s.)

---

[1] The Secret Committee consisted of nine members, two deputies from Holland, one from each of the other provinces, and the Greffier. Its proper function was to consider and report on remits from the States-General, but in emergency it frequently assumed the functions of the larger federal body. Votes were taken by head, so that Holland had two votes, whereas it had only one in the States-General. The Greffier had a vote in the Committee, though he had none in the States. See Sandwich to Newcastle, 2 October, 1746 (Brit. Mus. Add. MSS. 32,805, fo. 285). The minute of the Secret Committee of 2 July, 1746, which Gilles carried with him to France, was disclosed to Sandwich, probably by Bentinck, after the revolution had restored the Stadtholder. It appears that Gilles was present, that Van der Heim (sitting as one of the deputies from Holland) wrote the minute in his own hand, and it was not included in the Register. It was carried by a majority, Bentinck, Van Haren, and the Greffier Fagel protesting. The transfer of the negotiations from France to Breda and the events there prevented any action being taken on the minute, but it shows how near the Dutch came to breaking away from England. The copy of the document which Sandwich sent home is in the British Museum (Add. MSS. 32,808, fo. 217).

to Robinson found the Austrian Ministers in no mood
to accept the suggestion of a sacrifice to purchase
an immediate peace. To the gloomy picture which
England painted of the Netherlands, Austria opposed
the brightness of prospects in Italy. What was lost in
one country could be regained in the other. If England
was terrified by Prussia, Austria had insured against
that danger by the recent treaty of the two Empresses.
If Saxony had been lost, there was every prospect of
gaining Bavaria. If France was trying to detach the
Dutch, Austria had confident hopes of crippling France
by a separate treaty with Spain. Why talk of sacrifices in such circumstances? And, if sacrifices were
necessary, why should it always be Austria that was to
make them? Bartenstein must have enjoyed himself
when he penned these remonstrances and denounced
the iniquitous and ruinous conduct of an ally who negotiated behind his partner's back. Even allowing for
his habitual venom, the document, which Robinson
transmitted as an answer to Harrington,[1] was a sufficient warning to the English Ministers of the reception
which would be given to their announcement that they
had signed away Tuscany, Limburg, and Austrian
Gelderland without consulting Vienna. This strengthened Newcastle's case for immediate disclosure. Then
came the news of a complete Austrian victory on
15 June over the Gallispans at Piacenza. This victory,
trumpeted over Europe, would modify the Bourbon
demands for Don Philip, and put such a considerable
province as Tuscany out of the question. And almost
at the same time came Trevor's report of the parting
words of Puyzieulx, in which he had joined the Pensionary in demanding that an English envoy should
take part in the negotiations, and had declared that
France could not settle terms for Spain without consulting Madrid. This last statement took away the
strongest argument from the advocates of the separate
triple negotiation, and Harrington was compelled
against his will to write a letter to Trevor, which almost

[1] Robinson transmitted it, with an enormously long letter of
his own on 12 June, 1747 (S.P., For., Germany [Empire], 173).

completed Newcastle's triumph.[1] Not only did he
declare that the statements of Puyzieulx were wholly
inadequate to justify a final resolution on the part of
England, but he undertook that if France would send
a fully authorized person to some neutral town, England
would send either Trevor or another to negotiate about
a general peace, and instructed Trevor to urge the
States to make an immediate communication to the
envoys of the allies at The Hague, and if they refused,
Trevor himself was to make the communication, and to
send it on at once to Sir Thomas Robinson at Vienna.
This intelligence reduced the unfortunate Van der Heim
to despair. He had just obtained leave of absence to
spend a fortnight at Spa, and he implored Trevor to
send his remonstrances to Harrington and to delay
carrying out his instructions until a reply had been
received. Trevor, who had a real regard for the sick
man, and who advanced as a further excuse the absence
at the army headquarters of Rosenberg and Chavanne,
the Austrian and Sardinian envoys, yielded to the
request.[2] But the concession was useless. Harrington
replied that, as soon as the last dispatch had gone,
the English Ministers, assuming Dutch consent, had
given d'Argenson's project with the relative papers to
Wasner and Osorio for transmission to their respective
Courts.[3] This crushing news never reached Van der
Heim, who died of heart failure on his way to Spa.
Trevor regarded his death as a blow to the Anglo-Dutch
alliance, but trusted that Gilles, who was regarded
as the inevitable successor, would pursue the same
moderate policy.

Newcastle, with the support of the King and the
Lord Chancellor, and with the help of external circum-

[1] This letter is dated 20 June (o.s.), and is in S.P., For., Holland,
418 fos. 342, 381.   Three days beforehand, Harrington had
promised, much to Van der Heim's delight, to send the final
resolution.   This promise, after a further altercation in the
Ministry, he had to withdraw.   A modern Minister in such
circumstances would have resigned.

[2] Trevor to Harrington (most secret), 5 July, S.P., For., Holland,
419, fo. 11.

[3] Harrington to Trevor, 1 July (o.s.), *ibid.*, fo. 17.

stances, had trampled upon Harrington. He had got
rid of the policy of entrusting English interests to Dutch
diplomatists, who were so afraid of irritating France
that, though they received Trevor's summary of Harrington's instructions, they never informed d'Argenson
that the whole secret had been disclosed to the Courts
of Vienna and Turin.[1] In the confident belief that the
object was still to bring about a preliminary understanding between France and the two Maritime Powers,
and that an English plenipotentiary was to be sent, as
Puyzieulx had proposed, to avoid irritating delays, the
French Minister consented to the transfer of the conferences to Breda,[2] and selected Puyzieulx to represent
France. The same view was held by the Dutch, who
had made no communication to the allies, nor given any
approval to English action in the matter.[3] On the
other hand, Newcastle contended that the object of
informing the allies was to bring them into the negotiation, and that they must be invited to send representatives to Breda. The danger of this policy was that it
would so disgust the Dutch that they would purchase
their own safety by abandoning the war and making a
separate treaty with France. But Newcastle was
induced to run this risk by another extremely fortunate
event, the death of Philip V on 9 July, and the accession
of the surviving son of his first wife, Ferdinand VI. It
was universally expected that this event would put an
end to the domination of Elizabeth Farnese, the arch-
champion of Don Philip's pretensions in Italy, and that
it would be followed by a complete change of Spanish

[1] In his letter to Harrington of 8 July, Trevor says that the
Pensionary has sent his *précis* to Paris to strengthen the hands
of the Dutch plenipotentiaries. On 19 July he admits that he
had to withdraw this *précis* as inaccurate and substitute another,
which was given to Buys, as acting Pensionary. It subsequently
transpired that the first *précis* was not communicated to d'Argenson,
and that Buys never sent the second one to the plenipotentiaries.
See below, p. 175, for the importance of this.

[2] The transfer was necessary, because England, at open war
with France, could not negotiate on French soil. Breda was
technically neutral.

[3] The Dutch Government never did make any communication
or send any invitation to the allies. In fact, they denied that
Sardinia was their ally.

policy, which would dissolve the Family Compact as embodied in the Treaty of Fontainebleau. Hitherto, all attempts to detach Spain had broken down on the difficulty of finding a sufficient endowment for the son to satisfy the obstinate and ambitious mother. The new King was not supposed to be fond either of his stepmother or of his half-brother, and his wife, who was believed to be the predominant partner, was a Portuguese Princess, and had been brought up in a Court where the tradition was friendly both to England and to Austria. Newcastle jumped to the conclusion that with Portuguese assistance it would be easy to detach Spain from France, and that this would at once compel France to accept more moderate terms of peace. In these altered circumstances the difficulty about Don Philip might be got rid of altogether, or, at any rate, reduced in importance, and English public opinion might be gratified by the retention of Cape Breton. He had two strings to his bow. The Marquis of Tabernuiga, exiled from Spain as an opponent of Elizabeth Farnese, had for the last eight years been resident in England, where he had established intimate relations first with Carteret and later with Newcastle. He readily undertook to go to Lisbon, to open relations with the Court of Madrid, whither he hoped to be recalled, and to act as a mediator between Spain and Austria. At the same time Newcastle selected another friend, Benjamin Keene, who had been our envoy in Madrid before the war, accredited him to the Court of Lisbon, and gave him instructions to use that Court as a means of indirect communication with the Spanish Court, and, if possible, to obtain permission to return to a reconciled Spain.[1] Until the result of this double venture was ascertained, it was desirable to keep the negotiation in Holland going, but to avoid any final settlement. And, if it was at all possible, this must be done without provoking such a quarrel with the Dutch as would drive them into the arms of France.

[1] There is a copy of Keene's instructions, which were sent to Lord Sandwich for his guidance, in S.P., For., Holland, 424, fo. 148. They are not in the Portuguese State Papers.

It was not at all easy to find the right man for this delicate and very difficult task. Chesterfield knew more about Dutch politics and Dutch politicians than any other Englishman, but he disapproved of Newcastle's recent policy, and had fortunately refused to go.[1] Trevor was on the spot, and had been encouraged to believe that he would be chosen, in spite of his own professions of incapacity. But Newcastle ruled him out without any hesitation, as being the intimate friend of Harrington and Henry Pelham, and as being too sympathetic with the Dutch Republicans and their desire to put a speedy end to the war. Newcastle approached Nicholas Poyntz, who had an unproved reputation for notable ability and a knowledge of Dutch, having written a book on the Barrier Treaty, but he refused on the plea of ill-health.[2] In the end it was decided that, as no expert was available, a young man must be found of sufficient birth and capacity, who would have no pretensions to decide anything, and who would simply refer matters to be decided by the King and his Ministers. The choice ultimately fell upon the Earl of Sandwich, a neighbour and close friend of the Duke of Bedford, and a junior colleague of the Duke on the Admiralty Board.[3] It was understood that Bedford was only remaining at the Admiralty until his protégé, who had a hereditary interest in naval matters, had earned the right to take his place, and the latter's claim to such promotion would be increased if he could gain distinction in another field. Sandwich, who was just twenty-eight years old, had not been long enough in politics to make many enemies. Harrington had no

[1] On Chesterfield's refusal and its reasons see his letter to Trevor of 5 August (o.s.), in *Trevor Papers*, p. 149.
[2] Newcastle wrote to Poyntz on 23 May (o.s.) (Add. MSS. 32,707, fo. 237). Poyntz's elaborately servile answer is *ibid.*, fo. 255.
[3] See Henry Pelham to H. Walpole, 29 July, on the motives for the selection of Sandwich. Coxe, *Pelham Administration*, i., 332: " The King seems to like him very well. The reason to me is plain; he thinks he is a man not likely to give up Cape Breton, without which, the King knows, there can be no peace.   He thinks also that, as he is a young man, inexperienced in affairs, it will justify sending him without any positive or final instructions, which will of course leave everything *ad referendum*."

objection to him, and Henry Pelham was fully aware of the value to the Ministry of the Bedford interest. What attracted Newcastle to Sandwich was the fact that Bedford and the Admiralty in general were eager to carry the war into Canada, and therefore to retain Cape Breton as the key to the valley of the St. Lawrence.[1] The young Earl might be trusted, therefore, not to fall in with the Dutch desire to purchase peace with France by the surrender of the great English acquisition. The recovery of Madras, which was lost in the current year, was another naval interest for which the Dutch were not likely to show any enthusiasm. For these reasons Newcastle took to himself the credit of having pressed the selection of Sandwich, and he determined to take the guidance of the young diplomatist into his own hands behind the back of Harrington, to whose department The Hague and Breda properly belonged. Thus he would hold the two great diplomatic threads in Europe at the moment in Portugal and in Holland.

To Robert Trevor, after twelve years of continuous residence at The Hague, it was a mortal blow to be passed over in favour of an untried youth, who had neither training nor experience in diplomacy. But he was not altogether unprepared. For the last two months he had been conscious that powerful influences in England were opposed to the policy to which he had committed himself. He did not conceal his discomfiture and his growing sense that retirement would be forced upon him from Henry Pelham and Chesterfield, the two friends on whose sympathy he could confidently rely. The former, while recommending him to remain at his post, facilitated his resignation by procuring for him a commissionership of revenue in Ire-

---

[1] There are several references in the *Bedford Correspondence* to a projected conquest of Canada. On the Duke's desire to retain Cape Breton, Horace Walpole writes to Mann (16 May, 1746): " We are now, I suppose, on the eve of a bad peace; though, as Cape Breton must be a condition, I don't know who will dare to part with it. Little Æolus (the Duke of Bedford) says they shall not have it, that they shall have Woburn as soon " (*Letters* [ed. Toynbee], ii., p. 194).

land with a salary of £1,000 a year.[1] Trevor held on
for two more months, but he found himself for all
practical purposes superseded by his youthful colleague.
In November he resigned his office, and the ambitious
Sandwich took over the Embassy at The Hague in
addition to his commission to Breda.

[1] Henry Pelham to Trevor, 12 August (o.s.), 1746 (*Trevor
Papers*, p. 149). Trevor's grateful reply is on the next page.
He regretted his compulsory retirement the more because, before
he actually left The Hague, his other great friend, Lord Chesterfield,
had become his immediate superior as Secretary of the Northern
Department.

CHAPTER V

BREDA AND LISBON (AUGUST, 1746, TO JANUARY, 1747).

Sandwich and his task—His conspiracy with Newcastle—Moots at The Hague the admission of allies to the Conference— Pensionary Gilles unwillingly promises support—Conference opened with Puyzieulx—Sandwich proposes admission of allies—Consequent delay—Renewed deadlock at second meeting of Conference—Compromise proposed in interval— Ministerial crisis in England—Weakness of Premier— Harrington exchanges offices with Chesterfield—Sandwich Minister at The Hague—Compromise accepted at third meeting of Conference—Delay to obtain consent of the allies— Expulsion of " Gallispans " from Italy—Fall of Genoa— Invasion of Provence—Quarrels of Austria and Sardinia— Genoa expels the Austrians—Tabernuiga and Keene at Lisbon—Obstacles to a treaty with Spain—Don Philip— Attitude of Austria as to Italian problems—Attitude of Sardinia—Proposed Portuguese mediation—All progress blocked at Lisbon by opposition of allies.

THE fourth Earl of Sandwich has a somewhat unsavoury reputation in English history. Without entering into any controversy as to his later career, it may confidently be asserted that at the time he went to Breda he had done nothing to deserve such a reputation. He had already shown marked industry and ability at the Admiralty, where he was regarded, by Anson and others, as the destined successor of Bedford, whenever the Duke, who preferred his cricket and his conifers at Woburn to the public service, should think fit to make room for his protégé by resignation. In spite of his youth and inexperience, his selection for Breda met with general approval. He himself seems to have had no doubt of his being able to grapple with the difficult task entrusted to him, and only hesitated because he feared that during his absence some competitor might intrigue to forestall his claim to succeed to the First Lordship. His task was not made easier by the discord among his employers. His official instructions, drafted by Harrington, were the result of a compromise between jarring

views in the Cabinet.[1] Newcastle so far prevailed that
Sandwich was ordered to insist upon the admission of
Ministers of the allies to the Conference, and to reject
any claims on the part of France to transact business
on behalf of Spain. On the other hand, he was to do
all in his power to conciliate the Republican leaders in
Holland, and especially Gilles, who was expected to
succeed Van der Heim as Pensionary, while the negotiation was admitted to be a sequel of the negotiations
conducted by the Dutch envoys, so that its starting-
point would be d'Argenson's project with the objections
stated by Harrington in his letter to Trevor of 20 June.
Newcastle, however, was not content with his partial
victory in the Cabinet. He secretly handed over to
Sandwich the draft instructions which he himself had
prepared, together with the confidential document which
he had circulated to Cumberland and Hardwicke in
criticism of Harrington's first draft.[2] In this, strong
objections were made to any reference to the Dutch
negotiations on the ground that events had rendered
d'Argenson's project altogether obsolete, and that a
new start should be made. In the private instructions
Sandwich was told that there must be no neutrality for
the Netherlands, no transfer of Tuscany from the House
of Lorraine, and no cession of Cape Breton, unless some
substantial equivalent should be offered by France.
At the same time Newcastle arranged to carry on a
correspondence with Sandwich which should be kept
secret from Harrington, and gave him to understand
that his real mission was to prevent the Conference at
Breda from coming to any conclusion until it was
known how far Keene could succeed at Lisbon in
coming to terms with Spain, and how far France could
be humbled by an invasion of Provence. The test of
Sandwich's ability was to be whether he could so dis-

---

[1] The instructions are not in the Record Office, but are preserved at Hinchingbrooke in the Papers of the Fourth Earl.

[2] These documents, with Sandwich's autograph endorsement
" received from the Duke of Newcastle on my first going to
Holland " are in the Hinchingbrooke Papers, App. I. There is
a copy of the " Observations on Lord Sandwich's Instructions " in
the British Museum (Add. MSS. 32,805, fo. 140).

guise his policy of obstruction as to avoid driving the
Dutch into a separate treaty with France. Finally,
Sandwich was to establish close relations with Bentinck
and the Orange party, so that, in the last resort, if the
Republicans showed signs of being cajoled or intimi-
dated into submission to France, he might promote a
revolution to restore the Stadtholdership.[1]   Such a
revolution in favour of the King's son-in-law would not
only perpetuate the Anglo-Dutch alliance, but would
earn the grateful favour of George II.

Sandwich threw himself with great spirit and gusto
into the game prescribed for him by Newcastle, and
unquestionably played it with conspicuous success. As
he refused to go to Breda before Puyzieulx, he had to
spend some weeks at The Hague, where he broke it to
the Dutch Ministers, not only that England insisted
upon full communication to the Courts of Vienna and
Turin, but also that those Courts had received pressing
invitations from London to send Ministers to Breda.
Wassenaer and Gilles had already gone to Breda from
France, so the chief officials with whom Sandwich had
to deal were Willem Buys, the acting Pensionary during
the vacancy, and Fagel, who had succeeded his uncle
as first Greffier of the Republic. Fagel, who had a
hereditary attachment to the English alliance, offered
no objections, but Buys, a veteran Republican, who
had been Pensionary at Amsterdam and a Dutch envoy
at Utrecht, made the most vigorous protests against
this complete change in the character of the negotiation,
as certain both to alienate France and to cause endless
delays before peace could be arrived at. Sandwich
found himself somewhat handicapped by the presence
of Trevor, who had been so intimately associated with
all the previous negotiations, and by the Dutch conviction, which he admitted to be well founded, " that
England has more occasion for Holland than Holland

[1] Although there is no written evidence, which could hardly
be expected, the subsequent correspondence and Sandwich's
relations with Bentinck, which began at once, prove conclusively
that this was virtually settled between Newcastle and Sandwich
before the Earl left England.

has for England.''[1]   Luckily for him, Gilles, who had now been chosen Pensionary, came to The Hague and proved to be more reasonable than Buys.   He started with the same contention that the only way to make peace was for the Maritime Powers to adjust preliminary terms with France, and then present them to their allies, while France would do the same to Spain.   In support of this Gilles took his stand upon the wording of an important sentence in Trevor's précis of Harrington's despatch of 20 June.   From this sentence it appeared that Harrington promised to Van der Heim that he would make a separate treaty with France if reasonable terms could be arranged.   But Trevor's first précis had omitted the important words *dans l'interim*, and these altered the whole meaning of the sentence. The omission had been discovered at once in London, and Trevor had handed in a corrected version after procuring the return of the former document.[2]   This second document, either through carelessness or of design, Buys had never forwarded to Gilles, who was completely taken aback when Sandwich produced it, declared it to be the only document of which the Dutch Government was officially possessed, and pointed out that the " interim "

[1] Sandwich to Harrington, 2 September, 1746 (S.P., For., Holland, 421, fo. 13).   In a letter to Robinson on 9 November (Hinchingbrooke Papers) Sandwich wrote: " I fear in our present situation their [the Dutch] alliance is too necessary to us to suffer us to take any hasty step that may be likely to engage them in desperate destructive measures."

[2] The amended sentence ran as follows: " Et vous pouvez informer M. le Conseiller Pensionnaire en confidence que le Roy pourra même se croire en liberté de procéder à une conclusion, si de telles conditions pourroient *dans l'interim* être obtenues, que Sa Majesté pourroit les justifier à Elle-même par rapport à ses propres intérêts et à ses alliés par rapport aux leurs, en cas qu'ils refusassent de conclure sur des termes raissonnables."   It is obvious that the omission of the underlined words gives a wholly different meaning to the sentence.   Sandwich, who received on his arrival from Bentinck a number of accusations or insinuations against Trevor, was inclined to believe that the omission was not wholly accidental, and declared that Van der Heim had been heard to boast that he had a confidential assurance from Harrington which gave the lie to the whole of the rest of his despatch.   Sandwich's notes on Bentinck's assertions as to the relations of Trevor with Van der Heim are in the Hinchingbrooke Papers, App. I.

could only refer to the period before the opening of the general Conference.[1] Gilles had to admit that he had been completely misled, through no fault of the English Government, and could only implore Sandwich to postpone his demand for the admission of the allies until the Conference had considered those problems which primarily concerned the Maritime Powers. But Sandwich, who had no intention of allowing the question of Cape Breton to be raised at the outset, had now the upper hand, and used it to the utmost. He insisted that the King's honour was pledged to make the admission of the allies his first demand, and that the expedient proposed by Gilles would enable France to say that they began the Conference on one principle and then changed to another. Gilles had ruefully to admit that it would be disastrous for the allies to go to Breda and display their division on the first point at issue. If, therefore, Sandwich considered it his duty to raise at the outset the question of admitting the Austrian and Sardinian Ministers, the Dutch plenipotentiaries would be compelled to support him, even at the risk of alienating France. Sandwich conciliated him by promising that, if the allies were invited and didn't come, he would be willing to proceed without them. He already knew that the King of Sardinia had nominated Chavanne, his envoy at The Hague, to be his representative at Breda, and he had sent an urgent letter to Robinson to induce Maria Theresa to follow this example.

Sandwich's success in dealing with his first delicate problem made some sensation in official circles in London, and Newcastle, who claimed the credit of his selection, was loudly exultant. It was decided to entrust to Sandwich, rather than to Trevor, two other important matters, the preparation of a joint plan of campaign for 1747, and the obtaining leave from the Republic for the allied troops to take up winter quarters

[1] Sandwich narrated his interview with Gilles in a dispatch to Harrington on 13 September, 1746 (S.P., For., Holland, 421, fo. 28). Trevor also reported on the same day to Harrington the failure of Buys to send the amended document to Gilles, (*ibid.*, 420, fo. 42).

upon Dutch soil. Hitherto the troops had wintered in the Austrian Netherlands, but these were now so reduced by French successes as no longer to offer the necessary accommodation. Both commissions presented serious difficulties. The proposal as to a new campaign was certain to arouse Dutch suspicions as to the sincerity of the professed desire of England for an early peace. And the Dutch had no desire to provide winter quarters for foreign troops. The Pandours and other irregular forces of Austria were not likely to be pleasant guests, and the presence of enemy troops upon Dutch soil would furnish France with a convenient pretext for following them thither. And Sandwich himself was hampered by the continued discrepancy between the official instructions which he received from Harrington and the private guidance which was supplied by Newcastle. By one post came a letter from Harrington to say that, if Puyzieulx proposed d'Argenson's project, Sandwich was to reply by reading the criticisms of the project that had been sent to Trevor on 20 June.[1] The next post brought an agitated letter from Newcastle to say that he was to do nothing of the kind, that both project and criticism were out of date, and that the Cabinet would insist upon the revocation of Harrington's order.[2] The revocation duly followed, and a few days later Harrington wrote a moderate dispatch about the next campaign and the winter quarters, but evaded Sandwich's request for new instructions as to the terms of a future peace.[3] Newcastle however, on the same day sent him for his information, not direction, the full notes of the Cabinet meeting, together with his own proposals (not yet accepted) as to the altered terms which England should be prepared to accept.[4] In his plan there was to be no neutrality

[1] Harrington to Sandwich, 12 September (o.s.), 1746 (S.P., For., Holland, 421, fo. 48).
[2] Newcastle to Sandwich, 16 September (o.s.)., Add. MSS. 32,805, fo. 259.
[3] Harrington to Sandwich, 19 September (o.s.)., S.P., For., Holland, 421, fo. 72
[4] Newcastle to Sandwich, 19 September (o.s.)., Add MSS. 32,805, fo. 273.

for the Low Countries, however qualified, no establishment for Don Philip, and no surrender of Cape Breton,
even for an equivalent. Sandwich must have been in
some doubt as to how far it would be safe to follow the
suggestions of the sanguine Duke and to go beyond
the directions of his official superior. And his difficulties
were not diminished by the necessity, when he was
absent from The Hague, of entrusting a good deal of
business to Trevor, whom he suspected of a desire to
thwart his designs, and who was all the time carrying
on his own correspondence with Harrington. It must
be remembered that Sandwich, from the outset, was
in close relation with Bentinck and the Orange partisans
in three provinces which resented the predominance of
Holland, and was giving them informal assurances of
English support. On this subject he wrote carefully
concealed letters to Newcastle, who, by way of strengthening himself in his duel with Harrington, secretly
handed them on to the King.[1]

Before Sandwich had time to deal with his new
problems the Conference at Breda had been opened.
Puyzieulx arrived there on 29 September, and Sandwich
adroitly contrived to be there just an hour beforehand.
As Gilles was still detained at The Hague by the accession to his new office, the first discussion was delayed
till 4 October, when the three principal members met in
the residence of the Dutch envoys, Wassenaer being
absent at Utrecht. Puyzieulx opened the proceedings
by producing a bulky document, which Sandwich
assumed to be d'Argenson's project, either revised or
unaltered. Sandwich had succeeded in trapping Gilles

[1] Sandwich's secret letters to Newcastle, all necessarily written
in his own hand, were concealed in ostensible letters, also auto-
graphs, about election questions in Huntingdonshire. Whenever
possible, they were sent by a trusted messenger, but at times
they had to be transmitted by post. Newcastle, very nervous
as to their possible disclosure, wished that a safer mode of conveyance could be found. Sandwich's *feuillets*, as Newcastle called
them, are to be found in the British Museum (Add. MSS. 32,805 and
32,806). Newcastle's own private letters to Sandwich are at
Hinchingbrooke, some written by himself and some by Andrew
Stone, but copies of them are in the same volumes in the British
Museum.

into an admission that Harrington's objections to the project, although in the hands of the two Dutchmen, had never been communicated to France except verbally and informally.[1] As Harrington's letter to Trevor stated England's conditional willingness to cede Cape Breton, and as Sandwich knew that the Dutch wished to tie him down to that cession,[2] the latter was not ill-pleased with the reticence of the Dutch envoys, which he attributed to their excessive complaisance for France. He held that he was no longer bound by what had been said and done in the past, and that it was open to him to propound fresh terms. He would, therefore, anyhow have refused to accept Puyzieulx's version of the French project as a starting-point, but he had at the moment an additional reason for its rejection. He declared that it was useless to consider any details until they had settled the problem of procedure, that the Conference had now become public instead of private, that the allies of England must be consulted on all matters that concerned their interests, and that he proposed the admission of their representatives. Gilles, as had been arranged beforehand, supported the proposal. Puyzieulx, who must have known what was coming, professed to be taken aback by a proposition which was such a complete departure from previous procedure, and from all that the Dutch Ministers had agreed to in Paris on behalf, it was understood, of both the Maritime Powers. He accused Sandwich of a desire to delay and obstruct; otherwise he would be prepared to speak on behalf of his allies, as he, Puyzieulx, was prepared to speak for

[1] Sandwich obtained this admission by observing that France had a great advantage in knowing what our views were before recent events had improved our position. Gilles replied that the English views had never been given to France. Sandwich's secret letter to Newcastle of 16 September (Add. MSS. 32,805, fo. 245).

[2] Sandwich wrote to Newcastle on 30 August that Buys, in an unguarded moment, had said that " it could never be expected that Holland would be easy to see us enrich ourselves in a great branch of commerce, while they themselves are ruined by the loss of their most valuable possessions " (*ibid.*, fo. 207). See also Sandwich to Harrington, 23 September, in S.P., For., Holland, 421, fo. 64.

Spain. This gave Sandwich the dialectical opening for an argument which had been supplied from England. If the French plenipotentiary had powers to speak for Spain, then Spain was represented at the Conference, its character was already altered, and Austria and Sardinia were equally entitled to representation.[1] When Puyzieulx tried to retrace his steps and to minimize his authority from Spain, Sandwich was confirmed in the belief, inspired by Ammon, the Prussian envoy, that such powers as Spain had given were limited to the settlement of affairs in Italy.[2] This increased his obstinacy, and in the end Puyzieulx had to undertake to consult his Court on the question of the admission of other Powers, though he held out no hope of French consent. Sandwich gladly welcomed the delay, so the first round at Breda ended distinctly in his favour. He had put off all discussion of terms, and he had done so by means of a dispute in which the Dutch had supported him, so that the Republic could not make a grievance of the delay. And he had thereby gained time for the arrival of an Austrian Minister, which was doubly important, because the Dutch suspected the Court of Vienna of a desire to prolong the war, and Puyzieulx would certainly use the absence of a representative as proof that the allies were not so eager to take part in the Conference as had been represented. It was quite true that Bartenstein, elated by his recent Russian treaty, was unwilling to make peace at the present moment,[3] and Maria Theresa had no desire to co-operate at Breda with Dutch Ministers who had been so ready to sign away her husband's one possession. But the argument that the coalition must be kept together at last extorted her consent. Her first nominee

[1] Harrington suggested this argument in a dispatch of 19 September (o.s.).

[2] Sandwich reported to Harrington on 26 September that Ammon had told him Puyzieulx had full powers from Spain with regard to Italy, but not for commerce or any non-Italian problem (S.P., For., Holland, 421, fo. 70).

[3] Robinson to Sandwich, 10 September, 1746 (S.P., For., Germany, 174), describes Bartenstein as "the man the most difficult at this court to be brought to think of peace."

was Kaunitz, who had quitted Turin to be a sort of deputy-viceroy in the Netherlands, and when he refused on the ground of ill-health, she sent Ferdinand Harrach,[1] whose brother held high office at Vienna as Chancellor of Bohemia. Sandwich wrote to Robinson to urge Harrach to hasten his journey, as there would be danger in beginning the Conference without him and difficulty in postponing it till he arrived.

While Puyzieulx was waiting for the return of his courier from Versailles, Sandwich broached to Gilles his two supplementary commissions. Permission for the troops to occupy winter quarters in Dutch towns was obtained with unexpected ease,[2] though there were subsequent difficulties about the details of their distribution. The plan of campaign was a more complicated matter, as it required the concurrence of Austria and Sardinia, and in the end the Duke of Cumberland had to come over as a military expert to bring about harmony between the allies. But the mere mooting of these two projects rendered England more dependent upon Holland. It was impossible to ask the Dutch to fix a liberal contingent for a future campaign unless they were immediately gratified by assurances as to the continuance of the Breda Conference. Gilles began to press Sandwich with awkward questions as to what was to be done if Puyzieulx, as was expected, remained obdurate in his objection to the admission of the allies. This was a really serious problem, as the Dutch Ministers were not free agents. When the States, rather reluctantly, consented to allow them to support the proposal for admitting the allies, they had added an express proviso that the negotiations were not to be interrupted pending the arrival of their Ministers, and were not to be broken off on the emergence of any difficulty.[3] Sand-

---

[1] For Harrach's instructions see Arneth, iii., p. 266.

[2] Sandwich wrote to Robinson that leave had been granted on 24 October, 1746. Newcastle complimented Sandwich on his success, and declared that winter quarters " was a point thought impossible to be attained, until you attempted it " (Add. MSS. 32,806, fo. 114).

[3] Trevor sent a French translation of the Resolution on 30 September, 1746. It is in S.P., For., Holland, 420, fo. 80.

wich shrewdly suspected that Puyzieulx knew all about this Resolution, and that it would encourage him to insist upon exclusion. The Frenchman was assured that the Dutchmen were bound to continue in any case, and if England should break away, he would get his separate treaty with Holland, and the alliance of the Maritime Powers, which had been so disastrous to France in the past, would be at an end.

Sandwich was in a distinctly weaker position when the Conference met for the second time on 25 October than he had been at the first meeting. Then he had the support of Gilles; now he knew that, in the last resort, the two Dutchmen were bound to desert him. He had always maintained that the allies could not hold their own with the French plenipotentiary unless they were prepared to take as strong a line as he did, and declare that they would not continue the Conference unless the allied Ministers were admitted. This Wassenaer and Gilles were debarred from doing by their instructions. Fortunately Puyzieulx irritated the Dutch envoys by his unconciliatory tone.[1] He dilated upon the assurances they had given at Paris, taxed them with having deceived him in holding one language to bring him to Breda and then adopting a wholly different system, and declared that they could never have had any other design than to amuse him without thinking of any conclusion. Even Wassenaer, whom Sandwich had always regarded as the weaker vessel, resented this rating, and Sandwich did his best to foment the quarrel. In the end Puyzieulx so far calmed down as to undertake to make a new appeal to his Court, on condition that Sandwich would do the same to London. As soon as the Frenchman had left the room the two Dutch envoys appealed to Sandwich to find some way of getting out of the deadlock, which was due to no fault of theirs, but to the misfortune that they had only received the mutilated copy of the dispatch which Trevor had given to Buys. Sandwich admitted that

[1] D'Argenson in his Memoirs blames the hectoring tone of Puyzieulx at Breda, and contrasts it with his previous conciliatory attitude at The Hague.

they had good reason to believe that England would not insist upon admission, as the incomplete paragraph did " seem to intimate that we meant the invitation only as a matter of form, as that paper had much the appearance of a separate article, in great measure contradictory of what went before it." On the other hand, England had invited the allies to the Conference, and could not honourably withdraw the invitation. The only expedient which Gilles could suggest was that the Conference should be carried on between the three Powers, that everything should be fully communicated to the Ministers of the allies, and that the demand for their admission should be pressed at intervals. Sandwich replied that this could only be accepted with the consent of the allies, and that there must come a stage when they would have to insist upon their admission. To this the Dutchmen replied that the Republic would never undertake not to continue the negotiations without the consent of Austria, as such a pledge would put them absolutely in the hands of that Power. Wassenaer growled that they would have to save themselves, but Gilles " was invariable in his reasoning that no separate measures could have any other consequence than the ruin of both governments."[1] Sandwich was so alarmed by the situation that he began to think that it might be necessary to call in revolutionary forces to avert imminent disaster. In his secret letter to Newcastle, which he wrote on the same day, he said that the dispute might break the Conference, and added the significant phrase, " it is just at this time that I ought to have authority to give assurances of support to the well-meaning." To give point to the phrase he quoted the resolutions of the three well-intentioned provinces— Overyssel, Friesland, and Zealand—which an unnamed friend (almost certainly Bentinck) had extracted for him from the Register with his own hand. The secret of the Register must be rigidly kept.[2]

[1] Sandwich to Harrington, 25 October, 1745 (S.P., For., Holland, 421, fo. 169).
[2] This autograph letter of 25 October is in Add. MSS. 32,806, fo. 124. The resolutions of the three provinces are in *ibid.*, fo. 120.

Sandwich's public dispatch transferred the decision of the problem from Breda to London, as it was quite certain in the circumstances that Versailles would not give way. The pacific members of the Cabinet had no hesitation in accepting the expedient suggested by the Pensionary, and they found a precedent for it in the procedure adopted at Gertruydenberg in 1710, when the Austrian and English Ministers had no direct intercourse with the French, and the Dutch acted as go-betweens. Even Newcastle, the strongest advocate of harmonious action with the allied Powers, did not venture to advocate a breaking off of the Conference, which would have driven the Dutch into separation and frustrated all hope of procuring a creditable termination of the war. As to the suggestions in Sandwich's private letter, Newcastle knew that, whatever his own views might be, he could not induce his colleagues to run the risk of countenancing a premature attempt to bring about a revolution for which no adequate preparations had been made. With characteristic egotism, the Duke actually claimed to have devised the solution of the problem, which Harrington expounded to Sandwich in an official dispatch.[1] What he had done was to propose to the Cabinet the sending to Sandwich of an outline project of possible terms of peace, including the retention of Cape Breton, which his colleagues had rejected. Regardless of this decision, he sent the plan over with his private letter, with the stereotyped caution that he only sent it as a private friend, and that Sandwich must be guided by his public orders through the proper channel.

---

[1] This is so characteristic of Newcastle as to be worth recording. " I just flung out to my brethren last night the getting the consent of Count Harrach and Mr. Chavannes for your Lordship to treat publicly with the French and Dutch Ministers at the conferences, and communicate everything to the Ministers of allies, and concert with them what should be done about it. This proposal was then objected to, but I find it is since adopted, with a very good addition founded upon what was done at the Treaty of Gertruydenberg " (Newcastle to Sandwich, 14 October [o.s.], 1746, in Add. MSS. 32,806, fo. 114). There is something sublime about making this boast to a correspondent who knew that his own dispatch, which was before the Cabinet, had conveyed the suggestion from Gilles.

Sandwich had been afraid that the defeat of Charles of Lorraine at Rocoux would intensify the desire of the Dutch for peace, though he admits that the natural depression was counterbalanced by the sense that the Dutch troops, by their bravery in the battle, had recovered some of the credit which they had lost at Fontenoy. He was therefore relieved when Harrington's dispatch enabled him to conciliate the Dutch by the acceptance of the Gertruydenberg procedure, and was pleased with the evidence of Newcastle's confidence. He wrote to the latter that he was " quite a new person " since the receipt of his last letters, and that, if he succeeded in engaging the States for a new campaign, and in inducing the allied Ministers to consent to the proposed arrangement for their non-admission, he ought to be recalled, as his luck would be exhausted and his head swollen.[1] This complacency received a rude shock when he learned from the Pensionary that Harrington had communicated the decision of the Cabinet to Boetzelaer, the Dutch envoy in London. Sandwich had intended to represent the decision as the reluctant acceptance of a proposal which had been made by Gilles, and to demand in return Dutch assent to his condition that the approval of the allied Courts was necessary before the expedient could be adopted, and also Dutch accession to the plan of campaign. Deprived of this power of striking a bargain by Harrington's indiscreet disclosure, he remonstrated with ill-concealed anger to his official superior and with open indignation in his confidential letter to Newcastle.[2] These letters led to a Ministerial crisis. Newcastle carried the remonstrance to the King, who had detested Harrington ever since that Minister had taken the lead in the February resignations. Harrington taxed his colleague with having encroached upon his department by carrying on a private correspondence with one of his subordinates

[1] Sandwich to Newcastle, 1 November, 1746, in Add. MSS. 32,806, fo. 149.
[2] Sandwich's official letter to Harrington is in S.P., For., Holland, 421, fo. 188, and his private letter to Newcastle in Add. MSS. 32,806, fo. 151.

behind his back. In self-defence, Newcastle sent copies
of his letters to his brother, who sympathized with Harrington, and pointed out that he had carefully abstained
from giving directions to Sandwich and had only written
in his private capacity. Henry Pelham returned the
letters to Andrew Stone, with one of the most humiliating letters ever penned by a man who is included in the
list of British Prime Ministers, and the more astounding
as it was written to a private secretary.

" DEAR SIR,
" I send you back the Duke of Newcastle's private
letters to Lord Sandwich, together with what other
letters I have belonging to your office. I am obliged to
my brother for sending these letters to me, tho' undoubtedly you must know they cannot alter but confirm
me in the opinion I had before. When a minister here
writes to one of Lord Sandwich's consequence and knowledge of the state of affairs in this country, with an
incitement to go on with vigour, with assurances from
the King expressing of protection, with a known and
professed correspondence with some members of the
States, and with an acknowledgment of differences with
the natural correspondent of that province, with communication of papers unknown to some of the King's
servants here but known to be liked by the King; I say,
when this is the case, what avails it to any man of sense
to put in att the end : ' Pray remember I don't give any
orders ' ? I wonder I give you the trouble of these
remarks, but when I am alone, and consider seriously
our situation and the way in which we are going on,
I am too full of concern to have it in my power to act
as discretion should direct me. I see others can command themselves, if they take care not to put any thing
under their hands which they may be answerable for.
I am not fitt for the task that is put upon me. I have
too much private regard for my friends to do an act
which might commit them and put their affairs into confusion. On the other hand I have pride enough to be
terribly hurt att the necessity I see coming upon me to
appear to the world without the least influence in His
Majesty's councils, or attended to in any other manner
than to get the better of a dispute, or get rid of a scold,
or to secure payment of expenses contracted I don't

know how or when. *This* is the true state of the *case*, and *this* is desired to be the *case*. Forgive me, dear Stone, that I do so often repeat these things to you; if you could relieve me, I feel sure you would; but, as it is not in your power, it is some comfort to flatter myself that, tho' you may differ with me in my manner of acting and behaving, which I believe you do, yet you cannot, when you consider, differ very much in the matter which I have related to you, and that is all I can or ought to hope from one in your situation, let me be never so much, what I truly am, Dear Sir,

" Your most affectionate and faithfull servant,
                              " H. PELHAM."[1]

As Harrington could expect no help from so pusil-lanimous a Premier, he carried his complaint to the King, only to learn that his master had been a party to the whole of the private correspondence, and thoroughly approved of it. This was a last blow. It was bad enough that Newcastle should get secret letters from Sandwich for his own guidance; it was far worse that he should use them to guide the King. Harrington, not unnaturally, insisted upon resigning the seals, and Newcastle, without any consultation with his brother, induced the King to transfer them to Chesterfield, whose vice-royalty of Ireland was given as a solatium to Harrington. Why Newcastle nominated Chesterfield, why the King cheerfully accepted a man for whom he had always expressed his detestation, and why Chester-field took the office in conditions which virtually sub-ordinated him to a colleague whom he soon came to detest and despise, are problems which have never been adequately solved. Since the formation of the Ministry, Newcastle and Chesterfield had conducted a constant and fairly intimate correspondence while the latter was away at The Hague and Dublin, but their letters only serve to show the disagreement between their views. There must have been some bargain between the two men before they struck up that temporary alliance

---

[1] This autograph letter must have been communicated by Stone to the Duke, as it is to be found in the Newcastle Papers, Add. MSS. 32,709, fo. 65.

which startled contemporaries as much as it has puzzled later students of the period. And internal evidence makes it certain that the bargain must have included a promise on Chesterfield's part to use his knowledge of Dutch politics for the benefit of Bentinck and his friends. This, together with Newcastle's confident belief at the time that the Lisbon negotiation was going to bring about an agreement with Spain, would serve to explain why Newcastle refused at this time the King's suggestion that he should exchange the Southern for the Northern Department, which would free his correspondence with Sandwich from hostile criticism or supervision. And the assumption of some such bargain is necessary to explain the complacency with which Newcastle announced the change in the secretaryship to his fellow-conspirator at Breda. " I am persuaded your Lordship will be very well pleased with your new correspondent. . . . As it will be for the King's service and agreeable to your own inclination to write to my Lord Chesterfield upon all occasions with the utmost confidence and without the least reserve, I would by no means give your Lordship the trouble of writing so frequently to me as you have done."[1] Some three weeks later, with characteristic inconsistency, Newcastle complained that Sandwich was neglecting him by not writing, and enlarged upon the relations between the two Secretaries of State.

" You have every reason to be pleased with your new correspondent, but I have the vanity to think you have the obligation entirely to me; for the King was not only so gracious as to offer me, several times, to make any one Secretary of State whom I should recommend (and determined upon my Lord Chesterfield upon my recommendation), but His Majesty was pleased, for some days, to press me in the strongest manner to take the northern department, alledging to me how necessary it was that I should have the pen in my own hands, and how much trouble I had had in combating and disputing the work of others. [Newcastle

[1] Newcastle to Sandwich, private, 21 October (o.s.), 1746, in Add. MSS. 32,806, fo. 168.

replied that he and Chesterfield were in such agreement
that it made no difference who had the Northern Department.] And indeed Lord Chesterfield is so good
in writing all his letters in concert with me, that it is
just the same thing who has the pen; and your Lordship sees that the publick letters from the office now
are entirely agreeable to the private thoughts I used
to fling out to you in our private correspondence; and
for that reason I shall not trouble you with any business."[1]

The Ministerial change in England was an event
of substantial importance, though it only involved
the exchange of offices between two men, who remained
Ministers of the Crown. It emphasized the curious
ascendancy which Newcastle had gained in the Cabinet,
it weakened for some months the partisans of peace,
and it proved dangerous to the republican constitution
of the United Provinces. It also immensely added to
the importance of Sandwich. He received from Chesterfield his credentials to the Dutch Government, and, as
Trevor took this as a notice to quit, he was congratulated by Newcastle on becoming the sole English representative at The Hague. The peace plan, which Newcastle had secretly sent him some weeks ago, now came
to him with official sanction, though he decided to make
no use of it in the meantime, as some of the articles,
especially that which provided for the retention of Cape
Breton, were not likely to go down with the Dutch.
He was able, however, to take a firmer line in other
matters than he had done before, as he could reckon
upon Chesterfield's support for Bentinck in case it
should be necessary to employ strong measures to
keep the Dutch faithful to the English alliance.[2]

[1] Newcastle to Sandwich, private, 14 November (o.s.), 1746,
in Add. MSS. 32,806, fo. 202. An intermediate private letter
on 4 November (o.s.) contains the significant remark, "Your
friend [Bentinck] will now see that he may trust us, and now is
the time for him to improve his credit with the Republic" (*ibid.*,
fo. 177).
[2] The evidence for this is to be found at Hinchingbrooke, where
there are several private letters from Chesterfield to Sandwich,
which have so far escaped notice. From one of these, dated
18 November (o.s.), 1746, I extract this salient paragraph:

The third meeting of the Conference was held at Breda on 18 November, when Sandwich propounded the Gertruydenberg expedient as the only means of reconciling the French demand for the exclusion of the allied Ministers with the invitation which England had addressed to them. At the same time he proposed that acceptance of the expedient should be made easier for those Ministers by the transference of the Conference from Breda to The Hague. If Puyzieulx had been his own master, he would have broken off the negotiation at this stage, and enforced his threat that the French would attack Maestricht, now that that town had forfeited all claim to neutrality by the admission of troops belonging to the belligerent Powers. He was convinced that Spain was on the verge of making a separate peace at Lisbon, and that the negotiations at Breda were only continued in order to save Holland from a French invasion. But Puyzieulx was still bound to follow the letter of his instructions from d'Argenson, though he had ceased to observe their spirit. D'Argenson was assured in his own mind that Ferdinand VI, whose coming to the throne he had welcomed as involving the downfall of his personal enemy, Elizabeth Farnese, would never desert France, and that the acces-

---

" Bentinck's brother, I hear, has a fair chance of overturning the Rechleren interest in Overyssel: I wish that may happen. And, if it should, might it not be possible to improve that event to the advantage of the Prince of Orange, and consequently to ours ? His being made Stadhouder of that province, if it were possible to bring it about, would give him a plurality of provinces, and might be a step to *something else.* You may, therefore, in the utmost secrecy and confidence, tell our common friend, Bentinck, that though, in the present critical and delicate situation of affairs, it would be highly imprudent for us to appear, or even to be suspected of being in the least concerned in a matter of that nature, yet, if a sum of money not exceeding ten or twelve thousand pounds, secretly and properly distributed, would secure that affair in Overyssel, I will take care that that sum shall be forthcoming. I am sure I need not recommend either to you or to Bentinck the strictest secrecy and the most scrupulous circumspection in so nice an affair. Pray let me know likewise how you find the Prince of Orange's interest in the province of Holland. Does it rise or fall ? It was but low when I was there." This letter was more outspoken than Newcastle had ever ventured to be on paper.

sion of the new King, who was a nephew of Charles
Emmanuel on the mother's side, would facilitate his
favourite scheme of detaching Sardinia from the hostile
coalition.   He was equally convinced that the Dutch
were sincere in their desire for peace, that this would
be checked rather than stimulated by aggressive action
on the part of France, and that Dutch pressure would
in the end overcome any reluctance that might be
shown by England.   At all events, if the Breda Conference was to be fruitless, the blame for breaking it off
must not be incurred by France.   He had already
repented of having consented to the admission of the
direct participation of England, and to the consequent
transfer of the negotiation from Versailles to Breda.
And he had been resolute in his refusal to turn the
Conference into a Congress by the admission of Austrian
and Sardinian Ministers.[1]   But he had no objection to
the compromise which was now put forward, and,
indeed, was inclined to welcome it as inflicting a humiliation upon the Court of Vienna.[2]   He even went so far as
to suggest to Madrid that Spain should send an envoy to
Breda to co-operate with Puyzieulx in the same manner
as it was proposed that Harrach and Chavanne were to
aid the representatives of the Maritime Powers.   This
suggestion was destined to have rather disastrous results
for France, but they came after d'Argenson had ceased
to hold office, and he was sanguine enough to think that
he could have averted them.   Meanwhile, his instructions compelled Puyzieulx to accept Sandwich's proposal and to give a sullen consent to another suspension
of the Conference until it could be ascertained whether
Austria and Sardinia would agree to the expedient.
He showed his discontent by indignantly rejecting
d'Argenson's suggestion that he should spend the

[1] His letter to Puyzieulx on this subject of 19 October is quoted
by Broglie, *Saxe et d'Argenson*, i., p. 30.   His objections are
summarized in his *Journal et Mémoires*, iv., p. 352.

[2] Broglie (*op. cit.*, ii., p. 137) calls the compromise an " arrangement bâtard inventé par d'Argenson."   It may have occurred to
him independently, but there can be no doubt that, as a practicable
scheme, it was suggested in Holland, adopted by England, and
pressed by England at Vienna and Turin.

interval in strengthening his hold upon the Dutch Ministers by paying a second visit to The Hague. He objected with some force that it would be indecent for a French plenipotentiary to be present while the Duke of Cumberland was in the Dutch capital arranging with other allied generals for a new campaign against France.

Sandwich had scored another diplomatic success, and had by this time become a person of some note in Europe. Puyzieulx wrote of him disdainfully as " un blanc bec qui réunit l'esprit des belles-lettres à peu d'expérience et beaucoup de pédanterie," but the keen-eyed Frenchman saw through Newcastle's design of gaining time for the negotiation at Lisbon, and was angry that his instructions made it impossible for him to foil it.[1] Sandwich had done all that he had been instructed to do. He had again postponed all serious business on the question of procedure, as it would take five or six weeks to get the necessary answers from Vienna and Turin. In view of French consent, it was impossible for Gilles to adhere to his protest that the demand for the approval of Vienna would place the Republic at the mercy of Austrian caprice. In order to complete the partial triumph of England, it was neces-sary to induce the two allied Courts to waive their dignity and allow the exclusion of their Ministers from a Conference to which they had been invited. Sand-wich put all the pressure he could upon Harrach and Chavanne, and wrote urgent letters to Robinson and Villettes, while Newcastle and Chesterfield supplemented these letters and dealt personally with Osorio and Wasner. Sandwich, as usual, found Chavanne more inclined to be accommodating than Harrach, though neither could venture to pledge his Court without express permission. But, to the surprise of both Sand-wich and the English Ministers, Turin proved more

---

[1] When Sandwich asserted that George II desired peace, Puyzieulx replied: " Oui, my lord, il la veut avec l'Espagne et non avec nous, et tant que votre maître aura l'espérance de conclure quelque chose à Lisbonne, il vous fera jouer ici le rôle d'un soliveau " (Puyzieulx to d'Argenson, 7 October, 1746, quoted by Broglie, *op. cit.*, ii., p. 33).

obstinate than Vienna. Ulfeld and Bartenstein growled to Robinson that the proposal was an intolerable insult to Austria. Nevertheless, the English argument that refusal would drive the Dutch into a separate peace with France, and that this would render it impossible for England to continue the war, was not easy to answer. The argument was reinforced by resolutions of the provincial estates of Friesland and Overyssel demanding a speedy settlement, if possible with the assent of England, but if not then without it. The resolution of the estates of Friesland was the more significant because it was carried in the teeth of a protest from their Stadtholder, the Prince of Orange.[1] Austria also was engaged in what were regarded as promising negotiations at Lisbon, and as long as there was hope of gaining Spain, it was desirable to keep the Breda Conference going.[2] So at last Robinson was able to announce that Maria Theresa would consent to the continuance of the Conference, and withdraw her demand for its transference to The Hague, on condition that Harrach was kept fully informed of all that was going on, and that nothing that touched Austrian interests

[1] The news from Friesland was communicated to Chesterfield in the letter of a private correspondent, from which he sent the following extract to Sandwich on 18/29 November, 1746: " La Frise vient de prendre, par pluralité et malgré l'opposition du Prince d'Orange, son Stadhouder, et du Quartier des Villes, une Resolution bien étrange, et voici le précis. Cette Province y declare que considéré l'état deplorable de ses finances, et qui dans peu même ne lui permettra pas de payer les troupes qui se trouvent sur sa répartition, et que la continuation de la guerre entraineroit bientôt sa ruine totale, elle croît et prétend qu'il ne reste à la République que de redoubler ses efforts pour se procurer la paix, qu'on doit concerter pour cet effet avec la Grande Bretagne les mesures necessaires et constater un plan raisonnable, mais que, si inopinement cela souffre des difficultés, ou qu'on ne voit pas jour pour à y réussir, *la Republique se doit accommoder toute seule* le mieux qu'il luy sera possible, et que c'est l'unique moyen de se retirer du precipice où l'on se plonge de plus en plus " (S.P., For., Holland, 421, fo. 247. See also 422, fo. 18, and Chesterfield to Robinson, same date, in S.P., For., Germany, 175). The resolution was in itself alarming, but it was timely as an argument to be addressed to Harrach and Chavanne. The estates of Gelderland passed a similar resolution (*ibid.*, fo. 253).

[2] Robinson to Chesterfield, 30 October, 1746, in S.P., For., Germany, 175.

should be settled without her consent. Charles Emmanuel, on the other hand, anticipating a refusal on the part of Austria, expressed the strongest disapprobation of the proposal, and then succumbed to such a severe attack of smallpox that all business had to be withheld from him. As his Ministers refused to take any action without royal sanction, the whole business at Breda was held up by the negative attitude of Sardinia.[1] This was a serious matter for Sandwich, who had by this time, with the help of Cumberland, the accepted Commander-in-Chief in the Netherlands, completed an ambitious convention as to the forces which were to be supplied by each of the allied Powers for the next campaign. The Dutch would not agree to this unless they were assured that the peace Conference would continue, and this assurance could not be given as long as Turin held out. Sandwich, on his side, refused to go to Breda until the convention was signed.[2] In this dilemma Sandwich made a final appeal to Chavanne, who at last undertook, in view of the emergency and of the unexpected assent of Vienna, to assume that the approval of his Court had been obtained.[3] Sandwich was exultant. He got his military convention signed on 12 January, 1747,[4] and he was now ready to proceed to Breda. The question of pro-

[1] Sandwich to Villettes, 30 December, 1746 (S.P., For., Holland, 422, fo. 190), contrasts the docility of Vienna with the obstinacy of Turin, the exact opposite of what he had expected.

[2] Sandwich to Chesterfield, 3 January, 1747 (ibid., 424, fo. 1): "I have the satisfaction to think that I have made my bare return to Breda and my resolution to open the negotiation immediately the price of the conclusion of all measures relative to the next campaign."

[3] Sandwich reported his success to Chesterfield on 13 January (ibid., fo. 51). He says that Chavanne, in deference to his urgent representations, "determined to take upon himself tacitly to acquiesce in my going to Breda to open the Conference, upon my engaging to report to him regularly everything that passes in the negotiation in the same method as I shall observe with regard to Count Harrach." The Court of Turin approved of Chavanne's conduct as soon as its *amour propre* was satisfied by the assent of Vienna (Villettes to Robinson, 29 January, 1747, in S.P., For., Germany, 176).

[4] The text of the Convention is in Přibram, *Oesterreiche Staatsverträge, England*, i., pp. 736–51. Chavanne did not sign it till 22 February.

cedure had at last been solved, and he had now to face the problem of serious discussions as to the terms of peace. He had for nearly three months had Newcastle's ideas on the subject, and these had since, by Chesterfield's complacence, been transformed into something like official instructions. Their receipt had elated him so much that he declared it to be the happiest day in his life,[1] because he was freed from the original obligation, which he had come to regard as irksome and humiliating, to take everything merely *ad referendum* without any power of settlement. On the other hand, he had not made much progress, in his conferences with Gilles, towards any joint plan of preliminary terms to put forward at Breda. He had ascertained that the Dutchman desired some kind of neutrality for the Netherlands, and he had known all along that he would not support the retention of Cape Breton by England. For this reason he determined that, so far as he could control the order of discussion, these contentious topics should be kept till the last. He was fully conscious of the danger of entering a peace Conference in conjunction with an allied Power without any agreement as to the conditions upon which they were prepared to insist. But good luck had hitherto befriended him,[2] and he trusted with the confidence of youth that it would not desert him. It was in his favour that during the winter he had gained the warm approval of Cumberland, and that he could look for encouragement and advice in his task to the Commander-in-Chief.

While Sandwich was skilfully procrastinating at Breda and settling his military convention at The Hague, important events, both military and civil, were

[1] Sandwich to Chesterfield, 13 December, 1746 (S.P., For., Holland, 422, fo. 38).

[2] In one of his infrequent private letters to Newcastle at this time (28 December, 1746) Sandwich contends that it was extremely fortunate that the French objected to the admission of the allied Ministers. If they had consented and the Conference had begun in September, it would have been necessary to satisfy the Dutch on such questions as Cape Breton and the neutrality before they would have entered into any concert for a new campaign, whereas now "the price of military measures is barely the continuance of the Conference " (Add. MSS. 32,806, fo. 279).

14

taking place in Europe. There was no great change in the Netherlands after Rocoux. The French troops had not yet invaded Dutch territory, but they were in winter quarters near the border and could cross it at pleasure unless the allies should be able to raise a superior army to resist them. But in Italy very notable events occurred. The Battle of Piacenza in June and the surrender of the town and fortress in August were decisive as to the issue of the Italian war. Unless France was prepared to forfeit her superiority in Belgium in order to carry out the Treaty of Fontainebleau, there was practically no hope of gaining the proposed establishment for Don Philip by military force. It was more likely, if the Court of Vienna could get its own way, that his brother would have difficulty in retaining the Crown of Naples. The chance that the Gallispans might retain any part of their recent conquests was not improved by the successive deaths of Philip V and his daughter, the Dauphine, which seemed likely to put an end to the Family Compact. It was not easy, from the scanty and often conflicting reports, to gather what was going on at Madrid during the early months of Ferdinand VI's reign. Europe expected a complete change of policy from a King who was a nephew of the King of Sardinia, and from a Queen, supposed to rule her husband, who was a first cousin of Maria Theresa and brought up at Lisbon in traditions of friendship with both England and Austria. The expectation grew into assurance when Louis XV, pleading religious scruples, refused the offer of Ferdinand VI to send the Infanta Antonia to take the place of her deceased sister as the wife of the Dauphin. Vauréal at Madrid and all the partisans of Spain at the French Court, with Noailles at their head, advocated the marriage as necessary for the maintenance of the Spanish alliance. Ferdinand contended that a Papal dispensation would remove all religious difficulties. But Louis XV remained firm, and d'Argenson tried to buttress his declining credit by supporting the King with the arguments that French public opinion would be outraged if the heir to the throne should marry his late wife's sister, and that

France was never partial to Papal intervention. The King and his Minister were so far justified that, though Ferdinand did not conceal his chagrin at the rejection of his half-sister, the threatened rupture of the alliance did not follow. This would have required more energy and initiative than were to be found at Madrid. For thirty years Elizabeth Farnese had filled all offices in Spain with her creatures, and her stepson had neither the experience nor the strength of character to effect any immediate change in his Ministry. Spain was not yet prepared to break away from France. But the prophets of evil were not without some justification. There was a general assumption in Spain that the policy of the new Court would be wholly Spanish, and not French as in the later years of Philip V. D'Argenson might complacently assert that *être bon Espagnol, c'est être bon Français*, but this view was not prevalent at Madrid. There were Spaniards who recalled the days when Spain had fought against Louis XIV in alliance with Austria and the Maritime Powers.

The new spirit in Spain did affect its foreign policy, especially as regards Italy. One of Ferdinand's first acts was to send Las Minas, no friend of France, to supersede Gages as commander of the Spanish troops, and it was evident from the conduct of the new general that he had orders not to waste his forces in what had become a futile campaign. As the Spaniards were more numerous than the French, and the latter were in Italy rather auxiliaries than principals, Maillebois had to conform to the aims of his colleague. The retreat which he guided has been described by military experts as masterly, but it might have been rendered impossible or extremely hazardous and costly but for the discord between the Sardinian King and the Austrian General. Lichtenstein, who had won the original Battle of Piacenza, had been compelled by ill-health to resign his command, and the misfortune of seniority gave the succession to the Marquis Botta d'Adorno, who had returned to a military career after a disastrous experience as a diplomatist in Russia. Charles Emmanuel had the lowest opinion of Botta's character and capacity,[1] and, since the unfortunate negotiation with d'Argenson, no Austrian, from Maria Theresa downwards, had any trust in the fidelity of the Sardinian King. This discord enabled the Gallispans to retire with comparative impunity along the Riviera to Provence. Garrisons were left at Tortona in Piedmont and at Ventimiglia on the frontier, but neither could offer more than a temporary resistance. For all practical purposes Italy was evacuated. Genoa, deserted by the allies, surrendered to Botta, who avenged his father's exile by imposing the most humiliating conditions upon the unfortunate Republic.

The complete triumph of the allies in Italy was welcomed in England as a set-off to the disasters in the Netherlands, and also as promising to get rid of one of the formidable obstacles in the way of an agreed peace, the joint Bourbon demand that Don Philip should be endowed with a principality in Italy. It also offered an irresistible temptation to renew a plan, which Eugene and Marlborough had concerted in 1707, to invade France through Provence and capture the French naval base at Toulon. Such an enterprise, it was thought, would complete English naval supremacy in the Mediterranean, and at the same time, by compelling France to detach troops from the Netherlands, would give the Duke of Cumberland, if Sandwich could obtain his military convention, a decisive superiority of force in the forthcoming campaign. Newcastle threw himself into this project with even more than his accustomed impetuosity and optimism. He held that England was " entitled to demand some recompense for the disproportionate burthen that the war has laid upon this country."[2] But he found it no easy matter to enforce this demand. Neither Austria nor Sardinia was eager to embark on an enterprise to which they were bound by no treaty obligation. Their task under the Treaty

[1] Villettes wrote to Newcastle on 25 August, 1746, that Botta " is looked upon here to want the open frankness of a soldier and to be made up of the double dealing and all the artful cunning of an Italian Minister " (S.P., For., Sardinia, 51).

[2] Newcastle to Villettes, 26 September (o.s.), 1746 (S.P., For., Sardinia, 51).

of Worms had been to resist the Bourbon invasion of Italy, and this they had triumphantly completed. They were now entitled to their reward under the treaty— Austria to the expulsion of the Bourbons from the peninsula by the reduction of Naples, and Sardinia to the Marquisate of Finale and as much more as possible of the Genoese Riviera. Charles Emmanuel employed his main forces on the siege of Savona, and when that citadel fell he would be master of the whole Riviera di Ponente. Nothing but the threat that English subsidies could only be earned by compliance with English wishes, and the bribe that compliance would be met by increased payments, could overcome the reluctance of the two states to abandon or even to postpone the gratification of their own desires. Austria was the first to give way. It was not easy for Maria Theresa to combine her negotiation with Spain at Lisbon with an attack upon the Spanish King's brother at Naples, though she had a strong conviction in her own mind that such an attack was really the best method of forcing Spain to come to terms.[1] Also a Neapolitan expedition required the co-operation of the English fleet, which could not be obtained in the face of English disapproval. So Austria undertook to put off the reduction of Naples for the present, and made a great parade of her willingness to gratify England in contrast to the stubborn selfishness of Sardinia. Charles Emmanuel was much more difficult to deal with. He did not believe that the expedition would be successful, or that it would lead to any substantial withdrawal of French forces from the Netherlands. He declared that he was not at war with France, that he did not wish needlessly to provoke French hostility, and that if his troops invaded French territory they could only do so as auxiliaries of the Empress. In any case, he would not undertake the command, as the Treaty of Worms only gave him the position of Commander-in-Chief for the war in Italy. Nothing but his pecuniary and other obligations to England would induce him to contribute any troops to the expeditionary force, and these

[1] See below p. 211, n. 2.

could only be a small portion of his army, as he needed his men for the sieges of Savona and Tortona, and also for the defence of his frontier against the Spanish forces which were wintering in Savoy.[1]

To these initial difficulties was added the outbreak of a violent quarrel between Austria and Sardinia. It began with a revival of all the old suspicions at Vienna when it was learned that d'Argenson was endeavouring once more to conciliate Charles Emmanuel, this time by the suggestion that the Dauphin, following the Bourbon tradition which had always looked to the House of Savoy as a nursery of brides, might take as his second wife one of the King's daughters. Again the services of Mongardino were called in, and overtures, more or less formal, were made to the Sardinian Court. Charles Emmanuel was undoubtedly tempted, but family ambition was not enough to induce him to embark on a second Turin agreement. In December, 1745, he had been on the verge of ruin : in the following September he had achieved unexpected success. He was willing to give his daughter, but he must retain his present allies.[2] This was not enough for d'Argenson, and Louis XV put a stop to the negotiation by declaring that his son could not marry a bride who would require a safe-conduct to come to the wedding. The Dauphin had to send to Dresden for his second wife. The disappointment of Charles Emmanuel did not put an end to the Austrian

---

[1] These objections were summarized by Villettes to Newcastle in an immense letter on 30 September, 1746 (S.P., For., Sardinia, 51). Villettes had reached the Sardinian headquarters by sea, as ill-health made him unable to endure the hardships of the land journey.

[2] Villettes to Newcastle, 25 August, 1746 (S.P., For., Sardinia, 51), says that he had seen two letters from Mongardino, and had discussed them with the King and Gorzegno. " As far as I am able to judge by what passed with both, I do not think there is any reason to apprehend this Court will be so intoxicated with hopes of placing a daughter on the throne of France as to sacrifice the least point of their interest for it. Count Mongardin has been ordered to repeat the declarations he has already made to that effect, and to give the French Minister plainly to understand that tho' this new type of alliance be extremely agreeable to his Sardinian Majesty, it should never tempt him to act contrary to his engagements with his allies."

contention that his meditated disloyalty to the alliance was enough to forfeit the cessions made to him by the Treaty of Worms. At the same time, Sardinian claims to make and keep conquests on the coast provoked vehement protests from Vienna. Was this faithless ally to emerge, with Prussia, as one of the sole gainers by the war? If Sardinia took the Riviera di Ponente, Austria must have the Riviera di Levante. Meanwhile, Sardinia retaliated with more concrete charges. The surrender of Piacenza had been made to Austrian troops, and Austria took the whole of the captured artillery and other spoils. Charles Emmanuel claimed that half should be given to him. But the most acrimonious quarrel arose over the capitulation of Genoa to Botta, and the terms which Botta had exacted. If this was a civil treaty, it was a breach of the fourth article of the Treaty of Worms, which forbade any agreement with the enemy except in concert with the allies. If it was a military act, it required the sanction of Charles Emmanuel, who, by the sixth article of the treaty, was Commander-in-Chief of the allied forces in Italy. Either way, it was monstrous that Austria should levy for her own profit an immense indemnity upon the city in complete disregard of the services rendered by Sardinian troops and by the English fleet. Villettes, rather incautiously, was equally loud in denouncing the transaction as an insult to England as well as to Sardinia,[1] and induced Townshend, the naval commander, to disregard the capitulation and to continue the blockade on the ground that Genoa, having made no terms with England, was still an enemy Power. Newcastle, who had the strongest reasons for deprecating any quarrel

[1] Villettes to Robinson, 12 September, 1746, in S.P., For., Sardinia, 51, and *ibid.*, Germany, 174. Robinson was inclined to resent the terms which Villettes wished him to use in a representation to the Court of Vienna. It was not the first time that the two envoys had come into collision, each being inclined to criticize the other's Court. Chesterfield and Newcastle implored them to lay aside their differences, and urged that each should behave in his own Court as if he was the Minister of the other. This was a counsel of perfection and not easy to follow, as it would have made both extremely unpopular at their Court of residence.

at this juncture, reprimanded Villettes and sent Byng to the Mediterranean to supersede Townshend. Villettes consumed quires of paper in grovelling apologies. Austria, meanwhile, vigorously defended the conduct of Botta, and complained both of the language employed by Villettes and of the continued blockade of Genoa after the city had passed into Austrian occupation. As to Piacenza, Austria refused to admit that Sardinia had any just claim, but, at last, under pressure from England, offered *ex gratia* a third in place of a half of the spoil, an offer which Sardinia spurned as another insult. This squabbling about a fraction was bitterly denounced by the English peacemakers.

All this made it extremely difficult to adjust any agreement as to sending an army into Provence. It was not till the end of September that a convention settled that Austria should furnish two-thirds of the force and Sardinia one-third, proportions which were designed to show that Turin regarded the enterprise as standing wholly outside the Treaty of Worms. The command was entrusted to Browne, the most energetic of the Austrian generals, while Botta remained behind at Genoa. Charles Emmanuel accompanied the force during the reduction of Ventimiglia and the advance to Nice. Any attempt to induce him to reconsider his refusal of the command was rendered impossible both by the disproportion of his own to the Austrian contingent and by the King's subsequent illness. It was not till late in November that Browne crossed the Var at the head of some thirty thousand men. There never was any reasonable hope that such a force could take Toulon or make any substantial impression upon France. And any small chance of success was practically destroyed by events in Genoa. Botta had infuriated the citizens, but he had failed to take the elementary precaution of disarming them. The result was that between the 7th and the 11th of December a street riot grew into a formidable rising which compelled Botta to beat an ignominious retreat from the city which he had mal-treated. Until Genoa could be retaken, the troops in Provence were cut off from direct land communication with Italy, and had to get all their supplies by sea. The English Ministers were now as loud in their denunciation of the original capitulation as the Sardinians had been, and insisted that no such one-sided compact should be made in the future.[1] Even the sedate Lord Hardwicke wrote to Newcastle : " I wish Botta had been hanged when the Czarina would have had him hanged."[2] In Vienna Botta's earlier career was also recalled, and he was declared to be the evil genius of the House of Habsburg. But the merciful Maria Theresa was content to recall him and to entrust the command in Italy to Schulenburg.

While Newcastle all along based his most confident hopes upon the invasion of Provence, he had always a second string to his bow in the negotiations at Lisbon.[3] As soon as the news of Philip V's death reached England he had sent out the Marquis de Tabernuiga as a private agent of his own, in order to pave the way for Benjamin Keene, who was selected as a *persona grata et cognita* at Madrid. Tabernuiga was a Spanish noble, who had incurred the displeasure of Philip V and Elizabeth Farnese by questioning the legality of Philip's resumption of the crown on the death of his elder son, and maintaining that it should have passed to the younger son,

[1] On 23 December (o.s.) Chesterfield wrote to Robinson that Sardinia had complained, " and indeed not without some reason, of the impropriety (not to say the injustice) of that capitulation in which he, tho' an ally, and a very necessary ally, was neither consulted nor even mentioned " (S.P., For., Germany, 157). This was the sort of language for which poor Villettes had been severely reprimanded. Robinson was to urge that nothing similar should take place when Genoa was once more subdued.
[2] Hardwicke to Newcastle, 26 December (o.s.), 1746, in Add. MSS. 32,709, fo. 383. This refers to a famous episode in Russia. In 1743 a conspiracy to depose Elizabeth was discovered or invented, and Botta, previously Austrian Ambassador, was said to be implicated. The Tsaritsa demanded that Botta should be punished, and Maria Theresa's reluctance to admit the guilt of her representative led to a bitter and prolonged quarrel between the two rulers.
[3] For some unexplained reason, the Lisbon correspondence during the later months of 1746 is missing from the Portuguese State Papers at the Record Office. Fortunately the letters to and from Keene, and in addition the unofficial correspondence of Tabernuiga, are preserved in the Newcastle Papers (Add. MSS. 32,806–32,808).

Ferdinand. Now that Ferdinand was actually King, it was thought that this former offence would be counted to the credit of the Marquis, and that he might confidently reckon on his recall to favour at Madrid. Tabernuiga arrived at Lisbon in August, and persuaded the Spanish Ambassador to transmit a letter to Villarias, the chief Minister at Madrid, in which he demanded pardon for his conduct in the late reign, due to misinformed but well-meant zeal for the present King, and offered to earn his pardon by bringing about a reconciliation between Spain and England, based upon the security of Don Carlos in Naples and an establishment in Italy for Don Philip.[1] It must be remembered that when Tabernuiga left London the full extent of the allied successes in Italy was neither known nor foreseen. To this letter Villarias replied that the Marquis must not come to Madrid for fear of exciting suspicion in France,[2] that Spain would gladly come to terms with England as a step towards a general peace, and that the one essential condition was an *établissement convenable* for Don Philip.[3] Tabernuiga, himself a Spaniard, thought this a very reasonable demand, especially if England could, by extorting Austrian consent, purchase the recovery of the lost commercial concessions and the retention of Cape Breton.[4] And he explained that Spanish insistence upon the gratification of Don Philip was due to the desire of the new King to keep his too powerful half-brother at a distance from Madrid. As Admiral-General of Spain, Don Philip had the appointment of all naval officers, in addition to an immense revenue derived

[1] Tabernuiga to Villarias, 17 August, 1746, in Add. MSS. 32,806, fo. 25.
[2] D'Argenson (v., p. 30) says that the refusal to recall Tabernuiga was due to his remonstrances.
[3] Villarias to Tabernuiga, 26 August, in Add. MSS. 32,806, fo. 18.
[4] Tabernuiga to Newcastle, 5 September (*ibid.*, fo. 31): " Il faut contenter ce digne monarque dans le commencement de son règne. . . . L'Imperatrice-Reine ne peut pas manquer de se preter à donner cette preuve de reconnaissance à l'Angleterre, si Sa Majesté Britannique s'interresse pour cet établissement. . . . Est ce que Cap Breton ne restera pour toujours dans le pouvoir des Anglais." It is clear that the Marquis had grasped what was then the dearest object of the English Ministry.

from a 4 per cent. duty upon all imports and exports, with a gold pistole for every ship, large or small, that anchored off the coast of Spain. With such power, added to his rank as an Infant and as a son-in-law of the French King, it would be easy for him to form a powerful party with his younger brother, the Archbishop of Toledo and Seville, under the guidance of their mother, the formidable Queen-Dowager. It was only natural that the King should not desire to have so formidable a rival near his throne.[1] Tabernuiga might have added, if he had dared to commit it to paper, that the King's health was very uncertain, that both he and his wife were believed to be incapable of having children,[2] and that no self-interested Spaniard would venture too far in thwarting the wishes of Elizabeth Farnese, when her domination might at any moment be restored by the actual accession of one of her own sons.

Keene's official instructions, dated 11 August, the same day as those which Harrington gave to Sandwich, were extremely guarded.[3] On the two vital questions

[1] Tabernuiga to Newcastle, 21 September (*ibid.*, fo. 46).

[2] It is noteworthy that in all subsequent negotiations it was taken for granted that Ferdinand VI would leave no issue, and that Don Carlos would succeed him. But for this assumption, the settlement about Don Philip would have been even more difficult than it was. On this subject there are at Hinchingbrooke some letters between Bentinck and Fagel, when the former was at Aix-la-Chapelle. Bentinck wrote on 10 April, 1748, that he had questioned St. Severin as to what would happen if Ferdinand VI should outlive his wife and marry again. St. Severin replied that the impotence was on the King's part, that the late King had summoned a French surgeon to perform an operation on his son, but it had been unsuccessful. On the following day he added that Chavanne, who had been in Madrid at the time, confirmed St. Severin's story as to an operation, but declared that it had been successful, and that he had conclusive female evidence to that effect. Enemies of Elizabeth Farnese declared that the object of the operation was dictated by her, and was the complete opposite of that indicated by St. Severin. D'Argenson, *Journal et Mémoires*, v., p. 18: " Encore prétend on que de jeunesse il avait été maltraité par les chirurgiens de cette marâtre et rendu incapable d'avoir postérité."

[3] Keene's instructions are neither in the Record Office nor in the Newcastle Papers, but a copy, which was subsequently sent to Sandwich, may be read in S.P., For., Holland, 424, fo. 148.

of the security of Don Carlos and possible cessions to
Don Philip, he might proffer the King's good offices,
but nothing more. He was to make no sacrifice of the
commercial privileges of England. His main object was
to ascertain the conditions upon which Spain was willing
to make peace, and, as his mission had been disclosed
to Austria, Sardinia, and Holland, he was to act in the
closest concord with the Ministers of these Powers, and
especially with Rosenberg, who was to be sent out after
him by Austria, and who had recently been in intimate
intercourse with Ministers in England. Spain was to be
urged to send a Spanish Minister to Breda and not to
entrust the defence of her interests to Puyzieulx. But
before Keene could reach Lisbon the news had come to
England of the evacuation of Italy and the fall of Genoa,
which completely altered the situation. The result was
a supplementary letter from Newcastle, saying that in
the altered circumstances there could be no question of
giving anything to Don Philip, and that Spain must
come to terms with the allies as the only possible method
of saving Naples for Don Carlos. Newcastle repeated
the injunction as to co-operation with Rosenberg, who
was to go to Lisbon by the same packet that carried the
letter.[1]

Keene arrived at Lisbon in the third week of September, and speedily found that Newcastle had entrusted
him with an almost hopeless mission. Portugal, since
the war of the Spanish Succession, had lain contentedly
outside the main currents of European politics. The
King was an elderly epileptic, who had for some years
abandoned all political interests and given himself up
to religious exercises. The Queen, who acted as an
informal Regent for her retired husband, was a sister
of Charles VI, a stupid Austrian woman who was
devoted to her daughter, the new Queen of Spain, and
looked to her for such guidance as she could give. The
chief Minister, Cardinal Motta, was rather an ecclesi-
astic than a statesman. Keene set out with the belief
that he could use the Portuguese Government as a

[1] Newcastle to Keene, 26 September (o.s.), 1746, Add. MSS.
32,806, fo. 1.

channel of communication with Madrid. But he found himself hampered by the previous activity of Tabernuiga. Officially this activity was a complete secret at Lisbon, where the Marquis was supposed to be nothing more than an exile appealing for pardon. Keene discovered, however, that the Spanish Ambassador had betrayed the secret to Cardinal Motta, who had read all Tabernuiga's letters. This imposed upon Keene a double check. On the one hand, it would be diplomatically incorrect for him to show that he knew of the Spanish insistence upon some cession to Don Philip, because that information came through Tabernuiga, who had no status and was officially unknown at Lisbon. On the other hand, it was impossible for him to ask the Portuguese Minister to forward his letters to Madrid, when the latter knew that he had a ready-made means of communication with Villarias. So Keene was forced, against his will, to fall back upon Tabernuiga, to show him the instructions from England, and to get him to send a letter to the Spanish Minister expounding the reasons why nothing could be done for Don Philip, and the necessity of providing for the safety of Don Carlos.[1] To this letter there could be only one reply, that Spanish honour was pledged for Don Philip, and that Spain could not afford to make a separate treaty with England if nothing more was offered than a bare maintenance of the *status quo* in Naples.[2] Obviously Tabernuiga was too good a Spaniard, and too eager to curry favour at Madrid, to be of any further use to England. Newcastle realized this, and wrote in a private letter that he had better return to his wife in England.[3] Tabernuiga, however, was not under Newcastle's orders, and stayed on in the confident belief that he would soon be required as a Secretary of State in Spain. But he lost all political importance, and it would probably have been wiser on Newcastle's part never to have employed him.

[1] Keene to Newcastle, 29 October, 1746, in Add. MSS. 32,806 fo. 137.

[2] Villarias to Tabernuiga, sent on by Keene on 23 November, in *ibid.*, fo. 194.

[3] Newcastle to Tabernuiga, 2 December (o.s.), in *ibid.*, fo. 258.

Keene would now have been at a deadlock if the new Spanish Ambassador at Lisbon, the Duke of Sotomayor, had not opened relations with him, at first through a secretary, and later by secret interviews. But nothing came of them : the Spaniard could not drop Don Philip, and Keene was bound by his instructions to make no promise to the Infant. All that Sotomayor could suggest was that the Italian war should be left out of consideration, and that they should confine their attention to the settlement of the commercial disputes which had given rise to the original war in 1739.[1] To this Keene could not agree, as such a treaty would not detach Spain from France, nor would it prevent Spain from sending assistance to the French in Provence, nor would it satisfy in any way the allies of England. Meanwhile, Rosenberg, with whom Keene was ordered to act in concord, had arrived in Lisbon on 23 October. His presence made matters worse instead of better. He was quite willing to co-operate with Keene in refusing a cession to Don Philip, but he refused to consent to anything which expressed or implied a guarantee of Naples to Don Carlos. This rendered the conclusion of a separate treaty with Spain absolutely impossible. Newcastle had made up his mind that, in order to concentrate all available forces upon the invasion of France, and also in order to detach Spain from France, Austria must not be allowed to attack Naples. It had taken England some time to come to this decision, and it had not yet been clearly intimated to Vienna, but it was now definitely formed. It was this more than anything else which bound England to Sardinia during the remaining period of the war. Charles Emmanuel was at times an unsatisfactory and even an irritating ally, but he had never concealed his unwillingness to see Austria in possession of the Crown of Naples in addition to the Duchy of Milan.

Looked at closely, the Italian problem, which bulked so largely at Lisbon, was really a double one. The two questions, originally separate, which came to be inextricably mixed together, were the Bourbon claim for

---

[1] Keene to Newcastle, 12 November, Add. MSS. 32,806, fo. 171.

Don Philip and Maria Theresa's claim for a *dédommage-ment* for her cessions to Sardinia at Worms.   Down to the very end of the war Maria Theresa, egged on by Bartenstein, held obstinately to the contention that the Treaty of Worms entitled her, as soon as Italy was freed from foreign invasion, to demand the aid of her allies in the conquest of Naples.   If that aid were with-held, and, still more, if Austrian forces were diverted to some other purpose, then she was entitled to call upon Sardinia to disgorge the gains for which no equivalent had been received.   It was the old question of conditional or unconditional cession, which Carteret had endeavoured to conceal rather than to settle by a dexterous formula in the second additional article of the Treaty of Worms.[1]   Of course England contended that the equivalent was Sardinian assistance in the expulsion of the Bourbon invaders, and that Sardinia had also to be compensated for the loss of the revenue from Savoy. Austria replied that Sardinia was amply compensated by its share of the Duchy of Modena, and was prepar-ing to exact additional revenue from the coast towns of Genoa, where Austrian troops could only purchase sup-plies at preposterous prices, but that this did not affect the right of Austria under the treaty to regain her lost territories if she could not get Naples.   English Ministers adhered to their original interpretation of the Worms article, admitted that the complete expulsion of the Bourbons had been one of the war aims, but maintained that the failure to achieve it was not a breach of the treaty, but one of those accidents which in war it was impossible to avoid.   To Bartenstein the failure appeared to be deliberate rather than accidental, and the refusal to mulct a disloyal Sardinia was only another proof of the English determination to throw all the losses of the war upon Austria.   The controversy was interminable.

As long as England adhered to the resolution not to exact sacrifices from the allies, a resolution neoessitated by Newcastle's invitation of their Ministers to Breda, the endowment of Don Philip, without which neither

[1] See above, p. 66.

a separate peace with Spain nor a general pacification seemed possible of attainment, presented a still more insoluble problem.[1] Tuscany had been suggested by Trevor and Van der Heim. Although it weakened the security of Lorraine, d'Argenson had jumped at the suggestion, partly because it did not touch the Pragmatic Sanction, and partly because he thought it would satisfy Elizabeth Farnese, who had hereditary claims to the Grand-Duchy. But England had never given any official approval to the proposal, and Austria unhesitatingly rejected it. Its injustice was obvious, as the Emperor, whose sole dominion it was, was not even a belligerent. After the defeat of the Gallispans, all idea of the cession of Tuscany was absolutely dropped. A far more obvious endowment for the Infant was the Duchies of Parma and Piacenza, which had for a short time been actually held by a Spanish Bourbon. Their transfer would impose an approximately equal sacrifice upon both Austria and Sardinia. Maria Theresa might be induced to give up Parma and her strip of Piacenza, but only if she recovered her cessions in Lombardy. But Charles Emmanuel stuck to the Treaty of Worms, and would resign nothing that that treaty had given him. A solution which found some temporary favour at Madrid and at Lisbon was that Don Philip should keep Savoy, which was actually in his hands. But the allies had undertaken at Worms to procure its restitution to Charles Emmanuel, and England at least was loyal to that agreement. Villarias had thrown out a suggestion that an endowment might be found without any sacrifice

[1] It is important to remember that in all the negotiations about Don Philip it was assumed, at any rate on the part of the allies, that Don Carlos would succeed in Spain on the death of Ferdinand VI (see above, p. 205), that Don Philip would then become King of Naples, and that whatever should be given to him now would in that case revert to its present owner. Thus the cession would not be a permanent one but only for the lifetime, not expected to be long, of Ferdinand VI. But Austria and Sardinia, the two States most concerned, knew that these dynastic forecasts are not always fulfilled. As a matter of fact, although Don Carlos inherited the Spanish throne on the death of Ferdinand, Don Philip did not get Naples, so that he and his successors adhered to what he got in 1748, and there was no reversion to previous possessors.

on the part of either Austria or Sardinia.[1] This was
intended and interpreted to mean the island of Corsica,
which for a time came into some prominence in diplomatic discussions. It might be made more attractive by
adding the vice-royalty in Sicily. Maria Theresa was so
angry with Genoa after the rising against Botta that she
was inclined to dally with the idea of thus punishing the
Republic. Even England showed some inclination for a
solution which seemed likely to get rid of some difficulties with her allies, though it was contrary to all
English tradition to strengthen Bourbon naval power in
the Mediterranean. But Charles Emmanuel was recalcitrant. A Bourbon Prince in Corsica would be a mere
dependent upon France and a dangerous neighbour to
Sardinia. And at Vienna there was always the uneasy
thought, only thrust aside by a momentary temptation
to avoid loss by throwing it upon some other Power,
that any cession to Don Philip involved the abandonment of Naples. It would be preposterous to offer an
endowment to the younger while proposing to despoil
the elder brother.

Co-operation between Keene and Rosenberg at Lisbon
was impossible, and it was useless for Newcastle to
prescribe it. Rosenberg was constantly urging his
Court to coerce Spain by an attack upon Naples, and
Keene could not possibly concur in this.[2] Unless he

[1] This was in the memorandum which Villarias sent to Tabernuiga, and which Keene forwarded to Newcastle on 23 November
(Add. MSS. 32,806, fo. 195). In this document the Spanish
Minister said that if England desired peace, it would be easy to
find for Don Philip " a domain which would not disturb in any
way the neighbouring States."   Later Cardinal Motta, doubtless at
Spanish instigation, pressed Corsica as a serious proposition.   But
France, very creditably, refused to allow Genoa to suffer more
than it had done already.

[2] Rosenberg told Keene in his first interview that when he
went to see Motta he had " told the Cardinal that he did not
intend to make any advances to Spain, but, if that Court does
not speak first, the Germans will march directly to Naples and
take that city " (Keene to Newcastle, 29 October, Add. MSS.
32,806, fo. 141).   And when Keene communicated to his colleague
the answer from Madrid to Tabernuiga, Rosenberg said that the
only way to coerce Spain was to attack Naples, and that he would
advise his Court to that effect (Keene to Newcastle, 23 November,
ibid., fo. 192).   But Newcastle declared that Rosenberg, when

15

could guarantee Naples and get some concession for Don Philip, Keene had no hope of obtaining any agreement with Spain. His letters to Newcastle show that he despaired of success in his mission. And yet there was a widespread belief in Europe, inspired by the Spanish retreat from Italy and the notorious eagerness of Ferdinand VI to terminate the war, that a separate treaty at Lisbon either had been concluded or was on the verge of conclusion. Puyzieulx held this opinion at Breda, and d'Argenson, in spite of his boasted trust in the loyalty of the Spanish King, was so impressed with the current rumours that he took steps to avert the danger. To the Portuguese envoy in Paris, d'Acunha, he suggested that the King of Portugal should be invited to mediate a general peace, and that a general Congress should meet at Lisbon for this purpose.[1] The suggestion that Spain should concur in the invitation was conveyed to Madrid, and was welcomed by the Queen as a compliment to her native Court. Portugal could hardly refuse so flattering an invitation, though Cardinal Motta was clear-sighted enough to realize that Lisbon was geographically ill-suited for a European Congress, and that there was a curious inconsistency between the invitation to Portugal and the fact that France had a plenipotentiary at Breda engaged in a Conference, which might at any moment grow into a Congress, for the very same purpose which it was now proposed to carry out at Lisbon. Portugal, therefore, could only accept mediation on condition that all the belligerent Powers concurred, and that the rival negotiation at Breda should be abandoned.[2] This put the

---

in England, had agreed that Spain could never be gained unless Naples and Sicily were secured to Don Carlos (Newcastle to Keene, 2 December [o.s.], *ibid.*, fo. 326). Rosenberg must have received new instructions when he went to Lisbon.

[1] D'Argenson (v., p. 40) says that he did this with the approval of the King, but without the knowledge of his colleagues.

[2] A full account of the Spanish proposal to Portugal and of the Portuguese answer is to be found in a memorial presented to the Court of Vienna by the Portuguese Minister Carvalho. This document, with the Austrian answer to it, was sent by Robinson to Chesterfield on 7 January, 1747. With them went an answer to representations made by Robinson, into which Bartenstein

allies in a dilemma. It was obvious in both London and
Vienna that the proffer of mediation was a mere artifice
on the part of France to prevent them from using
the Portuguese Court for the purpose of obtaining
a separate treaty with Spain. But, as they had not
yet abandoned all hope of getting such a treaty at
Lisbon, they could not alienate Portugal by refusing
mediation, though they had no belief that it would
have any practical result, and no confidence in the
impartiality of Cardinal Motta, who would have to act
as mediator on behalf of his King.[1] Both Courts, therefore, expressed their acceptance of Portuguese mediation, but neither paid any attention to the condition
as to withdrawal from Breda. In fact, in view of the
attitude of the Dutch, such a withdrawal was out of
the question. It must have been some consolation to
London to learn that the conduct of Spain was equally
inconsistent. Keene wrote on 24 December that he had
received information from a friend " that the young
Queen of Spain had advised her mother that the famous
Mr. Macanaz, who has resided so many years at Paris, is
ordered to proceed to Breda to take care of Spanish
affairs at the congress."[2] Still more encouraging was
the news that at last a change of Ministry had taken
place at Madrid, and that Carvajal, reputed to be an
opponent of the Queen-Dowager, had become Chief
Minister.[3] This led Newcastle to hope that Spain would

poured the usual dose of vinegar. The negotiations with Spain,
he said, would not only be more advanced, but would probably be
finished by now, if the conquest of Naples had not been prevented
in September. Bartenstein also definitely stated that Rosenberg
could not act with Keene in giving any assurance as to the security
of Naples. All these documents, and also an interesting instruction to Richecourt at Turin, which touches the same topic, are
in S.P., For., Germany, 176.

[1] Keene to Newcastle, 24 December, says that Rosenberg, after
an interview with Motta, in which the latter said that he could
never conscientiously advise Spain to abandon the French alliance,
" has complained to the Queen of Portugal of the Cardinal's
partiality for the interests of France."

[2] Keene to Newcastle, 24 December, 1746, in Add. MSS. 32,806,
fo. 277.

[3] Keene to Newcastle, 13 December, ibid., fo. 262. The news
of the ministerial change came to Tabernuiga from a friend in
Madrid.

abandon the Portuguese mediation and accept direct
negotiation with the allies.[1] But this was for the future
to decide. The year 1746 closed without any realization
of the confident hopes with which Newcastle had sent
off Tabernuiga in July and Keene in August. Not a
single step had been taken in the direction of a separate
peace with Spain, and the Court of Portugal, which was
to bring about that peace, was diverted to a mediation
which nobody, and least of all d'Argenson, who had
initiated the proposal, took at all seriously. It was no
wonder that Keene declared that " no negotiation has
been attended with more confusion than this."[2]

[1] Newcastle to Keene, 23 December (o.s.), *ibid.*, fo. 292.
[2] Keene to Newcastle, 2 December, *ibid.*, fo. 219.

CHAPTER VI

SANDWICH AND MACANAZ AT BREDA (JANUARY TO MAY, 1747).

Ascendancy of Newcastle in England—Invasion of Provence—Continued quarrels between Austria and Sardinia—Evacuation of Provence—Wentworth's mission—Negotiations at Lisbon blocked by Austria—Prospective difficulties of Sandwich—Breda Conference postponed by recall of Puyzieulx—Fall of d'Argenson—Macanaz at The Hague—His extravagant demands—Fourth meeting of Conference—Protest of Macanaz and postponement—Fifth meeting and renewed adjournment—Renewed negotiation with Macanaz—Controversy with Newcastle about cession of Gibraltar—Chavanne procures withdrawal of demand for Gibraltar—Alienation of Sandwich from Chesterfield—Draft of treaty with Spain—Difficulty about Savoy—French invade Dutch Flanders—Revolution in United Provinces—Ill-founded jubilation in England—Spain drops Macanaz and adheres to France—Conference at Breda to be transferred to Aix-la-Chapelle—Chesterfield sends Dayrolles to The Hague—Indignation of Sandwich.

By the end of 1746 Newcastle had achieved the object which he had set before himself. He had freed himself, with the aid of the King, from all efficient control in his own department, and had become virtually a joint Prime Minister with his brother. This position he maintained until Henry Pelham's death,[1] when he stepped without opposition into the first place in rank as well as in power. But for eight years before that he had usurped supreme control of foreign affairs. The only restraint upon him was the necessity from time to time of getting the consent of the House of Commons to financial grants, which he could not hope to do without his brother's approval. But even in this matter

[1] Waldegrave, *Memoirs*, p. 11, calls the two brothers "joint Ministers." Newcastle was as supreme in Church affairs as at the Foreign Office. On 27 July (o.s.), 1750, he admitted to his brother that he was called "the ecclesiastical Minister" (Add. MSS. 32,721, fo. 471). And Henry Pelham wrote to a correspondent: "I seldom interfere in Church preferments, especially not in those of so great weight and dignity" (*ibid.*, fo. 502).

he usually got his own way in the end, owing to his persistent obstinacy and to the curious reluctance of Henry Pelham to maintain his own opinions against the ill-temper which the Duke never failed to show if any attempt was made to thwart him. Of course, Newcastle owed a good deal to the support of the Duke of Cumberland, whose favour he assiduously cultivated, and of Lord Chancellor Hardwicke, who was constantly called in to mediate between the two brothers.

During the early months of 1747, Newcastle, who was profoundly ignorant of all military affairs, continued to build the most sanguine hopes upon the invasion of Provence. He still held, in his own words, that " these operations on the richest and most exposed part of the French dominions must be regarded as the principal object of the war."[1] His hopes were based, not only upon Browne's early success, when the invaders advanced without serious opposition to Cannes, captured the islands off the coast, and laid siege to Antibes, but still more upon the military convention of 12 January, by which Austria was to employ sixty thousand and Sardinia thirty thousand men in France, over and above the troops which the two Powers deemed it necessary to maintain in Italy. If this bargain were carried out, it would be impossible for Austria to divert any substantial force to attack Naples, and it was not likely that Belleisle, with the dispirited troops of last year's retreat, would be able to make head against the Austrians and Sardinians. It was admitted that the loss of Genoa made communications more difficult and hazardous, but England had a sufficient squadron under Medley and Byng to secure transit by sea, and it was fully expected that Genoa would be easily and speedily recovered. The one great difficulty was the irreconcilable quarrel between Austria and Sardinia, each trying to throw upon the other as much as possible of the burden of the war, and the whole of the blame for any disasters that might occur. All conferences as to future operations became, said Villettes, acrid controversies as to the

[1] He had written thus to Villettes on 24 October (o.s.), 1746 (S.P., For., Sardinia, 51).

past.[1] Charles Emmanuel persisted in his demands for
his share in the spoils of Piacenza and Genoa, and for
the payment of his bills for supplies furnished to the
expeditionary force on its way through the Genoese
coast towns, which he now regarded as his property.
He declared that he was not bound by any agreement
to furnish troops or artillery for the siege of Genoa,[2]
and he refused to take any share in that enterprise,
which Austria declared to be necessary before more
troops could be sent to Provence, unless he was assured
beforehand that any future capitulation of the city
should be settled by a joint and equal agreement
between the three allied Powers. As Austria replied
that a recovered Genoa must pay the arrears of the first
indemnity before any other claim could be met, rejected
the demand for equality in the booty from Piacenza,
and denounced the charges for supplies to an allied
Power as indecently exorbitant, the King offered to
commute his pecuniary claims for a promise of Austrian
good offices to secure for him in the general peace permanent possession, not only of Finale, but of the whole
Riviera di Ponente. To this the reply from Vienna was
that if Sardinia kept the Ponente, Austria must have
the Levante.[3] It was not easy to get the better of Bartenstein in the war of pamphleteering which both Courts
indulged in.

Matters became worse when the news came that
Belleisle had received the reinforcements which had

[1] Villettes to Newcastle, 18 February, 1747 (S.P., For., Sardinia, 52).
[2] Villettes to Newcastle, 2 April, 1747, in *ibid.* Robinson to
Chesterfield, 16 April (S.P., For., Germany, 177), says that
Richecourt reported the answer from Turin to be " that the King
of Sardinia was bound by neither treaty nor convention to assist
the Austrians in the recovery of Genoa."
[3] Robinson forwarded to Chesterfield in the early months of
1747 several copies of Austrian replies to Gorzegno and of instructions given to Richecourt, the Austrian Envoy at Turin.
They throw a flood of light upon Austrian policy at this time
and upon the inveterate hostility with which every act of Sardinia
was regarded at Vienna. The documents are in S.P., For.,
Germany, 176. Villettes' dispatches in S.P., For., Sardinia, 52,
give the other side of the picture, and show that Richecourt was
accused at Turin of deliberate misrepresentation.

been refused to Maillebois; that the new Ministry in Spain, regarded at Vienna as creatures of the Queen-Dowager, had ordered Las Minas to abandon winter quarters in Savoy and resume co-operation with the French; and, finally, that Browne, finding himself confronted by a superior force and in danger of having his retreat and communications entirely cut off, had raised the siege of Antibes and had finally recrossed the Var. By the beginning of February the invasion of Provence was at an end. Sardinia at once declared that Browne's retreat, so contrary to that general's proved character, must have been due to secret orders from Vienna. Austria retaliated that if the King had sent the required artillery, which he had used in his own selfish siege of Savona, Browne could have taken Antibes and advanced to the Rhone. The only harmony between the two Courts was in blaming England for having failed to prevent the transport of troops and provisions from France to Genoa. The unfortunate Newcastle, to whom the evacuation of Provence was a far greater blow than it was to Maria Theresa and Charles Emmanuel, could only write in despair to Villettes: "It is very immaterial to what causes this unfortunate step may be chiefly attributed. The most evident one, and that which may be the most fatal, if not immediately remedied, is that jealousy, diffidence, and dissatisfaction which have so apparently prevailed both at Vienna and at the King of Sardinia's Court, and with all the respective generals and Ministers of those two Powers as to the conduct and view of each other, and I am sorry to say I am afraid the proper measures have not always been taken to remove them."[1] The last sentence was intended to rebuke Villettes for ill-timed partisanship. Newcastle himself had consistently preached the duty of reconciliation, but his "pathetic exhortation to the forgiveness of sins," as Gorzegno called it, had done more harm than good.[2] Charles Emmanuel, usually very circumspect in his communica-

[1] Newcastle to Villettes, 24 February, 1747 (S.P., For., Sardinia, 52).
[2] Villettes to Newcastle, 21 March (*ibid*).

tions with England, expressed his "concern that His Majesty should show so much indifference to his interests as to press him to heal the breaches between him and the Empress, while he took so little notice of the grievances that had caused them." Maria Theresa replied to the sermons which Chesterfield addressed to her through Wasner and Robinson by the stereotyped complaint that England was the champion of every Court except that of Vienna. So hopeless did it seem in the circumstances to look to the two Powers for a punctual fulfilment of the Hague Convention that the English Minister determined to send Lieutenant-General Wentworth to inspect and report upon the numbers and the equipment of their respective contingents.[1] His instructions, dated 6 April (o.s.), show that Austria was regarded as the more culpable of the two states. At Vienna, which he was to visit first, he was to insist, not only upon the sixty thousand men, but upon the acceptance of Charles Emmanuel as commander, upon a pledge as to no future exploitation of gains by Austria alone, and upon an equal division of the artillery and magazines taken at Piacenza. After expressing doubts as to whether Austria had been only half-hearted about Provence on account of a preference for an expedition against Naples, the document continued that, if either Court should fail to furnish the promised contingent, or should show indifference in the enterprise, Wentworth was to warn them "that we shall be obliged in those circumstances to take such measures as justice and prudence may suggest to us for the interest and security of our own kingdoms." This threat, which was also conveyed to the two Courts through Robinson and Villettes, might be interpreted to mean either the conclusion of a separate peace or the withholding of the promised subsidies.

The bitter disappointment in Provence and the neces-

[1] Newcastle to Villettes, 27 March (o.s.), 1747, says that the suggestion of sending a British officer to inspect the troops came from Sardinia through Osorio (S.P., For., Sardinia, 52). It was an astute move to conciliate England and to inspire distrust of Austria. The instructions to Wentworth are in the same volume of State Papers.

sary delays before Cumberland was ready to take the
field in the Netherlands compelled Newcastle and the
still submissive Chesterfield to concentrate their attention for a time upon the negotiations which were simultaneously proceeding at Breda and Lisbon.[1] At the
Portuguese capital matters were inconveniently complicated by the pretension of Portugal to mediate a
general peace. France had suggested, and Spain had
invited, this mediation, while Austria and England,
though their disinclination was ill-concealed, did not
think it good policy to refuse acceptance. But no one
of these Powers took the Portuguese mediation seriously,
and the other two interested states, Sardinia and
Holland, paid no attention to it at all. The only result
of its offer was to arouse Cardinal Motta's indignation
at the slight cast upon his Court by its virtual withdrawal, and to make him more reluctant to undertake
the minor task of reconciling Spain with the allies.
This detachment of Spain from France was still regarded
by Newcastle as a primary aim, and, in view of the
altered situation on the Italian frontier, he sought to
render it more feasible by withdrawing his original veto
upon any establishment for Don Philip and authorizing
Keene to offer Corsica, which might be held with the
vice-royalty of Sicily, if Spain could induce Don Carlos
to grant it.[2] This was a notable advance on the part
of England, but it was of little use unless it was also
supported by Austria. If those two Powers were agreed,
they did not anticipate any opposition on the part of
Sardinia, whose interests could not be said to be vitally
concerned by a cession which touched no Sardinian
territory. So Newcastle had perforce to renew his injunction to Keene to act in the matter with Rosenberg.

[1] The Portuguese State Papers at the Record Office, after a
curious gap in the later months of 1746, resume in January, 1747,
so from that date the correspondence between Keene and Newcastle can be followed either in them (vol. 46) or in the Newcastle
Papers in the British Museum (Add. MSS. 32,807).
[2] Newcastle to Keene, 7 February (o.s.), 1747. The offer
was to be made if Rosenberg would agree and Sardinia would not
oppose, " as his Majesty is persuaded he will not." This belief
in the superior ductility of Sardinia was constantly maintained
in England, but was very seldom justified.

This was necessary, but nevertheless ruinous to the project. England wanted to resume its Spanish trade; but Austria had no such interest in a separate peace with Spain except so far as it would help to induce or compel France to restore the Netherlands, and this was regarded at Vienna as the duty of the maritime Power. Rosenberg showed an inclination at one time to approve of Don Philip's retention of Savoy, to which Keene, pledged to defend the interests of Sardinia, refused to consent. But the Austrian envoy was equally obstinate in refusing to join in the suggestion of Corsica, because it would carry with it the security of Naples, and Maria Theresa would not grant such security unless she recovered her own cessions to Sardinia.[1] This was the old deadlock of the previous year. Austria must not be asked to satisfy at her expense both Charles Emmanuel and Don Philip. If England persisted in supporting the Sardinian King, then the Infant must go empty handed, and if Spain insisted upon his endowment as a necessary condition of peace, then peace could not be made with Spain with Austrian consent. Chesterfield summed up the situation in a letter to Robinson, to whom he sent extracts from Keene's dispatches. "You will take notice by them that there is something very particular in the late conduct of Count Rosenberg with regard to the negotiation now treating on at Lisbon under the mediation of the King of Portugal, since, if the Empress, as that Minister has given to understand, will not on the one hand agree to any establishment for Don Philip except the same be made at the expense of the King of Sardinia, or on the other hand either to

[1] Robinson's letters at this time (S.P., For., Germany, 176) are full of Austria's desire to regain the Worms cessions.. See his letters to Chesterfield and Sandwich of 8 March. To the latter he wrote: "The principal endeavour of the Empress will be rather to get back one inch of what she yielded to the King of Sardinia by the Treaty of Worms than to acquire one acre of the eastern side of Genoa, which, by the very cessions already made to his Sardinian Majesty, she can have little or no communication with from Lombardy." In the other letter he says that Maria Theresa would give Genoa and the whole Levante in order to recover Piacenza, and so secure the road from Lombardy to Tuscany (see above, p. 63).

Corsica or any other establishment for Don Philip if the possession of Naples and Sicily is at the same time to be secured and guaranteed to Don Carlos, it naturally follows that, not only no separate accommodation, but indeed no accommodation at all, can be concluded with his Catholic Majesty.''[1] It was clearly useless to parade the disunion between England and Austria by going to Motta or Sotomayor without a joint programme. It must have been almost a relief to Keene when the news came from Turin that Charles Emmanuel disapproved of the proposed cession of Corsica, and from Madrid that Spain had come to the same decision as France, that it would be monstrous to join in robbing a loyal ally. Keene expressed to Newcastle his regret that he had not been able to make any progress at Lisbon, and also his hope and belief that Sandwich would be more successful at Breda.[2]

When Sandwich, having signed his military convention at The Hague, prepared to go to Breda for a resumption of the Conference, he cannot have anticipated that his task would be easier than Keene's. Whereas Keene had one allied Power to deal with, Sandwich had three, and one of them was represented by two Ministers who had been engaged in the negotiation before Sandwich had entered it, and were certainly hampered, if not bound, by their previous transactions with France. Sandwich knew in outline the sort of terms upon which England desired to make peace, and he knew that they would not meet with the approval of any of those with whom he would have to act. Wassenaer and Gilles wished for the neutrality of the Southern Netherlands and for mutual restitution, which

---

[1] Chesterfield to Robinson, 31 March (o.s.), 1747 (S.P., For., Germany, 176). See also Chesterfield to Sandwich of same date in S.P., For., Holland, 424, and Add. MSS. 32,807, fo. 280.

[2] Keene to Newcastle, 20 March, 1747. In this letter Keene says that Macanaz at Breda, as an old opponent of the Queen Dowager, is more likely to bring about an accommodation than the Court of Lisbon, where the King is too ill to attend to business, where the Queen is more noted for her piety than for her knowledge of affairs, and where the Cardinal, himself too infirm for his job, is admitted by the Queen to be too partial to act as a mediator (Add. MSS. 32,807, fo. 191).

meant the abandonment of Cape Breton. After their discussions with d'Argenson they could hardly deny that they had accepted these fundamental conditions. They had no direct interest in Italian affairs, but they had committed themselves to the principle of an establishment for Don Philip, and had even proposed a more handsome one than either France or Spain was likely now to claim. Above all, they represented a party in Holland which was clamorous for peace, and was not likely to be deterred from it by the charge that they were injuring or deserting their allies. And this demand for peace might become irresistible if the French carried out their repeated threat and crossed the Dutch frontiers. The supreme problem for Sandwich was still, as it had been from the first, to prevent the Dutch from making a separate peace. He was not likely to get much assistance from his other colleagues. Harrach was sore at his exclusion from the Conference to which he had been invited. He refused to compromise the dignity of his Court by going to Breda, and insisted upon having all news of what passed transmitted to him at The Hague. If discussion came down to details, he was certain to be as obstructive as Rosenberg was at Lisbon. He had already begun to talk of the necessity either of carrying out the Treaty of Worms to its completion or of rectifying the injustice of its incomplete enforcement. And, as he had no power to conclude, and must refer everything to Vienna, he could cause endless delay.[1] The remaining Minister, Chavanne, was personally more congenial to Sandwich, and apparently more amenable. In fact, the two men were so intimate that some observers thought that the Sardinian Minister rather dominated the Englishman. But, when it came to be a question of his master's interests, Chavanne could be as tenacious as any Austrian. It was quite certain that he would not willingly resign any fragment of what had been given to his King at Worms, and he would cling

---

[1] Sandwich to Chesterfield, 13 January, 1747 (S.P., For., Holland, 424, fo. 51), anticipates that the immense delay caused by constant references to Vienna will exhaust the patience of the Republic.

as long as possible to Savona and the other Sardinian conquests on the Riviera di Ponente. Hence it was certain that any solution of the Italian problem which satisfied Austria would exasperate Sardinia, and *vice versa*. And it was quite possible that a solution would have to be found which would exasperate both. Altogether, Sandwich could count on finding his colleagues, both inside and outside the Conference, a difficult team to manage. And yet the second article in his instructions was that he was to keep the allies together. It did not improve matters that Sandwich and Newcastle were by no means on such intimate terms as they had been. The latter was beginning to chafe at the scantiness and formality of his protégé's letters, and Chesterfield had to urge Sandwich, in his own interests, to write a little more frequently to his former patron, and declared that he would feel no jealousy.[1]

Sandwich trusted to his good fortune to carry him through these difficulties, and again it did not fail him. Just as he and Gilles were starting from The Hague for Breda, the news came that Puyzieulx had been recalled to France, and that he had left for Wassenaer, whom he had always preferred to the Pensionary, a letter stating that he or another would return to Breda in a fortnight, and that Macanaz would accompany the French plenipotentiary, not as a member of the Conference, but as a consultant on the same footing as Harrach and Chavanne. This was the result of d'Argenson's advice

[1] Newcastle went so far as to complain to Cumberland of Sandwich's reticence. On 19 December (o.s.), 1746, he wrote to the Duke, after dilating on Sandwich's obligations to him: " I own I am not a little mortified in having been (as it were) totally forgot by his Lordship since my Lord Chesterfield has been Secretary of State " (Add. MSS. 32,709, fo. 352). Chesterfield's private letters on the subject (at Hinchingbrooke) are amusing. On 20 February, 1747, he wrote: " Pray continue to write separate letters to the Duke of Newcastle, if you would continue to be well with him, for he is a jealous lover of paper. Continue me only your friendship, which I value too much to regard forms." On 6 March he said he was glad Sandwich had written to Newcastle, as "little things hurt and please some minds." Newcastle would have been still more annoyed if he had known that the few letters he did receive were written at the suggestion of his colleague.

to Madrid that a Spanish Minister should be sent.[1] The reprieve was as grateful to Sandwich as it was distasteful to the Dutch,[2] whom Sandwich suspected of having come to a secret understanding with the French Minister. The postponement was prolonged, partly by a serious illness of Puyzieulx on his return to Versailles, and partly by the appointment of du Theil to take his place at Breda. To Sandwich's delight, Wassenaer, " who is of one of the best families of this country," expressed his dissatisfaction that France was sending a man " who, as I am informed, tho' a man of ability, is not a person of birth or figure in his country."[3] Sandwich eagerly fastened upon this objection, so characteristic of the eighteenth century, and insisted that he must apply to London for instructions before he could meet an envoy of inferior rank. Chesterfield, himself an aristocrat, replied that he must do what Puyzieulx would have done if the King had recalled Sandwich and sent his first *commis*. He must " refuse to treat with him unless he shall come dignified by a public character which may put him upon some foot of equality with your Lordship and Count Wassenaer."[4] Du Theil had to wait at Antwerp until the difficulty had been removed by his elevation to the rank of Minister Plenipotentiary.

The mystery of Puyzieulx's sudden recall was speedily explained. The Marquis d'Argenson had been suddenly dismissed from office by the French King, and his former subordinate was chosen to fill his place. The unfortunate campaign in Italy in the previous year had been fatal to the French Foreign Minister, whose futile negotiation with Sardinia was blamed for the surrender of Asti and all the subsequent disasters. The alienation of Spain, which had contributed to the ill-success in Italy, and had brought that Court to the verge of a

---

[1] See above, p. 191.

[2] Wassenaer remonstrated against Puyzieulx's departure on the ground that it would encourage the opponents of peace (Sandwich to Chesterfield, 18 January, 1747, in S.P., For., Holland, 424, fo. 71).

[3] Sandwich to Chesterfield, 31 January (*ibid.*, fo. 112).

[4] Chesterfield to Sandwich, 27 January (o.s.), 1747 (*ibid.*, fo. 122).

separate treaty with the enemy Powers, was another charge against him. The marriage of the Dauphin to a Saxon princess, of which d'Argenson tried to claim the credit, did him more harm than good, as it was really the work of Marshal Saxe, who detested the Marquis as the opponent of active operations against the Dutch. The Saxon Court, out of hostility to Prussia, was eager to reconcile France with Austria, whereas d'Argenson was the avowed enemy of Austria and clung to the Prussian alliance in spite of Frederick's infidelities. Finally, the prolonged negotiations with Wassenaer and Gilles, which had given undue importance to the detested Republic, and had so far brought nothing to France but humiliation at Breda, added to d'Argenson's discredit. Noailles, his inveterate opponent, gave the last impulse to the sluggish King by presenting a long and detailed indictment of the conduct of the French Foreign Office during the last two years.[1] Sandwich had no reason to regret d'Argenson's downfall. It seemed likely to free the Dutch Ministers from some of their past commitments, and it might be expected to bury in oblivion that project of peace which was such a bugbear to the English Ministry.

While the Conference at Breda was suspended, Macanaz arrived at The Hague at the beginning of February, and Sandwich had a series of meetings with him, at first at the house of the Neapolitan Minister, and later at the residence of George II's Hanoverian agent at The Hague. These meetings were kept as secret as possible from the Dutch Ministers. The old Spaniard is by far the most picturesque and arresting figure among contemporary diplomatists, and he undoubtedly exercised a sort of fascination over Sandwich, who had never met anybody like him. Macanaz had been a prominent Minister in Spain during the early years of Philip V, and had incurred the displeasure of

[1] Mémoire présenté au Roi par le maréchal de Noailles, le 15 décembre, 1746 (Rousset, *Correspondance de Louis XV et du Maréchal de Noailles*, ii., pp. 252-76). For the general hostility to d'Argenson and an estimate of his work as Foreign Minister, see Broglie, *Maurice de Saxe et le Marquis d'Argenson*, ii., chap. v.

the Jesuits by urging the King to assert the supremacy of the State over the Church. After Philip's second marriage with Elizabeth Farnese, the Inquisition had been strong enough to drive the obnoxious Minister from Spain. For over thirty years Macanaz had lived in exile, partly in France and partly in the Southern Netherlands, but he had never lost the confidence of the King, with whom he continued to correspond, nor his own keen interest in the politics of Europe. He had inherited the traditions of the seventeenth century, when the Spanish Empire, still undivided, had fought a series of wars against France, and had been allied with Austria and the Maritime Powers. To him the Utrecht settlement, with its partition of the European dominions of Spain and the humiliating loss of Gibraltar and Minorca, was an unmitigated disaster, and he still regarded the Spanish King as the lawful, though disinherited, possessor of the rights that had then been torn from his crown. The one period in subsequent Spanish history which he regarded with approval was when Spain had sought the Austrian alliance in 1725, when he had urged Prince Eugene to draw his sword for the recovery of Gibraltar. The later period of the Family Compact he regarded as imposing the degradation of servitude upon Spain. His mission to Breda was universally regarded as a sign that the Court of Madrid had determined to reassert its independence and to recover for Spain its former rank as one of the great, if not the greatest of, European Powers.

Macanaz was now seventy-seven years old, but by all accounts he had lost none of the fire of youth. Sandwich describes him as a decrepit old man, with only one tooth left in his head, and as pouring out with imperfect articulation a flood of mixed French and Spanish which it was extremely difficult to follow.[1]   In the very first

[1] Harrach quoted this description of Macanaz by Sandwich in a dispatch to his Court on 7 February (Arneth, iii., p. 469, note 28). On the same date Sandwich, in a private letter to Newcastle, wrote that " Macanaz is one of the most extraordinary personages I ever met with; he is seventy-seven years old, but of surprising vivacity. . . . He made use of an immense profusion of words, half French and half Spanish, and seemed to me

16

interview Sandwich extracted from him two extremely gratifying statements. In the first place Macanaz declared that he would not be content to remain outside the Conference with nothing but reports of what passed at the meetings, but would insist upon admission to full membership. This would enable Sandwich to reopen the whole question of procedure, and to retract his deeply regretted concession as to the non-admission of Harrach and Chavanne. If the Conference could be thus transformed, the Dutch Ministers would lose the advantage of their balancing position in a triangular discussion. The second assertion, no less valuable, was that, if France insisted upon excluding the accredited Minister of Spain and claimed a right to speak for that Power, Macanaz was prepared to come to an independent agreement with the allied Powers. Sandwich was somewhat less pleased when, in a second interview, the Spanish Minister dictated to him the terms upon which his Court was prepared to make such a peace.[1] In the first place, Gibraltar and Port Mahon were to be restored; the slave-trade was to be open to all Powers, and there was to be no *asiento;* Don Carlos was to retain his kingdom, and Don Philip was to receive "un appanage convenable au frère du Roi d'Espagne et dans les états mêmes qui ont appartenu au Roi d'Espagne n'étant pas dans les Pays-Bas." This last article, Sandwich explained in a marginal note, meant, according to Macanaz, Tuscany on condition that Lorraine should be restored to the Emperor. On these terms Spain would recognize the claims of Maria Theresa to the Austrias, Hungary, and Bohemia, would evacuate Savoy, and would withdraw the Spanish troops from Provence. Sandwich admitted that the terms were extravagant, and that they must be largely cut down. But he felt convinced that they were the out-

---

rather as one fond of his own project than as one desirous of making discovery of our intentions " (Add. MSS., 32, 807).

[1] Sandwich to Chesterfield (separate and secret), 7 February, 1747, in S.P., For., Holland, 424, fo. 132. The Spanish ideas of a peace are on a separate sheet (*ibid.*, fo. 136). There is another copy in Add. MSS. 32,807, fo. 39.

pourings of the fertile brain of a sanguine septua-
genarian, who had lost touch with the actual situation
of affairs, and he had little doubt that, if he could provoke an adequate quarrel between Macanaz and du Theil,
the former's indignation would induce him to consent to
more practicable conditions. From this moment Sandwich was buoyed up with the hope that he would succeed
in concluding that separate treaty with Spain which
Benjamin Keene, a far more experienced diplomatist,
had been vainly trying to bring about at Lisbon. Such
a treaty would earn for him the gratitude of Newcastle
and Chesterfield, and would amply compensate for any
falling away of the untrusted Dutch.

The English Ministers were more impressed than
Sandwich had been with the preposterous character of
Macanaz's suggestions, which were far in excess both
of the demands of d'Argenson and of those put forward
by Spain at Lisbon. The only article to which England
would consent was that giving security to Don Carlos.
Gibraltar and Minorca were out of the question; their
restitution had never been mentioned elsewhere. The
asiento could not be resigned in view of the losses inflicted upon our merchants by the interruption of the
slave-trade and the permitted ship during the war. As
for Don Philip, Tuscany was impossible; Lorraine could
not be recovered without another war, in which Spain
offered no help; neither Austria nor Sardinia would give
up territories to the Infant, and we cannot possibly ask
them, much less compel them, to do so. All that can
be offered to him is Corsica, and on that point Sandwich
may speak the same language as Keene at Lisbon.[1]
In addition to the official dispatches drawn up by
Chesterfield, both he and Newcastle wrote private
letters to Sandwich, in which we can trace the beginning
of a marked divergence between the two Secretaries.
Chesterfield wrote on 6 February (o.s.) : " Were nobody
here wiser than I, I confess I should be *tractable* upon

[1] Chesterfield to Sandwich (secret), 3 February (o.s.), 1747,
in S.P., For., Holland, 424, fo. 142 (also in Add. MSS. 32,807,
fo. 51), and 6 February (o.s.), *ibid.*, fo. 178 (also in Add. MSS.
32,807, fo. 67).

the affair of Gibraltar, rather than let the negotiation with Spain break off and throw the new King into the arms of France, from which I am convinced he is sincerely disposed to disengage himself. Nay, I am persuaded that, if we could, by the price of Gibraltar, purchase advantageous and unequivocal conditions for our commerce to America, the measure would be approved by all reasoning people. But this is by no means the opinion of *others* here, and we are not of a *tournure* to stand the least degree of popular clamour."[1] On the same day Newcastle wrote that he was not attracted by the overtures of Macanaz. " A peace with Spain attended with a breach with our allies would as inevitably fling us into the power of France, as the purchase of it by Gibraltar and Port Mahon would expose us to the condemnation and resentment of the nation."[2]

Whatever their differences on other matters, Sandwich's two correspondents agreed in urging him to keep up the negotiation with Macanaz, as likely to be extremely useful when he came to deal with the Dutch and French Ministers at Breda. Sandwich himself had made up his mind to do this, as the only way to checkmate Gilles and Wassenaer, whom he suspected more and more of having come to an agreement with du Theil to accept peace on the bases of mutual restitution and a neutrality for the Austrian Netherlands. It was not possible for him to make any progress for the moment in discussing terms with Macanaz, though he disclosed to the latter the English objections about Gibraltar and Tuscany. Everything depended upon the attitude which du Theil would take up as to the admission of other Ministers. Meanwhile, a private letter from Newcastle, asking for his opinion as to what terms would be likely to satisfy Spain, gave him the opportunity of expressing views from which he never wavered. He

[1] This autograph letter is in the Sandwich Papers at Hinchingbrooke.
[2] Newcastle to Sandwich (private), 6 February (o.s.), 1747, in Add. MSS. 32,807, fo. 71. Compare Newcastle to Cumberland of same date, *ibid.*, 32,710 fo. 7.

admitted that it was not easy to answer the question, because Macanaz " is so odd in his manners, his language, and his whole appearance " that his words are no trustworthy guide. He then continued : " In one of my former private letters I dropped a hint of the restitution of Gibraltar, and I must own that if we could at that price extricate ourselves out of the danger we are in hourly of being abandoned by our treacherous ally the Republick, could secure the possession of Cape Breton, could regulate our commercial dispute with Spain upon an advantageous foot, and could put it out of the power of the French to force us to any terms but such as we could wish both for ourselves and our allies, I should think our friends in England could never charge us with having given up the maritime interests of our country."[1] As Sandwich knew that Chesterfield shared his opinion and that Newcastle was the chief opponent, he thought it his mission to convert the latter. From this time his private letters, no longer disguised as in the time of Harrington, became as numerous and intimate as they had for some time been few and formal. But, as will be seen, Newcastle was not an easy person to convince against his will. He and his brother had their ears close to the electorate of these days, and they knew that public opinion would not tolerate the cession of Gibraltar.

As the time for the renewal of the Conference approached, the difficulty about du Theil's rank having been removed, Sandwich found his relations with his Dutch colleagues more and more strained. The Republican leaders were becoming alarmed by the growing hostility in the lesser provinces. The estates of Zealand had protested against a separate peace. The Province of Overyssel had elected Charles Bentinck, the younger brother of the Orange leader, over his Republican opponent.[2] The States-General, in defiance of the protest of the Province of Holland, had decided

[1] Newcastle's questioning letter of 10 February (o.s.) is in Add. MSS. 32,807, fo. 90. Sandwich's prompt reply on 24 February is *ibid.*, fo. 99.
[2] See above, p. 189, n. 2.

to recall van Hoey from France.[1] The Amsterdammers became convinced that they must obtain an early peace, or their ascendancy might come to an abrupt end. Gilles pressed Sandwich for some agreed ultimatum to put before du Theil. Sandwich replied that it was impossible as long as the Republic wanted the surrender of Cape Breton, an establishment for Don Philip, and a neutrality, "all of them very contrary to His Majesty's sentiments." The Pensionary said that peace was necessary for the Republic, and that, if Sandwich had expressed an English decision, he would be forced to speak a very different language at the Conference, which he had wished to avoid.[2] This made Sandwich more determined than ever to cling to Macanaz, from whom he had extracted a promise that " if he finds that France is concerting anything underhand, he will go any length with us except to a *declaration of war*."[3]

At the end of February Sandwich and Macanaz made their way to Breda, where the Conference was to reopen on 2 March, after a delay of six weeks. Chavanne, who was probably in the plot, undertook to follow them, but Harrach elected to stay at The Hague until the question of admission had been settled. On the day before the meeting, Sandwich and Macanaz met twice to concert the part which each was to play. The latter undertook " to take care if possible to throw the whole blame of Macanaz's being refused upon the French plenipotentiary, and if it was practicable to get an answer in his hand." The next day du Theil opened the proceedings by proposing to take d'Argenson's project as a canvas to work upon it, and to go through it point by point so that alterations could be suggested. Sandwich objected (1) that the project, largely inadmissible when it was first mooted, had been rendered still more so by recent events, and (2) that it contained articles relating to Spain, upon which he had been

[1] This decision was not actually carried out until after the subsequent Revolution.

[2] Sandwich to Chesterfield, 24 February, 1747, in S.P., For., Holland, 424, fo. 260.

[3] Sandwich to Chesterfield (secret), 15 February, in S.P., For., Holland, 424, fo. 229, and a copy in Add. MSS. 32,807, fo. 83.

warned by the accredited Minister of Spain not to treat
with the French Minister, who had no power to deal
with Spanish interests. Du Theil replied that he was
prepared to answer for Spain, and Sandwich asked if he
had any authority of later date than the instructions
given to Macanaz. Sandwich was dilating upon the
difficulty of conducting a Conference without the
presence of representatives of the Powers whose affairs
were being discussed, when the proceedings were interrupted by the entrance of Macanaz's secretary. He
presented a formal letter from Macanaz stating that he
had only learned at The Hague that there were objections to his admission, and also that of the Austrian
and Sardinian Ministers with whom he had to negotiate,
that he desired to have a categorical answer as to the
reasons for his exclusion, and that in the meanwhile he
hoped that they would proceed with nothing to the
direct or indirect prejudice of his master.[1] The secretary
having withdrawn, Sandwich continued that this added
to his grievance against France, that he could not
oppose the admission of a Minister from " so respectable
a Power as that of Spain," and that he proposed a
written invitation to Macanaz to attend. Du Theil said
that he could not consent either to admission or to a
written answer, and that he would explain verbally to
Macanaz that his admission would entail that of other
Ministers, to which France could not assent. The
secretary was recalled and informed that the members
of the Conference would call upon Macanaz and explain
the situation. Sandwich alone undertook to give the
explanation in writing.

In the long and jubilant letter which he wrote to
Chesterfield on the same day, Sandwich added that
" this proceeding struck a very great damp both upon
the French and the Dutch Ministers." Du Theil broke
the silence by saying that Macanaz's protest only
affected the articles which concerned Spain, and that
they could proceed with the others. But Sandwich
would not consent to this, which would have concen-

[1] A copy of this protest, in .Spanish, is in S.P., For., Holland,
424, fo. 288.

trated attention upon the forbidden subjects of Cape Breton and the neutrality. He contended that it had hitherto been understood that France spoke for Spain, and that he could not " proceed in the Conference upon a new system " without consulting his allies. Du Theil agreed to a postponement for this purpose, and added, with a malicious reference to Macanaz's extravagant demands, that Sandwich had better also talk with the Spaniard, "for that he imagined I should find Spain more tractable through the channel of France than through that of a Spanish Minister." The Dutch plenipotentiaries, who had kept silence during the discussion, were extremely perturbed by its result. As soon as du Theil had gone they appealed to Sandwich to find some expedient for continuing the Conference. He replied that he had previously met their wishes by removing difficulties created by our own allies, but that England could not be expected to remove difficulties created by an ally of France. However, he induced them to call upon Macanaz and assure him that they did not oppose his admission. By this means he carried out his purpose to throw the whole odium of exclusion upon France, and he concluded his letter with the exultant comment : " So public an instance of disagreement between France and Spain cannot in my opinion fail of turning to the advantage of His Majesty's interests."[1]

Not long after this Sandwich was alarmed by the arrival at Breda of another Spaniard, Aviz, who, it transpired, had been sent by Huescar, the Spanish Ambassador at the Court of France. He came nominally as assistant and subordinate to Macanaz, but, as Huescar was understood to have given du Theil his assurance that Macanaz would stand outside the formal Conference, it was shrewdly suspected that the newcomer's mission was to temper his superior's antagonism to France, and possibly to induce him to give way on the question of admission. Sandwich was much relieved when he learned that Macanaz was as firm as ever on this point. In order to drive home this wedge between

[1] Sandwich to Chesterfield, from Breda, 2 March, 1747, in S.P., For., Holland, 424, fo. 276.

France and Spain, Sandwich insisted upon another
meeting of the Conference as soon as du Theil's courier
had returned from Versailles. The former comedy was
repeated on 16 March. Macanaz's secretary reappeared
with a new version of the old protest that nobody but
himself was entitled to speak for Spain.[1] Du Theil
owned that he was still forbidden to consent to admission, and Sandwich at once declared that, in view of
this difference between the Courts of Madrid and Versailles, it was impossible to proceed with business until
either Macanaz and the other Ministers were admitted,
or Macanaz gave formal intimation that du Theil was
authorized to treat for Spain. Either alternative would
suit him equally well, but he must have one or the
other. On this the Conference was again adjourned,
while Macanaz and du Theil were to send couriers to
their respective Courts.[2] As this question of procedure
was never settled, the Conference of Breda, though it
remained in nominal existence for two more months,
never met again. Wassenaer remained on guard at
Breda, but Gilles had to return to The Hague to look
after domestic affairs, which were becoming daily more
difficult and disturbed. The failure to get anything
done at Breda made a profound impression in the
United Provinces, because it brought the State face to
face with the threat of a French invasion. The estates
of Holland stuck to their opinion that nothing but
a separate peace would avert the danger to which the
Republic was exposed by the selfishness of its allies.
But Zealand, more immediately threatened, was beginning to demand that preparations should be made for
a strenuous defence, and that an appeal should be made
to England for assistance.[3] Sandwich was sorely

[1] This protest is in *ibid.*, fo. 338. There is a translation of it
in Add. MSS. 32,807, fo. 184.
[2] Sandwich to Chesterfield, from Breda, in S.P., For., Holland,
424, fo. 336. There is a copy in Add. MSS. 32,807, fo. 182.
[3] Chesterfield, who was well informed as to Dutch affairs,
anticipated that Holland would prevail. In a private letter to
Sandwich of 6/17 March (at Hinchingbrooke), he said that he
feared slippery conduct on the part of the Dutch. The other
provinces may be well disposed, but " that province is the whole,

tempted to go to The Hague and to play his part in
what might prove a decisive drama. But he was detained at Breda for some weeks by his negotiation with
Macanaz.

This negotiation was going on in the interval between
the two meetings of the Conference, and for some time
afterwards. Chavanne was admitted to the secret
directly after his arrival at Breda, and probably knew
of it beforehand. Harrach was induced to follow him
on 7 March, and intimated that he was instructed to
co-operate in the negotiation with Macanaz just as
Rosenberg was co-operating with Keene at Lisbon
(rather an ominous comparison). He added that his
Court would like to know in which of the channels
England intended to bring the matter to a conclusion,
as one negotiation was apt to prejudice the other. Sandwich replied that he saw no harm in prosecuting both,
but that it would be better to conclude at Breda, as
that would have the most speedy influence in Holland.
Macanaz was now in direct touch with the Ministers of
three of the allied Powers. From the Dutch the negotiation was as carefully concealed as from du Theil, and
though Wassenaer and Gilles made several attempts to
draw Macanaz, the veteran, whose reticence was not his
strong point, succeeded in evading their queries with
the assertion that he could deal with no business until
the question of his admission had been settled.

The first concession extracted from Macanaz was the
dropping of the demand for the surrender of Minorca,
and a revised version of the Spanish demands, which
Sandwich in his covering letter seemed to think fairly
satisfactory, was forwarded to London on 10 March.[1]
But the English Ministers regarded them as quite as

---

and if she withholds her money or her troops, the good will of the
others won't signify much." And he went on to suggest that the
Prince of Orange might be made Stadtholder in that province.
But Sandwich must not let it be known that such a thing is thought
of in England. Advantageous as the thing would be, it would
be disastrous if the plan were suspected beforehand.

[1] Sandwich to Chesterfield, 10 March, in S.P., For., Holland,
424, fo. 308. Macanaz's revised proposals are *ibid.*, fo. 314.

inadmissible as the previous proposals.[1] The four major points of difficulty were Gibraltar, the *asiento*, the security of Naples, and the endowment of Don Philip. The first two concerned England alone. On the third England was assured of the support of Sardinia, and was prepared to take a strong line with the Court of Vienna. But on the fourth problem England was dependent upon the consent of the two allies most nearly concerned. The Maritime Powers had from the first vetoed any cession in the Netherlands. This left only Savoy or something in Italy. Sardinia, with English support, refused to give up Savoy, a cession which Austria was inclined to favour. Corsica had been proposed by England, and though both Austria and Sardinia had objections, those objections might be overcome. But Macanaz—much to his credit—would not listen to the proposal. From the very outset he declared that Corsica, even with the title of King, was wholly inadequate for the brother of a Spanish and the son-in-law of a French King, and that he would never consent to despoil a state which had incurred misfortunes through its attachment to Spain.[2] Nothing could be carved out on the mainland except out of Austrian or Sardinian territories, and neither would consent to this. In addition, Harrach was raising the same difficulties as Rosenberg had made at Lisbon. If Austria was to be called upon to resign all hope of getting Naples, then she was entitled to demand the restoration by Sardinia of the territories ceded by the Treaty of Worms. Finally, Chavanne, though Sandwich regarded him as a more amenable colleague than Harrach, was opposed to giving anything to Don Philip, and was uneasy lest Spain, in her zeal for Genoa,

---

[1] Chesterfield to Sandwich, 6 March (o.s.), *ibid.*, fo. 320, and in Add. MSS. 32,807, fo. 170. On the same day both Newcastle and Chesterfield wrote important private letters to Sandwich on the subject. Newcastle's letter, urging that Spain is asking too high a price for a bare neutrality, is in Add. MSS. 32,807, fo. 176. Chesterfield's letter is in the Sandwich Papers at Hinchingbrooke.

[2] This was reported to Chesterfield in Sandwich's letter of 2 March, and was frequently repeated when the English Ministers tried to press their proposal.

might demand the restoration of the whole Riviera di Ponente.[1]

Sandwich was now confronted by precisely the same difficulties which had wrecked Keene's efforts at Lisbon. But he had the confidence of youth and inexperience, he thought he had a card to play which had not been in Keene's hand, and he was convinced of the supreme importance of the task he was engaged in. For the last six months he had devoted his considerable acumen to the retention of Cape Breton and the avoidance of any certified neutrality for the Austrian Netherlands, and to the achievement of these ends without driving the Dutch into a separate treaty with France. So far he had succeeded, but the Dutch were approaching the breaking-point, and no tactical postponement of the Conference would suffice to hold them much longer. In this crisis, as it appeared to him, a treaty with Spain seemed to offer salvation. It would, he thought, secure Cape Breton, it would put an end to all need of a neutrality, and when France was paralyzed by the loss of the Spanish alliance, the Dutch would no longer have their present motive for making a separate peace. Somehow or other he had convinced himself that Gibraltar was the keynote in the Spanish demands. If the pride of Spain were gratified by the restored integrity of its mainland, Macanaz would be easy on the commercial problem and would drop Don Philip. Austria would have to give way about Naples, and, if she refused, the treaty could be signed without her. In comparison with the advantages which the treaty offered, the sacrifice of Gibraltar seemed to him, with all his naval traditions, a small matter. He set himself, in a series of almost impassioned letters, to convert the Duke of Newcastle, whom he regarded as the most influential of his opponents. But Newcastle, with one eye on the electorate and one on Vienna, with more

---

[1] It rather detracts from Macanaz's chivalrous professions with regard to Genoa, that the only reference to that State in his revised terms is a reservation of Spain's right to use her good offices for the restoration of Genoese freedom. This was specially emphasized by Sandwich as leaving it open to dispose of Genoese territory, and so to gratify Sardinia.

experience and a wider outlook, was not to be convinced by Sandwich's rhetoric. He pointed to the weakest point in the argument. Would a peace with Spain keep the Dutch loyal to the English alliance? Probably they would not venture to make a separate peace in any case, but nothing would be more likely to impel them to make it than the suggested treaty with a mere neutrality on the part of Spain. Again, was Cape Breton an equivalent for Gibraltar. " Many of your best friends, and formerly the most zealous advocates for Cape Breton, begin to think that Cape Breton alone without Quebeck and Canada will be such an immense expense and of so little use that the best we could do with it would be to purchase better conditions of peace." Finally, the Duke concluded with a warning which summarizes his policy at the time : " The cession of Cape Breton, I should hope, might be avoided ; the neutrality of the Low Countries can never, or ought never, to be consented to ; the establishment for Don Philip may be settled as things turn out. But the allies should be kept united ; and any peace upon that foot is better than a more advantageous one that is attended with disunion, coolness, and dissatisfaction amongst those Powers who ought ever, for their mutual interest, to be most firmly tied and united together."[1]

Sandwich was not dismayed by this depressing letter, but replied with an equally argumentative epistle in which he contended that France, if deserted by Spain, would not continue a hopeless war, and urged (which was probably true of the Duke of Bedford) that the depreciation of Cape Breton by his friends had been intended as an argument, not for its surrender, but for the conquest of Canada.[2] But his struggle was un-

[1] This letter of 6 March (o.s.), which is not discreditable to Newcastle, is in Add. MSS. 32,807, fo. 176.
[2] Sandwich to Newcastle (private), 24 March, in *ibid.*, fo. 201. In the plan of campaign drafted by Newcastle in the autumn of 1746 prominence was given to an English expedition against the French in North America. It was omitted from the draft convention submitted to the allies, as likely to convince the Dutch that England would never surrender Cape Breton. Both Bedford and Sandwich were eager supporters of the expedition, and were much chagrined when it was abandoned in February, 1747, in

availing. Every letter from England, both public and private, informed him that a treaty with Spain was impossible if Macanaz insisted upon the cession of Gibraltar. Very reluctantly Sandwich abandoned the struggle, and wrote on 4 April from The Hague, whither he had gone to watch the doings of the Pensionary, that this decision rendered the negotiation hopeless. In view of an anticipated General Election, he began to ask permission to return home in order to look after his political interests. To Newcastle, on the same date, he apologized for his obstinacy, and said that if he had known how resolute the Duke was about Gibraltar he might have been earlier convinced of his error.[1]

In this despondent mood Sandwich returned to Breda for what might be a final interview with Macanaz. Harrach and Chavanne, never very willing to leave the Englishman and the Spaniard alone together, hastened to follow him. Sandwich conveyed the news that Gibraltar was out of the question. Macanaz was much concerned, as the provision for Don Philip was by no means the principal object of Spain and was only urged " out of pique of honour." This was in rather startling contrast to the representations that had been made to Keene at Lisbon. Sandwich was equally unwilling to make Don Philip " a principal object," as it involved a collision with Sardinia and a probable breach with Austria. Macanaz was as resolute as ever in his rejection of Corsica. In the end Macanaz agreed that, if the reasons for the refusal of Gibraltar were given him in writing, he would send a courier to Madrid, though he could hold out no hope of success. This he regretted, as the King of Spain's intentions were " fixed upon forming a *Triumvirate* with England and the House of Austria."[2] Both in this and in later interviews Sand-

deference to naval opinion. See Newcastle to Sandwich, 31 January (o.s.), *ibid.*, fo. 43. Newcastle says that he and Bedford were alone in its support.
[1] The office letter to Chesterfield of 4 April is in S.P., For., Holland, 425, fo. 3. The private letter to Newcastle is in Add. MSS. 32,807, fo. 255.
[2] Sandwich to Chesterfield (secret), 11 April, 1747, in S.P., For., Holland, 425, fo. 19, and Add. MSS. 32,807, fo. 269. On

wich was agreeably surprised by the attitude of Aviz, whom he had hitherto regarded as a check upon the Anglophil tendencies of Macanaz. He was now inclined to regret that the second Spaniard had not been there from the first, as his keener practical sense might have cured the wild projects " which Macanaz by living for thirty years among books is too apt to give in to."

What Sandwich had failed to do was achieved by Chavanne, who was evidently an accomplished diplomatist. Two days after the former had gone back to The Hague he received a startling letter from the Sardinian Minister to the effect that Macanaz was willing that the two most difficult matters—Gibraltar and Don Philip—should be put aside, and that an agreement should be come to on the other points at issue between Spain and England. " Il m'a cependant ajouté qu'en se relachant sur l'article de Gibraltar, par les raisons que vous avés dit, il se croit en droit d'exiger que l'Angleterre s'oblige de se concerter avec ses alliés et le Roy d'Espagne son maitre, pour procurer dans la suite quelque accommodement à l'Infant Don Philippe." Chavanne added in a postscript that he hoped by this means to relegate both questions to the Greek kalends.[1] This letter, which Sandwich sent off by special messenger the same day, caused great relief in London, where Ministers were becoming extremely depressed by the apparent failure of the negotiation at Breda, by the increasing certainty that the Dutch would, willingly or unwillingly, be forced into a separate treaty, and by the probable disappointment of all the hopes that had been based upon the twin campaigns in the Netherlands and in Southern France which had been mapped out in the convention of 10 January. Newcastle, who saw in

the same day he wrote in a private letter to Newcastle that Harrach refused to come to any terms with Macanaz. "His expression was that if he was to offer him kingdoms, he could not venture to accept them " (*ibid.*, fo. 267). Throughout the Austrian Minister was as obstructive to the separate treaty with Spain as Rosenberg was at Lisbon, but with more courtesy and less vehemence.

[1] Chavanne to Sandwich, from Breda, 14 April, 1747, in S.P., For., Holland, 425, fo. 35, and Add. MSS. 32,808, fo. 9.

the letter a complete justification for his obstinate refusal of Gibraltar, was almost incoherent in his jubilation. He wrote to Sandwich that his letter

" contains the most comfortable and advantageous prospect of any letter I have yet seen. The thought of being able to make a separate peace with Spain, without either the cession of Gibraltar or the fixing an immediate establishment for Don Philip, exceeds indeed all my hopes, who am thought very sanguine here, however desponding you may think me. . . . If this scheme succeeds, Europe will be upon a better foot than it has ever been since the death of Charles the Second of Spain, and I will ever own, and every body must, the great share you've had in bringing about this great and surprising event. . . . No man alive is more for concluding than I am, and it is not a little *rub* in the way that shall stop me. The hope of a favourable peace with Spain was one of the favourable events that encouraged me to resist, as I did, the acceptance in any shape of d'Argenson's plan.

" I must laugh with you upon your dissertation upon my *despondency*. I showed it to the King, who daily sees and knows that I am the only man that have any hopes or expectations left. . . . When I said the spirits here were low and dejected, I did not mean my own, but, I am sorry to say, every body's else, even those who went with me last year. . . . I may say to you in confidence that, had it not been for my *single* opinion, we should now have been in a new confidential negotiation with the Pensionary upon the conditions upon which we would conclude a peace."[1]

This letter, and especially its last sentence, is of interest because it helps to solve a puzzle which is presented by a superficial reading of the correspondence. On the question of Gibraltar Chesterfield had expressed agreement with Sandwich, though he had been outvoted in the Cabinet. On the other hand, Newcastle had resolutely opposed the project and had carried the Cabinet with him. It would be natural to expect that Sandwich, who did not like being thwarted or criticized,

[1] Newcastle to Sandwich (private), 7 April (o.s.), in Add. MSS. 32,808, fo. 21.

would have remained, as he had been in the early months of the year, rather cool towards Newcastle and cordial in his relations with Chesterfield. But the very opposite was actually the case. From this time onwards Sandwich ceased to be on confidential terms with Chesterfield, while he became more intimate than ever with Newcastle. The explanation is to be sought at The Hague. Chesterfield, whose correspondents in Holland sometimes led him astray, seems to have made up his mind that the Republican party was going to hold its own in the States, that they would make peace with France, and that the only safe thing for England was to make peace too. For this reason he discouraged all further complicity with the Orange party, which he had at one time been inclined to encourage. For this neither Bentinck nor Sandwich ever forgave him. The alliance between the two English Secretaries of State was henceforth definitely at an end. There was no personal quarrel—Chesterfield did not seem to think it worth while—but they were now on opposite sides. Chesterfield had become again what he had always been at heart, an advocate of an early peace, " peace *quovis modo,*" as hostile contemporaries called it. Newcastle was determined, if he could guide events, to postpone a settlement until better terms were in sight. In this division Sandwich was heart and soul on the side of Newcastle, and he became more eager than ever to succeed in making his treaty with Macanaz.

On both sides of the sea there was a feverish framing of treaties. Sandwich and Macanaz, with the assistance of Chavanne, drew up one draft at Breda. Newcastle, always eager at this sort of work, wrote out another, which was sent off by Chesterfield to Sandwich on 11/22 April.[1] On its receipt, Sandwich and Macanaz reconsidered their draft, and produced a new version. Sandwich had hoped that he would be able to sign with the powers which he already held, but some unexpected

---

[1] Chesterfield to Sandwich (most secret), 11 April (o.s.), in S.P., For., Holland, 425, fo. 58, and Add. MSS. 32,808, fo. 41. The two drafts are both in the same volumes—viz., fos. 64 and 77 of the State Papers, and fos. 32 and 43 of the Newcastle Papers.

difficulties compelled him to refer them to London. The *asiento* was the principal commercial problem, and Newcastle would have liked to postpone it until the definitive peace. Macanaz insisted upon its abolition and upon the opening of the slave-trade to all nations. Sandwich was authorized to give way on this, provided Spain granted a free port and agreed to refer to commissioners the question of debts to the South Sea Company, but he must first get a satisfactory settlement of other points. Macanaz wanted a secret article reserving the right of Spain, after peace had been made, to find some expedient for the recovery of Gibraltar. This the English Ministers vetoed. There must be no mention of Gibraltar either in public or in secret articles. Macanaz also demanded that England should offer no opposition to an establishment for Don Philip, provided it could be found without compromising her with her allies. To this there could be no opposition, as the recent policy of England had been directed to find such a principality. But Macanaz further asserted that Spain must retain possession of Savoy until Don Philip's claims had been satisfied. England, in view of the pledges given to Sardinia in the Treaty of Worms, could not possibly assent to this. Sandwich found Macanaz much more difficult to deal with, both on political and commercial questions, now that the latter had lost all hope of Gibraltar. As long as there was any chance of gaining his great point, Macanaz had been very easy on other matters. Now he not only stuck to his secret article about Gibraltar and the retention of Savoy, but he put forward the extremely old Spanish contention that all commercial treaties since 1700 should be declared null and void, " under pretence of their having been made by foreigners, who have of late governed that kingdom, and have ever postponed the interests of that monarchy to their own private purposes."[1] This would have made short work of the *asiento* and the *navio permiso*. Sandwich had to rely upon the unexpected

---

[1] Sandwich to Chesterfield, 21 April, in S.P., For., Holland, 425, fo. 75, and Add. MSS. 32,808, fo. 28.

aid of Aviz to get the commercial clauses into tolerable
shape, but at last he had the draft preliminaries so far
completed that he was prepared to sign them except for
the one point of Savoy. It is true that Harrach, instructed like Rosenberg from Vienna, protested against
any security being assured to Naples unless Maria
Theresa received either the Worms cessions or some
other equivalent in Italy. Sandwich replied that it was
impossible to continue the war for conquests and equiva-
lents, and that the allies would do well to secure the
restoration of the Netherlands and Savoy, and otherwise
leave every party with its present possessions. These
ends could only be gained by detaching Spain from
France, and Spain could only be gained by abstaining
from all hostility against Don Carlos.[1] Sandwich had
for some time made up his mind that peace could only
be made by leaving Austria out.[2]

Before Sandwich could get his treaty finally adjusted
with Macanaz he had to leave Chavanne at Breda to
fight the battle for Savoy. He himself was forced to
hurry to The Hague, where it seemed every day more
difficult to prevent the conclusion of that separate peace
for which the provincial estates of Holland had been
pressing since December. The party in France which
always urged militant measures against the Dutch as
the only means of inducing them to come to terms had
gained the upper hand since the fall of d'Argenson. On

[1] Sandwich to Chesterfield (secret), 2 May, 1747, in S.P., For.,
Holland, 425, fo. 140, and Add. MSS. 32,808, fo. 105.

[2] On 17 April Sandwich wrote to Newcastle an autograph letter,
which is interesting in view of later happenings at Aix-la-Chapelle.
In this he said that, as regards Austria, Newcastle must agree
" that nothing is to be done in any pacifick negotiation if we
determine to act in everything fairly in concert with that Court.
I would not have your Grace imagine from what I am now saying
that I think our other ally, the King of Sardinia, in reality more
reasonable; but the present situation of his affairs makes him so
in effect; he has got all he expected, and will, I make no doubt, be
very glad to sit down contented with his present possessions, so
that I do not expect any obstructions from that quarter; but,
for the other, depend upon it, when you mean seriously to conclude, you must do it not only without their assistance, but
without their consent " (Add. MSS. 32,808, fo. 15). This was
an answer to Newcastle's sermon on the duty of keeping the allies
together.

17 April the French Government, through de la Ville, still technically French envoy at The Hague, issued a proclamation which came as near to a formal declaration of war as was possible without assuming that character.[1] France had no intention, it was said, of breaking with the Republic, but it was no longer possible to respect a neutrality which was abused by giving shelter and assistance of all kinds to the troops of Powers which were openly at war with France. The King had shown his regard for the Republic by using it as a channel for conveying his desires for peace since 1742, and by the deliberate postponement of an invasion of Dutch territories, fully justified last year, because the peace Conference was there conducted. But his last scruple had been removed by the open obstruction of the conferences at Breda in flagrant opposition to previous formal engagements with France. The French troops followed this proclamation by entering Dutch Flanders. Within a few days Sluys and three other strong places were in their hands. Zealand, the second most important of the Dutch provinces, was now open to invasion, and appealed to the Duke of Cumberland for assistance. Cumberland, who was preparing for his campaign against Marshal Saxe, could only spare some Dutch battalions, while the few Dutch ships that were fit to go to sea were ordered to cruise along the coast. The Pensionary Gilles was now face to face with the same crisis which had been fatal to the greatest of his predecessors in office, John de Witt. He had had ample time and warning, but was quite unprepared with any settled line of action. He denounced to Sandwich " the behaviour of England, who by refusing to co-operate in pacific measures had brought the Republic into their present danger and distress, and urged the unfriendly part of our refusing to explain ourselves upon the principal points of dispute, namely the establishment for Don Philip and Cape Breton."[2] But he dared not carry

[1] There is a copy of the French proclamation in S.P., For., Holland, 425, fo. 47. The covering letter of de la Ville, dated 17 April, is fo. 46.
[2] Sandwich to Chesterfield, 17 April, in S.P., For., Holland, 425, fo. 42.

out the oft-repeated threat of making a separate treaty with du Theil, as he feared that any servility to France might provoke a revolution in the provinces. Sandwich cared little for mere verbal reproaches, and was so re-assured that he returned to Breda to renew his direct communication with Macanaz. But he had made no progress, when news of the growing alarm in Zealand recalled him to The Hague, and he again left Chavanne in charge. As a last expedient, he wrote to Chavanne that Gilles was in constant communication with du Theil, and that Spain must conclude at once if the Dutch were to be prevented from making their separate peace. If Chavanne could obtain assurance as to the immediate evacuation of Savoy, he would take horse at once and be in Breda within eight hours.[1] At the same time he wrote to Chesterfield that he had deliberately exagger-ated the Pensionary's inclination towards France, and urged the prompt sending of naval aid to Zealand.[2]

Four days later, on 28 April, Sandwich wrote two important letters. In the first he reported that Macanaz had received no new instructions, and feared they were held up by Huescar at Paris in collusion with the French Government, which had been straining every nerve at Madrid to break off the Spanish negotiation with England. In the meantime there was a deadlock, as Macanaz dared not sign without either Gibraltar or an establishment for Don Philip, and if he failed to gain the latter he was ordered to insist upon the reten-tion of Savoy. Savoy was therefore the obstacle, and, until he had obtained that, Sandwich refused to give way about the *asiento*. In the second letter he an-nounced the momentous news of a revolution in Zealand. On the arrival of an English squadron the populace began to clamour for a Stadtholder, and the estates of the province, by the unanimous vote of the six towns, appointed the Prince of Orange to be Stadtholder, Cap-tain-General, and Admiral of Zealand. From Zealand

---

[1] Copies of the letter to Chavanne of 24 April are in S.P., For., Holland, 425, fo. 97, and in Add. MSS., 32,808, fo. 97.

[2] Sandwich to Chesterfield (secret), 24 April, in S.P., For., Holland, 425, fo. 93. Copy in Add. MSS. 32,808, fo. 93,

the movement spread to Rotterdam, Dort, Leyden, and other towns in Holland, which so terrified the Regents of that province that all danger of separate measures with France was at an end. The Pensionary's tone, said Sandwich, was now completely changed. He declared that he had been carried along by the torrent against his will, and that England, whose conduct he had so recently condemned, was the natural and inseparable ally of the Republic.[1]

The next day, a Saturday, Sandwich had even more momentous news to send. Deputies from Rotterdam came in the morning to demand that the provincial estates of Holland should follow the example of that town and confer the Stadtholdership upon the Prince of Orange. A popular rising broke out at The Hague, and the mob was only pacified by the appearance of Bentinck, who distributed Orange colours and promised the election of the Prince on the following Wednesday. Even after this rioters continued to demand the blood of the traitors who had sold them to France.[2] It was not till the evening that they began to disperse, and in the dark Bentinck took the trembling Gilles home in a coach decked with Orange colours.[3] This was the decisive day. On 3 May the estates of Holland fulfilled the promise given by Bentinck, and the proclamation was signed by that stanch Republican, Willem Buys.[4] On the following day the States-General elected the Prince as Captain-General and Admiral of the Union. As William IV was already Stadtholder of three provinces, and as Utrecht and Overyssel speedily followed the example of Zealand and Holland, he was the first

[1] These two letters to Chesterfield are in S.P., For., Holland, 425, fos. 112 and 118.
[2] Sandwich to Newcastle, 3 May (Add. MSS., 32,808, fo. 114), says that Löwendahl, after the surrender of Sluys, had the imprudence to say, in the hearing of many Dutch officers, that he came not to injure but to save the Republic, *et que ce qu'il faisait étoit de concert avec vos Messieurs*. This made a great impression. " I think it next to a miracle that it did not draw on the destruction of the Pensionary and many of the Dutch Regents."
[3] Sandwich to Chesterfield, 29 April, in S.P., For., Holland, 425, fo. 120.
[4] A copy of the proclamation is in *ibid.*, fo. 156.

member of his house to hold the office in all seven provinces.[1]

This sudden and complete overthrow of the great Republican party, which had guided Dutch policy for nearly half a century, and the elevation to considerable, though ill-defined, authority of George II's son-in-law, were hailed in England as extremely auspicious events. It is impossible to say how far Sandwich had any share in bringing them about. He had obeyed instructions to avoid publicity in his intercourse with the Orange leaders, and it was in the highest degree unadvisable, in the interests of both England and the Prince, to allow it be thought that the Revolution was in any way due to alien instigation. But the private correspondence of Sandwich with Newcastle and additional papers at Hinchingbrooke leave no doubt that he was from the outset on the most confidential terms with Bentinck, and it is quite possible that the latter had some financial aid from England. At any rate, without any imprudent boasting, Sandwich certainly took and received some credit for a change of government which he must have ardently desired. Newcastle, however, showed a characteristic eagerness to share in the credit. In his first congratulatory letter he wrote : " I think this turn in Holland will make our peace with Spain. . . . Your Lordship and I must have some secret satisfaction that a perseverance in the system on which you went to Holland has in some measure brought about, but in all respects enabled the King to profit of, this great and happy event ; whereas contrary measures and an acceptance, either last year of d'Argenson's plan of peace, or a confidential negotiation this winter with the present Pensionary upon the terms of peace, might have made His Majesty the instrument of defeating this very measure which he has always had so much at heart, and is so beneficial to this country and all Europe."[2]

[1] Historians have adopted the convenient but misleading practice of speaking of Stadtholders as if they were federal officials. It was essentially a provincial office.   The only federal position of the Orange Princes was that of Captain-General and Admiral.

[2] Newcastle to Sandwich, 21 April (o.s.), 1747, in Add. MSS. 32,808, fo. 101.   Three days later he wrote a longer letter with

Newcastle thought that the Dutch revolution would bring about peace with Spain. Sandwich, even more sanguine, thought that he would now be able to obtain the long-desired declaration of war against France, and also Dutch support for the retention of Cape Breton by England. None of these expectations were fulfilled. A cooler observer, like Chesterfield, knew from the outset that most of the confident hopes aroused by the elevation of the Stadtholder were doomed to disappointment. In spite of its momentary defeat, the Republican party was the strongest and most permanent element in the state. Its members held all the chief offices, both at The Hague and in the provinces. William IV, possessed of certain talents for discussion and exposition, was wholly without experience in administration, and, even if he had ventured on a complete change of officials, he had no trained followers to fill their places. Gilles, whom Sandwich now thoroughly mistrusted,[1] remained Pensionary, and his opinions had not changed as he had professed in a moment of panic. A Stadtholder was not a King : he was not even a hereditary magistrate. If William IV wished, as he did wish, to wield the same authority that his last great predecessor had enjoyed, and if he wished to transmit that authority to his descendants, he could only achieve these ends by getting the support of the men who wielded the chief influence in the provinces and the municipalities. And he could not hope to win this support if he acted against their convictions and their prejudices. Policy as well as personal pride forbade him to act as if he was the puppet of England. A father-in-law is not necessarily, or even frequently, a dictator. Even Ben-

---

more fulsome self-laudation. Among other things he claimed all the credit for sending aid to Zealand (*ibid.*, fo. 122). See also Newcastle to Hardwicke, 21 April, in Hardwicke Papers (Add. MSS. 35,409, fo. 21).

[1] It was at this time that Sandwich made his discovery that Gilles, when he went to join Wassenaer in the previous year, had carried with him leave, drafted by himself with Van der Heim, to conclude, if necessary, a separate treaty with France, and only to allow England a limited time in which to accede (Sandwich to Newcastle, 9 May, 1747, in Add. MSS. 32,808, fo. 128). See above, p. 164.

tinck might presume too much, like many king-
makers, upon the services he had rendered in reviving
the stadtholdership. And Bentinck, though half an
Englishman, was also half a Dutchman. He was willing
to go the whole way with Sandwich in opposing a
separate or a premature peace. But he had no interest
in securing Cape Breton for England, nor could he
advise William IV to go further in opposition to France
than France had gone with regard to the Republic.
All these considerations must have been brought home
to English Ministers during the following months, but
they were blurred to Newcastle and Sandwich in their
first exultation. Chesterfield was probably the only
Englishman who clearly grasped them from the first,
and who realized the danger of putting too much trust
in the assumed gratitude and loyalty of the Prince of
Orange.

The first disappointment was with regard to the
negotiation with Spain. Sandwich had all along built
too much upon Macanaz's personal hostility to France,
and had forgotten that there were important personages
at Madrid who did not share those views. He had had
ample warning as to the personal desire of Ferdinand VI
and his wife to provide a home for Don Philip in Italy
in order to keep him at a distance from Madrid. This
desire England could not gratify on account of the
opposition of Austria and Sardinia. The alleged preference of the recovery of Gibraltar probably existed only
in the imagination of Macanaz. If this had really been
the first object of Spain, Keene would surely have heard
something of it at Lisbon. But the treaty which Sandwich was ready to sign gave neither Gibraltar nor any
definite cession to Don Philip. Such a treaty offered
no temptation to Spain, whereas the Court of Versailles,
though not likely to give any promises about Gibraltar,
might be trusted to remain loyal to Don Philip, as the
son-in-law of the French King. These arguments were
sufficient to turn the scale at Madrid, and Sandwich
ought to have been prepared for their success. While he
was waiting at The Hague for the arrival of the Prince of
Orange to take up his new office, he received his first

warning in a letter from Wassenaer stating that du Theil was now prepared to admit Macanaz.[1] This startling news put the English envoy in a quandary. Now that he was assured against an immediate peace move in Holland he had no longer any use for the Conference. He had had no opportunity of discussing a programme with either the Prince or Bentinck, and he did not even know whether Gilles or Wassenaer would continue to be employed as plenipotentiaries.[2] As to Harrach and Chavanne, he could now insist upon their admission, but the motive for that insistence had gone, and he had good reason to know how little either of them, and especially Harrach, would contribute to harmony among the allies. To appear at Breda without any agreement at all as to what was to be demanded or refused would put all the honours in du Theil's hand. Before Sandwich could receive any instructions as to what he should do in this dilemma, another more shattering message arrived. On 12 May Macanaz's secretary—the man who had been so useful at Breda before—came with a message that Aviz desired a secret meeting. The wood on the way to Scheveningen was fixed upon, and there Aviz told Sandwich that French influence had prevailed at Madrid, that Macanaz's projects had been disapproved, and that the latter had received orders to continue the Conference as a full member but in concert with du Theil.[3] This was fatal, as Sandwich's trump card since January had been the rupture between the French and Spanish Ministers. He had now less use for the Conference than ever. Fortunately for him France shared his views, though for quite different reasons. France had been drawn into the Conference at Breda

[1] Sandwich to Chesterfield, 9 May (S.P., For., Holland, 425, fo. 170). In this letter he states the danger of going to Breda without an agreed plan. France would at once demand Cape Breton, and the Prince of Orange could not venture to oppose it until his power was more firmly established.

[2] Newcastle (to Sandwich, private, 5/16 May) thought that the Prince of Orange would never employ them. But it would have been dangerous to slight them at the outset. The postponement and transfer of the Conference removed this difficulty.

[3] Sandwich to Chesterfield (secret), 12 May, 1747, in S.P., For., Holland, 425, fo. 195, and Add. MSS. 32,808, fo. 150.

by d'Argenson's confident expectation that it would lead, if not to a treaty with both the Maritime Powers, which might serve as the basis of a general pacification, at any rate to a separate agreement with the Dutch, which would enable France to dictate terms. Since then d'Argenson had fallen. England had shown all along a determination to avoid even the discussion of a treaty, and the Dutch Revolution put an end to all prospect of a separate peace with the Republic. France must now abandon diplomacy and employ force. Peace must be sought on the battlefield, not in the council chamber. It was really preposterous to regard the Dutch any longer as neutrals, and Breda, which had been chosen as a technically neutral town, might at any moment be attacked by French troops. In such circumstances both international usage and French dignity required that the Conference, if it was continued at all, should be removed to some genuinely neutral meeting-place. This was the gist of a joint communication addressed by du Theil and Macanaz to the States-General—not to England.[1] In this the French and Spanish Courts proposed, not to break off the Conference, but to transfer it to some suitable town, such as Aix-la-Chapelle. As no Power could venture to appear as an avowed obstructor of peace, it was impossible for the Dutch to refuse the proposal, or for England to advise such a refusal. But it was clear that, at the moment, nobody wanted to renew the Conference, and so it remained in a state of suspended animation until the results of the campaign should impel one State or another to move for its resumption. Macanaz, after obtaining a sort of testimonial from Sandwich—a rather pathetic request from an old man to a young one—was sent to reside at Liège, whence he corresponded with the English envoy at intervals, and where he continued to dream of being recalled to high office at Madrid.[2]

[1] Sandwich reported the first rumour of this intention to Chesterfield on 16 May (S.P., For., Holland, 425, fo. 232), and the final notice to the States on 23 May (*ibid.*, fo. 252).
[2] In the Sandwich Papers at Hinchingbrooke (App. III.) there are some curious letters from Macanaz's secretary at Liège. On

Sandwich must have looked back with somewhat mixed feelings to the period of nine months during which he had been the accredited representative of England at Breda. He had been sent out, or rather he had concerted with Newcastle, to carry out a certain scheme, and he had done it with a mixture of luck and ingenuity. He had kept the Conference going all these months without ever touching upon its professed business and with only five meetings, each of which had broken up on the problem of procedure. And he had done this in spite of the ill-concealed indignation of his Dutch colleagues, and yet they had never made that separate treaty with France which they declared to be the inevitable result of obstruction. When all risk of this was over he admitted that his obstruction had been deliberate, which indeed they must have known. But this success, which at first elated him, was in the end more than counterbalanced by his failure to complete his treaty with Macanaz. To the end of his diplomatic career, and probably to the end of his life, he cherished a grudge against that overvaluing of ignorant prejudices which had prevented him from surrendering Gibraltar and so coming to satisfactory terms with the impulsive old man, in whose good faith he never ceased to believe. But, at the moment, even this disappointment was thrust into the background by a personal slight for which he never forgave the author.

For some weeks he had been impressing upon both

16 September, 1747, he wrote that it had been discovered at Madrid that Huescar had held up Macanaz's letters from Breda, and had urged the Spanish Government to adhere to France. On 20 March, 1748, he reported that Don Philip had written to say that Carvajal had lost the King's favour, that Macanaz was to be recalled, and that on his arrival the management of affairs would be placed in his hands. On 28 March a second letter announced that Huescar in Paris had withheld the promised supplies of money, and had remonstrated against Macanaz's return. But the old man was as confident, and his schemes as chimerical, as ever. He was prepared to strip France of all its seventeenth-century gains—Dunkirk and the towns on the Flemish border, Alsace, Lorraine, Franche Comté, Roussillon. Alsace and Lorraine with the border towns were to go to Maria Theresa, but Franche Comté was to be given to the King of Sardinia. It is not surprising that Maria Theresa thought Macanaz to be mad.

Chesterfield and Newcastle his urgent need for permission to return home for a time. His pretext was the approaching election, but it is probable that he also wanted to secure his succession to the Admiralty, which, according to rumour, Bedford was about to resign. As long as the new Government in Holland seemed insecure, and as long as there was a possibility of renewed meetings at Breda, compliance with his request was postponed, and Newcastle, in a private letter, warned him that persistence in the request might lead to the sending of a not altogether agreeable substitute or colleague.[1] Newcastle may or may not have known how prophetic this warning was, but exactly a week later he wrote that the King, in order to comply with Sandwich's request for leave of absence, " has been pleased to appoint Mr. Dayrolles Resident to the States, to be employed, as his uncle the late Mr. Dayrolles was, as second Minister in Holland."[2] Three days afterwards Chesterfield sent formal intimation from the Northern Office of the appointment of Dayrolles, who " is ordered to take your Lordship's advice in every thing that may be proper for him in his station to do."[3]

Sandwich had always a fairly high sense of his dignity and importance, and he considered that his recent services entitled him to special consideration from the Ministers at home. He would in any case have resented having a colleague thrust upon him without any notice or consultation, but his objections to this particular colleague were based upon something more than

[1] Newcastle to Sandwich (private), 28 April (o.s.), in Add. MSS. 32,808, fo. 142. " By the little experience that I have had, a Minister of rank, commissioned *pro interim*, has never been a pleasant thing to the resident one, as your Lordship must be considered at present to be."
[2] Newcastle to Sandwich (private), 5 May (o.s.), Add. MSS. 32,808, fo. 171.
[3] Chesterfield to Sandwich, 8 May (o.s.), S.P., For., Holland, 425, fo. 238. In a private letter (at Hinchingbrooke) written on 5 May, Chesterfield evidently felt the necessity of being somewhat apologetic. " As, during your absence from The Hague, whether by being here or hereafter at Breda, many things of form as well as of substance must be done, the King thought it necessary to have a settled Resident there, and that Dayrolles had a sort of hereditary claim to that employment."

wounded vanity. Dayrolles was regarded as a most intimate friend and confidant—scandal said he was an illegitimate relative[1]—of Chesterfield. Sandwich's suspicions as to Chesterfield's relations with the Republican leaders, and as to his continued correspondence with them in order to promote the conclusion of peace, had been turned into certainty by all that he had learned from Bentinck and others during and after the revolution. The statement that Dayrolles had a hereditary right to an appointment in Holland strengthened his conviction that this man, with his Dutch acquaintances and his knowledge of Dutch politics, had been specially selected to watch and report on his own intimacy with the Prince of Orange and his supporters. His indignation found expression in private letters to Newcastle, which not only throw light upon the writer's character, but also contributed in no small degree to sow dissension in the English Cabinet. In his first letter on the subject he says that the sending of Dayrolles "will add greatly to the necessity of my seeing your Grace, and knowing from you the foundation upon which I stand. Your Grace cannot think me so undiscerning as not to make my observations upon that measure, and indeed I believe I know more of the foundation from which it sprung than it was imagined I did, because, though it is impossible for me to be apprized of all that passes at home, yet I can generally discover any thing that has its rise upon this side of the water. . . . I have wrote privately to my Lord Chesterfield; I wish he may show you the letter; in which I hope I have given him reason to see that I did not think I deserved from him what he has thought proper to do in sending one to be a spy upon my actions. I have touched it so gently that he must look very close to see that I understand the meaning of Mr. Dayrolles' mission; tho', I own, I have had difficulty to hide my opinion, since the manner of doing it without giving me the least previous intimation, and the secret

[1] Horace Walpole (to Mann, 19 May, 1747) tells the story that Alexander Stanhope, a son of the first Lord Chesterfield, employed the elder Dayrolles as a clerk when at The Hague, and that the younger Dayrolles was the offspring of an intrigue between the Minister and his clerk's wife (*Letters* [ed. Toynbee], ii., 276).

foundation which I am satisfied it was built upon of some letters from hence from people who I should be sorry if they did not disapprove my conduct, have, I own, touched me so much that it will not be easy for me to get rid of the impression it has made."[1] Newcastle, unwilling to admit an intrigue of which he had no knowledge, tried to reassure Sandwich as to the appointment being due to letters from Holland. He acknowledged that Chesterfield had an extensive correspondence with some of his *old* friends, declared he used to see some of the letters before Chesterfield became Secretary, and defended Dayrolles as " a very honest fellow, a great friend of many of my friends, and an old acquaintance of mine." He owned that he had offered no objection to the appointment, and added that, if there was in any quarter a desire to do business through any other channel than Sandwich, he would undertake never to employ it.[2]

Sandwich, entirely unconciliated, replied that he was ready to follow Newcastle's " system," but that success was hopeless if once the Dutch pacifists knew that they had sympathizers in the English Ministry. " They will continue to act on the same supposition they did before (which notion they had at that time from the best authority) that the Ministry wish Holland would force them to a peace, and will consequently make it their business to clog all vigorous measures and to manifest as much as possible their disinclination and inability to continue the war. I own I suspect strongly that Dayrolles will be very likely to instill this sort of doctrine; your Grace thinks him an honest fellow, so do I, because I think him honest to his attachment, and I have seen a letter from him since I have been here (I mean several months ago) in which he spoke the same language of those to whom I take him to be most attached, and talked of the great necessity that England had for a speedy peace. I have pretty good information that some letters were wrote to Lord Chesterfield to desire him to come over in person to profit of the present

[1] Sandwich to Newcastle (entirely private), 23 May, in Add. MSS., 32,808, fo. 193.
[2] Newcastle to Sandwich (private), 12 May (o.s.), in *ibid.*, fo. 199.

opportunity, upon a supposition that I am not likely to turn it towards peace. I can easily conceive why Lord Chesterfield cannot leave England at this time, but a person sent directly out of his family[1] may convey his sentiments with as much authority as if they came directly from himself, and, as I consider the thing in that light, I own I can't be so indifferent about Mr. Dayrolles' mission as your Grace seems to be, and I shall never expect to succeed in any of my designs here when there is a channel open to convey another sort of language, which channel, as long as it remains open, will I have no reason to doubt be made effectual use of." A few days later Sandwich wrote again : " Bentinck considers the mission of Mr. Dayrolles in the same light that I do, and during my absence will communicate any thing that may be necessary for mine or your Grace's information thro' Mr. Keith's channel and no other, taking for granted (as I do more and more by considering the point) that the other is here in order to facilitate the execution of such purposes as are very contrary to your Grace's inclination."[2]   In this mood of anger and suspicion Sandwich quitted The Hague on 10 June and spent the next six weeks in England. During his absence he left the conduct of the Embassy, so far as he could, not in the hands of the intruding Dayrolles, but in those of Robert Keith, the Scottish secretary whom he had brought with him when he first came to Holland.[3]

[1] Dayrolles was Chesterfield's godson, and had lived with him as private secretary while the Earl was Ambassador at The Hague and Viceroy in Dublin.

[2] These two letters (private and entirely secret) of 28 May and 6 June are in Add. MSS. 32,808, fos. 220 and 258.

[3] Robert Keith, a cadet of the great Scottish family of that name, played an active part in diplomacy for the next fifteen years, first as Envoy at Vienna from 1748 to the outbreak of the Seven Years' War, and then in Russia during that war. He had to leave Russia after the revolution which placed Catharine II upon the throne, and spent the rest of his life in Edinburgh, where he was the intimate friend of Principal Robertson and Jupiter Carlyle, and where he was known as Ambassador Keith. His son, Sir Robert Murray Keith, who is frequently confused with his father by continental historians, was a still more famous diplomatist. See *Autobiography of Alexander Carlyle* (one of the best of books), and Mrs. Gillespie Smyth, *Memoirs and Correspondence of Sir Robert Murray Keith*, vol. i.

CHAPTER VII

BETWEEN BREDA AND AIX-LA-CHAPELLE (JUNE, 1747, TO MARCH, 1748).

Cumberland's defeat at Lafeld—Wentworth at Vienna and in Italy—Failure of Austrian siege of Genoa—Repulse of French attack on Piedmont—Subsequent inaction in Italy—Cumberland supports pacifists—Saxe-Ligonier overture—Opposition of Prince of Orange and Bentinck—Attitude of Newcastle—Controversies in English Ministry—Sandwich sent back to Holland—Saxe's extraordinary letter—Renewed controversy—Saxe formulates French demands—Sandwich entrusted with negotiation—Bentinck's mission to England—Interview of Sandwich with Puyzieulx at Liège—Fall of Bergen-op-Zoom—Depression of Newcastle—Sandwich and Bentinck reassure him—Negotiations with Wall—Military Convention for 1748—Difficulties about command in Italy and the Netherlands—Convention signed—Newcastle persists in opposing early peace—Legge sent to Berlin—Ministers nominated to Aix-la-Chapelle—Resignation of Chesterfield—Newcastle takes Northern Department—Bedford becomes Secretary of State and Sandwich First Lord of the Admiralty.

DURING the six weeks of June and July, 1747, that Sandwich spent in England, the General Election returned a very satisfactory majority for the Government,[1] but the allied cause met with two disasters on the Continent which rendered the convention of 12 January so much waste paper. In the Netherlands Cumberland never obtained his promised hundred and forty thousand men, both Austrians and Dutch being in default. And his army, when collected, was defeated at Lafeld on 2 July. The defeat was not in itself discreditable, as only part of the army was engaged, the retreat was effected without disorder, and the French losses were considerably

[1] Newcastle to Cumberland, 3 July (o.s.): " Your Royal Highness's great and eminent services have procured the King such a Parliament as none of his Majesty's late predecessors have ever seen. We scarce meet with any opposition, and those places where friends of the Government were never chosen before, are now the foremost in their demonstrations of duty and loyalty to the King, as the county of Middlesex, Westminster, and even the City of London " (Add. MSS. 32,712, fo. 23).

larger than those of the allies.[1] The beaten army was still able to cover Maestricht, and the only use that Saxe could make of his victory was to send a considerable detachment under Löwendahl to lay siege to Bergen-op-Zoom. If that fortress, the masterpiece of Coehoorn, held out, as was to be expected from the size of its garrison and the profusion of its stores, the campaign in the Netherlands might be regarded as drawn. There was no such panic in Holland after Lafeld as there had been after previous defeats,[2] nor was there any attempt on the part of Cumberland and the Austrian commander, Batthiani, to throw blame upon each other.[3]

The disaster in Italy was far more humiliating, as it was also more unforeseen. In spite of the recrossing of the Var, Newcastle believed in the possibility of renewing the invasion of France, and sent Wentworth in April to visit Vienna and Turin for the double purpose of preaching reconciliation between the two Courts and of urging them to carry out their engagements under the military convention. Wentworth arrived at Vienna early in May. He could not see Maria Theresa, who gave birth to an Archduke on 5 May.[4] But he went with Robinson to see the Chancellor, Ulfeld, who gave them a chilly reception. Austria was evidently annoyed both by Sandwich's negotiations with Spain at Breda and by Wentworth's inquisitorial mission. Ulfeld declared that Wasner had exceeded his powers by promising an Austrian contingent of sixty thousand men in Italy, and refused to give any pledge as to an early invasion of

[1] Cumberland to Newcastle, 3 July, calls the battle a "brisk but not very successful affair between our left wing and almost the whole of the enemy's army" (*ibid.*, 32,711, fo. 473).

[2] The Prince of Orange wrote to Newcastle on 12 July that the Dutch did not consider themselves defeated at Lafeld: only a left wing shattered because insufficiently supported (Add. MSS. 32,809, fo. 2).

[3] See Arneth, iii., 321, for the relations of the two commanders after the battle.

[4] Maria Theresa took the opportunity to pay a gratifying compliment to the Tsaritsa Elizabeth by asking her to be godmother (Robinson to Chesterfield, 8 May, in S.P., For., Germany, 177).

France. When Wentworth began to talk about England
being possibly forced to take other measures, Ulfeld
resented this as a threat, and growled : " How can we
enter France when Macanaz has been assured that we
shall not go into Naples ?"[1] That this last was the
real grievance is proved by the written answer given to
Wentworth, which concludes with a sentence characteristic of Bartenstein : " Pour contenter ses Alliés l'Imperatrice-Reine a postponé la conquête aisée d'un
royaume qui Lui a été promis par le Traité de Worms,
à une expedition des plus dispendieuses et difficiles. . . .
Il Lui seroit donc trop sensible si après avoir tant
sacrifié aux désirs de ses Alliés, son empressement à leur
complaire ne seroit pas pleinement reconnu."[2]

Wentworth was not much more successful at Milan,
where he went to visit Browne, who was now Commander-in-Chief of the Austrian forces in Italy. He
found Browne, though more courteous, almost as
reticent as Ulfeld, and the Austrian officers " very free
in their censure of the Piedmontese." As to the troops,
he thought the infantry defective and the magazines
non-existent.[3] He was much more favourably impressed
at Turin, and, like most observers, fell under the charm
of Charles Emmanuel. " No man was ever more
deceived than I am, if the King of Sardinia does not
deal fairly, and the most artful man living, by being
able to conceal the very appearance of it, though his
Ministers have not all the like good characters."[4] The
General's grammar is not very good, but his meaning
is quite clear. He must, however, have had reason later
to revise his estimate of the sincerity of the King, who
at the time assured him that he was eager to invade

[1] Wentworth to Chesterfield, 14 May, in S.P., For., Sardinia,
53; and Robinson to Chesterfield, same date, in S.P., For.,
Germany, 177.
[2] This answer, forwarded by Wentworth, and dated 8 May, is
in S.P., For., Sardinia, 53.
[3] Wentworth to Newcastle, from Turin, 3 June, S.Pı, For.,
Sardinia, fo. 53. As soon as Wentworth crossed into Italy, he
had to correspond with the Southern Department.
[4] This is in the above letter. It is only fair to say that the
sentence was put into cipher, and the grammar may have suffered
in the process.

France, and that he would furnish his full contingent of thirty thousand men.

From Turin Wentworth proceeded to Genoa, where he was completely disillusioned. Austria had insisted from the first that Genoa must be recovered before there could be any idea of a new entry into France. Charles Emmanuel did not oppose this decision, because the reduction of Genoa would help to secure his Riviera conquests, but he would take no responsibility for the enterprise, and refused to send any assistance until Austria had complied with his conditions. The siege of Genoa was therefore primarily an Austrian undertaking, and its conduct was entrusted to Schulenburg, Botta's successor, who had been envoy at Turin at the beginning of the war. He proceeded with more than the usual Austrian procrastination. Although the weather was quite open, it was not till April that he took his main force to the neighbourhood of the city, only to discover that it was inadequate without Sardinian aid. Charles Emmanuel demanded either a share in the prospective spoils or a guarantee of his hold on the Riviera di Ponente. The latter was unhesitatingly rejected at Vienna, but the Convention of Turin on 3 May promised a fifth of any indemnity levied on the city, and other booty was to be divided between the two parties in proportion to the troops employed. On this assurance Sardinia sent twelve battalions to serve under Schulenburg, and the siege ought to have commenced in earnest. But, when Wentworth visited the camp in the middle of June, he found that no complete blockade had even been attempted, and that the access to Genoa from the east was perfectly open. He laid the blame for this failure upon the divided authority between Browne at Milan, who had nominal control over all troops in Italy, Schulenburg, who had a special command before Genoa, and Pallavicini, himself a Genoese noble, who commanded all troops in garrisons and had sole control of finance.[1]

The delay in the siege operations enabled France to send soldiers to the aid of the Genoese. As access by

[1] Wentworth to Newcastle, 17 June (S.P., For., Sardinia, 53).

land was blocked by the Sardinian occupation of the Riviera, their transport had to be effected by sea. Several of the ships were sunk by the British fleet, but a sufficient number got through, and they carried French and Spanish officers as well as men. Among the entrants was Marshal Boufflers, who devoted all his energy and eloquence to the defence of the city. Meanwhile, the French and Spanish forces in Provence, under Belleisle and Las Minas, began to move. Their object was the relief of Genoa, but there was an acute quarrel as to method. Las Minas proposed to advance directly by the coast route, which was difficult in itself and would involve the successive reduction of the Sardinian garrisons in Ventimiglia, Oneglia, Finale, and Savona. Belleisle, on the other hand, wished to march from Dauphiné over the Mont Genèvre, and thus threaten both Piedmont and the Milanese. This would compel the Austrians and Sardinians to raise the siege of Genoa and to fall back for the defence of their own provinces. The dispute was referred by Belleisle to his own Court, which decided, on political rather than military grounds, in favour of Las Minas. It was necessary to check the evident inclination in Spain to conclude a separate peace, and it had always been held that in Italy France was only an auxiliary of Spain. The result of this decision was that the campaign began with the recovery of the county of Nice with its important harbour of Villafranca, which was thus closed to the British fleet. Thence the Gallispans proceeded to the attack on Ventimiglia, which only held out for eight days. The news of this danger from the west reached Schulenburg just as he had conveyed his guns by sea to the valley of the Bisagno in order to complete the encirclement of Genoa on the eastern side. A hasty council of war decided to reship the cannon and thus virtually to abandon the siege. A tardy reminder that there were other fortresses and a very difficult road between Ventimiglia and Genoa led to a reversal of this resolution, and the guns were brought back. Then came the news that Belleisle, in defiance of his Court, had detached a considerable force under his brother to cross the

mountains from Dauphiné. This compelled Charles
Emmanuel to recall his twelve battalions, and Schulenburg, who had been vainly trying for some time to
throw the responsibility of a decision upon the King of
Sardinia, chose to regard this as a virtual authority to
abandon the siege. Wentworth had already remarked
that he " seemed very sick of his enterprise."[1] The
only consolation was that in the mountains the Sardinian forces, with an Austrian contingent sent by
Browne, repulsed the French invaders in a sharp encounter on the Col de l'Assiette, where the younger
Belleisle was killed.[2]

The abandonment of the siege of Genoa was perhaps
the most important military event of the year, as it put
an end to all hope of effecting a diversion of French
forces by an invasion of Southern France. Newcastle
vainly urged that the French defeat on the Col de
l'Assiette should be followed by an inroad into Dauphiné.[3] All the old recriminations between Austria and
Sardinia broke out afresh, and their bitterness was increased by a report, communicated by Chavanne from
The Hague, that Rosenberg had, on 4 June, concluded
a separate treaty with Spain at Lisbon.[4] Its alleged
terms were that Don Philip should receive Parma and
Piacenza, and that Spain should assist Austria to
recover the cessions to Sardinia in the Treaty of Worms.
England refused to take any action in the matter until
the opinion of Sardinia had been received. Charles
Emmanuel was delighted that Austria should be accused
of an action as discreditable as his own meditated desertion of the allies in the winter of 1745-46. Robinson
was now instructed to question the Court at Vienna as

[1] Wentworth to Newcastle, 25 June (S.P., For., Sardinia, 53)
[2] For a good account of this battle see Spenser Wilkinson, *The Defence of Piedmont*, 1742-48, viii., 4.
[3] Newcastle to Wentworth, 24 July (o.s.), *ibid.*
[4] Sandwich to Chesterfield (separate and secret), 11 August,
S.P., For., Holland, 426, fo. 34. This was his first letter after
his return. The informant, a former secretary of Rosenberg
and a native of Milan, was sent on to England and there rewarded.
Chesterfield was inclined to disbelieve his story. See Chesterfield
to Sandwich (separate and secret), 7 August (o.s.), *ibid.*, fo. 56.
Chavanne got the story before Sandwich returned.

to the conclusion of the alleged treaty. The very un-satisfactory answer was that the agreement at Lisbon was purely conditional on the production by Spain of evidence that Charles Emmanuel had been a party to a treaty for the expulsion of Austria from Italy, that no such evidence had been forthcoming, and that therefore no treaty had been made with Spain.[1] This proof of a desire at Vienna to repudiate what to Sardinia was the most vital clause of the Treaty of Worms was fatal to any co-operation of the two States in an enterprise against France. But, even without this, a renewed invasion was out of the question. Neither Austria nor Sardinia had ever been eager, and had only been coerced by the pressure which England could exert as pay-master. Their object always had been, as Robinson expressed it some months ago, " to drive the enemy out of Italy, and to be contented with shutting the door upon them."[2] This had been achieved when the Chevalier de Belleisle fell in the Alps. No further inva-sion of Italy was attempted by the Bourbon Powers. Marshal Belleisle, dismayed by the disaster to his brother, the result of his own disregard of his instruc-tions, was content to strengthen the border defences. As Spain was still endeavouring to obtain her chief object—a principality in Italy for Don Philip—by negotiation, Las Minas was ordered to remain equally inactive. Maria Theresa had recovered the Duchy of Milan, and if she contemplated any further enterprise, it must be the promised conquest of Naples. Charles Emmanuel had got, not only the Austrian cessions in Lombardy with Finale, but the whole Riviera di Ponente as well. As long as he could keep these he had no desire

---

[1] Robinson to Chesterfield, 25 October, S.P., For., Germany, 178. Arneth (iii., p. 476) quotes two articles from the draft treaty, but does not say whether it was ever signed. It was certainly not ratified. Chesterfield to Robinson, 13 November (o.s.), accepts the Austrian denial, but strongly condemns their conduct in the matter. For Frederick of Prussia's well-informed estimate of the Austro-Spanish negotiation see Pol. Corr., v., p. 506.

[2] Robinson to Chetwynd (Foreign Office clerk), autograph, 22 February, 1747 (S.P., For., Germany, 176).

to waste his forces elsewhere. Both Sardinia and Austria had so concentrated their attention upon Italy that they refused to listen to English warnings that the war must be regarded as a whole, and that successes in one battlefield might be more than counterbalanced by losses in another.[1] Nor would Maria Theresa admit, what Robinson was always trying to impress upon her, that the recovery of her lost Netherlands was ample compensation for any sacrifice that she might be called upon to make in Italy. The unfortunate Wentworth spent the autumn of 1747 in attending futile military councils at Milan, which were called for the purpose of settling future operations. When he urged an invasion of France, and complained that so far nothing had been done to earn the increased subsidies paid by England, he was told that the recovery of Genoa was a necessary preliminary. If he agreed to that undertaking, the answer was that the defences of the city had been so strengthened that its capture was impossible. All that he succeeded in doing was to forbid Austria to renew that attack upon Naples which had been so disastrous in 1744. His pessimistic letters, which continued till his death at the beginning of December, convinced Newcastle, much to the delight of the Court of Turin, that the retreat from Provence, the humiliating failure before Genoa, and the subsequent refusals to take any active measures, were all to be attributed to Austria.[2]

---

[1] This point was cogently pressed by Hardwicke in a letter to Newcastle on 6 September (o.s.), Add MSS. 32,713, fo. 32.

[2] On 31 August Wentworth wrote: " I must own to your Grace there is something in the procedure of the Court of Vienna which I cannot account for. Every step taken by General Browne shows his unwillingness to advance to the French frontier. If the King of Sardinia did not obstinately refuse it (which your Grace may believe I use my best endeavours to support), he possibly might have already sent away one-third of the small body they have here. " When Newcastle attributed the inaction to the discord between the two Courts, Wentworth replied on 1 September that it was due to the bad condition of the Austrian army. On 15 September he wrote that Browne, whom he described as rather *homme de main que de cabinet*, had admitted to him the receipt of orders *pour menager ses troupes* (S.P., For., Sardinia, 53). Robinson to Chesterfield, 11 August, says that "all the Ministers bewail themselves what had passed, and above

As nothing more was to be expected from Italy, it became clear that the issue of the war was to be decided in the Netherlands. Here it was extremely difficult for even the most sanguine optimist to feel much hope. Even the Duke of Cumberland, upon whose support Newcastle had relied against his opponents in the Cabinet, was inclined for the moment, after his defeat at Lafeld, to join the pacifists. On 7 June (o.s.), New-castle had written in one of his confidential letters to the Duke, that " the Premier is bent upon a peace this summer," that the Chancellor "is every thing that is great and good," and that his fellow Secretary " is as much or more for peace than any body, but he will, if he can, avoid giving any opinion." As for himself, he wished for a " good peace," and so was not prepared to be too precipitate. He went on to say that he had a valuable ally. " I must on this occasion do justice to Lord Sandwich, who shows his ability and steadiness in pursuit of that system on which he set out. He has gained the entire and *sole* confidence of the Prince of Orange, the Greffier, and Bentinck, of which I have seen undeniable proofs. He holds the language he ought here ; and will be greatly serviceable in preventing any *damp* being cast upon the good disposition of the Prince of Orange. And it was a great satisfaction to me to see, by a letter he was yesterday honoured with, that your Royal Highness has the same opinion of his use and merit."[1] This letter remained unanswered until after the encounter with Marshal Saxe, when Cumberland sent an extremely damping reply, which contained the sig-nificant words : " I am more than ever convinced that the *brother* is in the right, that a good peace ought to be made this summer."[2] The key to this apparent fall-

---

all the total blame of it which, according to M. Wasner's letters, had been laid in England upon this Court singly " (S.P., For., Germany, 178).

[1] Add. MSS. 32,711, fo. 232. Newcastle begged the Duke to burn the letter after reading it, but he kept a beautiful copy for himself.

[2] Add. MSS. 32,712, fo. 1. The letter is undated, but there can be no doubt that it was written on the same day as that to Chesterfield.

ing away on the part of Cumberland is to be found in a letter which he wrote the same day to Chesterfield. Sir John Ligonier had been taken prisoner at Lafeld, had been treated with surprising generosity by both Louis XV and Marshal Saxe, and had been allowed to return for four days on parole to the allied camp in order to carry a surprising message to the Commander-in Chief. " The French King even took him out to show him the *feu de joye*, and the Marshal de Saxe owned to him that the battle was not worth winning at the rate they had bought it, since they could not cut us off from Maestricht, and that they had lost about 1,000 officers and 9,000 men, that the King of France disliked war, and that he (the Marshal) was sensible of the slippery path he trod, as he knew they would never forgive him being a German."[1] The message which Ligonier brought was a verbal one, but he had made notes of the conversation.[2] The gist of it was that Saxe would like to treat directly with Cumberland or some general named by him as to the terms of peace. The French King desired nothing for himself except the town of Furnes, and that only if England insisted upon the dismantling of Dunkirk. If, however, England would leave Dunkirk in its present condition, he would demand nothing but Cape Breton, and would restore all conquests in the Netherlands. Something was said about border disputes, but Ligonier had paid little attention to this. Cumberland replied that he would consult his father, who was as desirous of peace as the King of France, and that he personally would be proud to take part in such a negotiation.[3]

The arrival of Cumberland's letters made a sensation among the English Ministers. France had made overtures of a kind before, but they had always been addressed to Holland, even if they were intended to reach both the Maritime Powers. This was the first time that France had approached England directly, and this was as flattering to English pride as the direct in-

[1] Cumberland to Chesterfield, 10 July (*ibid.*, 32,711, fo. 587).
[2] Ligonier's signed notes are in *ibid.*, fo. 589.
[3] Cumberland's letter to Saxe is in Add. MSS. 32,711, fo. 591.

vitation to Cumberland was gratifying to that Prince and calculated to conciliate his father. Henry Pelham and Chesterfield were convinced that peace was at last within sight, and that Cumberland should be confirmed in his conversion by being allowed the honour of at any rate settling the first preliminaries. They were not prepared to give way to the protests of a bellicose Prince of Orange, or to the complaints of an injured Austria, or to the selfish greed of the King of Sardinia.[1] England had too long borne the heavy financial burden of a war in which it was now evident that the solitary gain, Cape Breton, could not be retained. If Newcastle had given way, there can be little doubt that the preliminaries of a peace might have been settled in the autumn of 1747, and that the three allied Powers would have been forced, however unwillingly, to accept them. But there were two men in Holland, William IV and Bentinck, who were convinced that the new Government would be ruined if the Dutch, so prominent in all previous negotiations, were now to be excluded, and that this Government, not yet very secure, required to be buttressed by the glamour of some military success. They had overthrown the Republican party, as William III had done in 1672, and they must justify their success, as he had done, by becoming the saviours of the state. They were prepared to appeal to the patriotism of the people for a grant of a levy of 2 per cent. upon all capital, and to join with England in the hiring of Russian troops even if, contrary to all precedents, they had to promise to bear half the cost. There were three people in England to whom they could appeal—the King, Newcastle, and

---

[1] The protests of the Prince of Orange were the loudest and most persistent. Those of Maria Theresa were more subtle, but equally efficacious. She professed her desire for peace, and gave powers to conclude to Batthiani and Reischach. But she insisted on her full share in the negotiation, and refused to give England any intimation as to her terms. See the ministerial answer to Robinson in S.P., For., Germany, 178. Chesterfield to Robinson, 14 August (o.s.), was as angry as if Austria had offered strenuous opposition. On the attitude of Charles Emmanuel, see Newcastle to Bedford, 22 July (o.s.), *Bedford Corr.*, i., 222. "He hopes France will not gain by *negotiation* what they are far from being able to gain by *force.*"

Sandwich. The last, who could be trusted to represent their point of view, was luckily in London, putting in a spell at the Admiralty, where he was still Second Lord, after having successfully settled his election business in Huntingdonshire. William of Orange undertook to write to George II and to Newcastle, while Bentinck wrote to Sandwich. The Prince also had to write officially to Chesterfield, as The Hague was in the Northern Department. The principal contentions in the letters were that the overture from Saxe was a trick on the part of France to sow dissension among the allies, and that the whole situation had been changed for the better by the new spirit among the Dutch, who were so far from being dispirited by Lafeld that they were prepared to supply both money and men far in excess of their previous efforts, so that another campaign ought to procure far better terms than France would be prepared to offer at the moment. A definite proposal was made to pay half the expense, if Hyndford could be instructed to procure thirty thousand Russians, either to join the allies in the Netherlands or to effect a diversion in Alsace. In addition, the Dutch would undertake to employ their ships in helping England to harry French commerce, though they still abstained from any declaration of war against France.[1]

In England it is not too much to say that everything depended upon the attitude of Newcastle, and upon the extent to which he could influence the King. The situation of the Duke was a difficult one. The representa-

---

[1] The Prince of Orange's letter to Chesterfield is in Add. MSS. 32,809, fo. 1, and that to Newcastle (autograph) in *ibid.*, fo. 32. Chesterfield's answer to the Prince is in *ibid.*, fo. 42, and also in S.P., For., Holland, 428, fo. 90. The gist of the answer was that there might be duplicity on the part of France, but, in view of the precarious situation in the Netherlands and Italy, it would be imprudent to reject the overture. England was pleased to hear of the intention to harass French trade. Newcastle's answer is in Add. MSS. 32,809, fo. 62. Bentinck's letter to Sandwich of 12 July is in the Sandwich Papers at Hinchingbrooke. In it he says that the overture to Ligonier, if accepted, will ruin all the plans made by the Prince and Sandwich. He thinks the whole thing was concerted beforehand either in Holland or in England. "Never was anything so scurrilously ridiculous as Sir John Ligonier's behaviour in this."

tions of the Prince of Orange and Bentinck irritated the
pacific members of the Cabinet, who declared that they
wanted deeds rather than mere words.[1] Henry Pelham
was reluctant to throw away money upon Russian
troops who would probably come too late to be of any
service. The official assurances from The Hague were
countered by Chesterfield's production of his reports
from Dayrolles.[2] It began to be doubted whether
Bergen-op-Zoom could hold out, and Cumberland
definitely announced that he could not attempt to
relieve the fortress without fatally exposing Maestricht.[3]
Even Hardwicke, upon whose support in the Cabinet
Newcastle largely depended, said that the Government
of Holland might have been changed, but the generals
and the troops remained the same. Against this chorus
of depression Newcastle could count upon little active
backing. Sandwich, who resented the treatment as a
negligible event of the Dutch Revolution which he had
helped to bring about, could be trusted to do all in his
power, but he was not in the Cabinet, nor was he, in
spite of his recognized services, altogether a *persona
grata* to the King. Newcastle could also reply to some
extent upon the sluggish but influential Duke of Bedford, who was intimate with Sandwich and was unwilling to give up Cape Breton unless Louisbourg was dismantled as Dunkirk had formerly been.[4] But Bedford,

[1] Newcastle to Sandwich, 28 July (o.s.). Add. MSS. 32,809,
fo. 111: " If the Stadtholder does not show that he can *act* as
well as *write*, and that the Republic has *power* as well as *will*, all
will signify nothing."
[2] The correspondence between Chesterfield and Dayrolles,
the latter being officially in charge of the embassy during Sandwich's absence, is in S.P., For., Holland, 428.
[3] Cumberland to Newcastle (autograph), 31 July (Add. MSS.
32,712, fo. 163). Chesterfield had asked on 10 July (o.s.) whether
Cumberland could defend Bergen-op-Zoom, Breda, and Bois-le-
Duc as well as Maestricht (*ibid.* fo. 81). The Duke replied to
Newcastle that he could not, but that those places ought to be
able to defend themselves, if the garrisons would fight and were
properly officered. Apparently Bergen-op-Zoom did not answer
to this description.
[4] Newcastle to Sandwich, 28 July (o.s.): " Our friend the Duke
of Bedford was violently against the giving up of Cape Breton,
on any account, in the state it now is " (Add. MSS. 32,809, fo. 111).

though a member of the Cabinet, was not one of the big
four who usually settled important business among themselves,[1] and it was always difficult to induce him to come
to London. In these circumstances it says a good deal
for Newcastle's courage that he did not hesitate to
throw himself against the current which was setting so
strongly in the direction of an immediate and decisive
separate negotiation with France. He took his stand
upon the fundamental principle that France would gain
more by breaking up the alliance than by the most
advantageous terms of peace. Therefore it would be
better for England to risk even a worse peace if thereby
the alliance could be maintained intact. He could not,
in the teeth of his colleagues and Cumberland, go so far
to gratify his Dutch friends as to propose the rejection
of the French overture, but he could, and did, insist
that there should be no secrecy about the matter, and
that the whole course of the negotiation should be disclosed to the allies. Newcastle's second point was a
more delicate one. Cumberland was avowedly pacific
at the moment,[2] and he was inclined to favour Austria,
which was behaving so badly in Italy, and to be
prejudiced against the Dutch, who by their own account
were making such strenuous efforts in the common
cause.[3] It would be in the highest degree dangerous to

Bedford remained of the same opinion on 28 January (o.s.), 1748,
that he would sooner give Gibraltar to Spain than Louisbourg
to France. " When I mention Louisbourg, I mean it unde-
molished; for was it otherwise, as I once advised, I should not
much care who had the possession of *L'Isle Royale* " (*Bedford
Correspondence*, i., p. 316).

[1] Newcastle to Hardwicke, 8 July (o.s.), writes, on receipt of
the Saxe-Ligonier overture: " We four must meet to-night "
(Hardwicke Papers, Add. MSS. 35,409, fo. 32). These meetings of
an inner Cabinet are frequently recorded at this time. Occasionally
a fifth Minister was called in—*e.g.*, on 29 July (o.s.), when an
important letter to Saxe was drafted, the Duke of Dorset was
present in addition to the usual four (Add. MSS. 32,809, fo. 133).

[2] Henry Pelham to Stone, 25 July (o.s.), Add. MSS. 32,712,
fo. 231: " I think with my brother that the Duke is pacifick,
tho' sorely against his will." Cumberland was " the Duke " to
his generation, as Wellington was to a later one.

[3] Newcastle to Hardwicke, 26 July (o.s.), complains that
Cumberland shows " a partiality in favour of the Austrians,

allow the Royal Duke to undertake a negotiation in which so many tender interests of the allied Powers were involved. At the same time it was equally undesirable to alienate Cumberland by showing this mistrust and by depriving him of the chance of concluding a soldiers' peace, which he evidently found attractive. It was also possible that the King might be annoyed by any disparagement of his favourite son. The only argument open to Newcastle was that the terms of peace could not be advantageous, and that it would be unfair to throw upon his Royal Highness the odium of concluding an unpopular treaty.

The first matter settled by the four principal Ministers was a compromise as to the Russian troops. It was agreed that the proposal should not be rejected, but that consideration should be postponed, as they could not affect the present campaign.[1] On the answer which Ligonier was to send to Saxe there was prolonged discussion. All that was agreed was that the proffered negotiation should not be broken off, and that Ligonier should send a colourless answer, expressing the King's desire for peace and a request for some more explicit statement of the French terms. The sending of Sandwich was broached by Newcastle, but was opposed by Henry Pelham and Chesterfield on the ground that Sandwich was not likely to contribute to the making of peace. Nothing was settled at the time on this point, and Newcastle had to sit down and write a letter to the Duke of Cumberland which must have cost him some care in its composition. After compliments on the Duke's heroism and regrets that it had not been suc-

---

who have both deceived and abandoned us, and such a spleen and resentment to the Dutch, who are at least endeavouring to do something for themselves " (*ibid.*, fo. 233).

[1] On 3 July (o.s.) Newcastle reported to the King that he had conferred with his brother and Chesterfield, and later with the Chancellor. " We are humbly of opinion that the Prince of Orange's proposal relating to the Russian troops should not be rejected, but only suspended, as not being the immediate object, nor capable of being of any use for the present campaign " (Add. MSS. 32,712, fo. 1). It is interesting to note how completely Newcastle, in these communications with the King, supersedes his brother, the nominal Premier.

cessful against the superior numbers of the enemy, he continued :

" Under these circumstances comes the overture made by the Marshal de Saxe to Sir John Ligonier. I wish I could say that the flattering appearances that seem to have made some impression upon Gen. Ligonier carried with them a probability of a good peace. . . . Your Royal Highness will see the strong remonstrances of the Prince of Orange against entering into this negotiation; and I may in confidence acquaint you that the Prince has still wrote more strongly against it in a memorial *pour sa Majesté seule;* and, though I do agree that it is unreasonable to expect that this country should continue the immense expense of carrying on the war purely to better and strengthen the Stadtholder's situation in Holland, I cannot, however, as a faithful servant of the King and my country, but be of opinion that it would be very unfortunate if, by a peace, the Republic of Holland should be thrown back into the hands of the French party, out of which it has been lately so miraculously delivered. [We should not reject the overture, but we should proceed cautiously, and in the utmost concert with the Prince of Orange and our other allies. Your Royal Highness's evident feeling that the military situation requires a speedy peace has induced me to concur in the answer sent to the overture. But I do not expect, at present, an advantageous peace for ourselves.] I cannot but, as a faithful servant of your Royal Highness, wish you may not be alone charged with this difficult and dangerous negotiation. For this reason I have pressed that Lord Sandwich may be immediately sent back to The Hague to give proper assurances to the Prince of Orange of His Majesty's friendship and support, to establish the most perfect concert with him and with the rest of our allies, both in measures of peace and war, and to take off from your Royal Highness, when proper, the burthen and weight of this transaction."[1]

Before the request for more precision could be copied by Ligonier and forwarded to Saxe, the latter, who had

[1] Newcastle to Cumberland, 10 July (o.s.), in Add. MSS. 32,712, fo. 73. The sentences in brackets are abbreviations.

received a copy of the General's notes of their conversation, wrote to him on 11 July that there were two serious omissions. Ligonier had forgotten to mention Spain, a problem on which Cumberland must be instructed, and Saxe had said at the interview that it would be difficult to moderate the pretensions of that Crown. And Saxe himself had forgotten to say that the Republic of Genoa and the Duke of Modena must be restored. In view of the importance of the negotiation Ligonier's parole was extended, and he might remain at the allied camp as a channel of communication between the two commanders.[1] This supplementary communication was still regarded as an inadequate statement of French terms, and therefore Ligonier was instructed to send on the letter as originally drafted in England.[2] At the same time Newcastle carried two points in the Cabinet. Sandwich, who had been consulted throughout, was to go back at once to The Hague in order to pacify the Prince of Orange and Bentinck, and full information was sent to the Courts of Vienna and Turin, with assurances that nothing would be concluded without full consultation with the allies.[3] Sandwich embarked at the Nore at the end of July, but was detained there for several days by easterly winds. While he was chafing at this involuntary delay, important discussions took place in which he was vitally concerned but could take no part.

Instead of sending a reply to the request for greater precision as to French demands, the impatient Marshal sent off on 30 July an extraordinary letter, in his own

[1] Saxe to Ligonier, 11 July (Add. MSS. 32,809, fo. 21). Ligonier acknowledged this two days later, and said that Cumberland had applied for instructions (ibid., fo. 19).
[2] This letter was not sent off till 28 July (ibid., fo. 80). Ligonier evidently expected to play a prominent part in the negotiation. He offered to go to Liège to meet Saxe, but, as such activity on the part of a prisoner of war would excite comment, he suggested that it would be safer to continue the negotiation by letters.
[3] Chesterfield sent the papers to Robinson on 10 July (o.s.) (ibid., fo. 47, also in S.P., For., Germany, 177). Newcastle gave the papers to Osorio on 16 July (o.s.), with a characteristic letter saying that it was very doubtful whether anything would come of the negotiations, and urging the King of Sardinia to make plans for the next campaign (ibid., fo. 75).

19

hand and his own spelling and grammar, which made a great sensation on its arrival in England. He began by saying that he was instructed to ask whether Cumberland would be authorized to treat and conclude, or merely to hear and report. He then went on to say that, if the Duke had full powers, matters could be easily settled. They could determine the principal points and then " autant que je puis en juger, l'on fera une politesse à l'Espagne, et l'on passera outre." The letter concluded with the suggestion that soldiers could force the hand of Ministers and politicians. " Les gens de cour et de ministère sont comme les femmes. Il faut deviner leurs desirs, et il est plus aisé de leur faire faire les choses que les leur faire dire." In a postscript he added that, as he had to show the letters which he received, any confidential communications should be sent on separate sheets and in separate envelopes.[1]

Cumberland forwarded this letter on the following day to Chesterfield, merely remarking that it was " in as extraordinary a stile as any letter I ever saw."[2] To Newcastle, on the same day, he characterized it as " either the frankest or falsest I ever met with."[3] But it was obvious that he inclined to the former estimate, and that he was more than ever tempted to pose as the peacemaker after his ill-success in the field. The King, also, was " mightily pleased with Saxe's letter ; thought it had an air of frankness and sincerity, and that France was disposed to drop Spain."[4] The words *politesse*

---

[1] There is a copy of this remarkable letter, with corrected spelling, in Add. MSS. 32,809, fo. 82.

[2] Cumberland to Chesterfield, 31 July, *ibid.*, fo. 78.

[3] Cumberland to Newcastle (autograph), 31 July (Add. MSS. 32,712, fo. 163). Cumberland's spelling and grammar are almost as peculiar as those of Saxe. He usually employed his secretary, Sir Everard Fawkener, to write for him. For other estimates of Saxe's letter see Newcastle to Hardwicke, 26 July (o.s.), in *ibid.*, fo. 233, and Hardwicke's reply (fo. 237). The Chancellor in this letter was more pessimistic than Newcastle liked : " I do not at present see the resources for carrying on the war, or mending our condition, and if there are none, it will grow worse and worse." It is remarkable how often Hardwicke agreed with Pelham and yet voted with Newcastle.

[4] Newcastle to Sandwich, 28 July (o.s.), Add. MSS. 32,809, fo. 111.

après quoi l'on passera outre made a profound impression. If they really bore the meaning attributed to them, the most dangerous snag in the negotiation—the establishment for Don Philip—would be evaded. Henry Pelham and Chesterfield renewed their insistence that Cumberland should be empowered, as Saxe suggested, to settle the preliminaries of peace. Newcastle had to fight this battle on delicate ground over again. He had one great advantage. George II had promised Sandwich, before he set out for The Hague, that, if the negotiation took place, he should be employed.[1] Newcastle and Hardwicke contended, against their colleagues, that it was neither possible nor politic that this promise should not be fulfilled. Newcastle had even obtained from the King an assurance that Sandwich should have the character of Ambassador, and very imprudently he conveyed the assurance to Sandwich, begging him at the same time to say nothing about it until an official letter came from Chesterfield.[2] At last a compromise was arrived at and an official letter was drafted for Ligonier to send to Saxe. Its purport was that the Duke of Cumberland had no power to conclude, but that, if France would state specific terms, a fully authorized Minister would be sent to the army to negotiate under the supervision and direction of His Royal Highness.[3] This, though not worded exactly as Newcastle had wished, was really a victory for him.[4] He had been aided by the support of Bedford, who wrote that " it appears to me absolutely necessary that the person who is to treat and finally conclude this peace with the

[1] In a private autograph letter, written on 20 July (o.s.) while he was waiting off the Nore for a favourable wind, Sandwich told Newcastle that the King had given him this assurance (*ibid.*, fo. 140). These letters from the yacht show how completely Sandwich considered himself at this time the Minister of Newcastle rather than of Chesterfield. His visit to England had completed his alienation from his official superior.

[2] Newcastle to Sandwich, 28 July (o.s.), *ibid.*, fo. 111.

[3] The letter is in Add. MSS. 32,809, fo. 119. Chesterfield's covering letter to Cumberland is in fo. 117.

[4] Newcastle had wished to add that peace would be furthered if properly authenticated Ministers from Austria and Sardinia and the States were appointed to assist his Royal Highness (*ibid.*, 32,712, fo. 284).

French ought to be the same who opens the outlines."[1]
The decision of the English Ministers put an end to
Saxe's dream of a peace imposed by the soldiers upon
the politicians.

The prolonged and acrimonious discussions in the
English Ministry were hardly finished when they were
rendered obsolete and unnecessary by the receipt of a
new letter from Saxe. On 5 August, only six days after
his own soldierly letter, he wrote a very different epistle,
which had evidently been dictated to him. In France
the politicians had resumed control. They probably
distrusted Saxe, apparently not very favourably disposed to Spain and inclined, like the Saxon Court, to
be lenient to Austria, quite as much as Newcastle distrusted Cumberland and Ligonier. In his new letter
Saxe declared that a settlement could be reached in
twenty-four hours if French interests alone were involved, but France could not desert her allies. Still, as
a proof of a genuine desire for peace, France would state
her proposals.[2] These were enclosed on a separate sheet,
and may be thus summarized :

1. France has no ambitions for herself, and has
resolved to surrender all her conquests in favour of her
allies.

2. Louisbourg and Madras (taken by the French in
1747), and all other conquests, shall be mutually
restored.

3. France must have either Furnes or leave to fortify
Dunkirk on the land side.

4. Arrangements shall be made as to the *enclaves* of
Hainault and other differences on the border of the
Netherlands.

5. Genoa and Modena shall be restored as in 1740.

6. France will guarantee Silesia to Prussia, as has
been already done by England.

7. No proposals are made on behalf of Spain, but
France would be glad to receive English proposals as to
the satisfaction of Don Philip and the settlement of

[1] Bedford to Newcastle, 3 August (o.s.), *ibid.*, fo. 321.
[2] Saxe to Ligonier, 5 August, in Add. MSS. 32,809, fo. 101.
The statement of terms is in *ibid.*, fo. 105.

trade disputes, and will do her best to promote a settlement.

This restoration of matters to the normal political plane was in a sense gratifying to Newcastle, because it seemed to justify and assure the employment of Sandwich. On the other hand, the definite pledge on the part of France to surrender the Netherlands, with the possible exception of Furnes, and the absence of any specific demand for Don Philip, gave great encouragement to the peace party. There were also difficulties with the King about Sandwich's official character. When his credentials as Ambassador were brought to the King he refused to sign them, on the ground that such a rank was justified neither by age, experience, or services.[1] He only agreed under pressure to the payment of an Ambassador's salary, and that only on the lower scale, the same as that paid to Lord Hyndford. This unexpected obstinacy on the King's part was attributed by Sandwich's friends to the machinations of Chesterfield, but Newcastle declared this to be quite unfounded.[2] It was, however, very awkward for Newcastle himself, as he had assured his protégé of this rise of rank, and had now to break it to him that it had been, at any rate for a time, refused. He had also to fight a battle with his colleagues about the answer to be sent to Saxe's last letter. Chesterfield proposed a detailed answer on the points raised by France. Newcastle argued that this would commit England too fast and too far, especially as to Cape Breton, and that it would be better to send a general answer and leave the

[1] Newcastle to Sandwich, 31 July (o.s.), Add. MSS. 32,809, fo. 121. Newcastle reiterates his injunctions to say nothing about his character as, but for the unofficial writer, he would know nothing about it. This was characteristic of Newcastle, who always liked, if possible, to gratify a correspondent, and to claim the credit of the gratification.

[2] Anson to Bedford, 22 August: " I own to your Grace that Lord Sandwich's situation appears to me a very disagreeable one; and the secret workings of Lord C. must be the true reason why he has not the rank in his way that his quality entitles him to " (*Bedford Correspondence*, i., 239). As against this must be set Newcastle's positive assurances in the above letter to Sandwich and also in one to Bedford (*ibid.*, p. 226).

rest to Sandwich.[1] As usual, the dispute ended in a compromise. The letter, as finally drafted, declared that England had not been the aggressor in the war, and had only defended her own territories and fulfilled her obligations to her allies. Two demands were made by England. Dunkirk must once more be in the condition prescribed by the treaties of 1713 and 1717, and France must repudiate the Stewarts to their remotest posterity. As to Louisbourg, in view of the French promise to surrender all conquests, His Majesty will allow the restoration of Cape Breton to be considered in the negotiation. No promise can be made as to matters which concern the allies of England, and the King can only treat in conjunction with them. The invitation to formulate proposals with regard to Spain was left unanswered. Finally, it was stated that Lord Sandwich, named for the first time, would conduct the negotiation under the guidance of the Duke of Cumberland with any Minister named by the French King. This letter was sent by Chesterfield to Cumberland to be copied by Ligonier and forwarded to Saxe.[2]

When Sandwich set out on his return journey at the end of July he was acutely reminded of his first start nearly a year ago. He was once more allied with Newcastle in a virtual conspiracy against his official superior, and was again pledged to carry on a clandestine correspondence with the knowledge and approval of the King. When he first landed in Holland he had been greeted by the news of the Austrian victory in the second Battle of Piacenza (sometimes called the Battle of Rottofreddo). As he waited at the Nore for a favourable wind the news reached him of the Sardinian victory

[1] Newcastle to Sandwich, 4 August (o.s.), Add. MSS. 32,809, fo. 133. The attempted division of the Newcastle Papers between foreign and domestic affairs is peculiarly irritating at this period. Nearly all the letters to and from Cumberland, which are almost exclusively about foreign affairs, are classed as domestic. The documents transmitted to and from him are some in one category and some in the other. The letters to and from Sandwich, on precisely the same affairs, are classified as foreign.

[2] Chesterfield to Cumberland, 4 August (o.s.), Add. MSS. 32,712, fo. 316.

on the Col de l'Assiette. He accepted the omen, and hoped that it was a sign that the good fortune which had attended him so far would not desert him.[1] He arrived at The Hague, after a very bad crossing, on 10 August, and found the Prince of Orange and Bentinck dismayed by the reports of despondency among English Ministers and by the decision to prosecute the negotiation with Marshal Saxe. The news that Sandwich expected to be entrusted with the conduct of the negotiation was not sufficient to reassure them, and it was decided to send Bentinck across the Channel to protest against the exclusion of the Dutch from matters in which they had hitherto played so prominent a part, to reassure England as to the resources and determination of the Republic, and to press for the most strenuous preparations for a new campaign, including the joint hiring of thirty thousand Russians. Very imprudently Sandwich intimated this mission to Newcastle, but sent no word to Chesterfield, who not unnaturally regarded Bentinck as having come to carry on an intrigue with his opponents in the Ministry. Sandwich was rather discouraged by his strained relations with the leading Dutchmen, and by the temporary loss of Bentinck, on whom he relied for help in guiding that rather difficult person, the Prince of Orange. He was still more dispirited by the unexpected refusal on the part of the King to give him the rank of Ambassador, and went so far as to consider the desirability of retiring into private life.[2] His spirits, however, partially revived when he received from Chesterfield definite assurances that he

---

[1] Sandwich to Newcastle (private), from the Nore, 23 July (o.s.), in Add. MSS. 32,809, fo. 95.

[2] Sandwich to Newcastle (very private), autograph, 15 August (Add. MSS. 32,809, fo. 125). This letter, to ensure secrecy, was carried to London by Bentinck. In a later letter to Bedford (secret, 29 August) Sandwich says: " It is not consistent with the opinion I have of my own condition, to continue at The Hague in a character so little removed from that of Mr. Dayrolles, either in the exterior part or in the point of confidence. . . . I thought from the first that the appointment of Dayrolles must have been meant to drive me out of my commission, and I am sorry to say that I begin to be convinced that it will have the desired effect."

was to be entrusted with the negotiation, together with instructions which were, on the whole, congenial. He was to insist upon the restoration of French conquests " in the condition in which they now are "—*i.e.*, without any further dismantling—and on the enforcement of previous treaties with regard to Dunkirk. The border disputes must be settled with the Empress and the States-General, the two states most immediately interested. France must be pledged to extend the repudiation of the Pretender to the remotest posterity " of whatever sex " : this to be a *sine qua non.* For Sardinia Sandwich was to try to obtain both Savona and Finale. The problem of Spain was familiar to Sandwich from his discussions with Macanaz. He was to obtain, if possible, a renewal of the *asiento,* at any rate for the years of *non-jouissance,* and England would consent to any establisnment for Don Philip which was approved by Austria and Sardinia, but would not force any sacrifice upon either of the allied states. Finally, " As the island of Cape Breton and the fortress of Louisbourg are the only acquisitions which the King has made during the long and expensive war, His Majesty had reason to expect an absolute cession thereof on the part of France at the general peace. [Chesterfield, when he penned this, must have realized the folly of expecting France to accept such an argument for retention.] But, if you are not able to obtain that, you are to insist upon a stipulation for the demolition of that fortress, and not to recede from that demand till you shall receive further instructions."[1] These instructions, and especially that with regard to Cape Breton, testify to another victory of Newcastle in the Ministerial debates. This he owed very largely to the support of Bedford, whose friendship with Sandwich led him at this time to take a far more active and prominent part in politics than he had hitherto done. He became a regular

[1] Chesterfield to Sandwich (secret), 7 August (o.s.), in S.P., For., Holland, 426, fo. 52. There is a copy of the letter in Add. MSS. 32,809, fo. 142. Newcastle's interesting comments on the instructions are in a private letter to Sandwich of the same date (*ibid.,* fo. 139).

member of the inner Cabinet in addition to the ordinary four. And he was for the time the ally of Newcastle.[1]

No sooner had Ministers settled the important problems of the answer to Saxe's letter of 5 August and of Sandwich's instructions than they had to deal with the unofficial envoy of the Prince of Orange. For some weeks Bentinck was an important and prominent personage in London. He was admitted to private audience by the King, and had several conferences with the inner circle of Ministers. Chesterfield did not disguise his annoyance that anybody should be sent from The Hague without any notice to himself.[2] This forced Bentinck into close and confidential relations with Newcastle, who eagerly undertook the congenial task of guiding the Anglo-Dutchman's footsteps.[3] A promise that England would take fifteen thousand Russians if the Dutch would take an equal number was obtained with ease. Chesterfield was not unwilling to demonstrate the cost of continuing the war,[4] and Henry Pelham was eager to commit the Dutch to the novel principle in this war of equality of financial burdens. The assurances as to military and financial resources were given verbally. But on the two main points—the overtures from France and the need for military preparations—Bentinck presented, on Newcastle's advice, a written memorandum, to which the English Ministers promised a

[1] Newcastle to Sandwich, 27 August (o.s.): " The Duke of Bedford is everything I could wish " (*ibid.*, fo. 256).

[2] Even Newcastle remonstrated against this *gaucherie* on Sandwich's part in his letter of 7 August (o.s.): " I could have wished you had mentioned to Lord Chesterfield Bentinck's design of coming over. . . . I am afraid some mistery by the secrecy is suspected in it, when in reality there is none."

[3] Chesterfield to Dayrolles, 25 August (o.s.): " Bentinck never comes near me nor speaks to me about business, though in my province, but confers wholly with his Grace " (*Chesterfield's Letters* [ed. Bradshaw], ii., p. 833). In this correspondence Chesterfield roundly denounces Bentinck and his " impetuous and impracticable temper."

[4] Chesterfield supported the hiring of Russians from the first, and Sandwich put it down to his desire to exaggerate the costliness of the war. For this reason Sandwich at first opposed the project, but came round when acceptance was demanded by the Dutch,

written answer.[1] On the first point the answer, largely
drafted by Newcastle, ought to have satisfied the envoy.[2]
As the French overtures had been made to England,
and as it would be impolitic to reject them off-hand, the
first interview with the French nominee must be conducted by Sandwich single-handed. But it was promised
that full and frank disclosure of what passed should be
made to the envoys of the three allies, that Sandwich
should consult with the Dutch Minister as to the terms
in which information should be given to the other two,[3]
and that nothing should be settled except in concert
with the allies. On the second point Newcastle was for
once deserted by Hardwicke, and Chesterfield carried
his proposal to avoid all specific promises, and merely
to give a general assurance that England would make
every effort to carry on the war in case the negotiation
should be unsuccessful.[4] To this answer Bentinck took
the strongest objection, and drew up a second memo-

[1] Bentinck's memorandum, dated 19/30 August, is in Add.
MSS. 32, 809, fo. 247. In a letter to Sandwich (at Hinchingbrooke)
of 1 September, he admits that it was drawn up at Newcastle
House with the Duke's aid.

[2] The ministerial answer (ibid., fo. 250), dated 25 August, was
drawn up by the inner Cabinet of five, H. Pelham, Hardwicke,
Newcastle, Chesterfield, and Bedford. Newcastle's proposed
draft is in ibid., fo. 215.

[3] This is in some ways the most important gain made by
Bentinck. It was put clearly by Chesterfield in his official letter
to Sandwich of 1 September (o.s.), in which he says that it had
been arranged with Bentinck " that your Lordship should first
acquaint the Minister of the Republic with the result of your
conferences with the person authorized to treat with you on the
part of France, and that afterwards you and the Dutch plenipotentiary were to concert together and previously agree upon
the terms in which you were to communicate what had passed
to the Ministers of the allies " (S.P., For., Holland, 426, fo. 125).
This was of no immediate importance because Sandwich had his
conference the day before this letter was written, and no Dutch
Minister was there at the time. But the distinction drawn between
the Dutch and the other allies paved the way for the subsequent
co-operation of Sandwich and Bentinck at Aix-la-Chapelle.

[4] Newcastle's account of the discussion is in a letter to Sandwich of 27 August (o.s.), ibid., fo. 256. In a previous letter of
14 August (fo. 191) he commends the prudent conduct of Bentinck, which he attributes to "my having had an opportunity
of putting him au fait of every thing before he had seen any
body else."

randum, this time without consulting Newcastle.[1] In
this he renewed his objection to the single-handed
negotiation, as being contrary to all that the two Maritime Powers had jointly struggled for at Breda, and
demanded that the priority of the Dutch over the other
allied Powers should be emphasized by substituting the
words *concert préalable* for *communion intime*.[2] He
also raised the old contention that " concert " with the
other allies might subject the Dutch to the caprices of
the Austrian Court. As to the second point, he denounced in the strongest terms the refusal of all details
as to what England would actually contribute to the
next campaign, if it should be necessary. This gave rise
to discussions which kept Bentinck in London, and so
caused him to miss the negotiations at the army headquarters to which William IV had promised to send
him. It is clear that the English Ministers, including
Newcastle, resented the tone of Bentinck's protest
against the separate negotiation in the first instance,
especially as Sandwich was only to hear and report. On
this point he got no concession. But Newcastle now
carried his previously rejected proposal, that England
should undertake to send no fewer troops than in the
current year, that she would induce Austria to do the
same, so that, if the Dutch provided the same number
as England, there would be, with the thirty thousand
Russians, an army of one hundred and seventy thousand
men. In addition, England would, in case of necessity,
join the Dutch in paying for an additional force of
Danes.[3]

[1] This second memorandum, dated 1/12 September, is in Add.
MSS. 32,809, fo. 301. Newcastle condemned the first part of it
in an explanatory letter to Sandwich of 4 September (o.s.), *ibid.*,
fo. 312. In a letter to Sandwich of 28 August (o.s.), Bentinck
complained that the answer to his first memorandum had been
embrouillée et tournillée by Chesterfield. In the same letter he
told Sandwich that any private letters which he did not wish
the King to see, such as letters criticizing Chesterfield, should be
sent under cover to Bedford. This letter is at Hinchingbrooke.
[2] Bentinck explained this demand in a letter to Newcastle of
1 September (o.s.), *ibid.*, fo. 292.
[3] The answer to Bentinck's second memorandum, dated
4 September (o.s.) is in Add. MSS. 32,809, fo. 306. Its general
tone is one of annoyance at his pertinacious objections. New-

While Bentinck was carrying on his controversy with Ministers in London, the correspondence between Saxe and Ligonier at last settled that the projected conference between France and England should take place at Liège, as conveniently near to the headquarters of both armies. Although there was no armistice, hostilities were tacitly suspended in the neighbourhood, though the siege of Bergen-op-Zoom continued. As England had selected a civilian, France nominated Puyzieulx, now Minister of Foreign Affairs. The Austrian representatives, Reischach and Batthiani, protested against any separate conference from which they were excluded, and declared that Sandwich had no authority to speak for Austria. But the cautious Chavanne, to whom Sandwich had communicated his instructions, had stayed behind at The Hague, and Holland had sent no Minister, and so the solitary protest of Austria was disregarded. The two old antagonists of Breda met again in a convent at Liège on 11 September. It was Sandwich's first introduction to what may be called first-class diplomacy. At Breda he had mainly been occupied with ingenious pretexts for evading all serious discussion, and in his intercourse with Macanaz he was dealing with an eccentric diplomatist. Now, for the first time, he was treating of matters which concerned the Great Powers of Europe with a Minister of the first rank.

Puyzieulx opened by raising the question of method. Neither could conclude without reference to their allies, but it would facilitate matters if they, as representing "the two principal Powers engaged in this war,"[1] could come to some agreement on the principal points at issue. Sandwich agreed, with the same reservation as to allies, that discussion might be useful. Puyzieulx then turned to the points raised in Saxe's letter of 5 August, which had probably been his own composition.

---

castle, who had in the main got his original proposals accepted, thought he ought to be satisfied.

[1] It shows how completely the character of the war had changed that Austria, the State attacked at the outset, was no longer regarded as a " principal Power," whereas that position was claimed by France and England, who were not actual belligerents until 1744.

1. Cape Breton.—Puyzieulx said that if England had decided to keep it, that would block all negotiation. Sandwich replied that he would not go so far, but that circumstances might arise which would lead to retention. Puyzieulx prompty closed the discussion by saying that there could be no compromise. The island must either be kept or resigned : France did not care which. But if it was kept, France would keep the Netherlands.

2. Dunkirk or Furnes.—Sandwich declared that peace must be based upon the confirmation of treaties, and treaties provided for the dismantling of Dunkirk. As for Furnes, the barrier was already too weak, and could not be further weakened. Puyzieulx replied that both were out of the question, and that France was indifferent as to which was chosen.

3. The *enclaves* of Hainault.—On this England was indifferent, and offered good offices to promote an agreement. Puyzieulx said that France would not be exacting, and might even accept English arbitration.

4. Modena and Genoa.—Sandwich declared that England had no objection to their restoration, but that a preliminary question was the claim of Sardinia to retain at any rate a part of its conquests. Puyzieulx answered that if England was going to support the territorial ambitions of Sardinia, an insurmountable obstacle would be raised to negotiation. Sardinia ought to be satisfied with the recovery of Savoy and Nice. Anyhow, neither France nor Spain would consent to the spoliation of their humble allies.

5. Don Philip.—This was admitted to be the most formidable obstacle in the way of peace. Sandwich repeated his prescribed formula. England would not enforce sacrifices on the part of her allies, and persuasion was not likely to obtain them. So he hoped France would agree to the renewal of former treaties, which would also settle the commercial disputes with Spain. Puyzieulx replied that France would not desert Spain on so vital a matter as the establishment for Don Philip, and that England would not find Spain easy to deal with on commercial questions.

Sandwich then raised a question which was not

touched in Saxe's paper, and demanded that France should repudiate the Stewarts, of either sex, to the last generation. Puyzieulx said: "Cela est pourtant bien fort et très humiliant pour le Roy." Even if France agreed to it, some concession, such as Dunkirk or Furnes, must be given in return.

Sandwich then declared that the result of the conversation was that Saxe's terms were to be regarded, not as a basis of negotiation, but as an ultimatum. Puyzieulx said that was so, and a further conclusion was that "the fruit was not yet ripe." France would, however, consent to a renewal of conferences, or even to a Congress, if a suitable place could be found. He did not expect much good from such a method, as the presence of all the interested parties would lead to endless confusion and delay. He added the significant words that "if we were inclined to concert any previous points together, it might be done as well and as privately at a Congress as elsewhere." Sandwich said that Aix-la-Chapelle had been suggested at Breda, and Puyzieulx assented. His office would prevent his attending in person, but the French King would send a proper Minister.[1]

At this point, when Sandwich thought the conference

[1] The account of this important conference is taken from Sandwich's official letter to Chesterfield of 11 September, 1747 (S.P., For., Holland, 426, fo. 135). There is a copy of the letter in Add. MSS. 35,409, fo. 90 (Hardwicke Papers). Broglie (*Saxe et d'Argenson*, ii., p. 252) professes to have collated Sandwich's report with that of Puyzieulx, and says that there is no substantial difference between them. He then adds: "Seulement Sandwich, par une raison facile à apprécier, ne dit rien de la perspective d'une négociation séparée pendant la congrès, dont Puisieulx fait mention." I do not know what the supposed reason might have been, but as a matter of fact Sandwich noted the words, and I have quoted them above from his letter. Arneth (iii., 342) says that the conference at Liège was held "in secret." This is preposterous, as full information of the negotiation was given by England to all the allied Courts, and two Austrian Ministers were present at headquarters and protested against it. Saxe in his letter to Ligonier of 2 September, stating that Puyzieulx will meet Sandwich at Liège, says that the interview cannot be secret, but that there should be no undue publicity (Add. MSS. 32,809, fo. 227). It was Arneth's cue to make the most of English unfairness to Austria, which provided him with a ready-made excuse for the forthcoming "diplomatic revolution."

over, Puyzieulx startled him by saying that Spain was about to send Major-General Wall to England to try to settle terms of peace, that this had been concerted with France, and that it would facilitate matters if France was allowed to send an informal agent to take part in the discussions. He suggested Bussy, who had been employed on similar errands before. Sandwich could only reply that he knew nothing about Wall, and that he must refer to his Court as to the admission of a French agent.

Sandwich gave a verbal report of the interview to Reischach, and, as there was no Dutch Minister at the army, wrote a detailed account to Fagel. The communication to Sardinia he reserved until Chavanne joined him. In England the news of Puyzieulx's attempt to dictate terms without discussion was regarded as putting an end to the negotiation which Saxe had proposed to Ligonier. The general conclusion, shared by Cumberland, was that France had never been serious in the matter, and that the only object of the overture had been to promote discord among the allies and to postpone preparations for carrying on the war.[1] Even if Puyzieulx had been more yielding in other matters, his refusal to agree to an unconditional abandonment of the Stewart cause would have been sufficient to cure George II and Cumberland of any desire for an immediate peace with France. The suggestion that France should send Bussy or any other private agent to England was scouted as impudent,[2] and Sandwich was instructed to find some means of conveying the refusal to Puyzieulx. There was a general consensus of opinion that preparations must be made for a new campaign and that Parliament must be asked to provide the necessary funds. Sandwich was held to have done admirably at Liège,[3] and was gratefully informed that he would be

[1] Newcastle to Hardwicke (autograph), 7 September (o.s.), Add. MSS. 35,409 (Hardwicke Papers), fo. 102.
[2] Cumberland to Chesterfield, 11 September (*ibid.*, fo. 96). There is a second letter, of 18 September, to much the same effect in Add. MSS. 32,809, fo. 321.
[3] Newcastle to Bedford, 8 September (o.s.): " Our friend Sandwich has done like an angel " (*Bedford Corr.*, i., 246). New-

sent to represent England at Aix-la-Chapelle. Sandwich himself was exultant. He had, without committing England in any way, obtained a statement of French terms, from which the obnoxious demand of a neutrality for the Austrian Netherlands had been excluded, and he had a virtual assurance that France would no longer oppose, as she had done at Breda, the admission of the allied Ministers to the forthcoming Congress.[1] He cheerfully undertook the task, now assigned to him, of arranging the contributions of the allies for the next campaign, which he thought would enable him to procure a " good peace." He paid no attention to the cold water administered by Chesterfield, who wrote to him in a private letter : " The conditions I confess are hard, and yet I cannot flatter myself that they will be mended by time."[2]

Newcastle's confidence was sadly shattered when the news came a few days later that Bergen-op-Zoom had been taken by storm, " more owing to want of vigour in the garrison than to the superiority of the enemy."[3] For the first time his belief in the magical results of the Dutch Revolution was shaken when he learned that the commanding officer was nearly ninety years old, and that the French had found both officers and garrison asleep in their beds. His depression was deepened when the Prince of Orange demanded that England should put as many troops into the field as the Dutch proposed to do, and made difficulties about a declaration of war,

castle to Cumberland, 12 September (o.s.): " I defy anybody to have acted more ably or more honestly than Lord Sandwich did in conference with Puisieux" (Add. MSS. 32,713, fo. 51; and 35,409, fo. 105).

[1] Sandwich's exultation is clearly visible in his private letter to Newcastle of 15 September, where he says of the Liège interview : " It is impossible it could have passed better, or that the negotiation could have taken a more advantageous turn than it now has; we are plainly masters of the form as well as of the essentials of the negotiation." This letter was sent under Cumberland's cover " to prevent notice being taken of my correspondence with your Grace."

[2] This letter of 11 September (o.s.) is in the Sandwich Papers at Hinchingbrooke.

[3] Sandwich to Chesterfield, 17 September, S.P., For., Holland, 426, fo. 43, and Add. MSS. 32,809, fo. 298.

which the English Ministers had at last categorically
demanded as necessary to demonstrate the unity of the
allies and to induce Parliament to grant supplies for the
continuation of the war. The Dutch seemed to forget
that they were defending their own country. Equality
of troops was contrary to all the precedents of the
Spanish Succession war, and the demand showed an
ungrateful disregard of the immense expenditure of
England in subsidies and the maintenance of the fleet.
What was the use of talking of " not irritating France
so as to engage them to break the ice "? Has not
France broken the ice sufficiently by invading Dutch
territory and capturing their strongest town ? Finally,
wrote the angry Duke, " Can anything be more absurd
than that the Republic should be pressing us every day
to continue the war, and decline at the same time declaring war themselves ?"[1]   It did not pacify him in the
least that Sandwich sent complacent reports of the
Prince's anticipated success in inducing the Provinces
to make the restored Stadtholdership hereditary. Something more was required to remove the prevalent impression in England of Dutch inefficiency. " The establishing of the Prince of Orange's succession alone will
not do it. And you must not be surprised to hear it
surmised that a management for the Pensionary,
D. S'cravemore [s'Gravemeer], and the pacifick party,
to bring them into that measure, may account for some
late appearances, and particularly for the tenderness
and backwardness in declaring war."[2]   Sandwich replied
with a long letter, giving a portrait gallery of the chief
personages at The Hague. He denied that the Prince
was deliberately making concessions to his former opponents, but pointed out that the constitution was still
republican, and that the Stadtholder could not be
expected to carry any measures, especially such an
extreme one as the declaration of war, without paying

[1] Newcastle to Sandwich, 25 September (o.s.), Add. MSS.
32,810, fo. 72.
[2] Newcastle to Sandwich, 29 September (o.s.), Add. MSS.,
32,810, fo. 86. The same suspicion was voiced by Bedford to
Sandwich on 19 October (o.s.) (*Bedford Correspondence*, i., 274).

some regard to the humour of the country. He admitted that the Prince was prone to take impressions not always from the wisest people, and that his cleverness enabled him to find arguments for his conduct even when it was on wrong lines. But a little patience and ingenuity would suffice to put him right, especially when Bentinck, his ablest adviser, had recovered from the illness which had incapacitated him since his return from London.[1] Newcastle thanked his correspondent for his " clear, honest and candid letter," but declared that it only confirmed his suspicions. " The present conduct of the Stadtholder is to me incomprehensible. He is, or has been, against all negotiations, and does not take one essential step towards carrying on the war." There is no inquiry into the conduct of the criminals who lost Bergen-op-Zoom, and the promised Dutch recruits are only on paper. "And yet the King must compleat his contingent to 70,000 men, to equal this uncertain, imaginary contingent of the Republick, and, after all, no declaration of war is to be expected." All that the Dutch promise is a vigorous answer to de la Ville, and it has taken them six months to give birth to that. Newcastle concluded that England was so alarmed about a possible French invasion that, so far from sending more troops to Holland, it would be necessary to recall ten or twelve battalions to defend the coast of Kent during the winter.[2]

Newcastle's fit of pessimism imposed a heavy burden of responsibility upon Sandwich and his intimate ally, Bentinck. They realized that no diversion was to be expected from Italy, and they had little hope, after the failure with Macanaz, of detaching Spain from France. Everything, therefore, depended upon the war in the Netherlands, where they planned to raise an unprecedently large allied army, which would compel France to

[1] Sandwich to Newcastle (private), 17 October, *ibid.*, fo. 116. This long and interesting letter was written out, partly by Sandwich himself, and partly by Robert Keith, who " is entirely to be trusted."

[2] Newcastle to Sandwich, 20 October (o.s.), Add. MSS. 32,810, fo. 162. See also a letter of Bedford on the same topics, 19 October (o.s.), in *Bedford Corr.*, i., 272.

moderate the demands which had been formulated at
Liège. In this way they would justify their Revolution.
They had certain advantages. The Prince of Orange,
for what he was worth, must perforce be on their side.
Cumberland, since Liège, was eager for a new campaign,
and he would carry his father with him. The Court of
Vienna was notoriously opposed to an immediate peace,
and had already announced its intention of supplying
one hundred and twenty thousand men for the next
year, half in Italy and half in the Netherlands, in addition to garrisons. Sardinia was equally hostile to a
Bourbon peace, which must establish Don Philip in
Italy. The weak spot was the English Ministry. Henry
Pelham and Chesterfield were avowedly against the
continuation of the war, and if Newcastle joined them
a decisive majority would be obtained and would be
able to coerce the King. Upon Sandwich and Bentinck
devolved the task of reconverting Newcastle to their
views, and of maintaining the allegiance of Bedford,
whom Bentinck thought he had gained during his recent
visit.[1] During October and November Sandwich employed every safe conveyance that offered itself to carry
his secret letters to the two Dukes.[2] In these he sought
to reassure them as to the power and determination of
the Prince of Orange, and as to the military and financial
resources of the Republic. Bentinck's letters were less
frequent and shorter, but equally positive and even
more outspoken in their denunciation of Chesterfield.[3]
In order to carry conviction, the two men induced
William IV to strain the constitution by giving a solemn

[1] Bentinck to Sandwich, 21 August (o.s.), from London, narrates
his relations with Bedford, whom he describes as " noble and
generous." The letter is at Hinchingbrooke.

[2] On one occasion Sandwich sent his own servant on the pretext
of private business, and Newcastle complained that the man gave
the secret away by applying to Chesterfield for a passport to
enable him to return to The Hague. He begged for more caution
in the future. Newcastle to Sandwich, 23 October (o.s.), Add.
MSS. 32,810, fo. 197.

[3] On 14 November Bentinck wrote to Newcastle: " Il me
semble claire et évident que my Lord Chesterfield est déterminé
à une paix *quovis modo*, comme Messieurs d'Amsterdam et leur
cabale ici l'étoient avant la Révolution. . . . Ici les choses sont
sur le meilleur pied possible " (Add. MSS. 32,810, fo. 249).

promise that the Republic would formally declare war at the beginning of the next campaign if the conference at Aix-la-Chapelle had failed before that date to procure peace.[1] At the same time the States-General approved an answer to de la Ville, who had issued a threat of renewed attacks against the Republic, and this answer only stopped just short of a declaration of war. The States further undertook to equip privateers and to put a stop to trade with France, while they begged England to concert measures for preventing neutral ships from stepping in to carry it on. One very obvious defect in Holland was the want of a good general. The Prince of Orange wished to remedy this by securing Field-Marshal Keith, who had quitted the Russian service, if George II would excuse his Jacobite record. In this design he was anticipated by Frederick of Prussia, and had to fall back upon Lewis of Brunswick-Wolfenbüttel, a member of a notable family of soldiers, who played a prominent part in later Dutch history.

The combination of persistent letters, promises,[2] and actual measures from The Hague produced their effect upon Newcastle, who was always ready to believe what he wished to be true. His conversion to a renewed advocacy of militant preparation may be dated from a private letter to Sandwich of 23 October (o.s.), in which he admitted that "things begin to mend extremely in Holland."[3] From this time he began to advocate that the Dutch demand for equality of forces, though demonstrably unreasonable, should be conceded. Sandwich had assured him that the Dutch declaration of war,

[1] This declaration of the Prince, dated 31 October, is in S.P., For., Holland, 426, fo. 357; and Add. MSS. 32,810, fo. 181. Sandwich, in his covering letter of the same date, says that the Prince wishes this document to be kept a profound secret, " as it would be attended with ill consequences if it should be known that he had taken upon himself to answer for things which, tho' he has the real, he has not the nominal, power to authorize him to engage for " (S.P., For., Holland, 426, fo. 350).

[2] The Dutch promises were not carried out. War was not declared, the trade with France was not stopped, and not a single privateer was equipped. See Newcastle to Sandwich, 8 February (o.s.), 1748, S.P., For., Holland, 431.

[3] Newcastle to Sandwich (private), 23 October (o.s.), Add. MSS. 32,810, fo. 197.

the Prince of Orange's authority, and his continued co-operation with England all depended upon this concession. Newcastle's conversion was unquestionably furthered by his desire to be on good terms with Cumberland, and by hopes of success in his negotiations with Spain. All through the summer the Spanish Minister, Carvajal, had continued to correspond more or less directly with Keene at Lisbon on the subject of a separate peace with England, and at one moment the virtual exile of the Queen-Dowager and her third son from Madrid to San Ildefonso had given rise to confident expectations of some result. So the mission of Wall, which Puyzieulx had so dramatically announced to Sandwich, was no great surprise to London. Newcastle took the actual conduct of the affair into his own hands. He had secret interviews with Wall, and also employed the Marquis Tabernuiga as an intermediary.[1] The negotiations followed the familiar line of those between Sandwich and Macanaz. Spain demanded Gibraltar and an establishment for Don Philip, and offered commercial concessions. Newcastle felt compelled, as before, to refuse Gibraltar, though both Bedford and Sandwich argued in favour of its cession. It remained to find something for Don Philip. Newcastle devised what he thought an ingenious scheme. The Infant was to have Parma and Piacenza, but Don Carlos must cede the *stato degli presidii* to Tuscany, while Sardinia was to be compensated with gains on the Riviera. He thought that the allies ought to be reasonable enough to accept this.[2] Sandwich, still eager for a treaty with Spain, urged him to take a strong line, fix his terms, and practically force the allies to give

[1] Tabernuiga also served as a link between Newcastle and Granville, who had been the Marquis's first patron in England. He also provided information about the Opposition leaders who consorted with the Prince of Wales at Leicester House. His letters to Newcastle offer a curious picture of politics and society in this period.

[2] Newcastle to Sandwich (private), 23 October (o.s.): " If Spain will agree on these terms, I think the Courts of Vienna and Turin cannot, in common sense, refuse them " (Add. MSS. 32,810, fo. 197). The scheme was expounded by Newcastle to Keene on the same date (*ibid.*, fo. 199; and S.P., For., Portugal, 47).

way by a *coup de main*.[1] But Newcastle clung to his
principle that the coalition must be preserved at all
costs, and this wrecked any chance of success. Austria
objected to a settlement of her affairs by England, and
stuck to her old contention that if she gave anything
to Don Philip, she must recover her cessions to Sardinia.[2] Even if Spain consented to mulct Genoa on
the Riviera, Charles Emmanuel would not consent to
a second Bourbon principality in Italy.[3] Don Philip
had failed to gain his establishment in war, and he ought
not to get it by negotiation. And so Wall had in the
end to depart with an absolute refusal of the Spanish
terms.[4]

Meanwhile, Sandwich, in the intervals of exhorting
his friends in England, was engaged in negotiating a
convention for the next campaign and in drafting plans
of peace which the allies could present at Aix-la-
Chapelle. The second occupation, in which Chesterfield and Newcastle also shared, was a perfectly futile
one, as previous experience had proved that there was
no conceivable plan on which the allies could agree, and
even if there had been, there was little prospect of
inducing or compelling France to accept it. In the other
task, although he had the valuable assistance of Cumberland, endless difficulties were encountered. Sardinia

[1] This was urged in Sandwich's long letter of 17 October.
[2] The Austrian objections are summed up in a dispatch of
Robinson, 22 November, S.P., For., Germany, 178.
[3] Sandwich reported to Chesterfield on 14 November that
Sardinia was opposed to any establishment for Don Philip, " as
a most dangerous measure, destructive to the tranquillity of
Italy and of all Europe, and as particularly ruinous to the King
of Sardinia, who will have a very powerful branch of the House
of Bourbon behind him, always ready to co-operate with France
in any attempt that may be made to molest him in his own
dominions " (S.P., For., Holland, 427, fo. 58).
[4] Newcastle summed up the negotiation with Spain in a private
letter to Sandwich on 8 March (o.s.). England was eager to come
to terms on the accession of Ferdinand VI, but " His Catholic
Majesty has hitherto put his interests and his negotiations, either
at first into the hands of those devoted to the Queen Dowager, or
afterwards into those of M. Maccanas, disavowed and unsupported
by the Court, or lastly into those of an Irish Major-General, who
saw every thing through a French medium, and was finally
determined in every thing by French influence " (S.P., For.,
Holland, 431).

was still suspicious of the alleged treaty of Lisbon
between Austria and Spain, and Chavanne pressed for
the inclusion in the first article, which confirmed existing treaties between the allies, of a pledge on the part
of Austria that no such separate treaty had been or
would be made. Batthiani rather increased suspicion
by answering that the convention was purely military,
and that he could not consent to the inclusion of any
political matter. Chesterfield instructed Sandwich to
support Batthiani's objection, whereas Sandwich himself was inclined, as usual, to side with Sardinia. And
the instructions from England became imperative when
Batthiani suggested, as a compromise, that all the allied
Powers should give an identical pledge. This, said
Chesterfield, was an insult to England. It was natural
that the Courts of Vienna and Turin, " being reciprocally suspicious and distrustful of each other upon every
occasion, should by this means find themselves reciprocally secured against each other." But the King of
England is irreproachable, and should be exempted
" from any expurgation of what is not so much as supposed to be insinuated with regard to him."[1] In the
end Chavanne had to withdraw his demand, but not
before it had given rise to a great deal of bad blood.[2]

There was all the usual friction at The Hague about
the amount of subsidies, and the conditions and dates
of their payment. Both Austria and Sardinia wanted

[1] Chesterfield to Sandwich, 8 December (o.s.), 1747 (S.P., For.
Holland, 427, fo. 202).
[2] Přibram (Œsterreiche Staatsverträge, England, i., 753, note 1),
referring to reports from Reischach and Wasner, says that England
at first supported the Sardinian demand, and only changed when
Austria proposed the reciprocal assurance. It is just possible
that Sandwich took this line, but, if so, he did it in defiance of
his official instructions. Chesterfield wrote on 10 October (o.s.)
that Batthiani was right about the military character of the
Convention, and that Chavanne should withdraw his demand
(S.P., For., Holland, 426, fo. 382). And on 17 November (o.s.)
he wrote still more strongly that the Court of Vienna could not
be asked to admit that the Empress had in some way failed to
fulfil her engagements, whereas the King of Sardinia had performed all his, " which is perhaps not so certain." Chavanne
should drop it (ibid., 427, fo. 108). Both letters were written
before the reciprocal assurance had been proposed. Přibram,
like Arneth, is inclined to exaggerate English unfairness to Austria.

more money, and Austria in particular insisted upon payment in advance, without conditions and without any inspection such as had been attempted by Wentworth in Italy during the current year. England haggled, but on most points Newcastle prevailed against his brother, and Sandwich had ultimately to give way. But by far the most serious troubles arose with regard to the command in the two prospective scenes of warfare. By the sixth article of the Treaty of Worms the command in Italy was entrusted to the King of Sardinia wherever he was present in person. Charles Emmanuel complained that this gave him no control over Austrian detachments, and demanded to have the command on the same terms as Cumberland held it in the Netherlands under the convention of the previous January. Austria objected vehemently to any alteration of the Treaty of Worms or to any forced interpretation of its terms. For weeks this controversy was waged with equal obstinacy and acrimony on both sides, and it was not till the last minute that Sandwich was able to extort a preposterous compromise, which must have broken down if it had ever been necessary to carry it out. By the fifteenth article of the convention the King of Sardinia was to have supreme command of the allied army, whether united or divided into detachments, but in complete conformity with the sixth article of the Treaty of Worms, which was quoted verbatim. In other words, the King was to command troops with whom he was not present in conformity with a treaty which prescribed that he was only to command troops with whom he was present. Only the imperative need of getting something or other signed to save his own credit can explain, though it hardly justifies, Sandwich's conduct in putting his name to so futile an agreement.

Quarrels between Austria and Sardinia were too familiar to provoke any surprise, but the dispute about the command in the Netherlands was quite unexpected. Austria offered no objection to a renewed appointment of Cumberland, and it was as prospective Commander-in-Chief that the Duke came over to The Hague in November to promote the progress of the military convention. But the Prince of Orange, always egged on to emulate William III, and already jealous of his younger brother-in-law,[1] now came forward with the assertion that he, as Captain-General of the States, could not allow an alien to command the Dutch troops who were defending their native land.[2] To the argument that he had no military training or experience, he opposed the oath which bound him not to sacrifice any of the prerogatives attached to his office. Every patriotic Dutchman, Bentinck as loudly as the Pensionary and other old Republicans, applauded this proper exhibition of national pride and self-sufficiency. Sandwich found himself in a most difficult and delicate position. He had every possible reason for desiring to stand well with Cumberland, but at the same time recent events had bound him by the closest ties to William IV and Bentinck. Cumberland magnanimously suggested that he and the Prince should divide the command, as had been done by Marlborough and Eugene—a comparison that was too ludicrous to be convincing.[3] This would have been a great relief to Sandwich, but it was promptly vetoed by George II, who declared that a divided command was a bad thing in itself, and that he would not allow his son " to be divested of any part of his command or to share it in any shape with any person whatsoever."[4] George II had no great love for his son-in-law as a man, and nothing but contempt for him as a soldier. But the Prince persisted in asserting that he could not submit to a superior in his own

[1] In his private letter from the Nore on 20 July (o.s.) Sandwich wrote to Newcastle of Cumberland's rupture with the Prince, which he feared at that time would make the Duke more inclined to peace (Add. MSS. 32,809, fo. 40).

[2] The Prince raised this question of the command at the end of October, not to Cumberland or to Sandwich, but to the Austrian commander, Batthiani. See Cumberland to Newcastle, 31 October, *ibid.*, 32,713, fo. 285.

[3] The comparison and the suggestion originated with Cumberland. See his letter to Newcastle of 31 October, in Add. MSS. 32,713, fo. 285; and Sandwich to Chesterfield of same date, in S.P., For., Holland, 426, fo. 313.

[4] Chesterfield to Sandwich (separate and secret), 30 October (o.s.), S.P., For., Holland, 426, fo. 389. See also Newcastle to Cumberland, 23 October (o.s.), in Add. MSS. 32,713, fo. 305.

country, and his wife, the Princess Royal, was eager to resent any slight upon her husband's dignity or talents. Bentinck had the impudence to write to Cumberland that Chesterfield had instructed Sandwich to demand the sole command for the Duke in order to prevent the conclusion of the convention, and by the ruin of all military plans to force the Maritime Powers to make peace *quovis modo*, " ce qui depuis longtemps a été sa marotte."[1] As a compromise, it was suggested that the Prince might command some fifty thousand troops which would be stationed on the border to guard Breda, but even this failed to satisfy him, as he still held himself bound to insist upon equality in the chief command, if this body should ever be joined to the main army. While the dispute was at its height, the Dutch suddenly raised another vexatious question by demanding that their fortresses should be garrisoned by allied forces in equal proportions. This novel attempt of a state to evade the primary duty of self-defence provoked great indignation in England, and Sandwich had to insist upon its withdrawal. This made the Dutch still more obstinate about the command, and the difficulty had to be solved by a secret article. The text of the convention merely said that the command should be settled between the Royal and the Most Serene Highness with the consent of their respective states (Art. 5). The secret article provided that Cumberland was to remain Commander-in-Chief as in the last year, but the Prince was to have the command-in-chief of one of the *corps d'armée*, and was to be consulted on all that concerned the safety of the Republic. An added sentence declared that the giving way of the Prince with regard to equality was not to be regarded as prejudicing the rights of the Captain-General of the Republic in the future. The two great difficulties having thus been solved or evaded, the convention was signed on 26 January, 1748.[2] As the number of men to be furnished by

[1] Bentinck to Cumberland, 10 December, Add. MSS. 32,810, fo. 322.

[2] The text of the Convention is printed in Přibram, *op. cit.*, i., 759-68.

England was fixed at sixty-six thousand, the Dutch affirmed their doctrine of equality by cutting down their proffered seventy thousand to the same number. In both cases the prospective Russians, in equal proportions, were included. The total army on paper in the Netherlands alone was to be one hundred and ninety-two thousand, and Sandwich was prepared with expedients to raise it to the two hundred thousand on which he had set his heart. He wrote in some triumph to Newcastle that this is " the greatest force that the allies ever brought together." It may not satisfy our opponents at home, but it makes an impression in France, where the Princes of the blood and others are denouncing Saxe and the militant party. And thirty thousand Russians, " the best troops in Europe," inspire fear. " My Lord, it is not the time to yield."[1]

Newcastle needed some encouragement. For the last three months he had been fighting almost single-handed in the Ministry against the advocates of immediate peace. To his great disappointment, Bedford, who had been his close ally in the autumn, had shown signs of joining the pacific section, now that all hope of retaining Cape Breton had practically disappeared.[2] All the difficulties raised by the Dutch and the exasperating conduct of the Prince of Orange and Bentinck had been weapons of which Chesterfield had made adroit use. Even Sandwich had to admit at one moment that the

[1] Sandwich to Newcastle (private), 26 January, 1748, Add. MSS. 32,811, fo. 53. Sandwich admitted his obligation to Greffier Fagel, who had been his chief ally in fighting the Pensionary on the twin questions of the garrisons and the Prince's command. " Why should the Prince receive the law in this manner ?" said the Pensionary. " Anything rather than receive the law from France," replied the Greffier. Bentinck, who wrote on the same day, declared that the Dutch gave way, not from conviction, but from necessity. He expressed his astonishment that people in England believed in getting admissible terms from France: " Voudrait-on envoyer carte blanche à Versailles ?" He again voiced his belief that Chesterfield had deliberately sought to obstruct the Convention (ibid., fo. 50).

[2] In order to facilitate its surrender, and to avert colonial protests, the Parliament of 1747 voted a sum of nearly £236,000 to reimburse the New England provinces for the expense they had incurred in the reduction of Cape Breton (Parl. Hist., xiv., p. 149).

Prince might " throw himself into the arms of Amsterdam."[1] And the fatal delay in sending full powers to
Swaart to conclude at St. Petersburg the convention for
the Russian troops was, considering the Prince's persistence in pressing for those troops, wholly inde-
fensible.[2] It was difficult to resist the contention that,
with such an untrustworthy ally, it was impossible to
expect better terms than those which Saxe had offered.
But Newcastle, buoyed up by the optimistic reports and
exhortations of Sandwich, doggedly maintained that
those terms could only be accepted in the last extremity,
that that extremity had not yet been reached, and that
a last effort should be made to obtain a better peace.
When Chesterfield asked him, as they emerged from the
Royal closet, " Pray, from whence comes all this good
news? I have read all the letters, and don't find it
there," Newcastle made the evasive reply that perhaps
they did not agree as to what was good or bad news.[3]
As had happened before, his obstinacy was not unsuccessful. With the help of Cumberland he extorted
the grudging consent of his colleagues to the Dutch
formula of equality of troops.[4] Parliament was induced
to grant what was then considered the huge sum of
eleven millions for the next year. Newcastle was fully
conscious of the heavy responsibility which he was
undertaking, and it was a great relief to him that the
military convention had at last been signed at The
Hague. In his elation he wrote at once to congratulate
Sandwich. " Two hundred thousand in Flanders, ninety

[1] Sandwich to Newcastle, 23 January, Add. MSS. 32,811, fo. 35.
[2] When Hyndford wrote to Sandwich that the convention was
held up by the Dutch envoy's lack of powers, Sandwich discovered that not a single step had been taken in the matter.
Even then he had great difficulty in inducing the Prince and the
Pensionary to forgo the normal practice of referring the matter
to the various provinces. Sandwich to Hyndford, 24 October, in
S.P., For., Holland, 426, fo. 296, and a letter of 26 October at
Hinchingbrooke. Newcastle wrote as late as 15 December (o.s.):
" Swartz's full powers still sticks in my stomach " (Add. MSS.
32,810, fo. 333).
[3] Newcastle to Sandwich (private), 19 January (o.s.), Add.
MSS. 32,811, fo. 85.
[4] Newcastle to Sandwich (private), 17 November (o.s.), Add.
MSS. 32,810, fo. 286.

thousand in Italy, and a fleet to sweep all before it ! I
begin now to talk a little big."[1]

On one point Newcastle found it necessary to give
way. Ever since Frederick had extorted the recall of
Laurence in November, 1746, England had been unrepresented at Berlin. It was not unknown that the
Prussian King resented this treatment, and the English
Ministers tried to insure against his indignation by
paying Russia to keep a body of troops on the frontier
of Livonia. There were not wanting advisers who held
that security could be more cheaply purchased by con-
ciliating Frederick, but George II was so hostile to his
nephew that such a proposal was certain to be rejected
by the King. In the winter of 1747-48, however, the
question became serious. There were sundry scares as
to a return of Prussia to the war, which would be still
more disastrous now than it had been in 1744, and it
was known that Frederick resented, and might even
forcibly oppose, the march of Russian troops across
Germany. It was another grievance to Frederick that
he had offered mediation to the Dutch, and that the
offer, at English instigation, had been declined. The
veteran Horace Walpole, the terror of successive Foreign
Secretaries, who spent his leisure in compiling reams of
advice on foreign policy, wrote one of his homilies to
Cumberland in December, contending that only one of
two things could save England—either a separate treaty
with Spain or a reconciliation with Prussia. Cumberland handed the document to Newcastle, who sought
to appease the formidable correspondent by maintaining that he personally had always been a persistent
advocate of both measures. Walpole, in a denunciatory reply, threw scorn upon Newcastle's professed support of a Prussian alliance, and accused him of having
ousted Granville from office only to follow Granville's
policy.[2] It is not possible to say, though contemporaries

[1] Newcastle to Sandwich, 22 January (o.s.), 1748, *ibid.*, 32,811,
fo. 102.
[2] Newcastle's letter to Walpole of 17 December (o.s.) is in
Add. MSS. 32,713, fo. 544, and the latter's reply of 28 December
(o.s.) is in *ibid.*, fo. 608. The reference to Carteret is noteworthy:
" I could say a great deal upon this subject, and particularly with

said it, that Newcastle was frightened by this denuncia-tion,[1] but it is a curious coincidence that it was im-mediately followed by his cordial acceptance of a pro-posal of Chesterfield that an envoy should be sent to Berlin to solicit Frederick's support either in the war, or in the making of peace. From this time the guarantee of Silesia in the general peace, which had startled the English and disgusted the Dutch Ministers when first propounded by d'Argenson, became a definite part of the English programme.[2] Sandwich, to whom New-castle communicated the design, eagerly welcomed it as he welcomed everything that might weaken France, and even offered to go himself to Berlin before the open-ing of business at Aix-la-Chapelle.[3] Newcastle refused to hear of Sandwich's leaving The Hague, but was en-couraged to persuade the King to consent to the sending of an envoy. After the usual scuffle as to who was the right man for the job, Henry Legge was selected, and was approved by Newcastle as an intimate friend of Bedford and likely to be congenial to Sandwich. One of Chesterfield's last official acts was to draw up Legge's instructions.[4]

---

regard to the difference between your Grace's way of thinking and acting since the removal of Earl of G—ville, and your thoughts and actions relative to peace and war before his removal: the reasons are obvious for this alteration, you stand in his place." As a matter of fact, Granville did at this time support Newcastle against the advocates of immediate peace. See Add. MSS. 32,811, fo. 131. See also Horace Walpole, *Letters*, ii., 302.

[1] Baron Clarke to Sandwich, 9 February (o.s.): " The Duke of Newcastle is frightened at shadows. Such another letter from Horace Walpole will make him change all his measures." The letter is at Hinchingbrooke. Charles Clarke, at one time M.P. for Huntingdonshire, was a Baron of Exchequer. He was an intimate friend of Sandwich, and kept him posted in London gossip. How he came to know about Walpole's letter is an enigma. Possibly the old man boasted of it.

[2] Bedford to Newcastle, 10 January (o.s.), 1748, Add. MSS. 32,714, fo. 42. See also Hardwicke to Newcastle, 29 December (o.s.), Add. MSS. 32,713, fo. 615.

[3] Sandwich to Newcastle (private), 5 January, Add. MSS. 32,810, fo. 408.

[4] For these instructions, 12 February (o.s.), see S.P., For., Prussia, 64. They were not issued until after Chesterfield's resignation, but Newcastle admitted that they had been drafted by his predecessor.

Meanwhile, the Conference at Aix-la-Chapelle, though long ago agreed to by all the Powers concerned, had been held up by difficulties as to passports and other formalities. Puyzieulx explained to Sandwich that he could not give to Maria Theresa the title of Empress, as France had never recognized her husband's election. A prolonged correspondence was necessary to solve such knotty problems, and it was not till February, 1748, that all was settled and the various plenipotentiaries nominated. Sandwich was to represent England without, as he had feared for a time, any colleague.[1] The Prince of Orange nominated Bentinck, as George II had desired, though there was some doubt in England as to whether he could be spared from The Hague. The estates of Holland added two others, Hasselaer and Catwyk, and the States-General insisted upon a fourth, the younger Van Haren, whom Sandwich regarded with special antipathy. It did not promise to improve Sandwich's chance of success that the State with which he was bound to be most closely associated was represented by a team instead of by an individual.[2] Maria Theresa sent Kaunitz, whom she had wished to employ at Breda; and Sardinia sent the experienced Chavanne. On the other side, France was to be represented by St. Severin, the Italian diplomatist who had won his spurs in the French service by negotiating the Franco-Swedish Treaty in 1738, but had later failed, through no fault on his part, to obstruct the election of Francis I. St. Severin had

[1] This question of a colleague, especially when he learned that Holland was to have several representatives, agitated Sandwich a good deal. He was especially alarmed lest Sir Charles Hanbury Williams, who applied for the job, should be sent to join him. Sandwich to Newcastle (private), 1 December, Add. MSS. 32,810¹ fo. 293.

[2] This difficulty was surmounted by Aix by the help of Bentinck, who kept Hasselaer and Catwyk in ignorance of all that was going on until the last moment when they were called upon to sign. Van Haren was prevented from going to the Congress by the ingenuity of Fagel. A letter of Bentinck to Fagel from Aix, dated 10 and 11 April, 1748, shows that it was arranged as early as the previous November that all really confidential letters should be transmitted through Sandwich to Bentinck, so that they could be kept secret from the other Dutch envoys. A copy of this letter is at Hinchingbrooke.

been thought of by d'Argenson for Breda, but Puyzieulx had been preferred and had profited by the preference to displace his patron. Spain nominated the Marquis de Sotomayor, who had been at Lisbon with Keene and had not been particularly helpful. Genoa and Modena also sent Ministers, but they never emerged from their obscurity until they were required to sign the treaty. The question whether interested but non-belligerent Powers, such as Russia and Prussia, should be admitted to representation was left to be settled at Aix-la-Chapelle. But it was known that the Tsaritsa desired to be represented, and England was pledged to support her claim.

As the time for the meeting approached the tension in the English Ministry became more acute than ever. The pacific section, now almost definitely reinforced by Bedford,[1] was in a distinct majority, but every recent precedent seemed to prove that they would be powerless against the combination of Newcastle with the King and Cumberland, and with Sandwich overseas, and that peace would be somehow or other postponed until the eleven millions had been spent in a successful or unsuccessful campaign. Suddenly, without giving notice to his colleagues, Chesterfield resigned his office. The immediate occasion was his failure to carry a small matter of patronage, and the published pretext was the state of his health. But the real reason was, as he avowed to his intimate friends, that he was tired of being a mere *commis*.[2] The incessant correspondence carried on between Newcastle and Sandwich, which he had at first contemptuously encouraged, had ended by exasperating him as it had previously exasperated Harrington. The wonder is, not that he resigned, but that he had held on to office so long. He refused to make any quarrel, and declared his intention of continuing to

---

[1] Newcastle to Sandwich (private), 19 January (o.s.), says that "our good friend" Bedford seems to have changed his mind and to be violent for peace (Add. MSS. 32,811, fo. 85).

[2] Chesterfield to Dayrolles, 26 January (o.s.): "I can no longer continue in a post in which it is well known I am but a *commis*" (*Letters*, ii., 846). This letter was written a fortnight before the actual resignation.

support the Government.[1] Newcastle, who had become
accustomed to a passively hostile colleague, and had not
resented opposition so long as he got his own way, was
disagreeably surprised by the sudden resignation.[2] He
had planned to carry on as things stood until the war
was finished and until Sandwich returned with sufficient
laurels to justify his promotion to be a Secretary of
State.[3] On one point he had no hesitation. He pounced
upon the Northern Department, which he had declined
rather more than a year ago, and thus secured the direct
supervision of the process of peace-making at Aix-la-
Chapelle. Chesterfield ruefully remarked : " The Duke
of Newcastle has taken my department; in truth he had
it before."[4] But it still remained to find a sufficiently
submissive colleague to take over the Southern Department. He could hardly abstain from suggesting Sandwich, who would be exasperated if he was passed over
without consideration, but it was impossible to press
his candidature against the ill-will of the King, who
seems to have realized Sandwich's defects more quickly
than Newcastle did, against the opposition of Henry
Pelham and other members of the Ministry, and against
the protests of the House of Commons, where Sandwich
was denounced as " the Minister of the Stadtholder and
not of the King."[5] Failing Sandwich, Newcastle would

[1] Newcastle to Sandwich (private), 9 February (o.s.): " I must
do my Lord Chesterfield the justice to say that he left the King's
service with great duty and decency to His Majesty, and with
the strongest assurance of his resolution to support the King's
measures to the utmost of his power " (Add. MSS. 32,811, fo. 197).

[2] Newcastle to Bedford, 14 January (o.s.): " The town is very
full of Lord Chesterfield's intention to resign the seals: I hope it
is without foundation, for it would be a most unfortunate cir-
cumstance if it should happen" (Bedford Corr., i., 308).

[3] As long ago as 17 July (o.s.), 1747, Chesterfield wrote to
Dayrolles (separate and secret) about the alliance between Newcastle and Sandwich: " The Duke of Newcastle has, I believe,
shown him my place en perspective, which possibly it may not be
in his Grace's power to dispose of " (Letters, ii., 827). Horace
Walpole to Mann, 5 June, 1747, says that Chesterfield's resignation was expected even then, and that Sandwich was looked upon
as his successor (Letters, ii., 277).

[4] To Dayrolles, 9 February (o.s.), 1748 (Letters, ii., 849).

[5] Newcastle to Sandwich (private), 19 February (o.s.), Add.
MSS. 32,811, fo. 239.

21

have liked to take Sir Thomas Robinson from Vienna, as was suggested by the Duke of Richmond, who had fathomed Newcastle's desire to have a clerk rather than a colleague in the office.[1] But he did not venture as yet to go so far in asserting his personal predominance. He would not have Henry Fox, the favourite candidate of the Commons, as likely to be too independent. In the end he fell back upon the Duke of Bedford as the best available choice. Bedford was, it is true, almost as pacific as Chesterfield, but he was thought to be too easy-going to assert himself too much. Then he was a friend and almost a patron of Sandwich, to whom he might be willing, when the proper time came, to resign the Secretaryship. The final argument was that Bedford's promotion enabled Newcastle to offer a sop to Sandwich in the First Lordship of the Admiralty, which had always been understood to be the object of his ambition. This was settled, and Chesterfield was propitiated by making his brother, John Stanhope, Second Lord in Sandwich's place. All this was explained in apologetic and regretful letters to the rather touchy young envoy at The Hague. He was reminded that he was now exactly in the same position

---

[1] Richmond to Newcastle, 9 February (o.s.), Add. MSS. 32,714, fo. 200. He was a vigorous opponent of the promotion of Sandwich, whom he described as " disliked by most people. He has flattered you and will continue to do so, but depend upon it, he is no more to be trusted than the last, and in the eye of the world is a much worse man. Yet how Totty [Bedford] and his father-in-law [Gower] will take his being refused, I don't know. 'Twould be a pity to lose them, yet the taking in this man, who is their only friend, will be the ruin of you." Richmond was a supporter of Fox, so his words may be discounted. A fortnight later he expanded his first letter: " I am not ' that Cabinet councillor' who won't bear your having one entirely your *commis*, for I most sincerely wish you had such a one, and Fox or Robinson would have been so, but all my argument is stopped at once by ' nobody in the House of Commons could have it.' I have then done, and the Duke of Bedford is Hobson's choice. But I must disagree with you about Sandwich, indeed the run against him is not so unjust as you imagine " (*ibid.*, fo. 235). Richmond's racy letters, of which there are many in the Newcastle Papers, give a most entertaining commentary on the politics of the period. He was a member of the Cabinet but not of the inner circle of trusted councillors.

that Lord Strafford had held at Utrecht in 1713—First
Lord of the Admiralty, Minister Plenipotentiary to the
States, and Ambassador at the Congress.[1] Sandwich
replied that he was more than satisfied with the settlement, and that he was glad to have escaped premature
promotion to an office " which must subject me at once
to a load of envy before I had got a footing to support
myself under it."[2] But, in spite of these professions of
equanimity, he seems to have found it difficult to
pardon those who were reported to him as having been
active in opposing his elevation.[3]

[1] Newcastle to Sandwich (private), 12 February (o.s.), Add.
MSS. 32,811, fo. 213. Bedford's letter on his acceptance of
office, also apologetic, is in *Bedford Corr.*, i., 323.
[2] Sandwich to Newcastle (private), 5 March, Add. MSS. 32,811,
fo. 269. See also his letter to Bedford of same date: " I should
deservedly be judged a very unreasonable person if I was not
thoroughly happy with the whole arrangement in consequence
of the late change " (*Bedford Corr.*, i., 327). There is a still
stronger letter to Henry Pelham of 6 March at Hinchingbrooke.
[3] Perhaps the letter which made the greatest impression on
Sandwich was one written by Clarke on 16 February (o.s.):
" Nothing was further from the Duke of Bedford's intention
than being what he now is, and both he and Lord Gower told
every body that you was to be S. for S.—then a push was made
for Henry Fox—then Pitt and Littleton exclaimed against your
being made, and said it ought to be an old experienced man,
and nobody so fit as H. Walpole—at last I am told the Duke of
Bedford was to be tried again, and Harry Legge was the great
agent and the most zealous in that scheme—then there was the
intention of keeping the Admiralty open, but that the Duke of
Bedford overruled and insisted upon your being named directly
—Harry Legge is a great man in Arlington St., remember that."
This letter is at Hinchingbrooke. Arlington Street means Henry
Pelham, who had a house there, and whom Clarke always regards
as an enemy of Sandwich. The result of this letter was a violent
antipathy on Sandwich's part towards Legge, which found expression when he discovered that Legge wanted to be associated
with him at Aix-la-Chapelle. See his private letter to Bedford
of 12 April, where he says: " I am not so blind as he imagines,
nor so unacquainted as I have appeared to him to be of his real
disposition during the time of the late change of Ministry "
(*Bedford Corr.*, i., 350). It is an astounding proof of Sandwich's
egotism that he should write thus to Bedford against a man
whose alleged offence was that he had supported Bedford against
Sandwich. Legge's conclusive defence was, as Anson discovered,
that he had only been active in procuring Bedford's appointment
after Sandwich's candidature had been ruled out. Anson, an
avowed partisan of Sandwich, had at first shared his suspicions

of Legge.   His letters to Sandwich on the subject are at Hinchingbrooke.

Sandwich also denounced Legge in private letters to Newcastle of 10 and 12 April (Add. MSS. 32,811, fo. 441; and 32,812,
fo. 1). Even Newcastle, though not well disposed towards
Legge, felt compelled to reply: " I own I think you carry your
suspicions about Legge too far " (*ibid.*, fo. 145).

CHAPTER VIII

THE PRELIMINARIES OF AIX-LA-CHAPELLE

NEWCASTLE was no sooner settled in his new office and freed from the humiliating necessity of secrecy than he proceeded, with his usual promptitude, to draw up instructions to Sandwich for his conduct at the approaching Congress. They were sent off on 12 February (o.s.), the very day on which Bedford received the seals and Sandwich was promoted to be First Lord. The preamble asserts that the efforts of His Majesty and his allies have preserved to Maria Theresa all her dominions in Germany and Italy, except what she has yielded by separate treaties; they have also restored the imperial dignity to the House of Austria, prepared the way for the recent Revolution in Holland, which gives weight and consistence to the Government and support to the common cause, destroyed the French marine, interrupted French trade, and deprived France of considerable territories in North America. These efforts are to be continued and even increased in the present year, but there is no hope of their renewal. For this reason it is necessary to consider the terms of a definitive peace. Its basis should be the mutual restitution of conquests,

311

with the proviso that Sardinia shall keep Finale, and that France shall renew its pledge to abandon the cause of the Stewarts. If the campaign should prove less successful than is expected, it may be necessary to give something to Don Philip. This should be arranged " with the least inconvenience," as His Majesty is very reluctant to demand any sacrifices from his allies, the more so as he strongly desires to maintain the coalition after the end of the war. Therefore, any concession to the Infant must be made with the consent of all the allies.[1] Four days later the instruction was added that Sandwich should demand the admission of a Russian Minister, and as this might give umbrage to the King of Prussia, that monarch should also be invited to send a representative.[2]

Newcastle's confident instructions, though they were not formally modified till six weeks later, were virtually obsolete by the time that they reached Sandwich, who received them with warm approval at The Hague. In a private letter, without any apparent appreciation of the importance of his news, Sandwich told Newcastle that the Dutch wanted to borrow a million, that Charles Bentinck was to carry the request to London, that Pensionary Gilles was hostile because such a loan would increase Dutch dependence upon England, and that this constituted a sound argument for acceding to the demand.[3] Before the arrival of this letter, Newcastle had already been alarmed by reports which had been brought over from The Hague by Count Flemming, the ubiquitous agent of Augustus III. According to Flemming, the Prince and Princess of Orange, irritated by the dispute as to the command of the army, were now as pacific as they had been bellicose in the previous year; the Stadtholder, in order to have his offices made hereditary, had thrown himself into the arms of his old opponents; and Sandwich, who was denounced in

[1] S.P., For., Holland, 431, and Add. MSS. 32,811, fo. 148. It may be noted that all idea of retaining Cape Breton has now been definitely abandoned.
[2] Newcastle to Sandwich, 16 February (o.s.), in S.P., For., Holland, 431, and Add. MSS. 32,811, fo. 219.
[3] Sandwich to Newcastle (private), 27 February, *ibid.*, fo. 227

England as more devoted to the House of Orange than
to that of Hanover, had lost all credit with the Prince,
to whose elevation he had contributed more than any
man except Count Bentinck.[1] The disquietude caused
by these reports became consternation when Charles
Bentinck produced, in support of his pecuniary demand,
a *Mémoire Instructif* in which William IV himself
painted the financial condition of the United Provinces
in the darkest colours. If these statements were
accurate, and it was difficult to disbelieve a document
which was brought by one Bentinck and had been seen
and presumably approved by his brother, it was clear
that Sandwich had been either a dupe or a criminal
accomplice, that the arguments employed for the postponement of peace had been utterly unfounded, and
that Chesterfield's information and Chesterfield's contentions had been more than justified and borne out.
The blow dealt to Newcastle's vanity and self-confidence
must have been almost intolerable. For months he had
stood almost alone in the Cabinet, upheld only by Royal
support, his obstinacy had committed the country to
enormous and now apparently useless expediture, and
he was exposed to the reproaches of his economical
brother and to the merciless lash of Chesterfield's gibes.
He had presumed to lead the state as a virtual Prime
Minister, and he had led it to peril and possibly to ruin.
He had exulted in a docile Parliament, but docility had
its limits, even in the eighteenth century, and Ministers
had been impeached upon less provocation than Newcastle might be held to have given. In the meantime,
he could only wait until the Duke of Cumberland, who
had been his accomplice since September in opposing
a precipitate peace, could cross over to Holland and
ascertain on the spot whether things were quite as bad
as they were represented to be in Charles Bentinck's
paper.

The correspondence[2] on the subject between the dis-

[1] Newcastle to Sandwich (private), 19 February (o.s.), Add.
MSS. 32,811, fo. 239.
[2] These letters are fos. 263, 287, 295, 321, 329, 341, 347, 367,
582, 398, in Add. MSS. 32,811.

illusioned Newcastle and the too credulous Sandwich is interesting as throwing light upon the characters of the two men, and is not on the whole discreditable to the former. He abstained at the outset from acrimonious complaints, and was despondent rather than querulous. It was only after considerable extra provocation had been given that he began to throw some of the blame upon the informer who had so grievously misled him. Sandwich, who had not at first actually seen Charles Bentinck's *Mémoire*, was obviously puzzled by Newcastle's sudden depression, and thought it necessary to deal out some of his old doses of encouragement. He declared on 8 March that things were 100 per cent. better than immediately after the fall of Bergen-op-Zoom; that France, with her trade gone and her East Indies threatened, could not afford to continue the war for the sake of Don Philip; that, even if the worst happened and Maestricht fell, the Russians would restore the balance, and therefore the rejection of Saxe's terms was fully justified and could be sustained at Aix. When Cumberland arrived at The Hague on 12 March with the text of Charles Bentinck's instructions, Sandwich tried to defend himself by throwing the blame on the envoy who had been fool enough to disclose so imprudent and damaging a document. Four days later, on his way to Aix, he tried to insinuate that the altered situation might justify an abandonment of the previous decision to retain Gibraltar. He took as his text an extract from a letter which Bedford had written to him on 28 January (o.s.), urging that peace should be made this summer upon admissible terms. "These terms may still be mended in case our friend Legge succeeds in his mission to the King of Prussia, and I think might be still more mended were all the King's servants hardy enough to make a separate and good peace with Spain, which I am confident they might do by giving up Gibraltar, and for which, I doubt not, valuable concessions in trade might be obtained in the West Indies. I must own that place seems to be of little or no utility to this country, and that the cession of it to Spain would not be near so dangerous as that of Louisbourg

to the French."[1] Sandwich expressed to Newcastle, as
he had already expressed to Bedford, his cordial agreement with the latter's contention, and begged that he
might be allowed to treat with Spain on the basis of
the cession of Gibraltar. On arriving at Aix on 16 March,
he renewed his denunciation of Charles Bentinck by
declaring that William Bentinck, who had come to represent the Republic at the congress, had never believed
that his brother would have the madness to disclose
the fatal document. " However he has had the madness, and has ruined our affairs by it, when they were
in the best situation they have been in for a long
time."

Newcastle was naturally nettled by this attempt of
a subordinate to reopen the question of Gibraltar, and
by the appeal to his junior colleague on a cardinal question of foreign policy; while he was exasperated by the
persistent blaming of Charles Bentinck, who had done
nothing but obey his instructions from the Stadtholder,
and by the repeated assertions, which he now knew to
be ill-founded, as to the improvement of the allies'
position. He described himself in one letter as astounded
at the discrepancy between the *Mémoire Instructif* and
Sandwich's previous reports. This was exactly what
his opponents had always said, and was a great triumph
for them.[2] If this new statement is true, why did we
reject Saxe's proposals, and why should changes have
been made in the Ministry? Three days later he
returned to the charge. Why did not the Prince confess
this bankruptcy before? How on earth did our old
friend Bentinck suffer such a paper, " such a libel on
our proceedings," to be brought here by his brother?
Our whole basis was to try a last campaign, and now

---

[1] *Bedford Correspondence*, i., 314. Sandwich, recalling his
negotiation at Breda with Macanaz, urged Bedford, in whose
department Spain was, to obtain leave for him to make the offer
of Gibraltar at Aix.

[2] Chesterfield to Dayrolles, 22 March (o.s.), 1748: " Charles
Bentinck is come here to contradict every word that his elder
brother said six months ago. . . . When the King heard the
purport of Charles's commission, he said Chesterfield told me six
months ago that it would be so " (*Letters*, ii,, p. 857),

that is said, at this eleventh hour, to be impossible. The Commons, previously so generous in their grants, now demand " any peace, peace at any rate, no ifs and ands." To Sandwich's letter from Aix he replied : " I own I don't taste the notion about Gibraltar. These times (as I have before observed to you) will not bear such strokes as those." And he utterly declined to join in blaming Charles Bentinck for producing the memoir. He was bound to do it. " He communicated it to me in confidence, and I should have deserved to be hanged if I had not communicated it in the same confidence to my brethren in the administration." The mischief lay, not in the production of the document, but in its truth. And when Cumberland's reports made it clear, not only that the financial position of the Dutch was quite as hopeless as had been represented, but that their military resources were no better, Newcastle at last wrote with a bitterness which he had previously restrained. " His Royal Highness's reports go much further than Lord Chesterfield's gloomiest forecasts, which I used to put down to prejudice, passion, and personal pique and resentment. We seem to have been all in a dream. It appears that the Dutch have no army at all, or any that they can or will employ. And yet it was the Stadtholder and Holland that caused us to reject Marshal Saxe's proposals, and to engage in the immense expense of this year. You must forgive me, my Lord, if I am a little warm. I am much provoked with your Dutch friends. I have gone through what no man ever did, from a blind dependence upon them ; and now I shall be sacrificed for my ignorance, obstinacy, and credulity. . . . I am pelted with pamphlets and papers every day : and God knows, if Maestricht is taken, whether some Parliamentary attempt may not be made. Many are ready for it ; and be assured that the part you and I have taken is sorely against the grain in this House of Commons." Cumberland's arrival had at last convinced Sandwich that his persistent optimism was out of date, and he could only reply to Newcastle's diatribes that he had been duped, that he was " in great measure the cause of your present uneasy situation," and that he was prepared to serve as scapegoat for his patron. But, with characteristic obstinacy, he reiterated his conviction that Charles Bentinck had blundered.

The real importance of the Bentinck disclosures, and of their confirmation by the Commander-in-Chief, lay, not in any question as to blame or responsibility, but in the compulsion they imposed upon Newcastle and his colleagues to change their views as to the possible terms of peace. On 29 March (o.s.) Newcastle wrote to Sandwich a "very private" letter, which was virtually a new instruction.[1] In his first directions Sandwich had been told that necessity might compel a demand for sacrifices on the part of the allies in order to provide for Don Philip. Although no actual disaster had yet occurred, it was now so imminent and inevitable that the forecasted necessity had arisen. It was therefore proposed that Don Philip should receive Parma and Piacenza, with the proviso that these duchies should revert to their present possessors whenever he should succeed to the throne of Naples or in case he should leave no heirs. Finale, as was agreed before, must be secured to Sardinia. "The King's honour is concerned in this; we cannot allow a Republic of Genoa to triumph over a King of Great Britain, and that in a point indifferent to France." To this scheme it was reckoned that the allies would be forced to consent: the Dutch, because it was their fault; Austria, "notwithstanding Count Kaunitz's way of talking relating to the Treaty of Worms, indemnifications, etc., which were never proposed or intended but in consequence of a successful war," because the Court of Vienna was really desirous of peace, even before they knew of the Dutch default;[2] and the King of Sardinia, because "he will be by this the only gainer by the war," by the retention, not only of Finale, "his principal aim," but also of all the

---

[1] This letter is in S.P., For., Holland, 431, and Add. MSS. 32,811, fo. 423.

[2] This was based upon reiterated assurances from Sir Thomas Robinson, and their substantial accuracy was proved by Maria Theresa's subsequent acceptance of terms which she loudly condemned.

cessions made at Worms except his share of Piacenza. If any objection should be raised by the allies, they must be reminded that Cape Breton was a bigger sacrifice than any demanded from them. If St. Severin should complain that the establishment for Don Philip was too meagre, he in his turn must be reminded that Spain, even with the help of France, had failed to conquer any territory for the Infant.

As to the other points at issue with France, Sandwich must refuse all cessions in the Netherlands, and must insist upon the enforcement of the Utrecht provisions with regard to Dunkirk. From Spain he must demand the restoration of the *asiento* and the *navio permiso*. Finally, in a " very secret " letter, written three days later, Sandwich was adjured to hasten the negotiation with St. Severin, and to show Chesterfield that " if his dull Dutch won't allow us to carry on the war, we can, when we please, make peace as well as he can do."[1] Newcastle sent copies of these letters to Cumberland, with the apologetic comment : " They are not in my usual and favourite strain. I am both concerned and mortified to write in this way. . . . The private letter to Lord Sandwich was by my brother's proposal. I think it can do no hurt. For indeed my friend Sandwich wanted some strong hint to cure him of his sanguine expectations."[2] The dispatch, without the secret letter, was also forwarded to Robinson, with instructions to urge that Kaunitz should be ordered to co-operate with Sandwich in promoting a treaty upon these lines.[3] This was the first formal intimation to Maria Theresa that she was to be called upon to make fresh sacrifices, though Wasner's reports and past experience had convinced both her and Bartenstein that such a proposal would sooner or later be made by the British Ministers.

[1] Newcastle to Sandwich (very secret), 1 April (o.s.), Add. MSS. 32,812, fo. 16.
[2] Newcastle to Cumberland, 29 March (o.s.), Add. MSS. 32,714, fo. 402.
[3] Newcastle to Robinson, 1 April (o.s.), in S.P., For., Germany (Empire), 180.

Newcastle must have been humbled when he followed his brother's guidance in foreign affairs. And he soon found it necessary to depart still further from his "usual and favourite strain." The reports from The Hague and from Cumberland's camp became more and more alarming. Not only were the Dutch unable to furnish or to pay their promised contingent, they could not, without an impossible loan from London, provide their stipulated proportion of the cost of the Russian troops. As Bestuzhev had adroitly stipulated that the Maritime Powers should be both jointly and severally responsible for the money, the Dutch default would throw the whole burden upon the British Exchequer. To make matters worse, Austria was not only squabbling with Sardinia about the conduct of the Italian campaign and demanding additional subsidies for a renewed siege of Genoa, but was also actually in default as regards the promised sixty thousand men for the Netherlands. Even if the men were there, which was more than doubtful, as the paper lists were notoriously untrustworthy, they were so scattered as to be largely useless for Cumberland's immediate task, the defence of Breda or Maestricht, whichever Saxe might determine to attack. When it became obvious that the advance against Breda was a mere feint, and when, taking advantage of Cumberland's fumbling moves, Saxe and Löwendahl had succeeded in concentrating their forces round Maestricht, the relief of that fortress became impossible. There was no longer the slightest possibility that the Russians could arrive in time to render efficient help. When Maestricht fell the whole territory of the United Provinces would be exposed to an irresistible French invasion.

Hitherto Newcastle's supreme guiding principle had been that the coalition must survive the war, and therefore no treaty should be made without the consent of the allies. This had brought him into collision with colleagues who were exasperated by Bartenstein's contentious memoranda, and not too appreciative of Sardinian professions. This principle he had now to abandon. France was not prepared to accept even his reduced terms, and neither Kaunitz nor Chavanne showed the slightest inclination to join Sandwich in supporting them. In view of these circumstances, and of the danger of Dutch desertion if Maestricht should fall, it was necessary to release Sandwich from the obligation to obtain the consent of the allies before signing any treaty. The letter in which Newcastle gave up what he had fought for ever since the issue of d'Argenson's project was written on 5 April (o.s.).[1] Sandwich was informed that the situation was so much worse that he must conclude before the French were masters of the Maes and of the whole Republic. He must not offend the allied Ministers, but they must not be allowed to ruin themselves and England. Dunkirk and Finale must be fought for to the last, but England cannot be sacrificed for Finale. By the next post he was more explicit. Sandwich may tell St. Severin that he is empowered to sign at once. The only outstanding difficulties are Finale and Dunkirk. He may offer to redeem Finale by repayment of the original purchase-money to Genoa, but if France is obstinate, as at Liège, for its restitution, he must give way. But if we are compelled to deprive the King of Sardinia of Finale, we are bound by both justice and honour to stand by him as regards the cessions made by Austria in the Treaty of Worms. As to Dunkirk, Sandwich must strive for the simple renewal of the terms of Utrecht and the Triple Alliance. But in the last extremity he may consent to fortification on the land side, and may also dispense with the supervision of commissioners, an indignity against which France had hotly protested, but without which French promises might never be fulfilled. Finally, when terms have been adjusted with France, they are to be submitted to the Ministers of the allies. If they make difficulties and want to refer to their Courts, Sandwich must say that necessity compels him to sign without them. In a separate letter of the same date Newcastle not obscurely hints that, if there is a

[1] Newcastle to Sandwich, 5 April (o.s.), in Add. MSS. 32,812, fo. 25.

choice between Finale and Dunkirk, the latter is to be preferred.[1]

In two of the letters of 8 April (o.s.) Newcastle added to Sandwich's burden detailed instructions to pay special regard to the interests of Hanover. Any guarantee that may be given to Prussia must be carefully worded so as not to include East Friesland, to which the Elector of Hanover has rival claims, and, if possible, Sandwich is to obtain payment of a debt due for Hanoverian troops supplied to Spain in the reign of Charles II. This somewhat belated regard for Hanover was due to the unpopular decision of George II to visit his Electorate in the summer, in spite of the critical position of his kingdom, of the remonstrances of his Ministers, and of the disapproval of his favourite son. Newcastle was faced with the unpleasant necessity, either of risking his newly gained hold over the King by allowing his fellow Secretary to go to Hanover, or to fulfil his proper function as Northern Secretary and cross the sea, to which he, and still more his Duchess, were notoriously averse.[2] In the end he hit upon a compromise. His trusted secretary, Andrew Stone, the universal confidant, was to accompany the King in order to conduct the necessary correspondence, while Newcastle was to follow as soon as the preliminaries of peace had been settled and the spring winds had blown themselves out. George II, who would have been quite satisfied with Stone alone and not at all displeased to be free for a time from Ministerial supervision, gruffly assented to Newcastle's proposal. Pelham and the other Ministers viewed with some alarm the prospect that, at a very anxious moment for the country, the Royal ear and the direction of foreign affairs would be monopolized by a colleague who had shown such symptoms of a desire to be dictatorial.

[1] There are three letters in all on 8 April (o.s.), of which the first is by far the most important. All three are in S.P., For., Holland, 431, and the separate letter is in Add. MSS. 32,812, fo. 25.

[2] On Cumberland's efforts to stop his father's journey, and for the discussions as to whether Newcastle should accompany or follow the King, see Add. MSS. 32,714, fos. 385, 387, 411, 417, 420, 471, 488, 534, 546; and Add. MSS. 32,715, fos. 1, 40, 66.

With Newcastle's letters went an urgent appeal from
Bedford that there should be no delay in putting an end
to the war.[1]   These were actually the last instructions
received by Sandwich before he finally signed the preliminaries.   The later dispatches were too late to affect
the terms, but they have a certain importance as illus-
trating the agitation in London, the hardening of the
resolve to act independently of the allies, and the increasing alienation from Austria.   On 15 April (o.s)
Newcastle wrote: "I am much concerned at Count
Kaunitz's behaviour.   The Court of Vienna talks big,
and are acting just like the Dutch.   I am afraid they
have not half their contingent in Flanders, and they are
doing nothing but quarrelling with their ally in Italy.
. . .   The difficulty about the inclusion of the King of
Prussia is abominable, and can't fail to create jealousies;
and the desire of getting back the cessions in Italy is
most unjust and monstrous. . . .   I hope you will not
be reduced to the necessity of signing singly, that is
without the Austrian and Sardinian Ministers."[2]   But
he evidently had little hope of Austrian concurrence.
On April 19 (o.s.), the very day on which the preliminaries were actually signed, he wrote a longer and
more elaborate dispatch, which had been approved by
the inner Cabinet—the Lord Chancellor, the Lord President, the Duke of Bedford, and Mr. Pelham.   In this
he renewed his condemnation of Austria.   The demand
for the recovery of the Worms cessions " will hereafter
discourage any dubious Power from taking part with the
House of Austria."   The objection to giving a guarantee
of Silesia implies a similar design to take back the
cessions to Prussia, which will drive that Power closer
to France, the very thing England wishes to prevent.
" Guastalla is a new demand, and you will treat it as
such."   It will give Vienna an additional cause of complaint.   The injunction to submit the terms to the
allies is repeated.   But, if they object, Sandwich must
sign without them, " to save the Republic from ruin."

[1] Bedford to Sandwich, 5 April (o.s.), *Bedford Corr.*, i., 340.
[2] Newcastle to Sandwich, 15 April (o.s.), Add. MSS. 32,812,
fo. 45.

The recent changes about Finale and Dunkirk do not directly concern Austria, and Newcastle has communicated them to Wasner and Osorio. " So the utmost regard has been paid to the allies through the whole proceeding."[1] This was evidently the aspect of the negotiation about which Newcastle had the gravest misgivings. But he recognized at last that the need of peace was more imperative than the conciliation of Austria and Sardinia. In a private covering letter he half apologizes for the apparent pusillanimity of his recent letters. " You may think I want courage and perseverance. I had both as long as I thought they were consistent with the interest of my King and my country. And I may say there is scarce a man in England that would have persevered so long as I did. . . . For God's sake, my Lord, look forward. Your friend Lord Chesterfield says you are now amused by St. Severin. Bring things to a decision. Get something signed if you can."[2]

Meanwhile, Sandwich, still little more than an amateur in diplomacy, had been left virtually single-handed to champion British interests at Aix. Hitherto, both at The Hague and at Breda Sandwich had had the invaluable assistance of a capable and trusted secretary of legation, Robert Keith. For some weeks before his departure from The Hague Sandwich had impressed upon Ministers at home the necessity, during the absence of himself and William Bentinck, of sending some agent of sufficient rank and capacity to keep a watchful eye upon the Prince and Princess of Orange, to checkmate the intrigues of the Pensionary and other leaders of the Republican party, and to strengthen the hands of the Greffier Fagel, the only Dutch official in whom Sandwich placed any real trust.[3] The difficulty in the way of gratifying Sandwich in this matter was

[1] Newcastle to Sandwich, 19 April (o.s.), Add. MSS. 32,812, fo. 80.
[2] Newcastle to Sandwich (private), 19 April (o.s.), Add. MSS. 32,812, fo. 100.
[3] Sandwich to Keith, 24 April (at Hinchingbrooke): " The Greffier is the only man in Holland that I now think fit to be trusted."

22

that there was already a resident Minister at The Hague
in the person of Dayrolles, that it was extremely undesirable to irritate Chesterfield by dismissing his
nominee, and that the King, who frowned upon all
extravagance upon embassies, would never allow three
men to be accredited at once to the States-General. As
both Newcastle and Sandwich suspected Dayrolles of
supplying secret information to Chesterfield, and of
intimacy with Chesterfield's old friends in the Republican party, Sandwich had carefully kept all confidential
documents to himself, and had only employed his colleague to deal with routine business, such as the issuing
of passports. In his own words, he had treated and
represented him as " an honest, insignificant, and
ridiculous fellow." Even if Sandwich had trusted Dayrolles, he would have stultified himself by suddenly putting business of the first importance into his hands.
And, therefore, at great inconvenience to himself, he
had to leave Keith at The Hague to serve as a channel
of confidential communication with the Stadtholder and
with Fagel. It was an anomalous situation at The
Hague, where Dayrolles, officially in charge, was superseded, in all important business, by a member of the
same service who was of inferior status and not formally
accredited to the Government of the State. There were
all the materials for a first-class departmental quarrel.[1]
Instructions to convey congratulations on the birth of
an Orange baby were sent to both men, but the actual
conveyance was performed by Dayrolles. On the other
hand, it was Keith who was called in to the States-
General to hear the expression of Dutch gratitude to
England for the conclusion of the preliminaries, and it
was Keith who went to Helvoetsluys to meet the King.
There can be no doubt that Dayrolles had a legitimate
grievance, but by Chesterfield's advice he abstained from
protest, which might easily have led to his own removal.

[1] In Chesterfield's *Letters*, vol. ii., there are a number which
refer to the relations between Keith and Dayrolles while Sandwich was at Aix. There are several letters at Hinchingbrooke
between Sandwich and Keith at the same time, but they are far
less personal.

His patience was ultimately rewarded when Keith in July was removed and promoted to Vienna.

The loss of Keith left Sandwich with no help except that of two volunteers who had gone out with him to get experience. One was his cousin, Edward Wortley Montagu, the disinherited son of the famous Lady Mary, and in later years a man of some distinction and more notoriety in Europe. The other was Richard Leveson Gower, the rather scapegrace son of Lord Gower and brother of the Duchess of Bedford, to whom Sandwich, an ill-qualified tutor, undertook to teach the elements of diplomacy and the virtue of economy.[1] This farming out of scions of great houses, so as to qualify them for salaries or pensions, was quite in accordance with the best Whig traditions. It was unfortunate that neither of them wrote so good a hand as Keith, nor could either be trusted to the same extent with secrets, so that Sandwich had both to write and to copy his private letters, and his work was seriously increased when dispatches had to be duplicated to Hanover and to London. However, he was grateful for such assistance as his two companions could give, and gave his superiors no peace until they extracted from a grudging Treasury the grant of an equivalent of Keith's salary between the two.

Sandwich was not lacking in courage, and he entered upon his task at Aix-la-Chapelle with that self-confidence which often irritated both his employers and his opponents. It was not altogether an easy task. He had to make amends for his criminally fatuous reports during the winter by obtaining the best terms he could in the interests of Great Britain, and he had to make those terms as satisfactory as possible to the allies. With William Bentinck, practically the sole Dutch plenipotentiary, he had long been on the most confidential terms, and the interests of the two Maritime Powers in getting rid of the French from the Netherlands were

---

[1] There are numerous letters at Hinchingbrooke in which Sandwich tried to promote the interests of his cousin, who was a year older than himself, and to excuse the extravagance of young Leveson Gower.

sufficiently identical to make co-operation at Aix both easy and imperative. The Sardinian Minister, Chavanne, had been intimately associated with Sandwich at Breda and The Hague, and was regarded by him as being almost as dependent upon England as Bentinck. In some ways he seemed even more dependent, for, whereas Holland had no other friend, Sardinia had three bitter enemies in France, Spain, and Austria, so that British support was the only visible shelter from their animosity. Kaunitz had not been at Breda, and Sandwich had no previous acquaintance with him. He found him, for the representative of a professedly allied Power, provokingly reticent and unaccommodating. But Sandwich's dispatches show that, until the preliminaries were signed, he never grasped the intensity and the danger of Austrian opposition. He must have known that Kaunitz saw St. Severin quite as often as he did himself, but neither reason nor imagination gave him any clue as to what passed in those interviews.

To Sandwich the one vitally important personage to deal with at Aix was St. Severin. He also was a stranger and a perpetual puzzle. There could hardly be a greater contrast than that between the outspoken and almost brutal tenacity of the English peer and the suave, supple, disingenuous demeanour of the Italian diplomatist, who was strangely chosen to defend French interests in the council chamber, as two other foreigners, Saxe and Löwendahl, were entrusted with the championship of those interests in the field. Neither Sandwich nor Newcastle could ever feel certain that the French envoy was not playing with them, and Chesterfield, a keenly interested observer, was convinced that he was doing so. But, against the possibility of French deceit, Sandwich, with some shrewdness, reckoned upon French exhaustion and a genuine desire in Paris for peace. With less wisdom he surmised that the forlorn position of the allies was unknown to their enemies, and that the Russian bogey was as terrifying in 1748 as it was assumed to have been to Fleury in 1735. As a matter of fact, St. Severin had visited Saxe's camp on his way to Aix, and had received ample assurance that

France could exert decisive military superiority in the
Netherlands long before the Russians, with their defective commissariat, could complete their sluggish march
through Germany. And there was no longer, as there
had been at the beginning of the previous year, any
possibility of a reverse on the side of Italy to counter-
balance the intended blow on the Dutch frontier.
Richelieu, who had taken over the command in Genoa,
was not only secured from attack by the discreditable
lack of concord between Austria and Sardinia, but had
a reasonable prospect of driving the Sardinians from
their conquests on the Riviera.

The military situation was as favourable as possible
for France, and the diplomatic position was almost
equally encouraging. The French allies—Spain, Genoa,
and Modena—were strangely slow in sending their plenipotentiaries to Aix. This freed St. Severin from any
pressing necessity to pay too scrupulous a regard to
alien interests, which was at first so hampering to Sandwich. Especially the absence of the Spanish Minister
precluded such inconvenient demands as those for
Gibraltar or Port Mahon, to which France, in deference
to the Treaty of Fontainebleau, would have been compelled to give at least formal support.[1] At the same
time, it made it impossible for Sandwich to open any
of those separate negotiations with Spain by which he
had hoped to weaken the hand of France. The consequent delay in convening any formal conference rendered
it less pressing to settle the troublesome question of
admitting representatives of Prussia or Russia. The
Tsaritsa Elizabeth loudly demanded a voice in the
settlement of Europe, and the Powers which had hired
her troops were pledged to give their support. But St.
Severin, on the ground that France was on the worst
terms with the Court of St. Petersburg, vetoed the proposal, and his opposition ultimately prevailed.[2] Nor

[1] St. Severin pointed to this as an advantage to England as
well as to France (Sandwich to Newcastle, 7 April, in S.P.,
For., Holland, 433).
[2] Sandwich to Newcastle, 7 April, in S.P., For., Holland, 433.
Finckenstein, writing to Frederick from St. Petersburg on 20 June,

did Sandwich press with much vigour for an invitation to Berlin. Newcastle's instructions on the matter were somewhat lukewarm, the Dutch were never ardent lovers of Prussia,[1] St. Severin had his own reasons for not desiring the presence of an ally whom it might be convenient to desert, and Kaunitz was openly hostile. From the Austrian point of view there was no Prussian question at Aix. Frederick had ceased to be a belligerent more than two years ago, his interests were sufficiently safeguarded by existing treaties, and there was no more reason for admitting his agent than for admitting one from Sweden or any other state. Frederick himself paid no attention to these discussions. He was determined that the guarantee of Silesia should be included, however incongruously, in the peace settlement, and, as soon as he saw that a treaty was imminent, he ordered Ammon, his envoy at The Hague, to proceed to Aix. Whether he was formally admitted as a party to the treaty was comparatively immaterial. But Ammon did not arrive till after the preliminaries had been signed.

Although St. Severin seemed to hold all the diplomatic and military cards in his hand, and though he did in fact hold every card except naval security and financial stability, he was not allowed to play his cards so as to gain what in those days of inter-state gambling were regarded as tricks. Rarely had France seemed so absolutely a dictator to Europe. Not even in the days of Condé, Turenne, and Luxemburg had she gained so complete a mastery of the Netherlands as had been secured by the three great victories and the innumerable successful sieges of Marshal Saxe. Not even in 1672 had the position of the United Provinces been so hopeless as in 1747-48, and the imitative restoration of a Stadtholder had not brought the same magical results. William IV was no William III, and the Dutch them-

---

declared that this exclusion of Russia was " l'affront le plus sanglant que la France pouvait faire à ce pays-ci " (*Pol. Corr.*, vi., 169 note).

[1] Sandwich informed Newcastle on 27 March that the Dutch were averse to the inclusion of Prussia in the treaty, and to the acceptance of any additional guarantee.

selves had lost the heroic spirit of the previous century.
And yet France seemed rather depressed than elated.
Frederick of Prussia was exasperated by French lamentations, which he interpreted as designed to drag him
back into the war. Over and over again he urged the
French Ministers to appreciate at their full value the
achievements of France. Not a rood of land in Europe
had France lost, her troops were nourished on foreign
soil, they had conquered magnificent provinces, from
which a fine revenue was drawn, and an irresistible
army stood on the frontiers of Holland. " Toutefois,
pour quelques vaisseaux qu'elle perd sur mer, la voilà
qui jette des hauts cris et se croit réduite à telle crise où
elle se trouva en 1709. "[1] Marshal Saxe, contemptuously
expressing his ignorance of politics, clamoured for some
gain that should be worthy of Fontenoy and Bergen-op-
Zoom. But neither Frederick nor Saxe had any interest
in American colonization, nor did they adequately appreciate the pressure exerted by sea power. There can be
no doubt that public opinion in France was eagerly
desirous of peace. The war seemed to have lost all
intelligible purpose, and even victories lost much of their
attraction when they were won by generals who were
aliens and Protestants. As long as the Marquis d'Argenson remained in office, French policy was still guided
by Belleisle's design to weaken and humiliate the House
of Austria. But this motive had lost much of its force
with the fall of d'Argenson. Louis XV in his youth was
a lover of pose. He had thrown himself ardently into
the war when popularity was to be gained by doing so.
Now he was satiated with the life of camps, the people
were tired of the war, and so he conceived the magnificent and novel gesture of giving peace to Europe as a
disinterested benefactor. It was openly avowed that
the campaigns in the Netherlands had been undertaken,
not to make conquests, but to force the enemies of
France to come to terms. This self-denial was justified
on the ground that any attempt to retain the occupied
provinces or any substantial part of them would only

[1] Frederick to Chambrier, 6 April, 1748, in *Pol. Corr.*, vi., p. 74.

perpetuate and strengthen the anti-French coalition, which would prevail against Louis XV as it had prevailed in the past against Louis XIV. And so the formula was coined and entrusted to St. Severin of mutual restitution of conquests and satisfaction for the allies of France. It was a flexible formula, and capable of almost endless variations in detail. But it did mean that France, for once in her history, was prepared to dispense with territorial gain.

As Puyzieulx had anticipated at Liège, it proved quite as easy to hold private conversations during what was nominally a Congress of all the belligerent Powers as it was when they were specifically arranged. In fact, the so-called Congress of Aix-la-Chapelle never met at all. Sotomayor, the Spanish plenipotentiary, did not arrive till 17 April, and St. Severin refused to hold any general meeting without him. When he did come he was involved in a quarrel with the Genoese envoy on a point of etiquette, and this caused further delay. Meanwhile, the French and English plenipotentiaries made considerable progress. Sandwich reported his first interview with St. Severin on 27 March, and was much comforted to find that the French terms had not been raised since the last year. St. Severin opened by saying that peace rested with France and England, the two Powers that were weary of war, but not unable to continue it. France was willing to offer the same terms as at Liège, and as she demanded nothing for herself, she was entitled to insist upon satisfaction for her allies. Sandwich, carefully following his original instructions, replied that restitution was simple and acceptable, but if satisfaction meant cessions to Don Philip and Genoa, there might be insurmountable obstacles. He further insisted that Finale must remain in the hands of Sardinia. St. Severin, on the other hand, was inflexible on the two points of an establishment for Don Philip and the restitution of the Riviera to Genoa. The problem of Dunkirk was not mentioned, nor that of the desertion of the Stewart cause by France. Sandwich expressed a confident belief that he would be able to make peace without any sacrifices on the part of the allies. To Kaunitz and Chavanne he merely reported that the French demands were unaltered, and both gave him to understand that their acceptance was out of the question.[1]

After a second interview Sandwich was not quite so hopeful. On 7 April he reported that the other two subjects of debate between France and England had been raised.[2] He had demanded that the fortifications at Dunkirk, which had been erected during the war, should be dismantled as prescribed at Utrecht and by the Triple Alliance of 1717. St Severin replied that these offensive conditions had been imposed upon France after an unsuccessful war, and that after a successful war France was bound in honour to insist upon their revocation, especially as the demand for Furnes had been withdrawn. From this time the problem of Dunkirk bulked very largely in the discussions. As to the Pretender and his descendants, St. Severin contended that no new provision was needed, as France was sufficiently pledged by existing treaties. Sandwich pertinently replied that recent events had shown how imperfectly France was bound by these treaties, and that the security of England demanded the extension of French obligations to include the Pretender's remotest posterity. On the other subjects no progress was made. St. Severin was adamant about Finale, and Sandwich sadly confessed that all hope of success in this matter depended upon Legge's efforts to secure the intercession of the Prussian King. Why Frederick should take the slightest interest in giving Finale to Sardinia, neither Sandwich nor Newcastle attempt to explain. Nothing could possibly have come of the appeal to Prussia, and fortunately the appeal was never made, as the preliminaries were signed before Legge had an interview with Frederick. Sandwich not only failed about Finale, but he was unable to extract

[1] Sandwich to Newcastle (secret), 27 March, in S.P., For., Holland, 433; and (private), in Add. MSS. 32,811, fo. 378. A summary account of the interview is given by Andrew Stone, in a letter to Bedford of 26 March (o.s.), in *Bedford Corr.*, i., p. 333.

[2] On this interview see Sandwich to Newcastle, 7 April, in S.P., For., Holland, 433, and Stone to Bedford, 7 April (o.s.), in *Bedford Corr.*, i., 338.

any clear statement as to what France would consider a reasonable endowment for Don Philip. And in this connection he made an almost incredible blunder, for which he was roundly blamed by both Newcastle and Cumberland. He suggested that Ostend should be handed over to England, on the ground that some maritime acquisition would commend the peace to English opinion and make it easier to obtain an establishment for Don Philip.[1] He represented the proposal as " an undigested project of my own," but St. Severin was bound to conclude that, whether Sandwich had definite instructions or not, it had at one time been seriously mooted in England. Ministers now hastened to disavow it, and Sandwich had to make a hasty and humiliating withdrawal. It is to St. Severin's credit that he seems to have observed the promise of secrecy which he had given. If the project had been disclosed, it would have placed the conduct of England in discreditable contrast to the parade of French disinterestedness, would have alienated the Dutch, and would have wholly justified Maria Theresa's exasperation.

The receipt of the second instruction, sent on 29 March (o.s.), which authorized the offer of Parma and Piacenza, enabled Sandwich to make more progress than had hitherto been possible, and his interviews with St. Severin became more frequent. He was, as usual, far more favourable to Sardinia than to Austria, and it is probable that Chavanne, as at Breda, did a good deal more prompting than Sandwich admitted in his dispatches. His first expedient was to treat the questions of Don Philip and Finale as alternatives, and to induce France to give way on the latter in return for British surrender on the former point. In this he utterly failed, and had again to declare that he could only look

[1] Sandwich to Newcastle (private and secret), 9 April, in S.P., For., Holland, 433. Sandwich explains that he has to write separately on this subject, as he showed his other letters to Bentinck. He adds that, even if this suggestion is refused by France, it will not prejudice the alternative plan of leaving a British garrison in Ostend. See also Newcastle to Sandwich, 5 April (o.s.), in S.P., For., Holland, 431; and Cumberland to Newcastle, 11 April, in Add. MSS. 32,714, fo. 411.

to Berlin for any hope of retaining Finale.[1] He then
tried to cut down Don Philip's principality to the single
Duchy of Parma. This St. Severin declared to be inadequate, and demanded in addition either Piacenza or
the district of Cremona. This latter alternative Sandwich quite rightly rejected, as it would have involved
an additional mulcting of Maria Theresa, to which Newcastle would never have consented. When he had given
way about Piacenza, St. Severin disagreeably startled
him by demanding the addition of the little Duchy of
Guastalla on the Po, as a natural complement to the
other two duchies. As Guastalla was in Austrian occupation, and Sandwich had no authority for its cession,
he struggled against this unexpected demand, and implored Legge to induce Frederick to procure its withdrawal. That the Prussian King had no earthly reason
to gratify Maria Theresa does not appear to have
occurred to him, and this illustrates his imperfect grasp
of international relations outside those which had come
within his immediate ken. The next problem was Don
Philip's tenure of his prospective dominions. By the
Vienna treaty of 1738, if the King of Spain died child-
less, Don Carlos was to succeed in Spain, and Don Philip
was to acquire the Two Sicilies. Sandwich insisted that,
when this transfer occurred, and also if Don Philip
should die without heirs, the territories now ceded to
him should revert to their present holders—*i.e.*, Piacenza
as far as the Nura to Sardinia, and the rest to Maria
Theresa. St. Severin at first refused, but it was expected
that he would give way on this point. The settlement
about Don Philip was now assuming a definite shape,
and Sandwich was still bound by his instructions to
obtain the assent of the allies. The Dutch, little
interested in Italy, offered no objections, but it was
otherwise with Austria and Sardinia. Kaunitz had for
some time been repeating the familiar formula that, if

---

[1] See his letter to Legge of 23 April in S.P., For.,'Holland, **433**.
He adjures Legge to represent to Frederick that the whole prospect
of peace depended upon Finale. The King was also to induce
France to desist from the demand of Guastalla. The whole idea
of Prussian intervention was preposterous, but the English
Ministers must share the blame with Sandwich.

the Treaty of Worms was to be adhered to, it should be
enforced as a whole and not merely in part. On 17 April
Sandwich extorted from him a definite explanation of
this formula. This was that, unless Austria acquired
Naples, or some other equivalent, all the cessions to
Sardinia were invalid. Austria would offer no objections to the proposed grants to Don Philip, but only on
condition that her other losses in Italy should be
recovered. Sardinia, said Kaunitz, had not deserved to
be the sole gainer by the war, and Sardinian acquisitions were forfeited by failure to fulfil the conditions
upon which they had been granted. Finally, he
declared that the Maritime Powers ought to oppose all
weakening of Austria, because it would make her a less
valuable ally. Chavanne, with more distress than indignation, declared that his master could never consent
to resign both Finale and Piacenza, and that he would
require a special guarantee of his dominions against the
obvious malevolence of Austria. Sandwich made a last
effort to gratify the Sardinian envoy by obtaining some
compensation for Charles Emmanuel on the Riviera di
Ponente, so that the King might gain his desired access
to the sea, but, as this would involve the spoliation of
Genoa, which had rendered such signal services to
France, St. Severin rejected the demand.

The last impulse to the negotiations on the part of
England was given when Sandwich received on 24 April
his third instruction (issued 5/16 April), which empowered him, if he should find it necessary, to sign
without the consent of the allies. In this final stage,
much to his surprise, the initiative passed to St. Severin,
who suddenly displayed an eagerness for a prompt settlement which he had hitherto concealed. On 28 April
Sandwich wrote to report the progress made in the last
three days. St. Severin adhered to the demand of
Guastalla, but agreed to the proposed terms as to the
reversion of the cessions to Don Philip. He had offered
to take Furnes and Ypres, and to allow the dismantling
of Dunkirk. In the end there was a compromise on this
thorny problem. The fortifications were to be retained
on the land side, but were to be destroyed where they

faced the sea. But there was to be no supervision of this destruction. Furnes and Ypres were to be restored with the rest of the Netherlands. Any other solution would have involved a rupture with Bentinck as well as with Kaunitz. Matters went so far that the two plenipotentiaries discussed how any recalcitrant Power should be coerced into accepting the prospective treaty. Finally, St. Severin, disgusted to find that Bentinck had been kept in touch with the whole course of the negotiation, warned Sandwich that Spain and Austria were planning a joint spoliation of Sardinia, and that he would do well to be very cautious with Kaunitz. Sandwich, always ready to believe the worst of Austria, and remembering his own discovery of Austro-Spanish negotiations at Lisbon, eagerly accepted the advice, and merely told Kaunitz that France was more unreasonable than ever and insisted upon Guastalla.

Just as Sandwich was closing this dispatch, St. Severin returned with the startling question whether he was prepared to sign at once, as he had learned since parting from him that a separate treaty had been virtually concluded between Austria and Spain. Its terms were that Austria was to be compensated for cessions to Don Philip by recovering what had been given to Sardinia. The only way to avert this complete upset of European relations was to sign the treaty immediately on the terms that had virtually been settled. Sandwich, taken aback by this sudden proposition, recollected that he had no authority to give way about Guastalla, or to sign without giving the allies a chance of concurrence. In the end, he collected his wits sufficiently to insist upon gaining at least the assent of Bentinck, whom St. Severin wished to exclude. He further demanded that proof should be given of the agreement between Austria and Spain. If that was forthcoming, he promised to sign the treaty on the following evening.[1]

On the following day (29 April) Sandwich went to

[1] Sandwich's dispatch of 28 May, and his second agitated letter (most secret) of the same day, are in S.P., For., Holland, 433.

St. Severin's house, and was met with the calm statement that the Austro-Spanish documents had been given
to him in such confidence that he could not disclose
them without breach of faith. As a matter of fact, he
had no such documents, and the whole story of the
projected separate treaty was a deliberate invention.
It was the time-honoured trick of the astute house-agent
who forces the hand of a hesitating client by conjuring
up an imaginary rival purchaser. Sandwich was no
simpleton, but he was too full of prepossessions in this
matter to see through the simple device. And even if
he had seen through it, he might well have thought
it worth while to feign deception. Presumably St.
Severin's haste was due to injunctions from the peace
party in France, who were afraid that, when once the
campaign was begun, the soldiers would take command
of the situation. If that was the case, it was probable
that the later terms would be far harder than those now
arranged. It would be a responsibility to sign without
reference home, but it would be a greater responsibility
to refuse to sign and to have to accept, a few weeks
later, a more ruinous treaty. Sandwich decided to take
what seemed to him, and probably was, the lesser risk.
The only use which he made of St. Severin's failure to
fulfil the stipulated condition was to insist upon delay-
ing signature till he had submitted the draft treaty to
the Ministers of the allies. As soon as he had extorted
St. Severin's consent to this, the two men, neither of
whom was a full-fledged expert in the art, set to work
to reduce to proper form the terms upon which they had
roughly agreed. Several of the articles covered matters
over which there had been no dispute, such as the
recognition of the Emperor, the renewed guarantee of
the Pragmatic Sanction (with the necessary deductions),
the guarantee of Silesia and Glatz to the King of Prussia,
and the restoration of all conquests in Europe, America,
and the East Indies. The armistice was to come into
force on land in six weeks from the signature, and at
sea in three months. On the more disputed questions
there was only occasional difficulty. The Duchies of
Parma, Piacenza, and Guastalla were to go to Don

Philip, but were to revert to their present holders in case of his death without children or of succession to his brother's kingdom of Naples (Art. 4). The King of Sardinia was secured in all his dominions, " et particulièrement de l'acquisition du Vigevanasque, d'une partie du Parmesan, et du comté d'Anghiera " (Art. 7). With regard to Dunkirk, St. Severin dexterously evaded any mention of actual demolition : " Dunquerque restera fortifié du côté de terre en l'état qu'il est actuellement, et, par le côté de la mer, il restera fortifié sur le pied des anciens traités " (Art. 3). The obligation of France to abandon the Stewarts was merely expressed by a renewal of Article 5 of the treaty of 1718, the so-called Quadruple Alliance. Genoa and Modena were to recover all losses. The *asiento* and the permitted ship were to be restored " pour les années de non-jouissance " (Art. 10). Sandwich succeeded without much difficulty in inserting the Hanoverian demands. George II was included in his capacity as Elector (Art. 8), and the other two contracting parties agreed to use their good offices to procure payment from Spain of his pecuniary claims (Art. 9). But St. Severin countered this by inserting a clause in favour of the Elector Palatine Charles Theodore, France's most loyal ally in Germany. His claim to Pleistein, a fief in the Upper Palatinate, which Austria had occupied in 1743, was to be settled in the general Congress (Art. 12). By Articles 17 and 18 the various restitutions and cessions were only to take effect when all the interested Powers had acceded. Finally, by a secret and separate article, the three signatory Powers agreed, in case of delay or refusal on the part of any of the other states, to concert measures for carrying out their agreement; and any state which persisted in refusal was to forfeit all advantages under the treaty. This shows how far Sandwich had been forced to depart from Newcastle's original principle that no sacrifice was to be forced upon the allies.[1]

Upon Sandwich now devolved the unpleasant task of

[1] The preliminary articles are conveniently printed in Broglie, *La Paix d'Aix-la-Chapelle*, Appendix, pp. 307–12. Přibram, *u.s.*, prints the definitive treaty, but not the preliminaries.

THE PRELIMINARIES OF PEACE

communicating these terms to Kaunitz and Chavanne. Chavanne may have had some warning, but Kaunitz certainly had no reason to expect this sudden denouement. It did not make Sandwich's task easier that at the last moment, in the presence of Bentinck, St. Severin, in a state of great agitation, tried to veto any communication except to the Dutch. When Sandwich remained firm, the French envoy denounced the article about the *asiento*, seized the copy of the preliminaries, and was with difficulty induced to return it. In constant fear that he might all along have been a dupe, Sandwich insisted that St. Severin should accompany him to Kaunitz, in order that there should be no question as to the fact of their agreement. The Austrian envoy, who had with good reason expected a wholly different solution, was completely taken aback when he discovered the actual state of affairs. Sandwich had prepared a defence beforehand by writing it to Newcastle. " I have not forgot to insert the acknowledgment of the imperial dignity, and the renewal of the guaranty of the Pragmatic Sanction, and as we have recovered all the Low Countries to the house of Austria (notwithstanding a formal offer of giving us our favourite point of Dunkirk in return for the cession of Furnes and Ypres), and secured them in the possession of all their dominions, except what is ceded by the present treaty, by the most efficient guarantees of all the contracting parties, I think they cannot have any just reason to complain of our treatment of them with regard to Parma and Guastalla, particularly if what Monsr St. Severin tells me is true, that they have offered much more than these two dutchies to Spain for the Infant, on condition of being restored to the possession of all they had yielded to the King of Sardinia by the treaty of Worms, and they have agreed besides with the court of Spain (as Monsr St. Severin informs me) to take even the dutchy of Savoy from him, though he would not tell me directly how that dominion was to be disposed of."[1] A promise of secrecy to St. Severin prevented

[1] Sandwich to Newcastle, 30 April, 1748, in S.P., For., Holland, 433.

Sandwich from making use of the last part of his argument, which would have caused a fine explosion if it had been brought forward in the latter's presence. To all the contentions as to British services to Austria, Kaunitz opposed a contemptuous silence. If anything, they served to aggravate the offence. To terms so destructive of the interests of his Sovereign he could not possibly assent, and he protested hotly, not only against them, but against the whole procedure by which they had been drawn up behind his back. Chavanne, however grateful he might be for the article which guaranteed to Charles Emmanuel the major part of his gains at Worms, could not possibly venture on his own responsibility to sign away both Finale and Piacenza. Having discharged his distasteful duty, Sandwich, with St. Severin, Bentinck, and two of the other Dutchmen, attached his signature to the preliminaries in the evening of the 30th April.

That the preliminary articles were open to criticism, and especially to the charge that they had been dictated by France, nobody knew better than Sandwich himself. The postponement of the armistice on land was a cowardly concession to the two Marshals of France, to enable them to gratify their vanity by a triumphal entry into Maestricht. Cumberland did his best to minimize wholly unnecessary bloodshed and destruction by arranging for a hasty surrender, and on the 10 May the great fortress fell. It was not flattering to British pride that the French concessions as to Dunkirk and the Stewarts were disguised under a mere reference to obsolete treaties. The article about the cessions to Don Philip was, in Newcastle's opinion, faultily worded, as it implied the possibility of female succession, whereas Parma and Piacenza were male fiefs of the Empire. This, he insisted, must be rectified in the final treaty. The only clause on which Sandwich boasted that he had got the better of St. Severin was that relating to the *asiento*, and in that matter his success was only short-lived. Cumberland, who was the first Englishman to receive the text of the agreement, bluntly expressed the military estimate of its tenor. "When you peruse the preliminaries and the conferences which led to the concluding to them, you will plainly see the insolence and vain discourse of a superior enemy, feeling his own strength and endeavouring without restraint to give the law to every other power : nay, St. Severin carried that sort of behaviour so far, that he even threatened Sandwich with further bad consequences to the alliance, if he did not think fit to subscribe in the manner he proposed immediately. From this behaviour of the French minister it is too plain that our situation and pacific disposition was thoroughly known to the enemy, and they took advantage of it." But he concluded that, though better terms might be hoped for, they could not be expected, that Sandwich had carried out his instructions against his personal inclinations, and that he must be vigorously supported. "Let the pacific party take the lead in applause. Otherwise, if we go too fast, they will do the opposite."[1]

Sandwich himself was at first extremely nervous and agitated at the thought of the responsibility he had assumed, and this is reflected in the letters which he wrote to Newcastle the day after the signature. He admitted that the wording of the preliminaries was hasty and in places obscure, that he had given way to St. Severin more than he ought, and that he had disobliged the allies, as was shown by their reception of the terms. "However your Grace must consider who we had to deal with; an enemy flushed with her superiority, and who was I fear but too well apprized of our weakness, and an Italian plenipotentiary, who I must acknowledge was the most difficult person I ever had to treat with, and, what is worse, who changed his language every day, and could not be depended upon for anything until he had signed and sealed." In a private letter he was still more apologetic. "I was forced to do what I doubt not I shall have reason to repent of as long as I live. . . . I hope to god (*sic*) you will

[1] Cumberland to Newcastle (private), from H.Q., 21 April/ 2 May, in Add. MSS. 32,714, fo. 508.

throw it all upon me, if that is necessary towards getting rid of your difficulties."[1]

This rather unnatural mood of diffidence and dejection did not last long. His first encouragement was the receipt of a kindly letter of approval from the Duke of Cumberland, whose opinion, he knew, would carry great weight with Newcastle. On 5 May he wrote in a very different tone. "I am now much revived, and begin to flatter myself that, except at the Court of Vienna, I shall be considered as having done an essential service to the public." He now welcomed the idea of having a colleague appointed, which he had hitherto regarded with a jealous fear that he might be deprived of the credit of terminating the war. He was not unwilling to be spared the uncongenial labour of translating the rather unconventional language of the preliminaries into the orthodox forms of a definitive treaty. Meanwhile, he asked leave to return to England, and admitted that he might be regarded as unfit to take part in the final adjustment, " as everything that is to be transacted with the Court of Vienna cannot pass through a more unacceptable channel than mine."[2]

This recovered buoyancy was fully justified by the reception given to the preliminaries in the three countries which were immediately involved. In France there was no hesitation about ratifying an agreement, in the framing of which the French plenipotentiary had played so obviously the dominant part. Maurice de Saxe growled that the King of Prussia had conquered Silesia and kept it, and he did not see why France should not do the same. But the overwhelming opinion of France, both in the capital and in the provinces, was in favour of the termination of the war upon any tolerable terms. St. Severin received full approval from Puyzieulx, only qualified by a reference to the brusqueness of his procedure and to the probable indignation of Spain. Ben-

---

[1] Two of these letters of 1 May are in S.P., For., Holland, 434; the private letter of the same date is in Add. MSS., 32,812, fo. 104.

[2] Sandwich to Newcastle (private), 5 May, in Add. MSS. 32,812, fo. 106.

tinck, though he had played a rather undignified part as the satellite of his English colleague, and had signed terms which he had taken little part in drafting, was applauded for having saved his country from disaster and the Prince of Orange from a probable loss of his recently restored offices. The Republicans, who had so consistently opposed any entry into the war, could not resent its abrupt closure, and Bentinck could confidently look forward to the restoration of his personal ascendancy at The Hague, which had so recently been seriously endangered.

Sandwich, to whom his colleagues complacently communicated the commendations which they had received, had not long to wait for that of his own Government. On 7 May the Cabinet unanimously recommended the King to approve the preliminaries, and George II, to whom they meant the removal of the last obstacle to his visit to Hanover, did not hesitate to assent. On the same day Newcastle wrote to thank the envoy for his prudent and spirited conduct, " and above all for your manly courage in taking upon yourself not to suffer this great, and now unfortunately for us this necessary work to miscarry for the single point of Guastalla. . . . Your conduct is universally approved. . . . The world is now much turned in our favour. My Lord Chesterfield congratulates us on our escape. . . . That which gives me the greatest comfort is to say that my Lord Granville, and all those that have been the great supporters of the war and favourers of our system, approve extremely of what is done. They own it is as right to do it now as it would have been wrong to have done it last year."[1] Chesterfield, who would not have subscribed to the last opinion, regarded the peace as a triumphant vindication of his own forecast, and expressed his verdict with characteristic malice. " Our escape is surely great in general, and the escapes of four persons in particular are almost miraculous. The Duke of Cumberland has escaped defeat and disgrace. The Prince of Orange has escaped being deposed, and the

[1] Newcastle to Sandwich, 24 April/7 May, in Add. MSS., 32,812, fo. 118.

Duke of Newcastle and Lord Sandwich being ——. . . .
Must not Bentinck now confess that either he lied like
a tooth-drawer while he was here, or else that he knew
nothing at all of the state of his country? And must
not Lord Sandwich confess himself a dupe, if he will
not acknowledge himself to be something worse."[1] A
few days later he complacently added : " My resignation made this peace, as it opened people's eyes with
relation to the imminent dangers of the war, and made
the continuation of it too strong a measure for our
Minister to stand."[2] Bedford had already come to the
same conclusion on different grounds. In his congratulatory letter to Sandwich he expresses the opinion that his
predecessor's resignation was the luckiest of events, as
if he had remained to instruct the British envoy we
should have had much harder terms.[3] Perhaps the
most convincing testimonial that Sandwich received was
to be told that his continued attendance at Aix, whether
with or without a colleague, was indispensable.

Meanwhile, the ratifications, commendation of plenipotentiaries, and rejoicings of peoples and politicians
in the three contracting states did nothing to bring
about a return of peace until the other belligerents
made up their minds to accept the terms so rudely
dictated to them. At the outset they were all recalcitrant. Even Genoa and Modena, for whom France had
secured such generous treatment, contended that restitution was inadequate without compensation. But they
were too obviously impotent to obtain any hearing.
Charles Emmanuel, whose assent was necessary to carry
out the settlement in Italy, and whose opposition was
denounced by Newcastle as gross ingratitude, was furious
at the loss of Piacenza and his long-desired corridor to
the sea. As a matter of fact, Newcastle should have
blessed his protests instead of denouncing them, for
Sardinian discontent was the one thing which commended the settlement to Vienna. If Sardinia had
obtained compensation for the loss of Piacenza and

---

[1] Chesterfield to Dayrolles, 3/14 May, 1748, in the *Letters*,
vol. ii., p. 865.
[2] *Ibid.*, p. 866 (13/24 May). [3] *Bedford Corr.*, i., p. 357.

Finale, as Sandwich had demanded, and Austria had received nothing in return for Parma and Guastalla and the Worms cessions, the anger of Maria Theresa would have been at once louder and more defensible.[1] But, whether England disapproved or not, the resistance of Sardinia could not be prolonged. The King had no supporter in Europe outside Great Britain, and Chavanne only waited for instructions from Turin to give his unconditional adhesion.

More serious was the opposition of Spain. If there were no such violent outpourings of wrath as would have been forthcoming in the days when Elizabeth Farnese ruled at Madrid, there was a very real indignation at the blow which had been dealt to the dignity as well as to the interests of Spain. To Spain the Treaty of Fontainebleau was as fundamental a charter as the Treaty of Worms was to Sardinia. By that treaty Don Philip had been promised a far larger dominion than the exiguous principality which was now offered to him. And, in addition, the hope had been held out that Spain would recover Gibraltar and Minorca, and would be enabled to cancel the hated commercial concessions which Great Britain had extorted at Utrecht. It is true that Sotomayor had come late to Aix, but he had come with the confident expectation that France would fulfil some at least of its lavish promises, and especially that Gibraltar, which several British politicians were known to be not unwilling to yield, would be recovered. None of these hopes had been realized. Don Philip was to have an establishment, but he was only to hold it during the lifetime of Ferdinand VI, who had no hope of issue, and it would then return to its present possessors. There was no word of Gibraltar or Minorca; of the maritime grievances, which had driven Spain into war in 1739, not one was redressed; and the *asiento* and the permitted ship were restored to Britain for an undefined period of *non-jouissance*, which was known to be reckoned in London at fourteen or fifteen years. And

[1] Even Newcastle realized this, and congratulated Sandwich on the failure of his demand for a strip of the Ponente. See his letter of 29 April/10 May in S.P., For., Holland, 431.

all this had been settled by France at a moment when France was in a position to dictate terms, and had only been communicated at the last moment to the Spanish Minister with a curt intimation that he must accept it as it stood. But Spanish indignation, however just, was, for the moment, as impotent as that of Sardinia. Even if Spain made up its mind to break away from the Family Compact and to ally itself with Austria, there was no hope of altering a settlement which France and the Maritime Powers were prepared to support. France, however, had no desire to lose the Spanish alliance, which was in many ways the sheet-anchor of French foreign policy,[1] and St. Severin did not hesitate to point out that the article about the *asiento* was open to various interpretations, and that it might be possible to gratify Spain on this point before the final treaty was made. With this rather meagre assurance, Sotomayor intimated the acceptance of the preliminaries by Spain.

Of all the malcontents by far the most exasperated and the most important, from the point of view both of the present and of the future, was Austria. To understand the depth and the character of Austrian indignation, it is necessary to go back to past occurrences at Aix-la-Chapelle, which were entirely unknown to Newcastle and to Sandwich, and which, if they had known them, would have given them a clue both to the puzzling vagaries of St. Severin and to the irritating obstinacy and occasional obscurity of Kaunitz. Maria Theresa and Bartenstein (Ulfeld, her Chancellor, was a nonentity in the matter of forming a policy, and leant upon Bartenstein's guidance) had long ago made up their minds that it would be difficult or impossible to make a peace in concord with England, and that it would be disastrous to allow England to take the lead in making peace. There were several black marks against the English record at Vienna, but the blackest were made against the Treaty of Breslau, the Treaty

[1] It became still more so after the renewal of the compact in 1761. The instructions to French envoys are full of such phrases as " Le Pacte de famille est fondé sur les liens les plus indissolubles." See *Recueil des Instructions, Autriche*, p. 477.

of Worms, the Convention of Hanover, and the Treaty of Dresden. At the moment, when the conference at Aix-la-Chapelle was only in prospect, three of these black marks seemed to belong entirely to the past. They were brought back into prominence when it was known that Britain favoured a one-sided, gratuitous, and, from the point of view of Vienna, a wholly irrelevant and uncalled-for guarantee of Silesia and Glatz to Prussia. This fact, combined with the sudden revival of a diplomatic intercourse between Britain and Prussia, which had been virtually interrupted for more than a year,[1] by the sending of Legge to Berlin and of Klinggräffen to the British Court, convinced Maria Theresa that her professed ally was drifting into threatening relations with her most bitter enemy. It was known that there were politicians in England who would prefer, if the alternative was before them, a Prussian to an Austrian alliance, and one of them, Chesterfield, was actually in office when the instructions for a British envoy were drawn up. Even if the worst fears of an Anglo-Prussian alliance or entente were not realized, it was obvious that, in the event of a future and probably sooner or later inevitable quarrel with Prussia, Austria would obtain no efficient support from either England or Hanover.

If the relations of England with Prussia were dangerous, those with Sardinia were for the moment worse. There can be no doubt that, at the time of the negotiations at Aix, the blackest mark against England was the Treaty of Worms. From the point of view of Maria Theresa that treaty was far worse than those of Breslau and Dresden. The latter treaties had doubtless been pressed and negotiated by British agents, but they had been extorted from Austria by the compulsion of

---

[1] Thomas Villiers, the negotiator of the Treaty of Dresden, quitted Berlin in August, 1746, after a residence of only six months. Frederic Laurence (or Lorenz), a Hanoverian, had been left there by Hyndford in 1744, and was still there when Villiers departed, but he was wholly inefficient and was removed by Chesterfield, at Frederick's request, in November, 1746. After that Britain had no agent at the Prussian Court until Legge was sent in 1748. See Lodge, *Great Britain and Prussia* (Oxford, 1923), 50, 63.

military disasters. For the Treaty of Worms there had been no such cogent reason : it was essentially the work of England. And England adhered to it as its handiwork, in spite of the notorious fact that Charles Emmanuel had been a virtual traitor to the alliance at the end of 1745. The common interest of England and Austria lay, if anywhere, in the Netherlands, not in Italy. To Maria Theresa the supreme interest in 1748 lay in Italy. The Netherlands must be recovered for her by the Maritime Powers. They must do it for their own sake. But for the maintenance of her Italian dominions she must depend upon herself alone. It had become clearly impossible to evade finding some dominion for Don Philip, but she would not allow England to find it at her expense. The Pragmatic Sanction had become a fetish to her, and she regarded the maintenance of her undivided inheritance as a religious duty to the memory of her father. If any portion of it was lost, the loss must be made good by an ample equivalent. It had been demonstrated that France would not suffer the spoliation of Genoa. It followed that Don Philip's endowment must be taken either from Austria or from Sardinia. If it came from Sardinia, then the Pragmatic Sanction was not infringed. But if, as seemed probable, it was held that Don Philip's Farnese blood entitled him to the Duchy of Parma, then Maria Theresa must extort her equivalent from Sardinia. To justify this she fell back upon her highly disputable interpretation of the Treaty of Worms. She had convinced herself, or Bartenstein had convinced her, that the failure of her allies to obtain for her the promised equivalent annulled the clauses assigning a part of the Milanese to Sardinia. She refused to listen to the British contention, pressed upon her by Robinson, that the cessions had been made to gain Sardinian support, that that support had averted the complete loss of her Italian possessions, and that the clauses as to compensation were a wholly distinct agreement, whose fulfilment was conditional upon a successful war. What she saw was that, if she recovered the whole of the Milanese, and if the cessions to Don Philip reverted to her on his accession to Naples or his death without male heirs, then the inheritance from her father in Italy would be once more intact. The obstacle in the way was the detestable determination of England to maintain the Treaty of Worms in the interest of Sardinia. There was only one way to overcome this obstacle. France, against whom.the treaty had been made, could have no attachment to it, and it might be possible to obtain better terms from the enemy than could be gained by the intervention of an untrusted ally. There was the further attraction that, if Austria could adjust separate terms with France, and could impose them upon the Maritime Powers, the hateful precedent of Utrecht would be reversed, and Austria would demonstrate that she was the predominant partner in the coalition.

The decision to make a separate treaty with France, without any communication to the allies, though it may be defended on the ground that, as events proved, they would not hesitate under pressure to demand sacrifices from Austria, was adopted at Vienna long before the diplomatists met at Aix-la-Chapelle, at a time when the British Ministers still hoped to avoid such a demand, and still longer before the idea of signing without the allies was adopted in London.[1] It found expression, both in the instructions given to Kaunitz, and also in the revival of those underground communications with Versailles which had from time to time been conducted through Saxon agents. Saxony, recently reconciled with France by a subsidy treaty and by a marriage alliance, and at the same time bound to Austria and Russia by past obligations and by a jealous hatred of

---

[1] The Duc de Broglie (*La Paix d'Aix-la-Chapelle*, p. 55) attributes the decision of the Court of Vienna to a discovery of the alteration of British policy caused by the mission of Charles Bentinck. He admits that it is a conjecture and that he has no definite proof. As a matter of fact, it is entirely contradicted by chronology. The date of the instructions to Kaunitz was 19 December, 1747, and of the grant of power to Count Loss, 16 February, 1748. The English decision to satisfy Don Philip at the expense of Austria was on 29 March/9 April. There can be no doubt that Arneth and other writers have exaggerated the scrupulousness of Maria Theresa, which was not always proof against the advice of her counsellors.

Prussia, was well fitted to act as an intermediary. Two brothers, Count Christian and Count Johann Adolf von Loss, represented Saxony at Vienna and Versailles respectively, and had instructions from Count Brühl to do all in their power to bring about a reconciliation between the two Courts. Through the Loss at Versailles Maria Theresa submitted a definite scheme of preliminaries which had been drawn up at Vienna, and was enthusiastically approved by Kaunitz. If France would accept them as they stood, Loss received powers to sign them on behalf of Austria. The essential point was that the Empress consented that a principality should be found for Don Philip on the mainland of Italy, which she had hitherto consistently refused. The principality was to consist of the two Duchies of Parma and Piacenza. But to this concession were attached three conditions: (1) On Don Philip's succession to Naples, or on his death without male heirs, both duchies (although Piacenza would be in large measure a contribution from Sardinia) were to revert to Maria Theresa; (2) other territorial arrangements in Italy were to be restored as they had been before the war—*i.e.*, Genoa and Modena were to recover everything—and the Treaty of Worms was to be annulled; (3) by a secret article[1] it was to be formally laid down that no guarantee of Silesia to Prussia was to be included either in the preliminaries or in the final general treaty. With regard to the special questions at issue between France and England, with regard to Dunkirk and the House of Stewart, Maria Theresa professed herself to be unconcerned, but she

[1] The wording of the proposed separate and secret article is of importance: "Quoyque Sa Majesté l'Imperatrice, Reine de Hongrie et de Bohème soit très éloignée d'enfreindre le traité de paix de Dresde, en cas que Sa Majesté la Roi de Prusse s'y tienne exactement; neantmoins il a eté convenu, que de même que dans les Articles Preliminaires signés aujourdhuy il est fait abstraction des interêts du dit Prince, et de la garantie de la Silésie, il en sera encore fait abstraction dans le Traité de Paix definitif à conclure. Cet article separé restera secret, et aura la même force comme s'il etoit inseré mot à mot aux Articles Preliminaires d'aujourdhuy, et sera ratifié et échangé en même temps." It was an obvious objection on the part of France that it was unusual and unnecessary to include in a treaty the exclusion of any possible provision.

was willing to hand over Furnes to France if England persisted in demanding the dismantling of Dunkirk.

These terms were not signed by Loss, because Puyzieulx suggested modifications of them and drew up a counter-project to be sent to Vienna. But in principle he may be said to have accepted Maria Theresa's proposals. He suggested that Don Philip should keep Savoy and Nice, which had been in Spanish occupation since 1742, and that Sardinia should be compensated elsewhere. He agreed that in Italy the *status quo* of 1740 should be restored provided that an agreement to that effect could be adjusted between Austria and Sardinia. And—most surprising of all, considering France's previous engagements—he assented to the exclusion of the Silesian guarantee from the treaty,[1] though he objected to the insertion of any article in the treaty, however secret, referring to that exclusion. This was the state of matters when Kaunitz arrived at Aix with both the Austrian project and the French counter-project in his possession. The settlement of a compromise between the two documents was now left to St. Severin and Kaunitz, and St. Severin was engaged in this negotiation all the time that he was carrying on those discussions with Sandwich which have been described above. The modern student can now put together the jig-saw puzzle which baffled Sandwich because many of the pieces were not in his hands.

---

[1] This willingness on the part of France to sacrifice his interests was not undiscovered by Frederick. On 20 May he wrote to Chambrier, his agent in Paris: " Il ne me reste presque point de doute que, si la France s'y était pu faire des convenances à son gré, elle ne m'eût sacrifié, en ce cas, pour se les procurer " (*Pol. Corr.*, vi., 118). And on 27 May he wrote still more definitely to the younger Podewils at Vienna, that the Court of Vienna is alarmed lest he should have discovered " ses chipoteries avec la France, ladite Reyne ayant insisté, à leur occasion, pour que la France agréât comme une condition *sine qua non* de ne point me garantir la Silésie et de promettre de ne vouloir point se mêler ni directement ni indirectement de la paix de Dresde " (*ibid.*, p. 125). Nevertheless, he thought it politic to conceal his wrath, and instructed Chambrier to express his gratitude to Puyzieulx, who claimed credit for the insertion of the guarantee. But his real gratitude was to England, and this increased his desire for an English alliance in the summer of 1748.

To comprehend and fully appreciate what followed it is necessary to grasp clearly the fundamental motive which guided St. Severin through the whole of the tortuous negotiations at Aix, both before and after the signature of the preliminaries. He was obviously in an exceptionally strong position. The two Powers with whom he had principally to deal were nominally allied together, but were really pulling in opposite directions, and both depended for success upon gaining the approval and support of France. His instructions forbade him to use his advantage in what would normally have been the most obvious way to gain territorial acquisitions. But he could use it, and he set himself to use it, to gain what might prove a far greater boon for France, the rupture of that alliance between Austria and the Maritime Powers which had so frequently stood in the way of France since 1689 and had foiled the original French plans in the present war. He had an easy game to play, and he played it with equal skill and gusto. He knew that Kaunitz and Sandwich distrusted each other too much to betray his confidence, and so he could safely lead each of them to believe that France was eager for an exclusive agreement with him. Both might at times have qualms as to the honesty of their too courteous antagonist, and Sandwich to the last was inclined to believe that he was being played with, but neither could find, what only the other could supply, overt evidence of his ill-faith. Of the two allied negotiators, Kaunitz was apparently the more confident and trustful, and his confidence seemed to be justified by the more rapid progress of his negotiation. At starting the discrepancy between the French and Austrian proposals seemed to be far less than the differences between France and England. And all difficulties in the way of an Austro-French agreement seemed to be removed when Maria Theresa herself offered to provide, partially at her own expense, the required compensation to Sardinia for the proposed temporary cession of Savoy and Nice to Don Philip. During the necessary interval that must elapse before Don Philip could succeed to Naples and restore the ceded principality, she would allow Charles

Emmanuel to have temporary possession of Parma and Piacenza, on condition that both should revert to Austria when he regained Savoy and Nice. This offer, which Maria Theresa's most eminent biographer extols as a marvel of equity and even of generosity,[1] would only postpone for a few years that restoration of the pre-war situation in Italy, which was to vindicate the Pragmatic Sanction. On the basis of this offer terms were rapidly adjusted, and both Kaunitz and the Court of Vienna believed that their separate treaty was assured, and that their allies and those of France would be compelled to accept them.

At the last moment, as has been seen, St. Severin threw over Kaunitz, and forced Sandwich, by falsely attributing to Austria and Spain what was really being plotted by himself with Austria, into a precipitate signature of preliminaries which were only put together at the eleventh hour. Clearly, if he wanted peace, he must come to terms with either Sandwich or Kaunitz, as he could not possibly bring them into agreement, and did not desire to do so. The only open question was which of the two should he choose as a party to a separate agreement with France. There were more envenomed disputes with England than with Austria, and therefore more contested points to settle. On the other hand, the more substantial advantages were to be gained by a settlement with England. Austria could only offer a partial peace; England could practically give a general peace. Also, England held pledges which were valuable to France. Austria, so far as France itself was concerned, was empty handed. A treaty with Austria would not terminate the maritime war, nor restore Cape Breton, nor put an end to the naval blockade which was strangling France. But if the Maritime

---

[1] Arneth, iii., p. 354, says that Maria Theresa was too honourable to impose upon Sardinia the sole cost of buying off Don Philip, and admits that, if no compensation had been given for Savoy and Nice, " Karl Emanuel dadurch für den Beistand, den er ihr doch immerhin geleistet hatte, nur schlecht belohnt werden würde." But he fails to point out that, under Maria Theresa's scheme, Charles Emanuel would be deprived of all the payment which had been promised to him for that support.

Powers and Sardinia, which must follow them, were to withdraw, Austria would be powerless without the subsidies of the former and without the military support of the latter. The Russian march would be arrested if the paymasters forbade any further advance. There was also a further substantial reason for preferring to conclude a preliminary treaty with England rather than with Austria. The Austrian project involved the exclusion of the guarantee of Silesia, although St. Severin resolutely refused to include any article which could be read as a repudiation of that guarantee. But mere exclusion would exasperate Frederick, and might drive him into the arms of the enemies of France. There were many at the French Court who resented Frederick's past desertions and his recent rather hortatory attitude, and who held that no excessive or hurtful regard should be paid to his susceptibilities. But no responsible statesman, and least of all the rather timid Puyzieulx, was likely wantonly and for no adequate gain to turn a powerful if rather annoying friend into a formidable enemy. After all, the essential thing was to break up the anti-Bourbon coalition. Other things being equal, St. Severin would have preferred to do it by exasperating Great Britain against Austria. But the same end would be achieved by exasperating Austria against Great Britain, and this was what he successfully accomplished.

That Austria should be exasperated was inevitable. The mere terms of the preliminaries were anathema at Vienna. This had already been demonstrated, though the news had not yet reached Western Europe, by the famous outburst of Maria Theresa when Robinson communicated to her the instructions which had been sent to Sandwich on 29 March/9 April. The unfortunate Sir Thomas received the document on 26 April. As Maria Theresa was pregnant, a condition which often embarrassed diplomatists, and the Emperor had gone hunting, he had to go in the first place to Ulfeld, who was not encouraging, and refused to discuss the interpretation of the Treaty of Worms, as Vienna had made up its mind on that subject. The same evening he had his interview with the Empress-Queen, who was prepared for his errand, and broke out at once : " You who had such a share in the sacrifice of Silesia, you who contributed more than any person in procuring the conditional cessions made to the King of Sardinia, do you still think to persuade me ? No ! I am neither a child nor a fool. Your accounts about the Dutch are exaggerated. A countenance may be still held, and there is still force to support that countenance. If you will have an instant peace, make it. I can accede, can negotiate for myself. And why am I always to be excluded from negotiating my own business ? My enemies will give me better conditions than my friends. At least they will not refuse a peace which they want as much as we, for any dispute remaining between me and the King of Sardinia about a little territory, more or less, or for the interpretation of a treaty. And who tells you Spain so much as desires Parma and Placentia ? She would much rather have Savoy. Place me where I was in Italy before the war, and I will establish the Infant. But your King of Sardinia must have all, without one thought or regard for me, but for him singly. Good God ! how have I been used by that Court ! And there is your King of Prussia too ! Indeed, indeed, all these circumstances at once rip up too many old, and make new wounds." When Robinson came to the words as to the reversion of Parma and Piacenza to their present possessors, she interrupted him : " ' Quoy ! retourner aux presens possesseurs ? Non, non, je perdrai plutôt ma tête,' and accompanied the expression with a gest of her hand to denote the action."[1]

This often quoted utterance has usually been regarded as a spontaneous outburst of indignation on the part of a justly offended woman. But there is ample evidence to show that it was a deliberate and carefully prepared exhibition of temper. Maria Theresa was, as she herself asserted, no fool, and she combined a good deal of craft

---

[1] Robinson to Newcastle (private), 1 May, 1748. Ever since this dispatch was printed by Coxe (*House of Austria*, iii., p. 353), it has been quoted by many historians, both native and foreign. But it was necessary to repeat it here, as it gives the most graphic and convincing picture of the attitude of Austria at the time.

with her feminine passion. She had as yet no conception that Kaunitz would fail to obtain his treaty, and her words were obviously designed to fit into the terms which she confidently believed would be the basis of her separate agreement with France. So long as this prospect was before her she could afford to speak her mind to the domineering ally who seemed to be no longer needed. And there can be no doubt that she did express her real sentiments as to the proposals from London. Her two sore places were Sardinia and Prussia, and England touched both on the raw. To give a guarantee of Silesia and the Worms cessions was an offence that could neither be forgotten nor forgiven. On these points her opinion never changed. But the situation was wholly different when she learned that the hated terms had actually been signed by St. Severin. Her anger was no less, but prudence demanded that it should be suppressed. She had, indeed, a double grievance now—she had been deserted by England and she had been provokingly duped by France. She could not annul the preliminaries, and she could not in the long run avoid accepting them. But the preliminaries were not the final treaty, and it was still possible to amend the terms in two directions. The distribution of territories in Italy might be modified, and the guarantee of Silesia might be made less unfair by imposing upon Frederick an equivalent guarantee of the Austrian dominions. The preliminaries confirmed only one part of the Treaty of Dresden, the ultimate agreement might include the whole. There were also other possibilities of improvement. But all these would certainly require the complicity of France, and might require the co-operation of England. Reasons of State compelled her to resist the first natural inclination to an outspoken denunciation of the treatment she had received both from her enemy and her ally. There was no second storm at the Hofburg, and Robinson, to his great relief, had to face nothing worse than a rather studied neglect.

Meanwhile, Kaunitz at Aix had to deal with an unforeseen situation, for which he had no guiding instructions from Vienna. That he was bitterly disappointed

24

and chagrined goes without saying. But his personal anger was directed less against Sandwich than against St. Severin. The British Minister had only done what Kaunitz himself had endeavoured and failed to do. He had indeed been much less reticent as to his intentions than Kaunitz had been. But the French plenipotentiary had, up till the last moment, fooled and misled his Austrian colleague with false assurances, and Kaunitz did not spare the lash of his wrathful invective. It was in vain that St. Severin tried to employ the same device which had succeeded with Sandwich, and excused his hasty signature on the ground that it was necessary to anticipate a secret treaty which was on the verge of being signed between England and Spain.[1] Kaunitz learned the lesson that St. Severin's word was not to be trusted, and this helped to guide his conduct in the negotiations which followed. But no expression of personal resentment could undo the fatal fact that three Powers had signed the preliminaries. Kaunitz protested verbally against them, on the ground that they had been negotiated without the knowledge or assent of the Empress-Queen, whereas the Treaty of Worms forbade any negotiation without mutual consultation and consent. At the same time he expressed the willingness of Austria to consent to the endowment of Don Philip provided the cessions to Sardinia were annulled. On 1 May he repeated this protest to all the representatives of the belligerent Powers at Aix, and accompanied it with very menacing language to the Dutch. Three days later the verbal protest was put into writing, and was circulated to all the Courts of Europe.

With the issue of the Austrian protest interest shifted to the various Courts, to which the representatives of the three signing Powers applied for ratification, and those who had refused to sign for instructions. Kaunitz especially waited with some eagerness and anxiety for

[1] Kaunitz to Maria Theresa, 30 April (quoted in Broglie, p. 154): " Sa confusion était telle qu'il ne trouvait qu'une excuse, les négotiations secrètes entre l'Angleterre et l'Espagne étaient fort avancées, il y avait lieu de s'inquiéter: l'Espagne pouvait prévenir la France. Voilà pourquoi il n'avait pu différer davantage à s'entendre avec milord."

communications from Vienna. When they came they coincided with the views which on calm reflection he had himself adopted. While his protest was approved, as demanded by the injured dignity of his Court, he was instructed to conceal his indignation at the way in which he had been treated, and to resume those confidential communications with St. Severin, without which no future improvement of the settlement could be effected. This was rendered easy by St. Severin himself, who had no desire to lose his hold upon Austria, and was as resolute as ever to sow dissension between Vienna and London. While he continued in daily intercourse to assure Sandwich that France would insist upon the enforcement of the preliminaries in the final treaty, he told Kaunitz that France had never desired or expected Guastalla, thus implying that this sacrifice had been wantonly imposed upon Austria by England,[1] and also assured him that the preliminaries were so loosely and vaguely worded that almost anything might be made out of them. The situation at Aix was essentially unaltered. Austria and England were leagues apart from each other, and France was free to advance in either direction at pleasure. As soon as this was clear, Austria had no longer any reason for rejecting the preliminaries, but every reason for proceeding to the pressing task of their elucidation and improvement. On 21 May ratifications were exchanged between the three contracting Powers. Two days later Kaunitz came to Sandwich and offered to sign the preliminaries with two reservations : (1) Austria was not bound to give anything to Don Philip unless Sardinia surrendered all its gains under the Treaty of Worms; (2) Austria was not to guarantee Silesia and Glatz unless Prussia also guaranteed Maria Theresa's dominions. Kaunitz added

---

[1] Robinson wrote to Stone on 15 May, " As for Guastalla, St. Severin has assured Kaunitz that France never demanded or expected it " (S.P., For., Germany, 180). Newcastle hastened to send this evidence of French mendacity to Sandwich (Add. MSS. 32,812, fo. 209): " Count Kaunitz has wrote word to his Court that St. Severin has told him that France never demanded nor expected Guastalla." See also Sandwich to Newcastle, 5 June (*ibid.*, fo. 244).

that St. Severin was not opposed to these conditions. Sandwich, however, had no hesitation in refusing to accept an adhesion which would have been equivalent to a wholesale alteration of the treaty in essential points. That afternoon St. Severin came to say that Kaunitz would accede to the preliminaries simply as they stood, and claimed that he had extorted this surrender by a threat that Sardinia would accede and disarm, the British Fleet would withdraw from the Mediterranean, and Austria single-handed would have to face France and Spain.[1] The explanation was almost certainly false, but the fact itself was true. Kaunitz himself came soon after and volunteered the statement that he would accede "sans reserve ni exception." This was a great apparent victory for England, and both Sandwich and Newcastle wrote congratulatory letters to each other. But it was marred by certain obvious drawbacks. Austria had obviously given way in deference to France, the enemy, rather than to England, the ally. Its continued alienation from England was demonstrated by the fact that Robinson, who had been pressing adhesion at Vienna, was not informed of the instructions sent to Kaunitz till a fortnight had elapsed from his acceptance.[2] And, finally, to the annoyance of Sandwich and the undisguised alarm of Chavanne, Kaunitz definitely refused, even after his unconditional adhesion, to withdraw the previous reservations which Sandwich had refused to accept.

The fact that Austria, obviously the most important and apparently resolute malcontent, was actually the first to accept the preliminaries[3] was decisive as to the

[1] Sandwich to Newcastle, 25 May (S.P., For., Holland, 434).

[2] Newcastle in a letter to Robinson of 7/18 June, enumerates among the misdeeds of Austria "the slight they have put upon the King's Minister, for above a fortnight together, by not acquainting you with the orders sent to Count Kaunitz to accede" (S.P., For., Germany, 180).

[3] The Duc de Broglie (op. cit., p. 185), after noting the other adhesions, says that Austria stood out alone, which is a curious reversal of the facts. The Duke gives a vivacious account of the negotiations, marred only by a curious disregard of chronology, which he explains, but hardly justifies, by the difficulty, in those days of slow locomotion, of estimating the length of time that must elapse before any document can reach its recipient.

conduct of the others. Chavanne gave in the adhesion of Sardinia on 30 May, "entirely owing to me," said Sandwich. On the same evening Genoa and Modena came in. Spain, whose delay was due almost as much to the traditional slowness of its government as to dissatisfaction, was the last to give its assent. France successfully insisted that only belligerent Powers should be invited to take part, so that Frederick and the Elector Palatine were not allowed to sign, although Article 23 of the preliminaries was so worded as to suggest that they were entitled, if not required, to do so.

By the end of May, 1748, the acceptance of the preliminaries by all the belligerent Powers (except Spain and Genoa, who did not sign till 28 June) was secured, and the tension at Aix-la-Chapelle was sensibly relaxed. All obstacles to Newcastle's journey to Hanover were now removed, and he set out in June to follow his master, visiting The Hague and Cumberland's camp on his way. Before he left he had made up his mind on one important point. He would do all in his power to restore the old relations between the Maritime Powers and Austria, and thus revive that "old system," which had been shaken to its foundations by the manner in which the preliminaries had been concluded, by Kaunitz's vehement protest against them, and by the captious reservations of Bartenstein[1] which had preceded and even accompanied the nominally unconditional acceptance by Austria. For this reason he had made up his mind to reject what he regarded as the insidious proposals made to Legge by the Prussian King that he should take the place of Austria as the supporter of the Maritime Powers against France. This attitude, which postponed for eight years any friendliness between England and Prussia, was attributed by

[1] Puyzieulx to St. Severin, 28 May, 1748, calls it "la plus captieuse pièce qui soit encore sortie de la boutique de M. de Bartenstein" (quoted by Arneth, iii., p. 485, note 28, and by Broglie, *op. cit.*, p. 209). Arneth (iii., p. 371) admits that Bartenstein was the author, and that it was characteristic of him to say yes and no at the same time. Arneth also unconvincingly contends that this disingenuousness contrasted with the usual straightforward conduct of Austria at this time.

Frederick, and even by Legge, to Newcastle's arrival at
Hanover and to an abject surrender on his part to the
prejudices of George II and his Hanoverian Ministers.
But the charge is unfounded, as the evidence is conclusive that Newcastle had formulated his policy in
this respect before he quitted London.[1]

[1] On 7 June (o.s.), just before starting, Newcastle wrote to
Cumberland: " My politics with regard to the King of Prussia are
that he should be gained by way of additional strength (if possible)
to the old alliance, but not be substituted in the place of the
House of Austria to form a new chimerical system " (Add. MSS.
32,715, fo. 166). He had known all along that the King was
hostile to any alliance with Prussia, and this had been confirmed
by recent letters from Stone.

CHAPTER IX

THE TREATY OF AIX-LA-CHAPELLE

Delay in converting the preliminaries into a treaty—Its causes—
Agreements between Sandwich and St. Severin—Question
of the *asiento*—Question of imposing reciprocal obligations
upon Prussia—Agreement to send back the Russians—
Intrusion of Hanoverian demands—Austrian quarrels with
England—Kaunitz obstructs the conclusion of a general
treaty—The question of the Barrier Treaty—Sandwich and
Bentinck propose to sign without Austria—Newcastle assents
on condition that France will grant provisional occupation
of the Netherlands to the Maritime Powers—Cumberland
disapproves—France refuses provisional occupation—Newcastle insists upon full communication to Kaunitz—Quarrel
with Sandwich and Bentinck—Controversy with Pelham—
Robinson sent to Aix—Disclosure to Kaunitz—Continued
obstruction by Austria—Newcastle reluctantly plans coercion
—First concession by Austria—England abandons Sardinia—
Du Theil's draft treaty—Hostages for Cape Breton—Compromise about the Barrier—Treaty signed by three Powers
—Accession of the other States—Newcastle's egotism—
" Peace without Victory."

BOTH Newcastle and Sandwich had good cause to congratulate themselves on the hasty conclusion of the
preliminaries. A prolongation of the war for the additional campaign which they had mapped out in January
would have involved their country in disaster and themselves in discredit. But, though they had saved themselves for the moment, they had only done so by
sacrificing the whole of their original programme. When
Sandwich set out for Breda in August, 1746, he had
undertaken, with Newcastle's guidance, to frustrate the
triangular negotiation which was desired both by France
and by Holland, and to bring about a peace with the
concurrence and co-operation of Austria and Sardinia,
so that the coalition might survive the treaty. And, in
the end, after all their boasted success in obstructing
the Conference at Breda, and in procuring the rejection
of Saxe's terms, they had been compelled to fall back
upon the rejected expedient of a triangular treaty,
bitterly protested against by the allies, and the best

defence they could offer for the terms was that they
were no worse than those which Saxe had offered. It
is not surprising that the alliance between the two men,
both rather thin-skinned egotists and intolerant of criticism, had been strained by this colossal failure. The
links which bound them together were already so thin
that only a little friction was needed to break them completely. That friction was supplied by the process of
converting the preliminaries into a definitive treaty.

Although the preliminaries had been so hastily and
faultily drafted that they had been followed by a whole
crop of supplementary declarations, their general meaning was sufficiently clear to make their conversion into
a comprehensible treaty a short and easy task if the
diplomatists concerned had desired. All that was needed
was the assistance of experts more skilled in the
technique of diplomacy than Sandwich and St. Severin.
This was clearly recognized in France and England, the
two states primarily responsible for the settlement, and
each of them sent an expert to Aix-la-Chapelle. Nothing
shows more clearly their preponderance in the negotiation than the fact that they were the only Powers to
take this precaution. But the real cause of the postponement of the final treaty till 18 October, and of the
continuance of European agitation and uneasiness
during these five months, was not the difficulty of drafting terms, but the strenuous endeavours of the malcontent Powers, and especially Austria, to obtain modifications of the terms in their favour. France could at
any moment have put an end to these manœuvres by
a firm declaration that she would abide by the preliminaries. But St. Severin could not resist the temptation to fish in troubled waters, and to stimulate that
discord among the opponents of France which, in his
eyes, was the only advantage which France could gain
by the war.[1] By encouraging the hopes of Austria, by

[1] Joseph Yorke wrote from Paris to Hardwicke on 25 February/
8 March, 1749 (Yorke, *Hardwicke*, ii., p. 15) that St. Severin
" declared that he did not build his reputation on the making
of the peace; that he would allow it to be called a good one or a
middling one, or even branded with the name of infamous; but
he founded his glory, as he said, on having sowed the seeds of

artfully parading British opposition as the sole obstacle to their realization, and by reserving the decision of France till the last possible moment, he succeeded not only in dividing the allies, but also in convincing Europe that France was its master and the arbiter of its fate. A belated attempt on the part of Newcastle to checkmate his policy by restoring the co-operation of Britain and Austria only served to strengthen the French position by irritating Sardinia and exciting the misgivings of the Dutch. A minor but not unsubstantial cause of delay was George II's unfortunate decision to go to Hanover. This necessitated a duplication of all official dispatches from Aix, and constant references from Hanover to London for the advice of the Ministers at home. Occasional efforts on the part of Newcastle to short-circuit business by giving directions to envoys without waiting for letters from London provoked a tart remonstrance from Henry Pelham that it was a waste of time for the home Ministers to read all the papers and frame a reasoned reply on matters which were already settled at Hanover.[1]

At Aix, Sandwich, who remained until the second week of August the sole British plenipotentiary with his two young assistants, Leveson Gower and Wortley Montagu (who had now received secretarial rank and pay), set himself to maintain the closest and most confidential intercourse with William Bentinck, and to avoid any unnecessary differences with St. Severin. Both he and Bentinck were convinced that St. Severin was the mouthpiece of the peace party in France and that it was imperative to obtain a settlement while that party retained its preponderance at Court.[2] This conviction

---

dissension between the Courts of London and Vienna, and having made an irreparable breach between them."

[1] See H. Pelham to Newcastle, 9/20 August, in Add. MSS. 32,716, fo. 28, and Newcastle's reply on 21 August/1 September (*ibid.*, fo. 99): " Is the King's business to wait till we get instructions from England ? Or is no opinion to be expressed in England on what is done here ?"

[2] Bentinck to Newcastle, 22 July (Add. MSS. 32, 813, fo. 116): "M. de St. Severin est l'homme de Monsr. de Puisieux et une ancienne connaissance de Madame de Pompadour. Je comprens

was strengthened by the moderation shown on several points by the French plenipotentiary. He allowed Sandwich to correct his slip about Don Philip's descendants, and to limit the succession to male heirs. He abandoned his original contention that the cessation of hostilities must date from the signature of the preliminaries by the three Powers on 30 April, and accepted Sandwich's view that in each case it must be reckoned from the accession of the particular Power to the treaty. This was a matter of considerable importance to England, because it took a long time to send instructions to ships in distant seas, and if Spain, which came late into the preliminaries, could claim that naval hostilities ceased within three months from 30 April, a very heavy bill might be presented in London for damage done by men-of-war whose officers knew nothing of the armistice. The questions of Dunkirk and the Stewarts, which had been prominent in the earlier discussions, were hardly mentioned in the later stages, except that Sandwich had to give a written assurance that England would not claim to send commissioners to inspect Dunkirk. A more serious problem arose about the security to be given for the surrender of Cape Breton. The preliminaries stipulated that colonial restitutions should be made *pari passu* with those in Europe. The Maritime Powers did not want to keep the French in the Netherlands a moment longer than was necessary ; and France would not evacuate the provinces until assured of getting Cape Breton. The only way out of the dilemma was to devise some form of surety. France proposed to retain in the meantime some towns in Flanders. Neither Sandwich nor Bentinck could agree to this, and the former suggested the old expedient of hostages. St. Severin

---

par les discourses de M. de St. Severin que l'homme de confiance de M. de Puisieux est le Maréchal de Noailles, et que ces trois personnes là veulent la paix et ont l'oreille du Roi de France." St. Severin naturally encouraged so useful a conviction. In a previous letter of 5 June (*ibid.*, 32,812, fo. 240) Bentinck says that St. Severin was bitterly hostile to Saxe and Löwendahl, whom he called *Diables de Sarmates* with other stronger expressions. See also Sandwich to Newcastle, 8 July, in S.P., For., Holland, 437.

accepted the suggestion on condition that they should be "persons of condition."

The only really serious difference with St. Severin concerned Spain more directly than France. The preliminaries stipulated that the commercial concessions granted to England at Utrecht should be renewed for the years of *non-jouissance*. These words were interpreted in London as covering all the years in which, as the result of past disputes, the annual ship had not been sent to the Gulf of Mexico. By including quarrels in the time of Alberoni and Ripperdà, the number of years, including those of the recent war, mounted up to fifteen. Spain protested vigorously against any attempt to take in these old quarrels, and reckoned that the years of *non-jouissance* were only four (1739-43), as the *asiento* was due to expire at the end of 1743.[1] St. Severin, who wished to make his peace with Spain, gave his support to this contention, and declared that the article in the preliminaries could only refer to the war which they brought to a close. The Dutch had no interest in supporting any mercantile monopoly or privilege of England. Sandwich, who had been inclined at first to boast of the vagueness of the clause as a creditable achievement of his own, was clear-sighted enough to realize that he had a hopeless case, and that it would be good policy to conciliate Spain by giving way with a good grace.[2] But Newcastle, always eager to secure the mercantile vote in England, refused to yield. The utmost he would consent to was that the question should be postponed by putting the disputed article into the final treaty as it stood in the preliminaries. This characteristically evasive proposal was rejected by both Spain and France, and so the problem of the renewal of the *asiento* remained till the last moment an obstacle in the way of a final settlement.

In spite of this difference, which was largely involuntary on Sandwich's part, there were some questions

---

[1] For the Spanish contention see Newcastle to Sandwich, 27 May (o.s.), in S.P., For., Holland, 431, where he narrates a discussion on the subject with General Wall.

[2] Sandwich urged this as early as 31 May. See his private letter to Newcastle of that date, Add. MSS. 32,812, fo. 219.

upon which he and St. Severin were in substantial agreement. Between them they coined a convenient formula, which Sandwich fathered upon St. Severin, for the exclusion of all irrelevant matter[1] and of all representation on the part of non-belligerent Powers. This enabled them to shelve finally the awkward problem of the admission of Ministers from Prussia and Russia. Neither could be admitted without the other, and the exclusion of one would serve to justify the exclusion of the other. Frederick, it is true, sent Ammon, his Minister to The Hague, to Aix as soon as he heard of the conclusion of the preliminaries. But Ammon, though he kept a watchful eye on his master's interests and sent regular reports to Berlin of what he could learn as to the course of the negotiations, was never regarded as accredited to the Congress, nor as having any voice in the settlement.[2] The formula also served to get rid of inconvenient proposals, such as the absurd suggestion from The Hague that the treaty should secure better treatment for Protestants in France and in Hungary. Even some questions, which had been definitely referred to the Congress by the preliminary articles, were ultimately excluded from the treaty and left for separate negotiation between the interested parties.

A delicate matter upon which St. Severin co-operated with Sandwich was the desirability of imposing upon the King of Prussia some reciprocal obligation to balance the unilateral guarantee of Silesia and Glatz which had been inserted in the preliminaries. Both Austrians and Dutch protested against the unfairness of the clause as it stood. The Dutch wanted a guarantee of their Barrier, and Austria clamoured for a Prussian guarantee of the Pragmatic Sanction. Newcastle, eager to reconcile Austria with the Maritime Powers, and after his arrival in Hanover more anti-Prussian than he had

[1] Both envoys were instructed not to admit irrelevant matter. See Newcastle to Sandwich, 27 May (o.s.), in S.P., For., Holland, 431. St. Severin's instructions of 17 June are quoted in Flassan, *Hist. de la Diplomatie Française*, v., p. 409.

[2] For Ammon's instructions see *Pol. Corr.*, vi., 97-99. He was accredited merely by personal letters from Frederick to St. Severin, Sandwich, and Kaunitz (*ibid.*, 108-110).

ventured to be in England, was prepared to gratify both demands. The difficulty was to find some suitable expedient. France and England had undertaken to procure the guarantee for Frederick, and had competed at Berlin for the credit of fathering the article in the preliminaries. Neither Power, therefore, would venture to risk a quarrel with Prussia by omitting or qualifying the article, and they knew that Ammon had been sent to Aix to watch their conduct in this respect.[1] Frederick refused to be bound by the preceding article which pledged interested Powers to " renew " the guarantee of the Pragmatic Sanction. He declared that he had never given such a guarantee and therefore could not renew it. He was willing to guarantee the German possessions of Austria, but Newcastle would not admit that this was sufficient.[2] Austria wanted a guarantee in the treaty of the whole Treaty of Dresden, but France had never been a party to that treaty, and objected to its inclusion, while Frederick vehemently protested that Austria had failed to give effect to the treaty by obtaining the promised guarantee on the part of the Empire.[3] Thus all attempts to bind Prussia to the maintenance of the Pragmatic Sanction proved futile. Nor was it easier to satisfy the Dutch. Frederick expressed his willingness to guarantee their Barrier,[4] but there was no mention of the Barrier in the preliminaries, and any attempt to bring it into the definitive treaty met with

[1] Article 20 of the preliminaries ran thus: " Le duché de Silésie et le comté de Glatz, tels que Sa Majesté Prussienne les possède aujourd'hui, seront garantis à ce prince par toutes les puissances parties et contractantes dans les présents articles préliminaires."
[2] Newcastle to Legge, 6/17 July, in Add. MSS. 32,813, fo. 58, and S.P., For., Prussia, 64.
[3] Frederick to Ammon, 5 September, *Pol. Corr.*, vi., 225, and *passim*.
[4] Frederick to Podewils, 3 October: " Je veux bien me prêter à garantir à la Republique de Hollande la nouvelle barrière qu'on va lui constituer dans les Pays-Bas, pourvu que la République se prête en même temps à me garantir toutes mes possessions de la Silésie et du comté de Glatz." In this letter Frederick lays it down that Ammon's primary task at Aix was to procure the insertion in the treaty of the guarantee of Silesia in the same terms as in the preliminaries (*ibid.*, 252-53). He expressed his gratitude to the envoy on receiving a copy of the treaty on 28 October (*ibid.*, 273).

opposition from Vienna. Matters might have been simplified by admitting Frederick as a contracting party, but this would have been a breach of the agreed formula and would have involved the admission of Russia, to which France was resolutely opposed. In the end the difficulty was evaded by inserting in the final treaty the article about Silesia without alteration (Article 22), and by contending that it was rendered conditional by the following article, also taken unchanged from the preliminaries, which provided that " all parties contracting and interested in the treaty should reciprocally and respectively guarantee its execution " (Article 23). It was a perfectly useless contention unless the other party accepted it. Frederick was not likely to pay much attention to a pious provision which he had never signed, about which he had never been consulted, and which carried with it no penalty. Newcastle, more and more committed to Austria as the treaty approached completion, expressed his regret that the article did not provide that any Power failing to carry out its guarantee should forfeit all advantages under the treaty.[1] As it was, Frederick exulted in getting his guarantee, which was all he wanted, and paid no attention to a merely nominal reciprocity.

If St. Severin may be regarded as having gone some way to meet Sandwich and the allies of England with regard to Prussia, Sandwich had to go still further to meet St. Severin on another equally delicate problem. No sooner had the preliminaries been signed and acceded to by the other Powers than France began to press for the retirement of the Russians as being no longer needed. There were strong political arguments against compliance. France already possessed a military superiority which made it difficult to resist her demands, and that superiority would be overwhelming if the allies lost the auxiliaries on whom such hopes had been built and such vast sums expended. Maria Theresa, who regarded the Russians as specially sent to her aid under the treaty

[1] Newcastle from Hanover to Sandwich and Robinson, 30 September, 1748, in S.P., For., Holland, 432.

of 1746, wished them to continue their advance, or at least to remain in Germany. She held that the French offer to disband an equal number of troops was delusive, because they were near at hand and could be easily recalled, whereas the Russians, once they returned home, were lost for ever. Charles Emmanuel, whose influence was diminished now that Italian affairs were virtually settled, urged the same arguments from Turin. It was a really difficult dilemma. On the one side were military weakness, the certain exasperation of Austria, and the more than probable wrath of the Tsaritsa, who aspired to control the balance in Europe, and who was already indignant at not receiving an invitation to Aix. On the other side was the danger of irritating France, who still held the Netherlands in her grip, and could at any moment raise her terms. France would regard an advance of the Russians as a hostile act, and demanded their retreat as a proof of pacific intent. Retirement would also be likely to conciliate the King of Prussia, whose goodwill was regarded by many influential persons in England as a matter of supreme importance. If Newcastle and Cumberland, the two men who regarded themselves as the dictators of English foreign policy, could have had their own way, they would probably have refused any further alienation of Austria, and would have decided to keep the Russians in Germany until peace had been signed. But what Cumberland called "the improper spirit of economy" was now rampant in England.[1] The Tory principle that England should avoid Continental war and rely upon her navy had deep roots in the country, and it now suddenly revived.[2] There was a general outcry for the recall of troops and for the cutting down of all military expendi-

[1] See Newcastle to Cumberland, 6 May (o.s.): "The spirit of economy begins to show itself" (Add. MSS. 32,715, fo. 20); and Cumberland to Newcastle (private), 20 May, where he expresses his pleasure that Newcastle has resisted "the improper spirit of economy" (ibid., fo. 40).
[2] Henry Pelham to Newcastle, 29 July, reports a meeting with Hardwicke, Bedford, Argyle, and Gower, at which they agreed that "the country is resolved: no land war, no more subsidies."

ture. George II and Henry Pelham, both economists by instinct, and the latter an inheritor of Walpole's distrust of Austria, had an uneasy sense that they had spent far too much upon useless Russians, and that, unless they could send them back before the winter, their expenditure would be doubled, and, if the Dutch should prove defaulters, would be almost quadrupled. When Newcastle, on his way to Hanover, visited Cumberland at the army headquarters, they agreed that they could not resist the combination of the King with a majority of the Ministers, and that the Russians must be sent back. Sandwich, who met them at the camp, received the necessary instructions, of which he thoroughly approved. There was no difficulty in coming to terms with St. Severin, and without a word to Kaunitz a military convention was signed on 2 August by which the Russians were to return and France undertook to withdraw thirty-five thousand men from the Netherlands.

No sooner did Newcastle arrive at Hanover on 8 July than he made the unpleasant discovery that the negotiations at Aix were likely to be hampered and English interests injured by the intrusion of wholly irrelevant Hanoverian demands. George II could never resist the temptation to utilize any negotiations in which he was engaged as King to get something for his electorate. English Ministers had come to regard it as an inevitable penalty to be paid for the retention of their conveniently Protestant dynasty.[1] The King had begun the familiar procedure with regard to the preliminaries while he was in England, and the moment he found himself in Hanover, with docile Ministers like the Münchhausens and Steinberg, and with only Stone to represent England, he set himself to carry it further. He had long desired to find some permanent endowment in Germany for his favourite son, the Duke of Cumberland. By the Treaty of Westphalia the Bishopric of Osnabrück alternated

---

[1] H. Pelham to Newcastle, 14 July (o.s.): " These accidents will always happen, more or less, whilst our Government continues upon its present basis " (Add. MSS. 32,715, fo. 353; Coxe, *Pelham*, i., 442).

between the Archbishop of Cologne and a cadet of the House of Brunswick. If only this inconvenient alternation could be got rid of, Osnabrück could be made into a hereditary principality and would be a most suitable appanage for the Duke. Frederick, who knew his uncle's weakness, had dangled this "Hanover bait" before him in his negotiations with Legge.[1] George was unwilling to be under any obligation to his nephew, whose good faith he distrusted, but the offer had been a tempting one and impelled him to find some other method of gaining his end. The Emperor was a good friend to Hanover and not so querulous as his wife about the conduct of England.[2] No opposition was expected from Vienna. The most obvious difficulty was the probable veto of France, the recognized guarantor of the Treaty of Westphalia, which it was proposed to infringe. This might be overcome if France could be induced to give an assurance that no opposition would be offered by Versailles. France was showing a good deal of acquiescence at Aix, and Sandwich was apparently on the best of terms with his French colleague. The opportunity seemed too good to be lost, and Stone, who could not presume to remonstrate, much less to refuse, was instructed to write to Sandwich that he should broach the matter to St. Severin.

Newcastle was in a quandary when he learned what had been done during the interval in which he had left the King without the guidance of an English Minister. It placed him in a very awkward personal position. Every Secretary of State in turn who had gone to Hanover had been exposed to the charge of pandering to the King's electoral prepossesions. And Newcastle had for the last two years made so much use of royal support that he knew himself to be particularly exposed to this odious charge. His coolness towards the advances of the Prussian King had already been put down to a desire

---

[1] On Frederick's offer with regard to Osnabrück see Legge's dispatches in S.P., For., Prussia, 64; Coxe, *Pelham Administration*, i., 437-445; and *Pol. Corr.*, vi., 57, 101, 201.

[2] Both Robinson and his successor, Keith, lay frequent stress upon the friendliness of the Emperor in contrast to the difficulties with Maria Theresa and her Ministers.

to make his court.[1] The charge would be irresistible if he confirmed the instruction already given to Sandwich to press this Hanoverian demand at Aix. At the same time it is only fair to say that the political objection bulked still more largely in his mind. Never had there been a more barefaced and noxious attempt to obtrude electoral demands into a negotiation in which vital English interests were concerned. And it was in direct contravention of his own orders that no irrelevant matters were to be admitted at the Conference. A demand of this kind would give St. Severin the power to put pressure upon the English Government. It was notoriously difficult to induce Continental States to distinguish between the dual personalities of George II as Elector and as King. Just as it was held to be legitimate in war to coerce the King by threatening his electorate, so it was equally open in negotiation to bribe the King by a favour to the Elector. And not only was it impolitic to give to the French plenipotentiary an additional pawn to play with, it was, as things stood, almost equally dangerous to incur any burdensome obligation to the Court of Vienna.

Newcastle's letters to his brother and Hardwicke give a graphic picture of the agitation into which he was thrown by this ill-timed scheme. Cumberland, whom he consulted upon every subject, expressed the best copy-book sentiments as to the desirability of avoiding any hindrance to the conclusion of peace, but it was not altogether safe to take such assurances from a Hanoverian Prince at their face value. It was not easy for a single Minister to set himself against the King, but Newcastle, by his own account, went further in expostulation than any of his predecessors would have dared to do. He tried to induce Münchhausen and Steinberg to add their remonstrances, but he might as

---

[1] In a long letter to his brother, undated but evidently written just after his arrival in Hanover, Newcastle defends himself against this charge. After expounding his view that it would be ruinous to accept a Prussian alliance if it involved the alienation of Austria, he continues: " Don't imagine I say this to make my court; it is my real opinion, and you know it has always been so " (Add. MSS. 32,715, fo. 257).

well have invited jackals to remonstrate with a lion. It
was some relief to him that George decided to send
Busch as an electoral Minister to Aix, but he found
himself compelled to order Sandwich to co-operate with
Busch. To this he added that the main negotiation
must not be obstructed. This letter he had to submit
to the King. " When he read that part of my letter,
his Majesty said, No, that is not my meaning, but why
may not I, as Elector, come to an agreement with
France that they shall give no opposition to it? And
that, I own to you freely, is what I dread."[1]
Newcastle's dread with regard to the Osnabrück
scheme proved to be ill-founded. Busch, who seems to
have had no formal commission to any state, left the
matter wholly in the hands of Sandwich, who could be
trusted not to be unduly urgent. St. Severin, after
playing with the proposal for some time, ultimately
rejected it as belonging to the category of irrelevant
topics.[2] But Busch had supplementary instructions of
which Newcastle at the time had no knowledge. The
preliminaries had included George II as Elector and his
electorate (Article 8). This did not satisfy George II,
who desired to substitute for " electorate " the words
"tous les Etats et possessions en Allemagne."[3] This
would cover, not only Bremen and Verden, of which he
had never received the imperial investiture, but also
certain mortgages in Mecklenburg which his father had
acquired as compensation for the expense incurred in
enforcing an imperial decree against the then Duke of
Mecklenburg. Sandwich was again called upon to

[1] Newcastle to H. Pelham (most secret), 14 July, in Add. MSS.
32,715, fos. 277-293. In this letter Newcastle says that he had
learned from Münchhausen—(1) that Maria Theresa had declared
that she would never consent to the King's proposal, and (2)
that, in spite of this, she and the Emperor had written that they
would not oppose it, if all the other parties should consent. This
letter is printed in Coxe, *Pelham Administration*, i., 437.
[2] Busch to George II, 2 August, says that St. Severin had
declared that France would not oppose if the Empire and other
parties to the Treaty of Westphalia gave their consent (Add. MSS.
32,813, fo. 191). But on 8 August he wrote that Sandwich had
submitted a separate article pledging France to assent, and that
St. Severin had rejected it (*ibid.*, fo. 239).
[3] George II to Busch, 27 August, in Add. MSS. 32,814, fo. 1.

support Busch, and this time his efforts were successful. The amendment was included in the final treaty (Article 20), but France exacted in return a concession to the Elector Palatine. In the preliminaries the Palatine claims were restricted to the fief of Pleistein. In the treaty this limitation was deleted (Article 18), and the undefined claims of the Elector proved a source of endless troubles to Newcastle in his subsequent efforts to bring about a reconciliation with Austria.

These Hanoverian complications agitated Newcastle enormously, but even he would have admitted that they shrank into insignificance as compared with difficulties in the relations with Austria. The two fundamental articles in his creed were that the Austrian alliance was the sheet-anchor of the English political system, and that the Treaty of Hanover in 1725, when England was allied with France against Austria, was the supreme blunder with which he had been associated.[1] Only the assurances of Cumberland that delay must result in military disaster justified in his mind the signature of the preliminaries without Austria and in the teeth of Austrian protests. When he heard that they had actually been signed, his first thought was that the Court of Vienna must be regained.[2] His letters to Sandwich at the time are full of the necessity of avoiding all *aigreur* and employing all *douceur*, in order that the old alliance may be strengthened and cemented.[3] With a complete absence of diplomatic subtlety, he repeated these assurances to Wasner, and was profoundly disappointed that his demonstrations of affection met with no response in kind. If he had been wiser, he might have foreseen that the more he professed his unalterable attachment to the Austrian alliance, the more Austria would take

[1] Newcastle to Cumberland, 23 October, 1748: " I was once catched in the year 1725, when the Hanover treaty was made. I got out of it in 1730 by the Treaty of Vienna, and I give your Royal Highness my word and honour, no consideration shall ever catch me again. Whenever it will go no longer on the old foot, I shall not help its going at all " (Add. MSS. 32,717, fo. 97).

[2] Newcastle to Cumberland, 26 April (o.s.): " The great point is to bring the Court of Vienna back " (Add. MSS. 32,714, fo. 534).

[3] See Newcastle to Sandwich, 13 May (o.s.), Add. MSS. 32,812, fo. 182.

advantage of his convenient devotion. In addition to
the manner and the contents of the preliminaries, and
to the supposed English advances to Prussia, Maria
Theresa had other grievances against England. There
were two pecuniary demands, both for £100,000, which
gave rise to intense friction between the two Courts.
Before Charles Bentinck's mission had exploded the
campaign of 1748, Newcastle had exulted in inducing
his unwilling colleagues to conclude a supplementary
convention by which that sum was to be paid for four
thousand Austrian horse. The convention had not been
ratified when George II went to Hanover, and both he
and Henry Pelham thought that payment might be
evaded, as the troops were no longer needed. This
repudiation of a contract, which was only formally incomplete, was denounced at Vienna as dishonest. Newcastle, always impotent against the King and his
brother, vainly protested against the folly of alienating
Austria by a piece of sharp practice at this particular
moment. In the end Cumberland, who had to live with
Batthiani, pointed out that the four thousand horse
troops were already on the spot, and that it was not the
fault of Austria that the hasty conclusion of the preliminaries prevented any use being made of them.
Henry Pelham gave way to the authority of the Commander-in-Chief, and Newcastle extorted the King's
consent at Hanover by pleading the approval of the
Chancellor of the Exchequer.[1] But the payment was
made with the worst grace, and only convinced the
recipient that concessions could be extorted by being
as disagreeable as possible. The other dispute proved
insoluble in 1748. Article 12 of the convention of
26 January provided that the last £100,000 of the
Austrian subsidy should only be paid when the commissioners appointed should certify the stipulated

_____

[1] See Pelham to Newcastle (most private), 7 July (o.s.), where
he says that his consent to payment for the 4,000 horse was extorted by his Royal Highness, but he never thought it right
(Add. MSS. 32,715, fo. 300). Newcastle had previously written
to his brother that he had only obtained the King's approval of
the payment by declaring that the Premier had consented (*ibid.*,
fo. 257).

number of troops in the Netherlands and in Italy. As no such certificate had been given, and as the deficiency of numbers in both areas was notorious, the payment was not made, and Hardwicke declared that an Act of Parliament or a new Convention would be needed to make it legal.[1] Newcastle pleaded that policy was more important than law in these matters, and Cumberland urged that it was not customary to be so scrupulous in inspecting military accounts. But Newcastle could not escape from Bedford's dilemma: either the troops were there or they were not; if they were not, the money was not due; if they were, there was no need for such a panic-stricken rush into a treaty with France.[2] And Cumberland could not deny that he himself had reported the Austrian deficiency. George II, backed by all his Ministers except Newcastle, would not listen to the idea of payment. Bartenstein was furious, and lost no opportunity of pressing his demand. And in the end his obstinacy and that of Newcastle triumphed. In 1749 Parliament was induced to sanction the payment, but it came too late to influence the negotiations at Aix-la-Chapelle.

These squabbles about money were resented by Sandwich because they added to the difficulties of his task. His chief trouble now lay, not in his relations with France, but in those with Austria. It is not too much to say that, in the later stages of the negotiation, his opponent was not St. Severin, with whom he thought himself upon the best of terms, but Kaunitz, the representative of an allied Power. This was what St. Severin had been playing for all along. There can be no doubt that he had encouraged Kaunitz to accede to the preliminaries by holding out the prospect of an improvement of their terms in the final settlement. It was with this prospect in view that Kaunitz terrified Sardinia by refusing to withdraw his protest and reservations of 23 May, although they were absolutely inconsistent

[1] Hardwicke to Newcastle, 24 June (o.s.), Add. MSS. 32,715, fo. 226.
[2] Bedford to Newcastle, 30 June (o.s.), Add. MSS. 32,715, fo. 265. The letter is printed in *Bedford Corr.*, i., 384.

with the professed simple acceptance of the agreed terms. What Austria would have liked would have been to leave Don Philip in possession of Savoy and Nice and to recover all the lands in Lombardy which Charles VI had held at the time of his death. Spain would welcome such a settlement, and for French assent a tempting bribe could be offered in Flanders. If the three Powers agreed to enforce such a settlement, there was no military force which could dispute their will. But it was realized at Vienna that neither Austria nor France was prepared for such a complete revolution in all their external relations, and especially that France was not prepared to face a continued maritime war which would almost inevitably lead to the complete loss of her Western colonies. And, therefore, when St. Severin, without any authority from Versailles, tried to draw Kaunitz into making extreme proposals, the latter refused to fall into the trap.

But between acceptance of the preliminaries as they stood and some chimerical scheme of transformation there was a possible middle course. In previous conversations St. Severin had often reminded Kaunitz that France was not a party to the Treaties of Worms and Dresden, and that both treaties had been concluded against French interests. He had also once observed that France was under no obligation to send troops to Italy to enforce the cessions to Sardinia. This parade of a disinterested attitude on the two questions which profoundly interested the Court of Vienna suggested that the sting might be taken out of the preliminaries if France would translate these *obiter dicta* into definite assurances. Accordingly, a treaty was drafted in the best Viennese Latin with two secret articles—(1) that France would not regard any subsequent attempt to regain the Worms cessions as a *casus belli*, and (2) that France would treat the guarantee of Silesia and Glatz " as the King of Prussia held them today " as a virtual guarantee of the whole Treaty of Dresden, that being the treaty under which he held them.[1] St. Severin was

[1] The text of these proposed articles is given in Arneth, iii., 485-86.

away in France when Kaunitz received this draft treaty, and it had to be given to the French secretary. But St. Severin got no encouragement from Puyzieulx to proceed any further in his Austrian intrigues. The motives which impelled France to seek a separate agreement with the maritime Powers rather than with Vienna were as strong as ever. The draft treaty had no chance of acceptance, and Kaunitz found himself for the second time duped by tempting assurances which were only designed to sow discord between the allies.

Foiled in his attempt to carry out instructions devised by the ingenuity of Bartenstein, Kaunitz fell back upon a policy of resolute obstruction, in the hope that during the delay friction might arise between France and the maritime Powers which could be turned to the advantage of Austria. For playing this game he had three very strong cards in his hand. In the first place, he contended that the stipulated restitutions should be made at once and not delayed till a general treaty had been concluded; secondly, he demanded that the Netherlands should be handed over to Maria Theresa without any conditions or limitations of her sovereignty; and, finally, he argued that it was absurd to end such a complicated war by a single treaty, and that it was necessary to follow the precedent of Utrecht, where separate treaties had been made between the various belligerent States. On all these points he came into collision with Sandwich. It is true that England had political and economic reasons for desiring to get the French out of the Netherlands, and for this reason was inclined to support immediate restitution. But, in view of the refusal of Kaunitz to withdraw his reservations, it would be extremely dangerous to hand over the Netherlands to Austria, as they were the only security for obtaining the promised cessions in Italy. France was bound to procure Don Philip's establishment, and England was equally pledged to maintain Sardinia in possession of its gains under the Treaty of Worms. And so, when Kaunitz urged that Articles 2 and 17 of the preliminaries promised immediate restitution on the accession of each state, Sandwich joined St. Severin in maintaining that these articles were governed by the 18th, which laid it down that restitutions should be simultaneous and *d'un pas égal*.

The obvious conclusion from this article, that the evacuation of the Netherlands must wait until Cape Breton and Madras had been restored, was evaded by Sandwich's offer of hostages for Cape Breton, though he failed at the time to demand that France should do the same for Madras. Confident that by this offer he had rendered a substantial service to Austria, he had two interviews with Kaunitz, on 14 and 15 July, when he urged him to join, as Bentinck and Chavanne had already promised to do, in promoting a general peace. The gist of Kaunitz's reply was that St. Severin had broken the preliminaries by tacking on [*accrochoit*] restitutions to the final peace, and that Austria could take no part in framing a general treaty, as his Court regarded such a procedure as ludicrous and impossible.[1] More than a week earlier Sandwich had made the still more startling discovery that Austria intended to repudiate the Barrier Treaty. This was a matter upon which the Maritime Powers felt themselves bound to stand together. In 1716 they had handed over the Southern Netherlands, where they had remained in occupation since the close of the war, to Charles VI on condition that Dutch troops should occupy a number of specified border fortresses, that Austria should pay 500,000 *patagons* (1,250,000 florins) towards the cost of their maintenance, and that no higher duties should be imposed upon imports until a new commercial treaty had been concluded. As no such treaty had been made, the Maritime Powers having deliberately evaded making one, the old duties, which were regarded by Austria as unduly favourable to the foreign trader, had remained in force until the French occupation. The whole treaty had always been resented at Vienna as an infringement of Austrian sovereignty. The question of tariffs was

---

[1] Sandwich's dispatches of 14 and 15 July, each written immediately after his interview with Kaunitz, are in S.P., For., Holland, 437.

not so prominent at Aix as it became later, though it was clearly alluded to by complaints as to "other provisions," a phrase of which Sandwich, perhaps truly, professed not to know the meaning.   The primary objections raised at the time were that the Dutch had proved themselves wholly incompetent defenders of a barrier designed for their protection, that many of the fortresses had been dismantled and were therefore useless, and that the provinces had been so ruined by the war that they could no longer pay the contribution fixed by the treaty.   Austria was determined to get rid of the treaty altogether, and Kaunitz opened the controversy in great style by declaring that it had been annulled when the Maritime Powers had concluded the preliminaries without consultation or concurrence on the part of Austria.[1] Sandwich and Bentinck, who had hitherto assumed that restitution applied to conditions of tenure as well as to territories, hastened to take up the gage which Kaunitz had thrown down.   They replied that, as there had been no war between Austria and the Maritime Powers, all treaties between them must be still in force.   France, against whom the Barrier Treaty had been drawn up, watched with ill-concealed glee the quarrel between the states which had concluded it.   In the dispute as to a general treaty against separate agreements, the Dutch were only concerned so far as the Austrian proposal was likely to cause delay.   But England denounced it with much more vigour as a transparent attempt to evade the guarantee of Silesia to Prussia and the Worms cessions to Sardinia.   St. Severin held as much as possible aloof from the contest, though Sandwich paraded him to Kaunitz as a champion of the single treaty.

The news of Austrian obstruction at Aix was a terrible

---

[1] Sandwich to Newcastle, 3 July.   Of this dispatch, which is of peculiar importance as coming just after Sandwich had talked to Cumberland and Newcastle at the army headquarters, there are two copies, one in 434 and the other in 437 of S.P., For., Holland. One was sent to Newcastle at Hanover, and the other to Bedford in London.   This duplication explains why so many important letters found their way to Woburn, and thence into print in the *Bedford Correspondence.*   Hence vol. i. of that correspondence is of peculiar value for the months during which George II was at Hanover,

blow to Newcastle. Ever since the signing of the preliminaries he had done all in his power to soothe the
injured feelings of the Court of Vienna. He had
quarrelled with all his colleagues, and had gone as near
as he dared to quarrelling with the King, about the
payment of their pecuniary demands, and, when the
second £100,000 had been absolutely refused, he represented it to Vienna as merely suspended. He had
reprimanded Sandwich for having instructed Byng to
cease naval operations in aid of Austria against Genoa,
and, in spite of Sandwich's argument that the order
was necessary to convince France of our good faith, and
that any success in Italy would make Austria more
reluctant to make peace, he had extorted from his
reluctant colleagues a grant of greater latitude to the
Admiral.[1] With the same motive he had thrown cold
water upon Legge's rather clumsy efforts to bring about
an alliance with Prussia, and risked the alienation of
Frederick by insisting that he must in some way or
other guarantee the Pragmatic Sanction as an equivalent for the gratuitous guarantee of Silesia and Glatz
in the preliminaries. He persuaded the King to appoint
Sir Thomas Robinson as joint plenipotentiary at Aix in
preference to Legge, who was supported by Henry
Pelham and Bedford, and claimed that he had received
a virtual promise of the post before he left England.[2]
There was a sound reason for preferring Robinson, as
an experienced diplomatist, over Legge, who was even
less of an expert than Sandwich. But Newcastle's real
reason was the belief that Robinson would be a *persona*

---

[1] Sandwich was guilty of a technical blunder in giving the
order to Byng, as, by an odd arrangement, the Mediterranean
squadron was not under the Admiralty, but took its orders from
the Secretary of State for the Southern Department. See Bedford
to Sandwich, 26 November, 1747 (*Bedford Corr.*, i., 297). On
Newcastle's conduct in the Byng episode see Sandwich to Newcastle (private), 26 May, 1748, in Add. MSS. 32,812, fo. 201; and
Bedford to Sandwich (most secret), 23 June (o.s.), in *Bedford
Corr.*, i., 381.

[2] Legge did not conceal his disappointment and chagrin. See
especially his letter to Newcastle of 20 July (Add. MSS. 32,812,
fo. 306. The letter is here a month out of place; it should be in
32,813).

grata to Vienna, and that his knowledge of the Austrian Court and his personal acquaintance with Kaunitz would make it comparatively easy to maintain or restore harmony at Aix.[1] On the other hand, Legge, as envoy at Berlin and as the known advocate of a Prussian alliance, would be in the highest degree distasteful to Vienna, where he would be regarded as the mouthpiece of that section of the Cabinet which was lukewarm, if not actually hostile, to the alliance with Austria.

Meanwhile, Sandwich at Aix, exasperated by Kaunitz's obstinacy and restrained by none of Newcastle's political caution, was prepared to make short work of the Austrian objections. If he had been an independent agent he would obtain the best possible terms from St. Severin, sign the treaty with the concurrence of Bentinck, and leave the other two allies to be compelled by their mutual differences and their isolation to come in afterwards. Hitherto he had been restrained by Newcastle's instructions to maintain harmony with Austria, and by the refusal to make any concession to Spain about the *asiento*. He knew that he could expect support from Pelham and Bedford, and in the middle of July he determined to make a desperate effort to convert his immediate superior upon both these points. Although his relations with Chavanne had been less cordial since the conclusion of the preliminaries, he anticipated little difficulty with Sardinia, and St. Severin had assured him that Spain would come in if the dispute about the *asiento* could be settled. The supreme obstacle, therefore, was Austria. On 14 July, after the first of his two interviews with Kaunitz, Sandwich supplemented his official dispatch by writing two private

[1] Newcastle to Robinson at Vienna (private), 16 July (Add. MSS. 32,813, fo. 33): " I hope your Court will take it, as it is designed, as an indication of our resolution to be well with them, if they will let us." This only shows how easily Newcastle could deceive himself into believing what he wished. He had ample reason to know that Robinson, associated with so many humiliations to Austria, was *persona ingratissima* at Vienna. Arneth (iii., 486) quotes a letter from Ulfeld to Kaunitz of 4 September, describing Robinson's departure: " Jamais Ministre a été congédié plus mal que celui-cy; mesme l'Impératrice a un peu trop chargé la dose,"

letters to Newcastle, in which he asked for authority
to conclude a separate treaty on the ground that it was
impossible to make peace " by a regular and formal
concert of every step with our allies." He declared,
in deference to his correspondent, that he was a convinced supporter of the Austrian alliance, but that a
too great compliance with that Court would ruin the
treaty. " I own, notwithstanding their fair words, I
cannot bring myself to think that the definitive treaty
can ever be signed otherwise than after the example of
the preliminaries, that is by some of the principal parties
agreeing upon the conditions they think adapted to the
present circumstances of the times, and leaving those
who are at first displeased to accede to those terms if
they desire to enjoy the advantages of them." Knowing Newcastle's weaknesses, he begged him not to let
Wasner know that there was any idea of signing without
Austria, as the matter must be kept a profound secret.[1]
Henry Pelham, after reading this letter, wrote to Bedford with unwonted enthusiasm : " Sandwich's letter
to the Duke of Newcastle is incomparable. I subscribe
to every word of it, and never had a thought of the
House of Austria but what is contained in the reasoning
of that letter. I hope he will keep firm, make his definitive treaty, and then he nor any one else need fear
the accession of all the other Powers."[2]

Newcastle was a very reluctant convert, but he could
not resist the evidence that Kaunitz had refused to
accede to a general treaty, that he had denied the
continued validity of the Barrier Treaty, and that, in
spite of his accession to the preliminaries, he adhered
to his reservations of 23 May with regard to the cessions
to Sardinia and the guarantee of Silesia. On 18 July
he wrote from Hanover to authorize Sandwich, if
Kaunitz's obstruction should make it necessary, to sign
the definitive treaty, in conjunction with the Dutch

[1] These two important letters are in S.P., For., Holland, 434.
A third letter of the same date (Add. MSS. 32,813, fo. 21) says that
he will consult with Kaunitz and Chavanne as far as he can, but,
if they refuse to go on with him, he understands that he is to
sign without them, provided Bentinck concurs.
[2] Pelham to Bedford, 7 July (o.s.), in *Bedford Corr.*, i., 403.

plenipotentiaries, on the basis of the preliminaries with the few amendments that had been already licensed. But to this authorization he attached an important condition. If Austria should refuse to accept the treaty, the Netherlands would not be evacuated. As it is essential to get the French out of the Netherlands as speedily as possible, France must agree, as had been done at Utrecht, to hand the provinces over to the Maritime Powers to be provisionally occupied by them until Austria shall accede. Only if France assents to this can the separate treaty be signed. In attaching this condition Newcastle forgot that in 1713 France was the defeated Power and the Netherlands were already in the hands of the Maritime Powers, whereas in 1748 France was victorious and in unassailable occupation of the Southern Provinces. And he failed or refused to see that the provisional occupation of her territories, which would enable the Maritime Powers to dictate their own terms for their surrender, would be a far more serious affront to Maria Theresa than the separate signature. With characteristic inconsistency, at the moment that he was exposing the Austrian alliance to the risk of imminent rupture, he expressed his unshaken allegiance to it. " I own," he wrote to Sandwich on the same day, " it is my opinion that the support of the House of Austria is necessary for His Majesty's interest and for that of the common cause, in contradiction to all new systems whatever, which can have their foundations upon nothing but theory and mistaken notions, which I hope will be discouraged every where."[1] It was equally in keeping with his usual practice that he gave to Sandwich the required promise of secrecy, and at once proceeded to break it. He could not resist the temptation to use the threat of separate signature as a means of inducing Austria to abandon her obstructive tactics at Aix. On 17 July, the day before he gave

[1] Newcastle's formal letter of 18 July, and the " most private " letter which accompanied it, are in S.P., For., Holland, 431. A third letter (it was quite usual for him when agitated to write three letters a day to one person) is in Add. MSS. 32,813, fo. 71. It is merely a repetition of what he had written before.

Sandwich his permission to conclude, and again on the following day, he sent a sort of ultimatum to be delivered by Robinson before he left Vienna, to the effect that unless Kaunitz received powers to sign without delay or reservations, and unless he withdrew his demand for multiple treaties, the Maritime Powers would sign a separate treaty with France.[1]

The licence to conclude without Kaunitz—liberally interpreted by Sandwich and Bentinck as leave to negotiate without him—was followed by rapid progress at Aix. St. Severin offered no objection to the proposal of provisional occupation of the Netherlands, but said that it must be referred to his Court. In the hope of purchasing consent a number of concessions were made to France. The convention about the Russian troops was signed on 2 August. Sandwich obtained leave to give a written assurance that no commissioners should be sent to inspect demolitions at Dunkirk. The belated demand that France should give hostages for the return of Madras was withdrawn. The request for the admission of a Russian representative was finally dropped. St. Severin drafted the project of a final treaty, and Sandwich and Bentinck prepared a counter-project. The chief obstacle to an agreement was Newcastle's obstinacy about the *asiento*. All that he would consent to was the insertion of the article in the preliminaries as it stood, leaving Spain and England to squabble about interpretation afterwards. Sandwich wrote that peace could be made in a few days if only France could have some little sop to throw to Spain. Bentinck, an old and familiar correspondent, wrote to Newcastle in the same strain. Both argued that surrender was neces-

---

[1] Newcastle to Robinson, 17 and 18 July, in S.P., For., Germany, 180. It was just at this time that Newcastle was doing his utmost to allay the disquiet caused by Legge's mission to Berlin. See his letter to Robinson of 16 July, a very lengthy one (*ibid.*), and a private letter of the same date in Add. MSS. 32,813, fo. 33. In the latter he attributes all the trouble to Bartenstein: " If they will talk such impertinent and offensive nonsense as they did in the paper of 23 May, Bartenstein will at last confound me and his own Court. I wish there could be any way to get rid of him, or to make him alter his whole system and conduct."

sary to strengthen the hands of the peace party in France, whose overthrow might result in the breaking off of the treaty.[1]

Newcastle's heroic resolution with regard to Austria lasted barely ten days. As late as 26 July he wrote to approve of all that had been done at Aix and to give an assurance that the King was resolute in support of Sandwich and Bentinck. Then misgivings began to arise. It was clear that the terms of peace were being dictated by France, and that the aim of France was to sow dissension among the allies. He received warnings from Hardwicke that it would be rather rash, in view of all the errors and inaccuracies of the preliminaries, to give Sandwich power to sign without first referring the terms to London or to Hanover.[2] But the greatest cause of disquietude was the disapproval of Cumberland, on whose support Newcastle relied to uphold him both with the King and with his colleagues. Few things, even in the family history of the House of Hanover, are more startling than the immense influence and even authority wielded by George II's second son at a time when his elder brother, the Prince of Wales, was jealously excluded from all knowledge of public business. Newcastle could hardly take any decision without consulting the Duke, and was in the habit of parading his approval as if it was a valid defence against all criticism.[3] Sandwich had been constantly instructed to send all his letters under flying seal to the Commander-in-Chief, and in several instances to take directions

[1] Sandwich to Newcastle, 8 July, in S.P., For., Holland, 437: "Monsr. St. Severin in all his late conversations with me insists upon the importance that it is to the success of the whole to hasten to an immediate conclusion, in order to prevent the military party in France, which is stunned and disconcerted with the suddenness of the blow, from gaining time to recover their strength and employ it, as they certainly would, to throw all possible obstructions and difficulties in our way."

[2] Hardwicke to Newcastle, 15 July (o.s.), in Add. MSS. 32,715, fo. 361. The letter is printed in Yorke, i., 658.

[3] Cumberland had to warn him that, though his approval might carry weight in some quarters, it would have none at The Hague, where he was regarded by his brother-in-law and his sister with undisguised jealousy. Cumberland to Newcastle (private), 29 August, 1748, in Add. MSS. 32,716, fo. 74.

from him. Disputants in England or in Hanover looked to the headquarters at Eyndhofen for arbitration. Before proceeding to Hanover, Newcastle had visited the princely oracle, and had there adjusted the policy which England was to pursue in the pressing problems of the moment.[1] Among other formulas, they had agreed that peace was not to be obstructed by any excessive tenderness for Austrian interests. To Cumberland, always inclined to favour the Court of Vienna, it appeared that this formula had been unduly strained when it was proposed that the allies of Maria Theresa should not only make peace without her, but should actually occupy her territories, which, he was uneasily conscious, they had rather ignominiously failed to defend.

Cumberland's opposition would in any case have been decisive with Newcastle, and it was the more so at the moment as the Duke had been invited to Hanover by his father to discuss the problem of Osnabrück, so that it would be necessary to meet this formidable critic face to face. On 28 July he wrote to Sandwich that His Royal Highness had raised difficulties as to any provisional occupation, had asked the pertinent question what would be done with the revenues during occupation, and had added: "Marshal Batthiani will look upon it as acting the part of enemies to the Empress by keeping her out of her own country." So Sandwich, and Bentinck with him, should urge upon Kaunitz the imperative need of concluding an immediate treaty on the foot of the preliminaries, and should tell him that, it he won't come in, the only way of averting the ruin of the Low Countries and of getting the French out of them is a joint occupation, in which case the revenues would be spent on the maintenance of the occupying troops. He must be pressed not to impose this unwelcome and distasteful compulsion upon His Majesty, and his answer is to be sent to Hanover at once. Meanwhile, the authority to sign the definitive treaty with-

[1] See Newcastle to Cumberland, 19 July, 1748, where he enumerates the agreements come to at their conference (Add. MSS. 32,715, fo. 310).

26

out the concurrence of Kaunitz is suspended until the receipt of further orders.[1]

To Sandwich, whose attention was concentrated upon the problem of harmonizing St. Severin's project with his own counter-project, this curtailment of his powers was in the highest degree unwelcome. On 2 August he replied that Kaunitz was as recalcitrant as ever, and that some secret article must be adjusted with France, as had been done in the preliminaries, for compelling Austria to come in. No progress can be made with a policy of consultation. "If we apply to Vienna, we are told that Kaunitz has full powers; if we apply to Kaunitz, he says he must refer to Vienna." Apparently, Newcastle wishes Bentinck and himself to communicate their project to Kaunitz, and thus let him into their whole secret. But this must surely be on the assumption that he will assist, which he refuses to do. At the same time, apparently without comprehending its full import, Sandwich supplied information which, to Newcastle's mind, destroyed the whole validity of his reasoning. This was the news that St. Severin, acting on instructions from his Court, had finally rejected all idea of giving to the Maritime Powers provisional occupation of the Netherlands, on the ground that the cessions and restitutions in Italy depended upon Austrian concurrence, and that all security for them would be lost if French troops evacuated the Netherlands.[2]

This was a very thunderbolt to Newcastle, who was also exasperated by the calm assumption in Sandwich's letter that he could still proceed to a separate signature of the treaty, although the express condition upon which permission had been granted had become impossible. For some time, also, he had been irritated by the hortatory and somewhat patronizing tone of the letters from Bentinck, who had calmly declared that he, Bentinck, took the same view about the *asiento*

[1] Newcastle to Sandwich, 28 July, in S.P., For., Holland, 431, and (very private) on same day, in Add. MSS. 32,813, fo. 154.

[2] This important letter of 2 August is in S.P., For., Holland, 435. It is printed in *Bedford Corr.*, i., 408. A private letter of the same date is in Add. MSS. 32,813, fo. 185.

clause that France and Spain did, that four years of *non-jouissance* was all that it had been intended to grant, and that the sooner England gave way the sooner peace would be made.[1] The intervention in a matter which did not concern the Dutch was intensely galling to a politician who had been accustomed to regard the Republic as a dependent, though not always a very trustworthy, ally. No sooner did he receive, on 6 August, Sandwich's letter of the 2nd than he sat down, without waiting for any communication with London, to draft a dispatch which altered the whole course of the negotiations at Aix. The gist of it is very simple. A separate treaty, without Austrian concurrence, and without provisional occupation, is worse than useless, as it will leave the French in indefinite occupation of the Netherlands. Kaunitz has now, under pressure from us and from France, virtually given up the demand that restitution should precede the treaty, so that evacuation cannot be brought about in that way. Newcastle is not prepared to cut down the period of *non-jouissance* at the dictation of France, and this is apparently the price to be paid for a separate treaty. The obvious conclusion is that all idea of a separate treaty must be abandoned, Austria must be induced to go along with us, and therefore Sandwich must communicate everything to Kaunitz, or, at any rate, wait till the arrival of Sir Thomas Robinson. Very unkindly, Newcastle went on to blame Sandwich for having kept the convention for sending back the Russians an entire secret from Kaunitz, who had complained through Wasner of this treatment. The convention must now be communicated to him, and " His Majesty hopes that, for the future, any such cause of uneasiness may be avoided."[2] Lord Hard-

---

[1] This last letter from Bentinck was written on 2 August, so that Newcastle received it with those from Sandwich of the same date (Add. MSS. 32,813, fo. 176).

[2] This crucial dispatch of 6 August is in S.P., For., Holland, 432. The usual accompanying private letter (in Add. MSS. 32,813, fo. 224) expresses resentment that Sandwich had written to Henry Pelham to defend Newcastle's policy, which, in Newcastle's opinion, needed no advocacy, and least of all that of his subordinate. The censure on the Russian convention was

wicke subsequently expressed the shrewd suspicion that the assurance of the withdrawal of the Russians encouraged France to refuse provisional occupation.[1] If the same conjecture had occurred to Newcastle he would doubtless have expressed his undeserved censure still more strongly.

Meanwhile, Sandwich, in cheerful ignorance of the bomb which was about to explode and of which he had unwittingly lighted the fuse, was trying to meet Newcastle's wishes by cultivating more friendly relations with Kaunitz.   On 4 August he wrote in a private letter that some concession to Austria might secure concurrence.   Although Kaunitz still protested about the Treaty of Worms, he seemed to lay the greatest stress upon the Barrier and the impossibility of defraying its expense.   This led up to a very secret letter on the same day, in which Sandwich said that he had obtained from the Austrian envoy a confidential admission (not to be betrayed, as it would ruin him at Vienna) that the threat of separate signature conveyed by Robinson had so softened his Court that, if persisted in, it would bring them in.   " Mons[r] Caunitz in his discourse with me said he owned we could make peace without them, if necessary, but then he added it would occasion such a breach between our two Courts as would never be to be repaired, and that it was as a friend to the sistem of the alliance that he wished this business might be finished with the harmony and good understanding between us which was necessary for our mutual safety." Hence Sandwich concludes that some gratification of Vienna about the cost of the Barrier (if it comes from Newcastle without any hint that Kaunitz suggested it) may gain the concurrence of the Austrian Court.[2]   Two

extremely unfair, as Sandwich had applied for and had obtained leave to make it, for the express purpose of encouraging the peace party in France.

[1] Hardwicke to Newcastle, 12/23 August (summarized in Yorke, i., 665), in reviewing the situation, says that before the convention about the Russians it seemed that France would agree to provisional occupation (Add. MSS., 32,716, fo. 46).

[2] The two letters from Sandwich of 4 August are in Add. MSS. 32,813, fos. 203 and 205.

days later he reiterated his warnings as to secrecy, and especially urged that neither Wasner nor Robinson should know that Kaunitz has spoken about meeting the expense of the Barrier. It is essential that Bartenstein should never hear of it, for " the truth of the matter is, I believe, that Caunitz depends greatly upon Mr Bartenstein, who is the person of the imperial court that supports the measures that are contrary to our in- inclination; and, though he sees the impossibility of carrying these measures through, yet he dare not appear to the other to have suggested methods of conciliation."[1] Sandwich was blissfully unconscious, as he wrote these letters, that he was supplying ammunition to be used against himself. The information that Kaunitz was becoming amenable served only to confirm Newcastle in the opinion that the idea of separate signature must be abandoned, and that it would be possible, as well as safe, to induce Austria to concur in a general treaty.[2]

Newcastle was confirmed in his decision, not only by the ill-judged letters from Sandwich, but also by the approval of Cumberland, and by the arrival at Hanover of Robinson, who reiterated his assurances, frequently expressed from Vienna, that Austria was as much in need of peace as any state in Europe, that its accession to the treaty was assured, and that the ungraciousness with which it was accompanied was only Bartenstein's way. On 11 August, probably in deference to Robin- son, who had magnified the efficiency of his own threats, he so far softened his previous instructions as to allow Sandwich to use the threat of separate signature, though he may not carry it out, if Kaunitz should prove obstinate and unreasonable.[3] But two days later, in a private letter, he indulged in a characteristic out- burst, beginning, " I believe you will be angry now with me in earnest." In this incoherent epistle he blamed

[1] Sandwich to Newcastle, 8 August, in Add. MSS. 32,813, fo. 241. It is printed in *Bedford Corr.*, i., p. 446.

[2] Newcastle writes on 13 August that Sandwich's account of Kaunitz's greater complaisance confirms him in his decision to conciliate Austria (S.P., Fr., Holland, 431).

[3] Newcastle to Sandwich, 11 August, in S.P., For., Holland, 431.

Sandwich for going too fast with St. Severin, and denounced at great length St. Severin's project, as if Sandwich had already accepted it, which, as the latter very properly replied, was far from being the case. He was angry at the insistence on limiting the period of *non-jouissance* to four years, and still more at Bentinck's support of the contention. " My good friend Bentinck is very apt of late to give up all our points." The general conclusion, though it comes in the middle of the letter, is that " we must have more management for the Court of Vienna. We can't conclude without them, though I am, if necessary, for making them believe otherwise. I could have wished that, when you saw this was the case, you had held your hand a little with St. Severin, and had been a little more gracious to Kaunitz, especially as his behaviour of late has given occasion for it. I can be as strong with the Court of Vienna as any body, as I was in the orders sent to Sir T. Robinson, which have had an extreme good effect, as you see : but if I have no *resource* (as in this case at present I have not), I must go on with prudence, and consider a little where things will end. You have often told me, my dear Lord, that you would follow my system ; I never desire you should when I vary from the old unalterable system for England."[1]

The arrival of Newcastle's dispatch of 6 August provoked something like a rebellion at Aix. Both Sandwich and Bentinck were aghast at being called upon to submit to Kaunitz all their confidential communications with France, including the draft of a secret article designed for the coercion of Austria. They feared two results : that it would give Kaunitz unlimited encouragement and facilities for the game of obstruction which he had hitherto been playing ; and that it might irritate St. Severin, who was just starting for Compiègne, if he found on his return that all his secrets had been given away behind his back. Sandwich laid chief stress upon

---

[1] Newcastle to Sandwich (private), in Add. MSS. 32,813, fo. 274; printed in full in *Bedford Corr.*, i., 447-52. Copies of this letter and of Sandwich's previous letter were sent to Bedford from Hanover, and so were found among the Duke's papers.

the former point, and Bentinck upon the latter. In fact, Bentinck went so far as to imply, if not to assert, that a pledge of secrecy had been given to St. Severin, and that it would be dishonourable as well as disastrous to break it. Sandwich, however, denied any binding promise, but feared that St. Severin would be less open and more stubborn after disclosure to the allies than he had been when he was dealing with the Maritime Powers alone. The practical conclusion of the two envoys was that Sandwich should suspend any communication to Kaunitz until their remonstrances had been considered and answered.[1] Sandwich's own letters (he wrote three private ones to accompany his public dispatch) were worded with some caution, but he committed the gross indiscretion of forwarding to Newcastle some rough notes which Bentinck had drawn up as material from which a strong protest against Newcastle's decision might be constructed. He added that he had had great difficulty in procuring Bentinck's consent, and that the document was forwarded in strict confidence.[2]

Sandwich's remonstrances and disobedience would in any case have exasperated Newcastle, but his anger was intensified by the calm admission that a British plenipotentiary had been induced by the advice of a foreign Minister to disregard the formal instructions of a veteran Secretary of State. And the perusal of Bentinck's outspoken notes added fuel to the fire. They were certainly never intended nor suited to be sent to Hanover. Bentinck began by asserting that he could not continue at Aix if the whole system was to be

[1] Sandwich threw the responsibility for this disobedience upon Bentinck, who, he said, " is so strong in that opinion [that Newcastle's plan would fail to bring in Austria] that he has formally insisted that I shall suspend the execution of your Grace's orders about communicating our counter-project to Count Caunitz. He thinks that, as long as his Court persists in her refusal of going on in our method of proceeding in a general treaty, it would be very imprudent in us to impart a measure to them of which they previously express their disapprobation " (Sandwich to Newcastle, 11 August, in S.P., For., Holland, 435).

[2] One of the private letters of 11 August is in S.P., For., Holland, 435; the other two (including the one which contained Bentinck's notes) are in Add. MSS. 32,813, fos. 256, 260. The notes themselves are in S.P., For., Holland, 435.

changed at the critical moment. The hostility of Vienna was no new thing, the Maritime Powers had had to deal with it all along, and they had fixed their plan when they signed the preliminaries. The only way to convince Austria that Bartenstein's policy was impossible was to adhere to that plan. In Bentinck's opinion the French objections to provisional occupation were well founded. In view of the inferiority of the allies St. Severin must be conciliated, and peace must be made while the pacific party in France has the upper hand. To lose St. Severin's confidence is to lose everything, and the allies may as well break off and renew the war. We are in the position " d'une ville qui a battu la chamade," and can only fix terms for capitulation. The longer we delay the worse these terms will be. These orders to Sandwich Bentinck regards as a breach of the concert promised by the Duke of Newcastle. If they are persisted in, Bentinck will return to The Hague and wash his hands of all responsibility. We shall be exposed in England and in all Europe as " des gens sans système et sans resolution. Bartenstein lui-même rira sous-cape de nous avoir fait peur."

Sandwich should have known Newcastle better than to suppose that he would be either conciliated or convinced by outspoken censure on the part of a Dutch politician. The Duke's one consolation, when he received this unpleasant communication, was that by this time Sir Thomas Robinson had arrived at Aix with instructions to manage Kaunitz, to moderate the impetuosity of Sandwich, and to devise some compromise which would enable the allies, on St. Severin's return, to speak to him with a single voice. Meanwhile, he sent to the two envoys imperative instructions to communicate everything to Kaunitz, while he informed Sandwich in a separate letter that he had laid everything, including Bentinck's confidential notes, before the King, that His Majesty adhered to his previous position, and that there was no need to take or to impose the necessity of arguments on the subject.[1] It

---

[1] Newcastle to Sandwich and Robinson, and (private) to Sandwich, 18 August, in S.P., For., Holland, 432.

would have saved much ink and temper if he had
adhered to this self-denying resolution. But when both
Sandwich from Aix and Bentinck from The Hague continued to write defences of their policy, and when Bentinck sullenly adhered to his refusal to return to the
Congress, Newcastle's itch for controversy proved uncontrollable. Not only did he answer their letters, but he
sent them with elaborate and bitter commentaries to all
his correspondents—to his brother, to Lord Hardwicke,
to Bedford and, above all, to the Duke of Cumberland,
who had to be called in to keep Sandwich in the right
path and also to induce the obstinate Bentinck to
return. His eagerness to defend himself was intensified
when he found, to his intense chagrin, that Henry
Pelham and his oldest ally, the Lord Chancellor, were
disposed, not only to approve the policy, but also to
defend the conduct, of Sandwich and Bentinck. From
this moment his letters become steadily more numerous,
longer, and more vituperative. "Sandwich is abominable." "Never was man used as I have been by the
folly, vanity, and ignorance of my Lord Sandwich. . . .
And his friend Bentinck to declare that he never would
have sent that paper if Lord Sandwich had not assured
that I would not take it amiss. Call me fool; tell me
I don't know my own business; and then suppose I will
not take it amiss."[1] Such phrases abound in these
letters, and when Sandwich, in despair of pacifying the
Duke, tried to drop the controversy, the latter was so
piqued that he urged him to say all that it was in his
mind in order that it might be answered. Every event
and every expression of opinion at Aix or elsewhere
were pulled into the controversy to justify one side or
the other.

Perhaps the most irritating of all Newcastle's corre-

[1] The great bulk of the letters to and from Newcastle are in
Add. MSS. 32,716, and 32,814, *passim*. On 24 August he wrote to
H. Pelham (*ibid.*, 32,716, fo. 53): "Put yourself in my situation,
and you must think I have been greatly provoked. Would my
Lord Townshend have been as moderate as I have been in these
circumstances? He would have complained of Bentinck to
the Prince of Orange, demanded his recall, and have immediately
recalled my Lord Sandwich. But I have acted otherwise. There
was a design to bully me; but that design has not taken place."

spondents was his brother, who could never refrain from expressing his antipathy to the Court of Vienna and his contempt for Newcastle's system. At the same time he had an exasperating habit of saying that foreign affairs were not his province, that his opinion in such lofty matters was worthless, and then proceeding to express his opinion with disconcerting emphasis. On 22 August, when he first learned of the dispute at Aix, he wrote: "Why does she [Maria Theresa] refuse to come into a general treaty? Plainly because she will not give the same security to our ally the King of Sardinia and the King of Prussia as she is willing to do to France and Spain. Is this acting upon the old system, or is it decent with regard to the King of this country? It is this behaviour of the Court of Vienna that provokes me. . . . I own, Brother, it has given me great concern to see you run so fast into declaring that you will do nothing without the Court of Vienna. I am not in love with Sandwich and Bentinck, but I like them better when they pursue ends which I think necessary and practicable." A week later he wrote still more brutally: "I heartily wish you had kept Mr Bentinck's paper to yourself. It is writ with spirit and though I agree in the doctrines, with an acrimony I did not expect from that quarter. . . . I never had an ill opinion of the Bentincks, but I did not conceive the elder to have had either the parts or the passion which he shows on this occasion. . . . Dear Brother, are they mad at Vienna, or have they any subterfuge, which we here cannot find out, and no one abroad has ever suggested?" He went on to say that we might have had a better peace, and our allies too, a week after the preliminaries, and saved a million. "All this millstone of debt is due to the weakness and want of good faith of a single Power."[1]

While this acrimonious correspondence was going on Newcastle steadily pursued his policy of carrying Austria with him in a general treaty. Robert Keith was summoned from The Hague, where he left Dayrolles in sole

[1] These two letters of 11 and 19 August (o.s.) are in Add. MSS. 32,716, fos. 41 and 76.

possession, to Hanover, whence he was dispatched to act as temporary substitute for Robinson at Vienna. His instructions were to press for a single treaty, and to demand that the Low Countries should be received on the basis of the Barrier Treaty, leaving it open to adjust subsequent modifications. Delay at this stage would leave the French in the Netherlands till next spring, and would necessitate the continuance of useless expense. The instructions closed with the old threat. " Had His Majesty been disposed to conclude separately with France, the King might have done it long ago. Nothing but the last extremity will ever oblige His Majesty to come into that measure. But, if the Court of Vienna will destroy themselves, the King must take care not to be destroyed with them."[1]

Before Keith's embassy could produce any results, two critical interviews had taken place at Aix. Robinson came from Hanover with instructions to keep a watchful eye upon Sandwich and to carry on a private correspondence with Newcastle. To the latter's intense annoyance, the new plenipotentiary allowed himself at the outset to be overborne by his more imperious colleague, and consented to delay compliance until the remonstrances of Sandwich and Bentinck had been answered. It was only on the receipt of renewed and more imperative commands that on 20 August the two envoys carried all the vital documents, the French project, the counter-project, the draft secret article, and the correspondence about the recall of the Russian troops, and laid them before Kaunitz. It was impossible to keep anything back, because all confidence would be destroyed if France and Spain should show him the unmutilated documents. The secret article was excused by the expression of a hope that no occasion for it would arise. Kaunitz's reception of his visitors was characteristically reserved. He pointed out that the revelation was strangely late, and that it was still more odd that Chavanne had been informed and he had not. Sandwich replied that the delay was due to his own per-

---

[1] Keith's instructions are dated from Hanover 13/24 August (S.P.,¶For., Germany, 181).

sistent refusal to co-operate. On the details of the suggested terms, and especially on those which concerned Vienna, Kaunitz was resolutely reticent, and merely declared that he would send all the papers to his Court and await instructions. Until a reply could be received no further progress could be made with Austria.[1]

Three days later, St. Severin having returned from Compiègne, it became necessary to disclose to him the fact that Great Britain had abandoned the idea of a separate treaty with France. The French representative, who was himself expecting a supervising colleague, and whose latest instructions were to press for a speedy settlement, gave the British envoys a convenient opening by admitting that he had discussed the terms with Huescar, the Spanish Ambassador to the French Court. This enabled them to say that they had done the same with their allies, and especially with Austria, as Robinson had brought a more favourable estimate of the attitude of that Court. To their intense relief, St. Severin took no umbrage at this unexpected disclosure. "He seemed a little startled at first upon our telling him that we had communicated the whole in writing to Count Caunitz, which he intimated would be likely to do hurt to our affairs, but upon our assuring him that the communication was made but the day before, and that consequently he was full time enough to proceed in the same manner with Sotto Mayor, he passed it over without laying any further stress upon it."[2]

The news that the revelation had produced no apparent change in the attitude of St. Severin was a source of great exultation to Newcastle, who made the most of it in his correspondence as giving the lie to the gloomy forecasts of Bentinck. But his self-satisfaction was sorely shaken by the refusal of Austria to show any compliance in return for the tardy communications made by the Maritime Powers. Even the growing coolness between the Courts of Hanover and Berlin seemed

[1] Sandwich and Robinson to Newcastle, 21 August, in S.P., For., Holland, 435.
[2] Sandwich and Robinson to Newcastle (private), 24 August, in S.P., For., Holland, 435.

to make no impression at Vienna. Keith reported wholly unsatisfactory interviews with the Austrian Ministers and with the Empress. Ulfeld refused to discuss the Treaty of Worms and said that his Court had made up their mind on the subject. Bartenstein talked at large about diplomacy, and Keith left him no wiser than he came. Maria Theresa was within three weeks of her confinement, and the bashful newcomer dared not agitate her by dwelling on the threat of separate action which he had been instructed to convey. The British Court was reproached at Vienna for a criminal partiality for Sardinia, and the Barrier Treaty was denounced as an insulting infraction of Austrian sovereignty and as an intolerable burden upon the exhausted provinces.[1] And Robinson could report no better news from Aix. Kaunitz continued to insist that peace could only be made by separate treaties, and refused to discuss any details with the British envoys until his answer came from Vienna. Even if he had been less reserved, the question of the Barrier, which had now become the most prominent subject of dispute between the two Courts, could hardly be profitably debated during the absence of Bentinck. In the absence of Austrian co-operation, the British envoys found themselves forced into closer intercourse with Chavanne, who now pressed three urgent demands on behalf of Sardinia : (1) the formal withdrawal of Kaunitz's protest and reservations of 23 May ; (2) the prohibition of any future union of the crowns of Spain and Naples ; (3) the granting of a " corridor " through Genoese territory from Piedmont to the sea. Although these demands were in the highest degree exasperating to Austria, and though Newcastle characterized them as " absurd," Robinson inserted them in the revised project which he and Sandwich were now drawing up.

In the later days of August, Newcastle's confident hopes of securing Austrian concurrence in the treaty sank to zero. So far his change of attitude had apparently been completely unsuccessful, and in his despondency he began to revert to the possible necessity of

[1] Keith's dispatches are in S.P., For., Germany (Empire).

signing without Austria. How could this be reconciled with the imperative need of terminating the French occupation of the Netherlands? France had refused to hand them over to the Maritime Powers because that left France no pledge for the fulfilment of the promised restitutions to Genoa and Modena or the cessions to Don Philip. In some way or other this legitimate pretext for refusal must be removed, and the only expedient that presented itself was the coercion of Austria by her former allies. On 23 August he wrote privately to Robinson that Kaunitz's obstinacy " may force us at last to do what we so much desire to avoid."[1] Five days later he filled in this ominous suggestion by proposing a secret article, engaging by force, conjointly with France and Sardinia, to procure the cessions and restitutions in Italy, and even to send a squadron to the Mediterranean for that purpose. " This is a sad expedient to be driven to, but this is better than leaving Flanders to France."[2] On 8 September he went so far as to suggest to Henry Pelham that either Robinson or Stone should be sent to Paris to propose a formal agreement by which, in return for French consent to provisional occupation, the Maritime Powers should pledge themselves (1) not to restore the provinces until Austria should accede purely and simply to the treaty, and (2) to procure by force Don Philip's establishment and the cessions to Modena and Genoa.[3] Meanwhile, he induced George II, acting in his electoral capacity, to send to Vienna a definite threat that if Maria Theresa did not concur he would be forced into an alliance with Prussia, and also a warning that her continued obstinacy would probably produce in England a Ministerial change which would remove from office the well-wishers of the House of Austria.[4]

[1] Newcastle to Robinson (private to yourself), 23 August, in Add. MSS. 32,813, fo. 321.
[2] Newcastle to Robinson (private), 28 August, in Add. MSS. 32,814, fo. 34.
[3] Newcastle to H. Pelham, 8 September, in Add. MSS. 32,716, fo. 129.
[4] Newcastle to Bentinck, 30 August, in Add. MSS. 32,814, fo. 64 (printed in *Bedford Corr.*, i., 481–88). See also Newcastle

Fortunately for Newcastle he was not compelled to carry out any of his threats. On 13 September, Kaunitz received the long-expected comments of his Court upon the documents which had been submitted to him on 21 August.[1] They were not at first sight reassuring, as they were drawn up in Bartenstein's best controversial style. He denounced the whole conduct of Sandwich and Bentinck both before and after the conclusion of the preliminaries. He declared that the Barrier had contributed to the ruin rather than the defence of the Netherlands, the *anti-mural* of the Maritime Powers, that the unfortunate towns must be restored to their rightful ruler, and that, if Dutch troops were subsequently admitted, there must be no demand that the devastated provinces should bear the cost of maintenance. He threw scorn on the proposal of a single general treaty. The first article would restore peace between Powers which had never been at war with each other. Modena had nothing to do with the East and West Indies. Anglo-Spanish quarrels did not concern other states. Austria had been attacked *de son chef*, and should therefore make peace *de son chef*. Finally, he categorically rejected all the recent demands of Sardinia, but offered to accept Article 7 of the preliminaries if it was inserted without either addition or subtraction.

This offer to confirm the Worms cessions to Sardinia was the first departure of Austria from the policy of obstinate obstruction which had hitherto been pursued. It was rightly hailed at Hanover as far more important than all the vinegary paragraphs that preceded it. It was not without precedent that Bartenstein should be most vituperative when his Court was prepared to give

---

to H. Pelham, 28 August, in Add. MSS. 32,716, fo. 69, where the Duke claims to have advised the King to take this step.

[1] Bartenstein's document is entitled " Remarques sur les deux projets de Traité definitive, et les observations y relatives, qui ont été communiqués à M. le Comte de Kaunitz par Messrs. les Plenipotentiaires de sa Majesté Britannique le 21 Aout, 1748." It is to be found, with Sandwich's covering letter of 13 September, in S.P. For., Holland, 435.

way.[1] From this moment Newcastle determined to do all in his power to induce Austria to be a signatory of the treaty and not merely an accessory after its signature. The major questions in dispute at Aix had by this time been narrowed down to four : (1) the dispute about the *asiento*, in which France was the champion of the interests of Spain, and no Power was concerned to support the English claims; (2) the quarrel between Austria and the Maritime Powers about the Barrier; (3) the recently advanced claims of Sardinia, of which the most notable was for a corridor to the sea; and (4) the form of the settlement, whether by one or by several treaties. The Sardinian problem was virtually solved by Bartenstein's memorandum. For once England failed to support Sardinia. Newcastle especially was so impressed by the Austrian concession that he refused to chill the nascent goodwill of Vienna by urging any further demands.[2] Chavanne made a gallant struggle, and at the last moment Osorio came from Hanover to Aix to back him up. But all their efforts were unavailing. Kaunitz stuck to his instructions, while France had no love for Sardinia and would not allow an inch of territory to be taken from Genoa. The desertion of England, which Chavanne bitterly resented after his recent friendly relations with Sandwich and Robinson, was the last blow. The article about the

---

[1] Robinson, who knew Bartenstein well, shared and encouraged Newcastle's optimism. On 16 September he wrote in a private letter: " I am little concerned at Bartenstein's papers. I know the nature of the fellow to stick out as long as he can, but that nobody runs faster into a thing when once it is necessary and ripe " (Add. MSS. 32,814, fo. 204).

[2] Newcastle to Sandwich, 21 September (Add. MSS. 32,814, fo. 244): " I love Sardinia and its interests, I am in disgrace at Vienna for supposed devotion to them, but I won't break with the Court of Vienna and let France keep Flanders to satisfy the King of Sardinia against the Queen of Hungary's *petitorio*." On 8 September, in defending himself to his brother against the charge of being the dupe of Austria, he had pointed out that at Vienna he was equally denounced for attachment to Sardinia. " Bartenstein says our partiality to the King of Sardinia keeps us out of Flanders." On 21 September, in addition to the above letter to Sandwich, he wrote privately to Robinson to blame him for having inserted " those absurd Sardinian demands in his draft project."

Worms cessions was taken verbatim from the preliminaries and inserted in the treaty. Isolation was equally fatal to England in the matter of the *asiento*, and it was finally decided to cut down the period of its renewal to the four years of interruption during the late war.

The decision as to the form of the ultimate settlement rested obviously, not with Austria, but with France. Hitherto, St. Severin had sided with Sandwich in supporting a single treaty. But on 5 September he had been deprived of the sole conduct of the negotiation by the arrival of du Theil, the veteran *commis* of the French Foreign Office, who was to play to his colleague the same part that Robinson was playing to Sandwich.[1] Newcastle surmised, and rightly, that the sending of du Theil was a proof that France was genuinely desirous of peace. The newcomer startled diplomatists at the outset by intimating a preference for separate treaties. But, when he explained that he meant identical treaties to be signed by all Powers on the same day, Kaunitz rejected the suggestion as even more preposterous than the single treaty. That settled the matter, and du Theil set himself, with a deliberation which exasperated Sandwich, to draft a general treaty on the basis of the preliminaries, merely putting in the necessary corrections and amplifications. The other diplomatists had to wait impatiently until the oracle had spoken. The draft was disclosed at Aix on 23 September, communicated to the English plenipotentiaries on the following day, and forwarded by them on the 25th. It was greeted with a chorus of satisfaction at Hanover, London, and Cumberland's headquarters. As regards direct English interests nothing had been altered for the worse except the article about the *asiento*. But there was one small point which touched English pride in a raw place. Du Theil had restored to the treaty the original French demand that the hostages for Cape Breton should be peers of the

[1] Newcastle to Pelham, 2 October, says that France was dissatisfied with St. Severin and sent du Theil, just as we were dissatisfied with Sandwich and sent Robinson (Add. MSS. 32,716, fo. 318).

realm. Such a provision would provoke an outcry from Parliament, and especially from the House of Lords. Sandwich and Robinson were instructed to procure the restoration of the words " persons of rank and consideration," which had been accepted in the preliminaries. It was with the utmost difficulty that this concession was extorted, and it could only be obtained by the acceptance of a secret article to the effect that these words were to be interpreted as meaning peers. This compromise failed to satisfy the constitutional scruples of the Lord Chancellor, and in the end two young peers had to be found, one at Hanover and one at Cumberland's camp, who were willing to accept French hospitality and a handsome allowance from England for a few months. They were hurried off to Paris in order to induce the French Ministers to return the peccant secret article, and thus preserve intact the honour of England and the privileges of its peerage.

Even if England had been less satisfied with du Theil's proposals, it would have been impossible to reject them, as on 25 September, the day on which they were sent out from Aix, without any communication with the allies or with the Commander-in-Chief, Austria had concluded a convention with France for the mutual withdrawal of thirty thousand men from their respective forces in the Netherlands. It was a gross insult to the Duke of Cumberland and to Great Britain, which had contributed so largely to the maintenance of the Austrian troops, and the anger in high quarters was not diminished when Kaunitz defended the action of his Court on the double ground that the Maritime Powers had done the same thing in sending back the Russians and that £100,000 of the last subsidy were still unpaid. Henry Pelham, though he shared the general indignation and suggested that Cumberland should come home at once with the British contingent, was not altogether displeased with an act which demonstrated that the war could not possibly be renewed and that Austria must be prepared to come into a general peace.[1]

[1] Pelham to Newcastle 23 September (o.s.), in Add. MSS. 32,716, fo. 354.

While the English plenipotentiaries were settling the delicate problem of the hostages, they had also to grapple with the task of inducing the allies to accept the treaty. There were now three possible malcontents—Austria, Sardinia, and Holland. It proved impossible to cajole Chavanne and Osorio. No appeal to the past services of England and no contention that Sardinia, after all, was the sole belligerent to gain anything by the war, could induce them to sign a treaty which failed to give effect to the last Sardinian demands. There remained Kaunitz and Bentinck. When Bentinck went off in dudgeon to The Hague, he was not merely angry at the English change of tactics at Aix; he was genuinely afraid that Newcastle's eagerness to conciliate Austria might impel him to urge concessions with regard to the Barrier. He tried to induce Sandwich to follow him in the hope of committing England to joint action in the matter. In this he failed, as Sandwich prudently refrained from adding to the wrath of Cumberland and Newcastle, who would have regarded his going to The Hague as flagrant insubordination. Charles Bentinck was then sent to Hanover to press upon Newcastle the danger of losing Dutch goodwill.[1] But all was in vain. William Bentinck returned at last to Aix with instructions to insist that the treaty should only restore the Netherlands to Austria on the foot of the former treaties. Kaunitz refused to accept any such terms. Du Theil had declared that he would accept any solution which commended itself to Austria and the Maritime Powers. This became in the closing stages the dominant issue at Aix, and, as Bentinck had feared, England behaved, not as a partisan, but as a mediator. Newcastle had already deserted Sardinia to please Austria, and he now demanded sacrifices from Holland with the same object. Bentinck found it quite impossible to obtain either recognition or renewal of the Barrier Treaty. But in the course of the negotiation

---

[1] There are copies of Charles Bentinck's reports from Hanover to Fagel in Add. MSS. 32,814, fos. 312, 329. It would be interesting to know how Newcastle obtained possession of these letters, which were certainly not intended for his perusal.

Kaunitz let fall the observation that the Dutch garrisons might return to the towns which they had previously occupied. This was fastened upon by Sandwich and Robinson as a possible basis of compromise, and at last, with immense trouble, a form of words was found which both Kaunitz and Bentinck agreed to accept. The sovereignty of Maria Theresa was to be recognized, but the French were to hand over the Barrier towns to Dutch troops. Nothing was said as to payment for their maintenance or as to the retention of the old import duties.[1]

This was a substantial victory for Kaunitz and an equal defeat for Bentinck, who had no authority to accept such terms. Yet it was Bentinck who signed the treaty, with the other Dutch representatives, and it was Kaunitz who refused to sign. Newcastle might have learned what his brother and Hardwicke constantly dinned into him—that concession was the last way to win the Court of Vienna. The more he proclaimed his desire to carry Austria with him, the larger and the more insistent became the Austrian demands. Kaunitz was not satisfied with having evaded admission of the validity of the Barrier Treaty. He insisted that an imperial diploma should be required for the transfer of Parma and Piacenza to Don Philip, and that the claims of the Elector Palatine should be once more cut down to the fief of Pleistein. As both these demands were refused, he held aloof when the Treaty was signed on 18 October by the same three Powers which had signed the preliminaries. This abstention was enjoined from Vienna as a demonstration of discontent at the subordinate part which had been allotted to Austria in the negotiation. Kaunitz may well have vowed in his own mind that Austria under his guidance would henceforth

---

[1] The final wording was as follows: " Les villes et places dans les Pays-Bas, dont la souveraineté appartient à l'Impératrice Reine de Hongrie et de Bohême, dans lesquelles Leurs Hautes Puissances ont le droit de garnison, seront évacuées aux troupes de la République." Sandwich and Robinson explain how they persuaded Bentinck to accept these words in defiance of his instructions in their dispatch to Newcastle of 13 October (S.P., For., Holland, 436).

make treaties *de son chef*, and not under the patronage of another Power, however benevolent. But Austria had no intention of continuing the war, and Kaunitz gave in a formal accession to the treaty on 23 October. Spain, pacified by the concession about the *asiento*, had already acceded on the 20th, the delay of two days being the Spanish protest against subordination to France. On the 25th the representatives of the five contracting Powers signed a supplementary convention by which they undertook to carry out the provisions of the Treaty even if any of the Powers concerned should refuse concurrence. This was designed to coerce Charles Emmanuel, who churlishly delayed his accession till 20 November. He had to restore his conquests on the Riviera to Genoa in return for the recovery of Savoy and Nice.

Newcastle was at his worst in the weeks following the conclusion of the Treaty. Never was his egotism more nauseating. He claimed for himself the whole credit that peace was made, that it was made without further difficulty and delay, and that Austria acceded so quickly.[1] He declared that if Sandwich had been allowed to follow his reckless course, Austria would not have come in, the French would still be in the Netherlands, and the old alliance would be at an end. He therefore clamoured for the fullest recognition of his services to the State, and whimpered like a spoiled child if the allowance of praise fell short of his expectations. Henry Pelham exasperated him by refusing to be coerced into undeserved laudation. He countered his brother's pretensions by asserting that it was du Theil's coming which made the peace, and not any ingenious manipulation of diplomacy from Hanover. As to the conciliation of Austria, what had it come to? Kaunitz had refused to sign the treaty. Austria had only acceded because the continuance of the war was impossible.

---

[1] Newcastle to Pelham, 20 October, 1748: " I have the secret comfort of thinking that I have, not only greatly, not to say almost singly, brought it about" (Add. MSS. 32,717, fo. 70). In this volume may be found all his querulous letters to his brother and to Hardwicke, some of which are quoted or referred to in Yorke, *Life of Hardwicke*, i., 678–85.

Kaunitz had tried to make ratification conditional on the payment of the £100,000, and Newcastle had been compelled to renew his unwarranted assurances. When Keith asked for an audience to compliment the Empress, Maria Theresa had curtly refused to receive him on the ground that the treaty was a subject of condolence rather than congratulation.[1] The unkindest cut of all was that the Premier agreed with Sandwich and Bentinck that, but for the interposition of Newcastle, the treaty might have been made at least two months earlier, with a proportionate saving of public money.[2] Newcastle was angry with his brother, but he was still more angry with Sandwich, who had committed the unpardonable offence of adhering his opinion, in defiance of all the letters that had been written from Hanover to convince him of his error. "I am determined," Newcastle wrote to Robinson, "never to have any Minister in my department who tells me he is wiser than I am."[3] The favoured pupil of two years ago was no longer either a pupil or a favourite. Sandwich wished to remain at The Hague during the winter in order to draw his Ambassador's pay and to straighten out Dutch affairs with Bentinck. He was curtly told that the King expected him to take up his duties as First Lord. Newcastle congratulated the King on the royal insight which had enabled him to see how unfitted Sandwich was to be made a Secretary of State.[4] To the pedestal from which Sandwich had been deposed, Robinson was exalted. He had done what he was told to do, and had welcomed his instructions instead of remonstrating

[1] Keith to Newcastle, 6 November, 1784, S.P., For., Germany (Empire), 181.

[2] See especially Newcastle to Hardwicke, 27 October, in Add. MSS. 32,717, fo. 128 (there are excerpts in Yorke, i., 680); and Pelham to Newcastle, 25 October (o.s.), *ibid.*, fo. 184.

[3] Newcastle to Robinson, private, 22 October (Add. MSS. 32,815, fo. 55). This is a letter of congratulation on the signature of the treaty, and its cordiality contrasts with the chilliness of the private letter to Sandwich on the same day (*ibid.*, fo. 53). See also Newcastle to Hardwicke, 20 October, in Yorke, i., 680.

[4] Newcastle to Pelham, 18 August: "The King is very angry and said, *My Lord, this man would not have done for Secretary of State;* to which I answered, *Your Majesty always thought so*" (Add. MSS. 32,716, fo. 21).

against them. Although Robinson was not likely to
please either the Prince of Orange or Bentinck, Newcastle wanted to send him to The Hague for the winter,
which would have been a mortal insult to Sandwich.[1]
This project, however, was foiled by the argument that,
with Dayrolles on the spot and Lord Holderness nominated as Sandwich's successor, it would be monstrous
extravagance to employ a third person, especially as
Robinson was also drawing an Ambassador's salary.
And so the two Englishmen who signed the treaty ter-
minated their uneasy partnership[2] when ratifications of
the treaty had been exchanged. Both returned to England : Sandwich to become more closely allied than ever
with Bedford and to be a thorn in the side of Newcastle ;
Robinson to receive a comfortable commissionership
with a seat in the House of Commons, and to be exalted,
when Newcastle became Premier, to a parliamentary
eminence for which he was wholly unfitted.

The Treaty of Aix-la-Chapelle is perhaps the nearest
approach in history to that " peace without victory "
which President Wilson at one moment seemed to
regard as the ideal ending of a war. It cannot be said
that this particular peace gives much support to the
President's view. The war in its erratic course had
raised a number of problems, but the treaty settled none
of them. The war had opened with a general breach

---

[1] Newcastle to Pelham, 5 November: " I send you a copy of a
curious letter from my friend Sandwich. It was a most notable
project he had taken into his head, to be First Lord of the Admiralty and Ambassador at The Hague at the same time, in order
to direct the foreign affairs in both places. But that can't be
upon the present system. Sure, the thought of leaving Robinson
at The Hague to cool and quiet things, is right " (Add. MSS. 32,717,
fo. 182).

[2] In their private letters Sandwich and Robinson frequently
profess their regard for each other, but these reiterations are too
numerous to be convincing. Each tried to conceal this correspondence from the other. On 19 September, Robinson writes
to Newcastle that Sandwich gets him into his closet and keeps
him there until the courier has started (Add. MSS. 32,814, fo.
600). It is obvious from the letters that there was a great strain
between the two men, and that Sandwich knew that Robinson
was Newcastle's watch-dog. Newcastle suspected a private
correspondence between Sandwich and Bedford, and wanted
Robinson to find this out.

of paper guarantees; it ended with the enactment or renewal of a number of guarantees, which were not likely to be more strictly observed than those which had been broken eight years before. Rather curiously, the one part of Europe which enjoyed a substantial period of rest after 1748 was Italy, where the settlement had been most vigorously contested, and where it seemed in the highest degree artificial and insecure. Elsewhere there was no approach to quietude. It was quite certain that a clause in the treaty was not enough to enable Frederick of Prussia to enjoy his unrighteous gains in peace. The renewal of the *asiento* for four years was a mere evasion of the disputes between England and Spain which had kindled the war in 1739. The imperial title had been restored to the House of Austria, but the imperial authority was challenged by the rise of Prussia. The stage had been set for a great struggle between France and Great Britain in America and in Asia, but the curtain had fallen before the first act had been completed. Thanks largely to the war, the North of Europe had become a powder-magazine where the slightest blunder might give rise to an explosion. And, finally, Europe had lost such measure of stability as had been given by the traditional grouping of the Great Powers. The Family Compact, if not repudiated, was for the time suspended. And the anti-Bourbon group had fallen to pieces. The negotiations at Aix-la-Chapelle had shown that the Barrier Treaty, long regarded as the bond between Austria and the Maritime Powers, was really a dissolvent. England could only regain the allegiance of Holland by restoring the Barrier; and England could only hope to conciliate Austria by removing what was regarded in Vienna as an intolerable and degrading servitude. For the next seven years Newcastle made frantic efforts to find some escape from this dilemma, but they were doomed to failure. The " old system," which he had idolized for the thirty years of his official life, was shattered, and he had contributed to its downfall. His whole policy rested upon the conviction that England could not face France without the active aid of the two traditional allies, and he had lost them both.

At the last moment of despair he clutched at the Prussian alliance, which he had deliberately rejected in 1748. But this would not by itself have saved him, and he would have come down to history as the architect of his country's ruin if he had not found what he had so long dreaded—a masterful colleague in William Pitt.

INDEX

412